Fourth Edition

Educational Facilities

Planning, Modernization, and Management

Basil Castaldi
Educational Consultant

Allyn and Bacon
Boston • London • Toronto • Sydney • Tokyo • Singapore

Series Editor: Ray Short
Series Editorial Assistant: Christine M. Shaw
Production Administrator: Annette Joseph
Production Coordinator: Holly Crawford
Editorial-Production Service: Linda Zuk/WordCrafters Editorial Services, Inc.
Cover Administrator: Linda K. Dickinson
Cover Designer: Suzanne Harbison
Manufacturing Buyer: Louise Richardson

Copyright © 1994, 1987, 1982 by Allyn and Bacon
A Division of Simon & Schuster, Inc.
160 Gould Street
Needham Heights, MA 02194

Library of Congress Cataloging-in-Publication Data

Castaldi, Basil.
    Education facilities : planning, modernization, and management /
Basil Castaldi. — 4th ed.
      p. cm.
    Includes bibliographical references and index.
    ISBN 0-205-15201-5
    1. School plant management.   2. Educational planning.   I. Title.
LB3241.C37 1994
371.6—dc20   93-12602
                                    CIP

Printed in the United States of America

10 9 8 7

To My Wife Angela,
to My Daughter Linda and Son Paul,
and to My Grandchildren Allison and Alex

Contents

PART II   Procedures and Criteria for Long-Range Planning   63

PART III Fundamental Elements of Educational Facility Planning 160

**PART V   Modernizing, Maintaining, and
Operating an Existing Facility   378**

Preface

As was true of the first edition, this book is a comprehensive treatise on the planning, design, remodeling, and maintenance of educational facilities. It is intended to serve the needs of students and practitioners. It is organized so that it can be used as a basic textbook by the student in educational administration, and as a sourcebook for the practitioner. The fundamental concepts and associated theory concerning the planning of educational facilities are of equal importance to both groups. The difference lies primarily in the emphasis placed on theory or on practices by each group. The student is perhaps a little more interested in the theory than in the practices. The practitioner, on the other hand, must often produce concrete solutions to the real problems of educational administration and attaches far more importance to the practice than to the theory. The difference between these two groups lies in the point of view. The student examines practices to better understand the theory, while the practitioner utilizes theory to justify practical solutions. It can be seen, therefore, that theory and practice are not mutually exclusive. They strongly supplement each other depending upon whether the reader is a student or practitioner.

The organization of the subject matter presented in this text is intended to blend theory and practice. The first few chapters of this book deal primarily with theory, principles, and techniques related to the educational planning of school buildings, including the application of selected principles of educational psychology. These initial chapters contain theoretical considerations that serve as a basis for the development of a long-range educational plan and for the planning of specific educational facilities in any school district. The practices are introduced only as needed to illustrate the operational aspects of the theory. The remainder of this text offers a rich source of timely and practical information that reflects the state of the art in the planning of functional and futuristic educational facilities.

This book has been expanded to include specific information on the planning of child-care facilities. There is a growing and pressing need for such facilities in our ever-changing society. In conducting the research on this topic, the author soon discovered that there is a dearth of information on the planning of such facilities. Architects have encountered the same difficulty. A number of excellent articles discuss many aspects of child-care services, but touch only lightly on housing. The author has diligently examined the developmental programs recommended by accreditation agencies for child-care services, and has relied on his long years of experience to determine the approximate physical space required for each activity. Furthermore, he has applied his knowledge of functional planning of educational facilities in suggesting various types of specialized spaces and their relationship to each other. The author has also proposed a technique designed to simplify the planning of child-care facilities. It is believed that this is the first comprehensive treatment of child-care services from curriculum to facility.

This book is designed also to satisfy the needs of a variety of users. It provides a comprehensive treatise on educational facility planning for the student. It contains a wealth of information on curricular matters for the architect. And it offers suggestions and solutions to a wide variety of problems related to educational facilities confronting school officials, school maintenance personnel, college and university officers, boards of education, citizens' committees, and the planners of child-care facilities. In order to assist these readers in addressing specific problems, each chapter is a self-contained unit consisting of a cluster of closely related topics that address a major aspect of educational facility planning. Thus, readers need not peruse the entire text to find answers to a problem of immediate concern.

▶ 1

The Evolution of Educational Facilities

INTRODUCTION

It should be stated at the outset that this book is envisioned as a broad-based guide for school officials, members of boards of education, school administrators, school maintenance personnel, educational consultants, students of school administration, and school architects. The text is organized so that readers may refer only to the sections that interest them. Part of this book deals with curriculum development—principles of learning applicable to the planning of school facilities that promise innovations in educational methodology. Another part concentrates on the process and activities related to the identification of educational needs for the foreseeable future. A third focus of this publication is on the actual planning of a specific type of school facility that has been recommended by the Board of Education. Such a recommendation by school officials may involve the construction of a new facility or the modernization of an existing school building. And finally, this text includes material on the maintenance and operation of a school building and on techniques for saving energy.

This book looks at educational facilities from both a theoretical and a practical point of view to meet the needs of both student and practitioner. Students preparing for positions in educational administration will be interested in the principles that underlie the suggested application of the theory. Practicing school administrators such as superintendents of schools, college presidents, school principals, and deans of administration will find the variety of specific and pragmatic suggestions of immediate value. This dualism of purpose, however, should not be construed to mean that students are not interested in practice or that practitioners see little or no value in theory. But as a practical matter, the student frequently has more time to value in theory. But as a practical matter, the student frequently has more time to examine the "why" of the practice, while the hard-pressed practicing administrator—who often must provide an immediate solution to a problem—has little time to deal with theory.

In the first case, the objective is to arrive at a feasible ideal solution through the application of accepted principles. In the second instance, school administrators seek to find practical answers in the shortest possible time, using the theory and principles to support their recommendations to their respective boards. Principles and concrete solutions to problems are not mutually exclusive. Each reader will place a different emphasis on theory or practice depending upon the situation. For example, the school principal who is asked to submit a set of recommendations to the superintendent of schools within a few days as to how he could best use his present school building under a given set of circumstances would find it very helpful to focus immediately on the suggested practices that apply to his problem. In preparing this report, however, he would find it advantageous to review the principles and theory appropriate to his situation in order to support his recommendations. Clearly theory and practice are mutually supportive. The student needs some knowledge of the practices to better understand the theory, and the practitioner can take advantage of certain basic principles to bolster his recommendations. Principles and practices serve both the student and the practitioner.

THE "THINGS" OF EDUCATION

For centuries, very little attention was given to the "things of education." Education was envisioned primarily as people—teachers and learners. School buildings were incidental to the learning process. Wherever the Athenian teacher could conveniently hold a discussion with a small group of learners, that was where the school was. Education was primitive and uncomplicated in those days. Parents simply selected a teacher and sent only their boys to him. Oftentimes the school was nothing more than a teacher and a few students meeting on the open stairs of an ancient temple.

Recent advances in instructional methodology, educational psychology, and programmable learning technology have stimulated the development of a wide variety of effective teaching aids. These new instructional tools have had a profound effect on modern educational thinking about the "things of education." Today's school building is more sophisticated in design and function. More than just a shelter for its occupants, it is a complete educational tool, capable of supporting a wide variety of learning experiences. The electronic revolution and the availability of sophisticated teaching aids have introduced a multitude of exciting and innovative features in the design of futuristic school buildings—from kindergarten to graduate school.

Updated Hardware 2010

The new teaching devices are an important addition to the collection of educational hardware. Hardware alone, however, is educationally useless. It must be coupled with an ample supply of related educational software—films; transparencies; magnetic tapes; and a variety of computer disks, including flexible ("floppy"), rigid, and laser videodiscs on which commercially prepared computer programs for instructional uses are recorded.

Excellent school facilities and dedicated teachers are the basic ingredients of a good educational program. As important as "the things of education" may be, they do not per se produce first-rate instruction. It cannot be assumed that functionally designed school buildings containing a wide variety of modern teaching aids will automatically improve the quality of the educational program. The importance of skillful teachers cannot be overstated. On the other hand, a skillful teacher working in a well-designed and highly functional school building, supplied with a wide array of electronic and visual teaching aids, can achieve a level of instructional effectiveness that far exceeds what is possible when the necessary "things of education" are not provided.

EXTENDED USE OF EXISTING BUILDINGS

During the period of increasing birthrate and expanding school enrollments immediately after World War II, the solution to overcrowded classrooms was, in most cases, a new building. The major questions, under those circumstances, were what new building and where should it be located? Today the problem assumes an *now* entirely different form. With the significant drop in birthrate, the former problem of overcrowding is less pressing. In a few suburban areas, there is still some residual overcrowding; but, for the most part, the major educational challenge stems from obsolescence. To be sure, obsolete school buildings existed even then, but the need for new capacity was so great that it was often fiscally impossible to replace obsolete schools and construct new ones simultaneously.

With taxes rising higher and higher, and with a significant increase in taxpayer resistance to the construction of new school buildings, it might be extremely profitable to explore the ways and means of making existing buildings more educationally effective. A way must be found to overcome obsolescence and to provide for a moderate increase in building capacity without overburdening the taxpayers of the school district. We must begin to look more seriously at the buildings we have. These buildings represent a sizable capital outlay, and every conceivable avenue should be explored to protect this investment without shortchanging the students.

As will be discussed in detail in Chapter 17, remodeling is not always the most economical solution to the problem of obsolescence and additional capacity. On the other hand, we can no longer afford the luxury of abandoning school buildings simply because they are old, educationally obsolete, or both. No school building should be recommended for disposal by a school district until an in-depth study is made.

Undoubtedly there are situations in which the cost of remodeling is not in the best financial interest of the school district over a 50-year period, but would adequately meet short-range needs. For example, a heavily bonded school district might have two options. It could remodel an existing building for one million dollars with an expected useful life of 15 years, or it could construct a new one for three million dollars with an expected useful life of 60 years. Simple mathematics dictates that the new three-million-dollar building is the "better buy." However, let us, for a moment, examine the financial impact of these two options on the school district. The school district is already heavily in debt and is paying for a number of recently constructed school buildings. Taxes for other services are also high. Its tax leeway is approaching an alarming level. Under these circumstances, would it be better to consider some form of installment purchasing to provide for its educational needs? Build what is needed in the foreseeable future for the smallest capital outlay and accept the penalty that must be paid, because the school district is not in a position to take full advantage of long-range financial benefits.

Admittedly, this approach is pragmatic, but more and more school districts will be confronted with a similar situation in the not-too-distant future. The recent period of rapid enrollment growth has left many school districts in precarious financial straits. For some time to come, such school districts must make the best use of existing facilities until they can recover some of their borrowing potential. Several sections of this book deal directly with the ways and means of getting the most education out of existing school buildings.

PROTECTING THE CAPITAL INVESTMENT OF THE SCHOOL DISTRICT

Maintaining the educational efficiency and the aesthetic attractiveness of school buildings concerns both educators and boards of education. But new buildings do not always fare too well in this regard. Understandably, the public often assumes that a new building requires little or no further attention. Actually, a building is new only when the keys are turned over to the Board of Education. From that day forward, it starts to get old. The mechanical equipment begins to wear, the intensity of the artificial lighting visibly declines, metal surfaces tarnish, and painted areas accumulate a film of condensed air pollutants. The well-known aging process has set in.

These changes are slow, subtle, natural, and cumulative. In addition, normal use accentuates the problem of maintenance. Students contribute to the soiling of floors and walls and the expected wear and tear on surfaces. Also, there is a substantial amount of unpredictable damage, due to abuse or misuse of the building or teaching equipment. Consequently, new school buildings may deteriorate due to lack of proper maintenance.

A long-range program of preventive and restorative maintenance that protects the initial capital outlay is important to the school district. Maintenance should be conceived of as an ongoing activity designed to keep the educational function and environment of a school building at peak efficiency. This is more likely to result in maximum educational return per maintenance dollar. Various suggestions concerning the maintenance and operation of a school building are presented in Chapter 18.

AN HISTORICAL PERSPECTIVE ON EDUCATIONAL FACILITIES

Space for learning has undergone dramatic change over the past two thousand years. In the beginning there were no educational facilities at all. There were no classrooms, and there were no desks and chairs. Plato and Aristotle met with students to exchange and discuss ideas in the open air at any convenient location, perhaps in the shade of a temple or a wall. Since then, educational facilities have become effective laboratories of learning, where teachers and students benefit from the latest advances in educational technology and instructional methodology. The once rudimentary space for learning is now a complex enclosure that controls the environment and supports the learning process.

It is difficult to imagine that school architecture is a relatively recent development. In fact, prior to World War II, school buildings were not viewed as specialized public buildings. Some of them reflected Greek or Roman architecture. Others were simple, uncomplicated nondescript buildings housing a rather traditional curriculum. Schools were generally utilitarian structural envelopes that simply protected teachers and pupils from the elements. In essence, they were shelters in which teachers cited and pupils recited, and where the "things of education" consisted primarily of benches, tables, books, pencils, paper, pens, and perhaps a slate blackboard.

At the risk of reiterating certain historical facts that are quite familiar to many educators, it is fascinating to examine the development of educational facilities over the centuries in relation to corresponding educational practices. Until recently, little or no attempt was made to design school buildings for specific educational functions. It may take some readers by surprise to learn that school buildings did not become architectural entities until the middle of the twentieth century!

For centuries architects envisioned architecture as an overall science of building construction without a view to school design per se. Until recent times, a school building was not considered a vehicle of architectural expression. In fact, school buildings did not attract the serious attention of architects until mass education was established in many countries about a century ago.

The development of architecture in relation to school buildings is traced through three periods of history. The first is the Hellenistic Era. Although there was some development of church grammar schools in Italy, France, Germany, and England during the fifteenth and sixteenth centuries, a review of the historical literature reveals no special interest in school facilities as a form of architecture at that time. Consequently, the second phase of this study jumps to the Early American and post–Civil War period. The third phase is the Twentieth Century.

THE HELLENISTIC AND ROMAN PERIODS

The Status of Architecture (500–200 B.C.)

During this period, architecture focused on the design of early forms of Doric temples found in Italy and Corinth (Figure 1-1). When choosing materials to construct these temples, the builders began with softer stone that could be easily shaped. Later they used marble. Its superior strength became more important than the ease of working.

Architecture during the fourth century B.C. produced public buildings that were magnificent and imposing. They were designed in a monumental style (Figure 1-1) that has persisted for centuries. The interior design of these monuments changed from time to time. Greece emphasized municipal functions, so the interior spaces of Greek monuments were generally planned as series of long narrow halls to house council chambers, record offices, and law courts.[1] The Romans, at a later date, felt the need to provide forums in many of their centers of population. While the exterior style of the Roman monuments did not depart greatly from that of the

FIGURE 1-1 **Doric Architecture, 500 B.C.**

Greeks, internal design and placement changed drastically. Typically, a central open area was surrounded by buildings that provided spectator and circulation space for the populace attending forums.[2]

The Status of School Buildings (500–200 B.C.)

During the early part of the Hellenistic and Roman eras, a "school" was not associated with a structure. Wherever the teacher was, there was the "school," regardless of the physical environment. A teacher and his small group of students constituted the "school." Teaching sessions were held outside in the open air (Figure 1-2), usually sheltered by a public building.

Around the year 100 B.C., the demand for schools reached a significant level as the education of boys became an accepted part of the culture. Although not compulsory, education "was considered to be a private concern of the family."[3] For the most part, the Greek and Roman schools were quite similar in many ways. They

FIGURE 1-2 **The Open Air Classroom, 500 B.C.**

did differ, however, in one respect. The "Romans placed greater emphasis on rhetoric the art of thinking on one's feet."[4]

Since education was not universal at that time, class enrollments in Roman schools were quite small by today's standards. Class sizes ranged from two or three students in a small group to several scores of students in a lecture situation. But they never reached the multitude of students we find in schools today.[5]

Schools, as places to teach and learn, were not associated with physical facilities until the end of the Hellenistic and Roman periods. Early instructional spaces, sometimes called schools, were rudimentary and housed a rather primitive educational program. Except for the *palaestra* (gymnasium), educational space was simply an existing room where teacher and students assembled. Thus, at that time, a "school" was wherever space was available.

The educational program of the Greek boy of this period was quite simple. Three basic areas of learning required only three teachers—the *chitharist* or teacher of music; the *grammaticist* or teacher of reading, writing, and arithmetic; and the *paedotribe* or teacher of gymnastics. What little educational equipment there was (Figure 1-3), the pupil supplied:

FIGURE 1-3 **An Early Grade School**

- Plaques of baked earth upon which the alphabet was written
- Several styli
- Wax tablets
- A counting board using pebbles of different colors for thousands, hundreds, tens, and units
- Quills, ink, and papyrus
- Simple musical instruments, such as the lyre or the flute[6]

According to Cubberley,[7] the grammaticist and the chitharist originally occupied the same room for instructional purposes, but later separated and taught in two adjoining rooms. The palaestra was usually found in another building where pupils reported for instruction in gymnastics.

Educational facilities during the Roman Period (about 100 B.C.) had not improved much over those in Greece one or two centuries earlier.[8] Classes might well have been held under a portico, in a shed, in a booth in front of a house, or in a recessed corner of a room shut in by curtains. The equipment found in these ancient schools consisted of a chair for the master, benches for the pupils, and a bundle of rods *(ferula)* for the instruction.[9] The meeting place of the pupils and teacher was incidental to the instructional process.

THE EARLY AMERICAN PERIOD (SEVENTEENTH CENTURY)

Early American Architecture

During the first part of the seventeenth century in America, shelter was the primary concern of the early settlers. There was little choice in construction materials, so builders used whatever materials were available. In the eastern part of the country, stone was used for foundations and wood for the upper levels. In the west, masonry, stucco, and adobe were the major materials used for construction. Shape and form were of lesser concern to the builders of Early American structures.

Toward the end of the seventeenth century, there was some evidence of interest in architectural design. For the most part, Early American architecture followed whatever was in vogue in England at the time. The lack of trained architects, the inexperience of the builders in working with classical forms, and the necessity of using wood and bricks instead of stone produced an architecture that was interesting but undistinguished. Architectural interest at that time was focused primarily on public buildings (Figure 1-4), such as Craigie House in Cambridge, the old State House in Boston, and Independence Hall in Philadelphia.

FIGURE 1-4 **Seventeenth-Century American Architecture**

Early American School Buildings

American school buildings were so simple and so utilitarian in this period that they failed to attract the attention of architects. In all probability, the practical and resourceful citizen in the seventeenth century felt no need of architectural advice in planning a school anyway. To him, a school was a simple structure with a fireplace on one end, chalkboards on the west wall, and windows on the east wall. Since natural illumination was the only source of lighting, the visual environment was far from satisfactory on overcast days.

Figure 1-5 shows a typical "Little Red Schoolhouse" built in 1828—located in Shrewsbury, Massachusetts. Many educators and historians have written about the Little Red Schoolhouse with affection and admiration, but Gulliford points out that most of the early schoolhouses were not red at all. They assumed the color of whatever construction materials were available in the vicinity of the school site, such as logs, rough-sawn vertical boards, stone, and adobe.

These early country schools did not provide a stimulating learning environment. They were frequently crowded, poorly ventilated, and drab, and were equipped with a whipping post. Gulliford also pointed out that:

the interior arrangements and equipment did not lead particularly to attentiveness or order in the classroom.[10]

FIGURE 1-5 **A Typical Little Red Schoolhouse**

FIGURE 1-6 **A Seventeenth-Century American Classroom**

Seventeenth- and eighteenth-century American schoolhouses had progressed very little beyond the ancient notion that they were simply shelters in which pupils and teachers might come together. They did include some furniture: benches and tables for the pupils and a podium for the teacher (Figure 1-6).

THE POST–CIVIL WAR PERIOD

Post–Civil War American Architecture

Roth points out:

During the second half of the nineteenth century, the decline of architectural conception and creative thought was approaching the lowest possible level characteristic of a deeply uprooted and contradictory epoch. The architects in that period held on to certain vague traditions which in no way correspond to modern times. The fact that school buildings became a state concern (during this period) furthered their erroneous development from the start.[11]

No evidence of any distinct relationship between schoolhouse design and architecture appeared until the latter part of the nineteenth century. In big cities, where the structurally complex buildings needed could no longer be planned by laymen, the advice and services of architects were sought at last.

In its incipient stages, school architecture was more or less an adaptation of other forms of architecture without much regard to the needs of education. As Roth says, "The design of the ordinary school building took no account of its nature or various functions. The solution adopted was nothing but an addition of classrooms, one exactly like the other."[12]

During the latter part of the nineteenth century, schools were designed as architectural works of art rather than as educational facilities. Schoolhouses of that period were outsized buildings, characterized by unfunctional and undifferentiated space organization and unfunctional and noncreative design.[13] Many such schools are still in use with their large corridors and imposing lobbies, stately columns, and useless parapets. Architectural emphasis was clearly on shape, form, and style, not on the functional aspects of school plants.

American School Buildings

Knight provides a detailed description of Early American schoolhouses, as they were commonly called at that time (Figure 1-7).

FIGURE 1-7 **The Nineteenth-Century American School**

The great majority of the schools of New York state in 1844 were officially described . . . as naked and deformed, in comfortless and dilapidated buildings with unhung doors, broken sashes, absent panes, stilted benches, yawning roofs and muddy mouldering floors. . . . Only one third of the schoolhouses were reported in good repair, another third in only comfortable circumstances, while more than 3,300 were unfit for the reception of either man or beast.[14]

The battle for free public schools in the United States was fought and won between 1820 and 1850. Through the efforts of Horace Mann, Henry Barnard, and others, the value of free public education came to be recognized, and in time the public school became an accepted institution in the United States. Schoolhouses of many types began to rise throughout the country. The more elaborate schools were, of course, erected in the cities; simple one- or two-room structures sufficed for the rural areas. By and large, the school building itself was still viewed as a place where the teacher could instruct pupils in a sheltered environment. The schoolhouse was still a long way from a learning laboratory. In fact, as noted above, a few school buildings were still "unfit for the reception of either man or beast."

THE TWENTIETH CENTURY

The Consolidated School Movement

At the turn of the twentieth century, the size and shape of American schoolhouses were greatly influenced by the consolidation movement that spread rapidly throughout the country. Thousands of one-room schoolhouses were abandoned immediately following World War I and students were transported to so-called grammar schools housing grades one through eight. Kindergartens were included in a few urban school systems.

The consolidation movement was directly responsible for the rapid development of multiclassroom school buildings. They appeared in various shapes and sizes. For the most part, they continued to serve primarily as shelters designed to protect students from the weather. The interiors remained simple and rudimentary, with copious blackboards and screwed-down furniture.

One-room schools have not become extinct, however. According to Muse, there were still 837 one-teacher schools in rural America in 1984.[15] Some of these schools are located in remote and sparsely populated areas where consolidation is neither practical nor economically justifiable.

Recent research reveals that current one-room schoolhouses are capable of providing good education for students in isolated rural areas.[16] The availability of video programs transmitted via satellite (Chapter 2) has the potential of dramatically enriching the educational program in one-teacher schools. Thus, the outlook for the one-room school is quite promising.

The Emergence of School Architecture

According to Roth,

> . . . *Schools were either castles or palaces and their architectural style either Gothic, Renaissance, or Baroque, or a combination of styles. Whatever their shapes or forms were, they in no way resembled a school (in the functional sense). The child's own scale was not taken into consideration, either practically or emotionally. Out-sized entrances, corridors, stairways seem to be particularly selected by the architect for his "artistic" effects with the well meant aim of contributing to the child's education in art.*
>
> *It would be wrong and unfair to blame the architect alone. The absence of unbiased pedagogical conceptions, and of a curriculum based on them were as much a cause of mistaken evolution, as was the lack of close collaboration between the architect, educator and building authorities.*[17]

During this period, schoolhouses were, for the most part, not architecturally exciting. The effect of European architecture was noticeable in some school buildings (Figure 1-8), and a few schools built earlier in the century did reflect the classical influence, but the majority of them were structures without architectural

FIGURE 1-8 **The Classical American School**

character. Many looked like large boxes enclosed by red brick walls and covered by a steep slanted roof. The large boxes were subdivided into four or eight smaller, uniform, cubicles called classrooms. Sometimes the attic space under the slate roof was used as an assembly hall. At that time, these buildings undoubtedly represented the best conceivable answer to the school housing problem, but, as Roth points out, neither the architects nor the educators really had a clear understanding of the educational tasks to be accomplished.[18]

As we approach the twenty-first century, many educators and architects are aware of the need for functional planning of school buildings. Unfortunately, a few boards of education and school administrators still do not recognize the need for cooperative action between educators and architects. Some school districts still ask an architect to design a school on the basis of the information listed on a single sheet of paper. This information may include the grade level and number of pupils to be housed in a school and, perhaps, the number of the various types of spaces desired. To ask an architect to design a school without giving him or her a complete set of educational specifications requiring perhaps 50 or 60 pages of educational information is ridiculous and unfair. Until it is generally recognized that educational facility planning is a team operation involving architects, educators, and boards of education, schools will continue to be built to meet housing rather than instructional needs, and many will include the shortcomings of the schools of yesterday and today. According to Roth: "The development of school buildings up to the present time must be considered faulty for, indeed, it has not achieved the standard required by sound and valid pedagogic principles."[19]

During the latter part of the twentieth century, the development of school buildings was rapid, innovative, and dramatic. Immediately following World War II, architects became quite excited about "bringing the outside into the building." Accordingly, large expanses of window-walls were built into school buildings. Beautiful vistas and natural light in great quantities were the order of the day. This development created problems of controlling heat buildup within the buildings during certain parts of the year and glare from direct and reflected sunlight. The 1960s ushered in the era of the "finger design." Energy losses and gains were very high due to the large expanses of outside walls. But with a plentiful supply of inexpensive energy at that time, this design posed no significant problems. During the 1970s, air conditioning of school buildings was widely accepted. But due to the large amounts of energy required for air conditioning, architects became greatly concerned with the heat gain of a school building during hot days when air conditioning was required. In order to solve this problem, architects introduced the controversial "windowless" school. And finally, the enormous increase in the cost of energy following the Iranian revolution in the 1970s introduced a multitude of changes in the design of educational facilities for the purpose of conserving energy and facilitating energy management. These and other developments are discussed in detail in various parts of this text.

THE BIRTH OF PROFESSIONAL EDUCATIONAL FACILITY PLANNING

As mentioned earlier, for centuries school buildings were rudimentary shelters that simply protected teachers and learners from the elements. It was not until the first quarter of the twentieth century that educators began investigating the possibility that there might be a relationship between learning and the design of instructional spaces within a school building. A few educators of that era sought to determine whether or not the design of a school building imposed limitations on the quality of the educational program. Not surprisingly, these early studies suggested that there was a perceptible relationship between the design of teaching spaces and the increased number of instructional activities that could be accommodated within them. This finding signaled the beginning of educational facility planning.

The Pioneers of Educational Facility Planning

The profession of educational facility planning developed slowly prior to World War II. Among the pioneers in the field was Nicholaus Engelhardt, Sr., a professor at Teachers College, Columbia University, in the 1920s. Engelhardt had a keen and inquisitive mind. He did not hesitate to use innovative and untried approaches in attacking problems confronting school plant planners. He was successful in blending theory and practice in resolving issues and problems associated with the planning of school plants. He developed basic techniques for conducting school facility surveys that are still valid today. (The educational survey process is discussed in detail in Chapters 3 and 4.) He devised several methods for making both long- and short-range enrollment projections. Many of his reports and studies published prior to World War II greatly influenced the planning and design of educational facilities constructed during the middle of the twentieth century.

Immediately following the end of World War II, there was a phenomenal increase in the number of educators and architects involved as professional planners of educational facilities. N. L. Engelhardt, Sr. was joined by N. L Engelhardt, Jr. and Stanton Leggett, who conducted school surveys for local school districts and advised architects in designing functional school buildings. The list of educational facility planners of that period is quite lengthy. Among the most prominent professional leaders in school plant planning during the middle of the twentieth century were Henry H. Linn and Felix McCormick at Columbia University; John Herrick, Arthur Wohlers, and Marion Conrad at Ohio State University; Donald J. Leu at Michigan State University; James D. MacConnell at Stanford University; and W. D. McClurkin at Peabody College. During this period, Charles D. Gibson, a member of the Bureau of School Planning in California, made significant progress in the quality of lighting provided in school buildings. In addition to educators, a few architects were also pioneers in the design of innovative school buildings. The two most prominent school architectural firms of that era include Perkins and Will in Chicago, and Caudill, Rowlett and Scott in Houston.

THE FORMATION OF AN EDUCATIONAL FACILITY COUNCIL

In 1921, three concerned educators, Samuel Challman of Minnesota, Charles McDermott of New Jersey, and Frank H. Wood of New York, met in a hotel room in Atlantic City to discuss the possible formation of an organization to deal with the problems of school plant planning. The original intent of the proposed organization was "to promote the establishment of reasonable standards for school buildings and equipment with due regard for economy of expenditure, dignity of design, utility of space, healthful conditions, and safety of human life.[20]

The above-mentioned triumvirate together with other concerned educators met a year later, in 1922, and created a national organization to develop minimum standards of school building construction and equipment from the standpoint of meeting educational needs. The members of the group agreed to meet from time to time to share ideas and to collectively prepare specifications to serve as national standards for school construction and equipment. The founders named this embryonic organization the National Council on Schoolhouse Construction.

For over a quarter of a century, the Council, as it was often called, served as an information center for anyone engaged in the planning of school buildings. Its primary function was to develop minimum standards for school building construction and make them available to school plant planners.

In 1930, however, the Council introduced a new service for school administrators throughout the United States and Canada. Instead of simply responding to requests for information, it began publishing guides for the use of anyone engaged in a school building program. These guides focused primarily on the dissemination of specific minimum standards for the planning and construction of school buildings.

The impact of these guides on the planning of school buildings was overwhelming. The influence of the Council on Schoolhouse Construction far exceeded the expectations of its founders. School districts began to rely more and more on the Council for technical information concerning the planning of school buildings. Under these circumstances, the Council felt that it had an obligation to reexamine the content of its guides and to reevaluate its goals and objectives. Thus, in 1946, the Council set new policies and guidelines for material contained in its publications. Fearing that minimum standards might become maximum practice, the Council de-emphasized minimum standards and promoted basic principles of sound educational facility planning in all of its subsequent publications. The main thrust of the new policies was to encourage innovation and creativity in the planning of educational facilities. The Council also broadened the scope of educational facility planning. It changed the designation of "school building planning" to "school plant planning" by including the school site as an integral part of the planning.

Over the years, the National Council on Schoolhouse Construction has been a positive and dynamic force in the field of educational facility planning. The Council has been flexible and innovative in meeting the challenges of an unsettled society. The influence and membership of the Council has grown dramatically. The name of the National Council on Schoolhouse Construction was recently changed to the Council of Educational Facility Planners International. Its membership is no longer restricted to educators and education-related persons. It has a roster of several hundred members including persons from a wide variety of disciplines. Little did the three founders of the Council ever dream in 1921 that their brainchild would ultimately influence the nature of school buildings throughout the world.

NOTES

1. Michael Raeburn, *Architecture of the Western World* (New York: Rizzoli International Publications, 1980), p. 51.

2. Ibid., p. 61.

3. W. F. Connell, *A History of Education in the Twentieth-Century World* (New York: Teachers College Press, 1980), p. 10.

4. Ibid., p. 26.

5. Stanley F. Bonner, *Education in Ancient Rome* (Berkeley: University of California Press, 1977), p. 131.

6. Elwood P. Cubberly, *The History of Education* (New York: Houghton Mifflin, 1948), pp. 26–29.

7. Ibid., p. 30.

8. Ibid., p. 36.

9. Russell Sturgis, *History of Architecture* (New York: Doubleday, 1916), p. 142.

10. Andrew Gulliford, *American Country Schools* (Washington, DC: The Preservation Press, 1984), p. 159.

11. Alfred Roth, *The New School* (New York: Frederick Prager, 1957), p. 24.

12. Idem.

13. Ibid., p. 26.

14. Edgar W. Knight, *Education in the U.S.* 3d ed. (Boston: Ginn and Co., 1957), p. 416.

15. Ivan Muse, Ralph B. Smith, Bruce Baker, *One-Teacher School in the 1980s.* Fort Collins, CO: National Rural Education Association, 1987, p. 14.

16. Idem.

17. Roth, op. cit., p. 26.

18. Idem.

19. Ibid., p. 24.

20. *Guide for Planning School Plants.* National Council on Schoolhouse Construction (now, Council of Educational Facility Planners, International). (Nashville, TN: Peabody College, 1953). Foreword.

► 2

Educational Practices and Technological Developments

PREVALENT EDUCATIONAL PRACTICES RELATED TO EDUCATIONAL FACILITY PLANNING

Both administrative policy and classroom methodology have some bearing on the design of educational facilities. Almost without exception, planners routinely provide for those classroom practices that are already operating in the school district. But they do not always include other innovative concepts that are likely to improve the educational experience. A few of these neoteric concepts and practices are presented here. They and others can be examined for possible implementation during the planning stages of an educational facility.

Many exciting educational practices are being introduced from time to time in various school districts. Some are the product of imaginative classroom teachers who are on a never-ending search for more effective teaching methods. Others are conceived in more theoretical settings in colleges and universities. Regardless of their origin, some new educational concepts eventually become an accepted part of the curriculum.

Innovations are proposed and applied in quick succession. Curriculum seems to be in a constant state of flux. Some concepts are terminated, some are continued, and new ones are introduced. Educators jokingly point out that, if one makes no changes for a sufficiently long time, present practices will someday be seen as promising innovations. Under this recycling concept, a traditional school system could become a pioneer in education, simply by waiting for the others to complete the cycle. Many educators compare curriculum to a pendulum: as public attitudes and values change, the curriculum changes with it. It should not come as a complete surprise, therefore, when an old concept is revived and reintroduced in the school curriculum.

It is sometimes assumed that all innovative practices and imaginative concepts are good because they are new and exciting. This position is not always tenable, however. Some innovations are readily accepted. They persist over a number of years. Some that are tried and dropped without much fanfare are called fads. Others continue in practice in an atmosphere of uncertainty and controversy. In recent times, "the windowless school concept" and "the open space plan" have been subjected to considerable controversy. Their fate apparently has not yet been decided.

The design of functional futuristic school buildings requires superhuman capabilities. School plant planners should not only be superbly endowed with creative powers but they should also be able to clearly distinguish between those educational concepts and practices that will persist for a long time and those that are likely to be short-lived. Obviously, it is humanly impossible to perform this task with any degree of certainty. At best, planners can study a large number of concepts and practices and identify those that best fit into the philosophy of the people who will be served by the proposed school building.

The concepts and practices that follow are judged to be educationally sound and administratively feasible. But educational facility planners should not limit themselves to this small list. Other ideas should be considered. On the other hand, innovations should not be incorporated simply because they appear to be new and exciting. In some instances, it might be wise not to introduce new practices upon the completion of a new or modernized school building, particularly if the community, the staff, and the students are not yet ready for such changes. In these instances, school plant planners should design the school building so that these features can be added at a later date.

Promising Instructional Practices

Negotiated Learning

The concept of negotiated learning is not new. It is a revival of the learning method familiarly known as "the contract method," "independent study," or "multioption instruction." The application of this concept has much merit for those students who can profit from it. In general, its success depends upon the skill of the teacher in preparing and using well-conceived units of instruction and upon the initiative and resourcefulness of the student. When both are present, the results from this approach to individualized instruction can be gratifying to both teacher and student. Negotiated learning allows the student to participate in shaping the learning experiences that he or she will undergo in achieving certain predetermined educational outcomes that may be in harmony with personal goals.

Implications for School Plant Planning.   There are no special design features associated with this concept. Obviously, it requires a teacher office or faculty work station of about 120 square feet. The trend is to provide offices for teachers, even at the secondary level. Thus, where this facility is provided, nothing special is required to accommodate the negotiated learning approach.

To learn on an individual basis, students need space in which to study, experiment, and discuss. A student enrolled in this program is assigned to a carrel for an indefinite period of time. Clearly the number of carrels should equal the number of students anticipated in this program. Normally, carrels are not assigned. Students using the learning resources center simply find a vacant carrel and use it. Under the concept of negotiated learning, however, a student station is reserved for each student. These carrels should contain lockable drawers and lockable bookshelves where students can store their books and work materials.

The Open Laboratory Concept

The open laboratory concept can be applied to any learning situation requiring students to perform experiments, gain skills, or conduct demonstrations of basic principles—for example, science laboratories, secretarial science laboratories, and engineering science laboratories. This approach is not overly complicated. Students are free to do laboratory work at their convenience, provided they reserve the space in advance. A faculty member is always on duty in each open laboratory to assist students and to make certain that all safety and health precautions are taken.

Implications for School Plant Planning.   The spaces most affected by this concept are the laboratories where this method of instruction is used. The laboratories must be large enough to accommodate the carrels, where students primarily listen to tape recordings. It is recommended that carrels comprise half the laboratory capacity. Some planners feel that a one to three ratio is sufficient. It often is, but during busy periods laboratory experiment stations often remain vacant because too few carrels cause a bottleneck.

If space is at a premium, the amount of area allocated to each carrel can be kept at a minimum by omitting chair space. It is not unreasonable to expect a student, unless physically handicapped, to stand in front of a carrel and listen to a tape for five or six minutes at a time. Under these conditions, the area for each carrel can be reduced from about 20 square feet to approximately 12. In a biology laboratory serving 24 students, for example, it would require an additional 144 square feet to accommodate the suggested 12 carrels. These could be located in an alcove or along a wall that is not exposed to heavy student circulation. Also, these carrels should be supplied with local lighting and a 120-volt outlet for tape players and other audiovisual equipment.

The Epideikic Method of Instruction in the School of the Future

The epideikic method, defined as the demonstration-inquiry method of teaching, relies heavily upon the combination of teacher demonstration and student inquiry. In this age of science and advanced technology, it is appropriate to introduce the demonstration type of instruction whenever possible in the school curriculum. Students should be able to observe demonstrations of basic principles in the sciences and the humanities and then to make inquiries stemming from their observations. As pointed out earlier, the inquiry method of instruction, used judiciously, has a definite place in the school curriculum. The epideikic concept is basic to both the inquiry and the presentation forms of instruction. The school of the future can encourage and facilitate both by including features that support, encourage, and stimulate demonstration.

Implications for School Plant Planning.   This concept is applicable to all areas of instruction. Whenever the word "demonstration" is mentioned, however, it is generally envisioned as applying to the physical sciences. To be sure, many demonstrations do arise from the physical world about us, but teachers may often use the demonstration method to reinforce instruction in, for example, the social sciences. A colony of ants viewed through glass shows the distribution of labor and specialization of activity in an organized society. A group of imaginative teachers working with a receptive planning committee can suggest many ingenious features that will promote the demonstration type of instruction. One obvious suggestion is to provide a demonstration area in classrooms or large-group instructional spaces. The minimum requirement in an elementary school building, for example, would be one demonstration table with sink, utilities, and electricity in each instructional space. In instructional spaces having a capacity of more than 10 students, a closed-circuit television unit should be provided with one 21-inch monitor per 25 students. The school of the future would probably include television monitors in the same ratio in spaces where large-group instruction is conducted. The epideikic concept should also play a part in the design of spaces that can be converted into large teaching areas through the use of operable partitions.

As mentioned earlier, teachers do not motivate students; this they must do for themselves. But teachers can provide experiences that are most likely to energize students to become motivated to learn. This objective has been foremost in the conscious or unconscious thinking of successful teachers for centuries.

In planning school buildings, both architects and educators can do much to assist teachers in stimulating desire for learning. Provision should be made for every reasonable type of demonstration and simple experiment in the physical and social sciences. Demonstration, a powerful stimulation to student motivation, can be the means of arousing intellectual curiosity at the elementary school level. Both the method of presentation and the content of instruction must arouse and hold interest if we expect to awaken students from their frequent classroom lethargy.

Cooperative Learning

Cooperative or collaborative learning is a modern version of the old practice of students learning from each other. According to Watson and Rangel, "A popular teaching strategy of the 1980s, cooperative learning, may continue well into the 1990s. . . ."[1] It is a group process whereby students share information, understandings, and experiences in a team setting. The role of individual members of the team may vary from one team to another depending upon the purpose underlying the operation of each team. A cooperative learning group may perform as a heterogeneous team in which each member functions as an individual interacting with other members of the team. Or, the group may operate in a teammate-interpendence mode in which the performance of each member contributes toward the achievement of the team as a whole in accordance with goals set forth by its members. Finally, the team may function as a team-interdependent group whereby each team engages in friendly competition with other teams having similar goals and objectives.

From the standpoint of educational facility planning, most classrooms can accommodate the activities associated with cooperative learning without much difficulty. The rearrangement of book shelves and storage cabinets can often provide the necessary spatial separation for independent group activities conducted within a classroom. While the success of cooperative learning depends largely on the resourcefulness of the classroom teacher, the selection of highly mobile furniture and cabinets facilitates the implementation of this instructional activity.

Students teaching one another, however, is not a new concept. It is perhaps as old as teaching itself. It is not unusual to find students teaching concepts or skills on an informal basis to one or two of their peers. This practice is beneficial to both the teaching student and to those being taught. The teaching student strengthens his or her knowledge or skills in order to transmit them clearly to his or her peers, while the learners profit from having concepts explained in simple language that they can readily understand.

It is not suggested, however, that peer "teachers" replace professional classroom teachers or that students be used regularly as teacher aides. Although this concept is educationally sound, it should be used judiciously. It might be considered in situations where class sizes have increased to intolerable levels due to severe budgetary restrictions. Under these circumstances, it may be used as a stopgap measure to ease the excessive burden imposed on the classroom teacher.

Relevant Administrative Policies and Concepts

The Variable Group Size Teaching for Secondary Schools

One intriguing concept being considered for secondary school and college-level instruction could virtually eliminate the conventional instruction of students in classes or sections. Under the variable group size concept, primary attention is given to the curriculum and the individual learning experiences that it includes. The entire curriculum is analyzed to determine the most effective group size for each learning experience. Such an analysis would clearly indicate that, for some experiences, a 1:1 ratio is best—one teacher instructing a single student. For other types of learning, the ratio might well be one teacher for three or four students, or one teacher to 15 learners. For still others, the ratio could be one teacher to as many as 150 or 300 or 500 students. This approach treats learning in a realistic and sensible fashion, providing for tutoring where it is needed and for large group instruction where that is effective. The overall cost of instruction to the school district is not changed materially under this plan. The increased cost of teaching groups smaller than the conventional 25 or 30 students is offset by the saving in instructional time when a single teacher teaches large groups of 150 or more students.

Implications for School Plant Planning.   School plant planners should give serious thought to this concept in designing schools. It goes much further than the mere installation of randomly scattered, movable partitions throughout the building. Such half-measures are not justifiable. It would be wiser to include destructible partitions rather than costly movable ones.

A school building planned for variable class size must contain spaces that can be divided and subdivided easily by the teacher at any time. The major requirement, in this instance, is a system of interlocking operable partitions having a noise reduction coefficient of about 38 decibels. Spaces should be capable of accommodating groups of 6, 15, 30, 60, 90, 150, and 300 students.

The number of spaces required for groups of a given size depends upon the nature of the educational program. It is suggested that the following formula be used to determine the requisite number of *instructional areas* (not rooms):

$$T = 1.25 \frac{E}{C} \cdot \frac{n}{N}$$

where:

   T = Number of areas needed (rounded off to the closest whole number)
   E = Total number of students requiring space for a given group size
   C = Number of students in a given group or class
   n = Number of minutes that a given group size meets per week
   N = Number of minutes in the school week

Example.   Let us assume that an elementary school program calls for 275 students to meet in groups of 16 for 10 percent of the time. Suppose further that there are 1,500 minutes in the school week based on a 5-hour school day. The students would meet 150 minutes per week (10 percent of 1,500) in groups of 16.

$$T = (1.25) \frac{275}{16} \cdot \frac{150}{1,500} = 1.25 \, (17.19)(0.1)$$

$$= 2.15 \text{ teaching stations}$$

This means that two areas (teaching stations) will be required on a full-time basis to satisfy the needs of 275 students divided in groups of 16. The computation is repeated for all of the other groupings. The total number of areas needed is the sum of the individual computations.

The Variable Class Size Concept for Elementary and Middle Schools

Many educators agree that certain learning experiences in elementary and middle schools can be imparted just as effectively to groups of 300, 150, 75, and 50 as they can to the conventional group of 25. On the other hand, there are some learning situations in which the traditional group of 25 is far too large. In fact, a ratio of one student to one teacher is required for transmission of certain knowledge or skills. There may be other learning experiences where the group should consist of 2 or 3, 6 or 8, or 12 to 15 students.

Implications for School Plant Planning.   In view of the growing acceptance that grouping for instruction should vary according to the character or complexity of the learning activity, educators are beginning to plan elementary and middle school buildings to accommodate groupings of various sizes. Teachers are being provided with offices where they can work with individual students. A few small seminar-type rooms that can be subdivided by operable partitions are being included in elementary schools to meet the need for small group instruction. And conventional classrooms are being designed so that three or four of them can be joined to form a large instructional space for a single group.

Modular Scheduling

For years educators have shown a keen interest in some form of modular scheduling. Under this concept, unit modules vary in length from 15 to 20 to 22½ or 30 minutes. The number of minutes is immaterial. It is the number of modules included in a time block that is significant. Time blocks vary in size, depending upon the nature of the learning. Two or more unit modules may comprise a single time block for a given teaching period on certain days of the week. Consequently, the length of time a student spends in a given class may vary from day to day.

From time to time, educators have expressed fears that high school students would become confused under a schedule that varied from hour to hour and from day to day. In practice, however, these fears are unfounded. In one school district, for example, modular scheduling was introduced in the middle school. When the author inquired how students managed to remember their schedule as it changed from day to day, the answer was simple: each student was asked to make a copy of his or her schedule and paste it inside their locker door. Thus, every morning each student was reminded of his or her schedule for the day.

Implications for School Plant Planning.   Modular scheduling greatly increases the movement of students during the school day. Under traditional secondary school scheduling, students move from one location to another at intervals ranging from 45 to 60 minutes. If modular scheduling is employed, students move much more frequently. Under these conditions, special attention should be given to student circulation patterns and to the design of corridors that expedite student movement. The walls separating the corridors from classrooms and laboratories should be soundproofed in order to minimize disturbances for students engaged in classroom activities while other students are travelling from one room to another. A building of compact design is also desirable.

Team Teaching

The idea of team teaching goes much further than the cooperative efforts of teachers currently practiced in conventional schools, and the structure and procedures associated with the implementation of this concept are receiving greater attention. A team of teachers with talents and abilities in different fields of instruction can develop the curriculum and methodology most likely to achieve the objectives set cooperatively by the team itself and by the school administration. The school of the future designed for team teaching should provide space where three or four teachers can plan together, space where a single teacher can prepare materials for large group presentation, work space where other types of instructional materials can be produced, and space where 90, 120, 180, or 300 students can be instructed as a single group, as well as in groups of 30 or fewer.

Implications for School Plant Planning.   A seminar room about 300 square feet in area should be provided for each two teams. An office should be planned for each teacher. A workroom having an area of approximately 400 square feet should be planned, preferably near the library. And classrooms should be grouped so that the opening of a number of movable partitions would convert several of them into a single, relatively square space with good sight lines to the podium. Team teaching can also be effective in schools that cannot convert several traditional classrooms into a single large one. When large-group instruction is desired, such schools can use the auditorium, multipurpose room, or cafeteria. Schools designed for convertibility of ordinary spaces into larger or smaller ones, however, possess the flexibility essential to the application of the concept of variable group size, discussed above.

The Nongraded School

The nongraded school concept has special significance for the planning of both elementary and secondary school facilities. In its application to secondary schools, this idea revolves more closely around a well-developed guidance program than it does around any special features that might be built into the school. Although school facilities in themselves strongly influence the quality of the educational program, it is felt that the cooperative efforts of administrators, staff, and guidance personnel are fundamental to the success of the nongraded system at both the elementary and secondary levels of education. Obviously, under this concept, the number of guidance counselors must be sharply increased.

Implications for School Plant Planning. Basically, the nongraded school concept depends on the organization of groupings within the various "year of school" levels. The major requirement is that rooms housing students in sequential year levels be contiguous. In schools or subject matter areas having more than one room per year level, the spaces should be sequential within a given group. For example, in a six-grade elementary school building, one group of instructional spaces would house year level 1–6 in sequence. A second group of spaces would contain a second sequence of six rooms, etc. Such an arrangement facilitates the movement of students from one room to the other for certain aspects of their instruction. In addition, the nongraded school should contain one seminar-type room having an area of about 350 square feet for each group of about six teachers.

The Open Campus

Some secondary schools are implementing the open campus concept to provide greater student freedom. Under this concept, students are treated as adults. They are allowed to engage in a wide variety of activities within the building and, in some cases, may even leave school if they have no class in a given period. On the face of it, the concept has considerable merit. It should make students responsible for using their time wisely.

The open campus concept, however, has become a nightmare. In one particular secondary school, students were permitted complete freedom within the building during their free periods. While students could work in the library, go to a study area, or confer with a faculty member, most of them, in this instance, chose to socialize in the corridors. These corridors were so noisy that conducting classes in these areas was impossible. Some of the students engaged in all sorts of pranks. It was reported that a teacher in a room adjoining a noisy corridor heard a loud pounding noise coming from the direction of the corridor. Upon investigation, the teacher discovered that two or three boys had stuffed a girl into one of the large corridor lockers reserved for faculty storage. Vandalism became a problem because students given a greater latitude of freedom were not provided with activities in advance. This picture seems gloomy. It is. The above describes an actual situation, and the lesson to be learned is, "Don't institute an open campus in a facility that is not designed for it." It was not the philosophy of giving students greater freedom that was faulty, but the lack of facilities that would permit students to use this freedom wisely.

When a school facility is in the planning stages, consideration should be given to special needs if the open campus concept is to be adopted. In existing school buildings, the introduction of the open campus concept should be delayed until the proper facilities can be provided. Without such spaces, the open campus concept can become a real disappointment.

Implications for School Plant Planning. The open campus concept requires spaces for a wide variety of activities. These spaces can provide educationally enriching experiences for many students enrolled in a secondary school. A secondary school housing the open campus concept should

1. provide two or three classrooms where films are shown throughout the school day. Any student who has a free period can choose a film to watch.
2. include two or three television-reviewing rooms. Each room's television should be turned to one of the major network stations.
3. provide a student lounge where students can socialize. This space should be planned for some form of passive supervision.
4. include a snack bar.
5. feature a recreation room with Ping Pong tables and other equipment.
6. be designed so that noisy spaces do not interfere with the instructional process in other parts of the building.
7. be planned to minimize vandalism. There should be no isolated, out-of-the-way alcoves, rooms, or corridors where students could loiter.
8. take full advantage of glass walls. These isolate noise but maintain visual contact among students.

The Open Space Plan

Despite the great deal of national interest in the design of school buildings without partitions, some educators are beginning to have second thoughts. There are many strong arguments favoring the open space plan and an equal number of good reasons against it. Most objective planners have mixed feelings and usually compromise in designing school buildings. The single large space is interrupted only by supporting columns, including a number of partial walls—floor to ceiling—supplemented by folding partitions. Both sides of this issue will be discussed in detail below.

For the Open Space Plan. The large expanse of space is psychologically liberating. One feels free in both movement and thought. Since partitions are often light, movable visual screens, the spaces for instruction *can* be changed in size and shape—at will and at once. The omission of walls allegedly reduces the cost of the building substantially. The open space plan lends a feeling of informality to the learning process. Students feel less regimented. There is likely to be a greater intermingling of both students and teachers. The open space plan facilitates the grouping and regrouping of students and tends to encourage change, experimentation, and innovation.

Against the Open Space Plan. Confusion and a laissez-faire attitude is often present in the "school without walls." Since there are no corridors under the open space plan, students simply roam from area to area, passing from one teaching space to and through another. Although there are as yet no validated research findings on the quantity and quality of learning in the open space plan, it can be hypothesized that the amount of learning is open to question. From a first-hand qualitative study of the open plan school, the author found himself straining to hear the teacher from a position in the rear of the room. After two or three hours, fatigue set in.

In discussing the open space plan with students, all seemed to like it, but both the writer and the students identified two major shortcomings. Subjects that require concentration are more difficult for students to master. Students complained particularly of mathematics. The subject matter was not usually very exciting, while the topic on the other side of the screen seemed more interesting. Also, sufficient chalkboard for student work was lacking. The other serious drawback concerned audiovisual materials which are clearly incompatible with the open space plan. The school administration had a ready-made solution: construct three audiovisual rooms. The open "classroom" is not used while the class is in the audiovisual room, so any savings in walls is spent in constructing audiovisual rooms to supplement the open space plan.

Many teachers liked the "liberated" feeling of the open space plan, but stated that constant background noise forced them to concentrate so much on hearing that they were physically fatigued by the end of the day.

Implications for School Plant Planning. The open space plan is a mixed blessing. Ideally, it would be desirable to plan space in such a way that the open plan atmosphere and informality could be produced whenever it was desired, and that effective teaching spaces could be created through the simple operation of folding partitions when it was educationally advantageous to do so. Imaginative school planners may wish to face the challenge of designing a school facility that contains the advantages of the open space plan without its deficiencies.

Flexibility in Space. The proponents of the open space plan also extol the virtues of flexibility in space. While this is theoretically possible, faculty members using the open space plan indicated that the space allocated to a given class activity is rarely changed in actual practice. From a practical point of view, the "flexible" space becomes almost inflexible. In a given high school, the open space plan consisted of the space normally occupied by 29 conventional classrooms plus space for corridors. Spaces for classes were loosely related to patches of colored tile on the floor. The colored patches also served an aesthetic function. Classes were located randomly within the open space. A mathematics class, for example, could adjoin an English class, a social studies class, and a foreign language class. Under these conditions, increasing the space in one class could not be done without encroaching on the space occupied by another group of students. Thus, the potential flexibility that was built into the open space plan could not be realized under normal operating conditions. In fairness to the open space plan, however, if a comprehensive team teaching approach were employed in the instructional program, flexibility of space could be achieved. On the other hand, the degree of flexibility in a conventional building is limited by the number, length, and arrangement of folding partitions and the configuration of the walls in a given area.

The School-within-a-School Concept

Under the school-within-a-school concept, a large secondary school is envisioned as two or more secondary schools operating independently on the same school site. Each school has students randomly assigned to it at all grade levels. Each school has its own administrative guidance and teaching personnel, and each is planned to operate as though it were located separately in another part of the school district.

For at least a decade, the school-within-a-school idea has been gaining considerable support. In areas where the population is so concentrated that enrollments in excess of 1,500 students must be educated at one location, this concept, sometimes called the "house plan," should be seriously explored. A word of caution is in order, however. Some school districts resort to the school-within-a-school concept, not because of high population density, but because they want a single football or basketball team—clearly an indefensible rationale for planning any kind of high school. After all, some students must be transported over fairly long distances if, let us say, 2,500 students are to be enrolled in one school. The money spent in transporting pupils from home to school represents a necessary but noneducational expenditure, and such funds, whether they are from state or local sources, might be better utilized in direct support of the educational program.

Implications for School Plant Planning. When a secondary school is likely to have an enrollment of more than 1,500 students, boards of education and school planners should seek to provide multiple school plants in two or more parts of the school district, except in highly congested areas such as New York, Los Angeles, Chicago, Dallas, Boston, and Philadelphia. A superintendent of schools once defended the planning of a single large high school in a sparsely settled school district by pointing out that students were bussed anyway. So, "What difference does it make?" Actually, it makes a considerable difference in cost—much more than the superintendent implied. In this situation, two secondary schools would have cut the bus mileage almost in half, not to mention the time students spent on the buses. Unless there is a compelling reason for building secondary schools with capacities greater than 1,500, the planning of one or more 1,200-student secondary schools should be given serious consideration.

FUTURISTIC TECHNO-EDUCATIONAL SYSTEMS

It can be assumed, a priori, that the design of educational facilities reflects the educational thinking and architectural philosophy at the time when school facilities are proposed, planned, conceived, and constructed. The end product at any given time represents a blending of prevailing architectural concepts, dominant educational practices, and promising curricular innovations. The well-planned educational facility not only provides for the accepted and conventional educational practices that are widespread at that time but also includes features that can accommodate a few of the more promising foreseeable educational concepts of the future.

There are many well-designed and educationally effective teaching aids on the market. They range from a simple slide projector to a sophisticated computer. An early teaching aid at the turn of the century was the arc lantern. This projector was extraordinarily simple. It consisted of a slide holder, a relatively large lens, and two rods of carbon that produced a very bright electric arc. While this bulky device worked fairly well, it was noisy, not portable, and somewhat troublesome to operate.

The next generation of teaching aids marked the beginning of the widespread use of supplementary instructional devices. The development of high-intensity light bulbs inaugurated a new era in projection techniques. The arc lantern was soon replaced by the slide projector, and the movie projector became a common piece of educational equipment. Most schools owned at least one movie projector, which was shared by several teachers in a school building. During this same period, a group of enterprising scientists invented the vacuum tube, which made it possible to produce a powerful distortion-free record player suitable for classroom use. Enterprising educators exploited these relatively simple educational tools to the maximum.

Today, electronic teaching devices have become extremely sophisticated and highly specialized. A few of them are programmable and many are completely automated. Once the starting button is depressed, the equipment requires no further attention. To be sure, the movie projector and slide projector have been significantly improved. They are lighter in weight, simpler to use, and brighter in intensity of image. While the record player is still widely used, the tape recorder-player is gradually replacing it in the classroom. The ingenious overhead projector is supplementing the chalkboard, and its application is far more effective than the chalkboard in the presentation of materials in a sequential pattern. Also, the capability of superimposing transparent overlays on the overhead projector to depict changes in situation, statistics, or statements makes it far superior to the traditional chalkboard.

The most exciting electronic devices, however, have yet to be fully exploited. To be sure, educators are aware of their capabilities and potential, but their future use depends upon the adaptability of the teachers and upon the ingenuity of school administrators to provide staffing, equipment, and the necessary software. These electronic devices are becoming rapidly attuned to the specific instructional techniques underlying the educational process. According to Van Horn, "New instructional delivery systems will generate a new sense of hope in our schools, because (now) we have a way to increase the useful work of schools exponentially."[2]

The computer is well recognized as an invaluable educational tool. In addition to its ability of communicating information to students, it is perfectly suited for controlling the operation of a wide variety of teaching devices currently available in many school systems. Curriculum planners have yet to capitalize on this unique feature of the computer, particularly in the area of integrated audiovisual instruction.

More specifically, computers can be programmed to display a series of interactive instructional materials for instant use by the student in a logical and prearranged sequence. For example, the computer can be programmed to trigger a videotape player, a television set, and an audiotape player, a movie projector, an overhead projector, and filmstrips and slides so that each display appears at the proper time within the desired sequence of learning experiences included in the curriculum. This educational tool holds much promise for creative and adventurous educators.

The Merging of Video and Computer Capabilities

Continuing improvements in the display capabilities of video screens and computer monitors will present more options for discriminating educators. Just a few years ago, it was relatively easy to differentiate between video and computers. The former presented an audiovisual message while the latter communicated solely by words and numbers. The rapid development within these two fundamental technologies is blurring the line of demarcation between them.

Technical improvements in the output capabilities of computers over the past few years have been outstanding. They are capable of producing artificial speech. They can be programmed to produce moving images along with still alphanumeric symbols. The phenomenal increase in computer memory will significantly improve the quality of computer graphics.

Simultaneously, video equipment is becoming more sophisticated and versatile. Its output produces high-quality natural sounds and high-definition pictures. Its output can be recorded on videotape or videodisc and any segment of the recording can be programmed to be shown in any predetermined sequence.

These two technologies are reaching the point where the differences between them in the quality of displayed images will soon become indiscernible. It is suggested that educators and school plant planners keep abreast of developments in both of these technologies and exploit them for educational benefits.

Advanced Computer Development

Microcomputers are now exponentially more powerful than they were just a decade ago. Additionally, the speed of operation of modern microcomputers has increased tenfold. Several programs can be run simultaneously in today's microcomputer. This feature is extremely important for multiprogramming the various types of audiovisual devices in accordance with the sequences required by any integrated instructional program.

Computers have both an internal and an external memory system. As mentioned above, the internal memory of computers has increased enormously and is still expanding. The external memory is stored on computer disks or tape. The stored data can be transferred from the external source into the computer for processing at any time.

The most outstanding advances in external memory for computers have occurred in the field of optical memory systems. Optical disks about 5 inches in diameter can store diagrams, pictures, animation, motion video, and voice, along with alphanumeric symbols. The capacity of optical computer disks is overwhelming. For example, one disk can store the entire educational program for a student from kindergarten to grade 8 in mathematics, reading, language arts and science.[3]

Futuristic Developments in Video Technology

The development of laser videodisc technology has revolutionized the educational capability of video as an instructional tool. According to Van Horn, a single videodisc the size of a phonograph album holds 108,000 randomly accessible still pictures plus four hours of single-channel video.[4] These developments are indeed impressive. They have the potential of modifying the educational process during the twenty-first century.

These extraordinary advances in computer technology suggest that some changes should be made in the current educational process in order to take advantage of these new instructional tools. As most educators well know, such changes are evolutionary and occur slowly. Until teacher training institutions instill in future teachers the basic skills and knowledge required to exploit the educational potential of modern technology, little change is likely to occur in the classrooms of the world. On the other hand, progressive school districts can take advantage of the benefits of modern technological advances right now by setting up local training programs for a core of teachers within a single school district or a combination of districts.

Emerging Instructional Delivery Systems

Software, also known as courseware, is being developed to cover an entire curriculum in many fields of education. Some of the developers of such courseware work directly with school districts in creating programs that are tailor-made for their needs. These learning systems are referred to as Integrated Learning Systems (ILS) or Integrated Instructional Systems (IIS). Several vendors of such courseware are investing millions of dollars in developing learning systems that can be used in microcomputers already available in many school districts.

The advent of television satellites, cable television, and fiber-optic transmission lines is providing educational capabilities that were only a dream just a few years ago. These new technologies are making it possible to disseminate ILS programs, for example, over large geographical areas. They provide a practical and affordable vehicle for the enrichment of instructional programs in small school districts and in isolated one-room schools. Also, instructional programs transmitted via satellite or over fiber-optic lines can be received by microcomputers in homes as well as in schools. Thus, homebound students can continue learning during periods of recuperation.

PRACTICAL APPLICATIONS OF ADVANCED VIDEO TECHNOLOGY

Technological improvements in high-definition television and in user-friendly programming of videocassette players is stimulating the use of video displays for educational purposes. Videocassette recorders and players significantly enrich the instructional program. Educational television broadcasts have increasingly supplemented the instructional materials available to the classroom teacher. Satellite technology has greatly expanded the geographical coverage for the effective dissemination of excellent instructional materials. The advent of fiber-optic telephone communication systems is making it possible to transmit video programs at affordable costs from widely separated instructional materials centers, from school district to school district, and from school to school within a school district.

Television

Television is a powerful medium for group instruction. Its use is growing rapidly as the number of educational television broadcasting stations increases. The content and nature of the programs is increasingly focused on the special needs of the public schools. In some instances, the programs are coordinated with the instruction that takes place in the school districts within their range. Some stations employ educational coordinators who work directly with local school districts in maximizing the impact of their television programs on the education of the students in the area.

Although television emerged as a widely accepted communication medium after World War II, it has yet to fully penetrate the everyday teaching activities in the classroom. Practically every school in America has at least one television set at its disposal for educational purposes. Unfortunately, many of them are used only for special events, such as rocket launches, presidential addresses, and matters of world import. The vast number of high-quality television programs, both on the air and cable, provide a rich source of educational material that can be integrated into the local school curriculum in a systematic fashion. This potential has not yet materialized. It is incumbent upon educational facility planners to do everything within their power to promote and facilitate the expanded use of video equipment as an effective educational tool.

Videotape recording has greatly enhanced the effect of educational television on the schools. Videotape recording makes it possible to record programs broadcast by educational television at any time during the day or night. These programs can then be reproduced in the classroom immediately or at any time later.

Videotape recording offers great challenges and opportunities for classroom teachers. Since educational television programs can be recorded on tape for 24 hours during the day, the number of programs available to school districts has almost tripled. Once a program is recorded, it can be rebroadcast throughout the school over closed circuit television or directed to one classroom at any predetermined time. Thus, the classroom teacher can introduce a television program at the most appropriate time during the instructional process. Stated differently, the teacher can show a television program whenever the class is ready for it.

Teachers may also use videotape to diagnose their own teaching techniques. The teacher may ask the staff from the instructional resource center to set up a television camera and videotape recorder in his or her classroom. The teacher would activate the equipment and record all of the classroom activities for a period of time. Later during the day, in privacy, the teacher could play the videotape and make a self-evaluation of his or her performance. This use of videotape equipment often leads to self-improvement without fear of embarrassment.

Facility Planning for Television. Educational facilities for television range from rudimentary space for storage of one or two movable sets to a sophisticated closed-circuit television system complete with a magnificent commercial-type broadcasting studio. Neither situation is immune to public criticism. In all probability, the first can be questioned on the premise that such austere provisions will have no significant impact on the quality of the educational program. The second can be challenged on the grounds that the expenditure of funds for such an elaborate system cannot be justified in terms of the educational return per dollar expended. A defensible position—with respect to the effective use of television as an educational tool—lies somewhere between these two extremes.

To be effective, televised and video-recorded programs must be smoothly integrated into the ongoing school curriculum. Instructional television must be capable of delivering specific programs to students at times when they are ready to receive them and when they can dovetail into the regular school curriculum. Consequently, live programs should be prerecorded on videotape or disc, for use at a more propitious time later.

In designing an educational facility for instructional television, three basic functions must be satisfied. There must be a space where equipment for receiving both airborne and cable television signals may be installed. There must be a specially designed television processing center where such programs are recorded on videotape or disc. And there must be an efficient means of delivering these programs to the classrooms. The technology is available; two feasible methods are described in the following two paragraphs.

The first method is the most efficient and least labor-intensive way to deliver television programs into the classroom. This relatively straightforward approach includes three major components, two spatial and one electronic. It calls for a television receiving room of about 500 square feet, where television signals are received and recorded on videotape or disc. This room should also contain electronic equipment and switching devices capable of reproducing the stored programs and directing them to a given classroom at a predetermined time when it can fit exactly into the curriculum. The second element of the system is a closed-circuit television wiring network interconnecting classrooms and other instructional spaces and the television receiving room. And finally, this system includes a permanently mounted television set in each instructional area. It would also be helpful, but not essential, to provide a simple, unsophisticated television broadcasting studio of an area of about 300 square feet. This space, located near the television receiving room, would be equipped with a portable video camera, a video recorder, and associated instrumentation for originating television programs. The omission of a studio would present no problem. Any classroom wired for closed-circuit television could be used for originating television programs, provided portable video equipment is available. And finally, from the standpoint of operation and supervision, it would be advantageous to locate the television receiving room and ancillary spaces within the learning resources center complex.

The second method, less costly but more cumbersome, consists of two major components. This system features a television receiving room similar to the one described above and a complement of several portable television sets mounted on frames with casters. The number of television sets depends on the financial resources of the school district. It is suggested, however, that the number of sets equal one quarter the number of classrooms. The operational aspects of this system are somewhat more complicated than the fully electronic system described in the preceding paragraph. A television set—together with a video player and videotapes—must be wheeled into the classroom by a television technician who is responsible for setting up the equipment and removing it at the end of the presentation. To be sure, there are substantial savings in initial capital outlay: no closed-circuit wiring network and fewer television sets to buy. It should be pointed out, however, that these savings may eventually be wiped out by the additional cost of television technicians needed to operate this less-expensive system.

The heart of a functional instructional television system is the television receiving center with its video-recording equipment. This facility is an essential part of both of the systems described in the preceding paragraphs. It can be stated categorically that, if the system does not include the television receiving center with its capability of recording and playing back recordings, television as an instructional tool will be ineffective.

Planning Core Facilities for a Future Closed-Circuit Television System. In situations in which funds are not available to plan the television facilities under the first option described in the preceding section, it might be feasible to plan a less sophisticated television production, processing and distribution system. A space of approximately 500 square feet could be designed as a multipurpose television facility. It should be planned for receiving and recording television programs from outside sources. It should contain *lockable* spaces for storing videotapes and television equipment, taking into account the precautions listed in the next section, "Facility Planning for Video Recorders."

Thus far, the plan described above provides minimal space for only one component of a functional television system in a school facility. Television programs can be received, recorded on videodiscs or tapes and stored for future use by classroom teachers. And there is also space for originating and recording educational materials developed by the school staff or students using camcorders.

A second vital component of any minimal television system must include a functional and effective means of conveying recorded television programs to the classroom. Obviously, unless there is some way of bringing recorded educational television programs into the classroom at a strategic time designated by the teacher, the television room described above represents a waste of time, energy and money. Consequently, when funds are extremely limited, it is suggested that the nucleus of any television system consist of the multipurpose room specified above *together* with the low-cost distribution system described in the previous section.

As discussed earlier in this chapter, television production, processing and storage facilities should be clustered around the learning resources center. In terms of long-range planning, it is prudent, therefore, to locate the space initially designed for limited television service in the same area recommended for full-scale television facilities. Under this plan, the core of a future comprehensive television system is already in place.

Facility Planning for Television Viewing.   The viewing of television programs in regular classrooms generally presents no serious problem. Such spaces are usually sufficiently large to satisfy the needs of a closed-circuit television system. While no additional classroom space is needed for this purpose, however, special care should be taken to make sure that the sight lines are free and clear of building supports, wires, pipes and suspended cabinets.

Space is needed in classrooms for the temporary storage of video materials such as tapes, discs and video players. Normally, classrooms contain about 100 square feet of storage space in the form of closets, cabinets and shelving. Consequently, there should be ample storage space in these viewing areas for video materials and equipment. If a closed-circuit system were installed in a school building, however, all of the storage needs related to video would be centralized in the television distribution center.

Video Recorders

Scientists and engineers have succeeded in recording television programs on magnetic tapes and videodiscs. This development augers well for education. Educators are just becoming aware of the potential of this electronic breakthrough. At first glance, it appears to be similar to photographic films that produce motion pictures. To be sure, both methods record images for future showing, but this is where the

similarity ends. Videotape recorders reproduce images instantaneously. No processing is required. This procedure provides the immediate feedback that can strongly
reinforce learning in some selected situations.

Facility Planning for Video Recorders.　The video recorder-player units themselves present no serious problem. Their space needs are the same as those discussed
under "Facility planning for television" above. Storage space for the videotapes
associated with the recorders, however, require special attention. First is the choice
of location. It must be remembered that videotapes and videodiscs are generally
shared by several teachers within a school building and, in many instances, by
teachers throughout a school district, in which case appropriately designed space is
needed for only temporary storage. The storage room for videotapes and discs
should be easily accessible to users.

The presence of strong magnetic fields has a deleterious effect on magnetic
videotapes. Storage space must *not* be located near electrical transformers, which
are often present in electrical distribution centers. When alternating current loads
are fairly high, over 100 amperes, strong alternating magnetic fields are generated
in the vicinity of the conductors carrying such a current. This alternating magnetic
field removes the magnetic recordings on the videotape and destroys its usefulness.
Architects and educational facility planners should be constantly on the alert for
places in the building where high alternating electrical currents are present, in order
to avoid placing video storage spaces near them. A masonry wall separating a
distribution center from an adjoining room does not provide sufficient magnetic
shielding for the storage of magnetic tapes.

Abnormal temperature ranges and dust can also ruin magnetic videotapes.
Temperatures should range somewhere between 50 and 125 degrees Fahrenheit.
Normally, this requirement is not a problem, unless heating pipes run through the
storage space. Finally, videotapes should be stored in spaces that are relatively free
of dust and dirt. Precautions should be taken to prevent air containing such contami-
nants from circulating through spaces designed for the storage of videotapes.

Interactive Television Systems

Interactive television systems can effectively teach hundreds of students individually or in groups widely separated from one another. One type is already in its
experimental phase of development; another is still in the conceptual stage. Both are
described briefly in the following paragraphs.

The system that is being tested experimentally is discussed in considerable
detail by Tom Pate in an article appearing in a recent issue of an educational
journal.[5] It consists of a 4-channel, 50-watt instructional television network serving
a large group of students in the Houston area. Students located in widely separated
schools can both see and hear the master teacher broadcasting from a studio in
Houston. The master teacher, on the other hand, can hear the students over an FM
(frequency modulation) radio network, but cannot see them. There seems to be

considerable support for this approach to large-group instruction in Texas. The final verdict has not yet been reached, but experimental results thus far look very promising.

Another method of teaching large groups of students through use of electronic devices involves television, telephone, and radio. At the present time, it exists in concept only. As soon as it is put into operation somewhere and an efficient procedure developed, the worthwhile goal of mass education will be brought closer to reality. Granting the External Degree in England and elsewhere is an excellent example. What is needed is a means of educating hundreds of people at a time without a large capital outlay. The proposal is a practical and financially feasible approach to mass education, particularly at the college and university level. Under this concept, a student might earn college credit toward a degree or become sufficiently proficient for a diploma or certificate. Each institution would determine its own procedure and standards for the nature of the recognition it wishes to give for such extramural instruction.

The proposed procedure is as follows: A presentation is made over a local television station or over an educational television station for one hour by a recognized authority in the field or by a member of the college or university staff. Upon termination of the telecast, a panel of three or four faculty members from a given department at each institution granting awards would receive telephone calls from students at home. Students registered in the course could call the institution, using an ENTERPRISE number (also known as 800 number) at no cost to them. A moderator would keep about 10 students in contact with the panel at a time. This discussion involving 10 students and three panelists would be simultaneously broadcast by radio. The discussion period by radio could cover a period of about two hours. If the moderator allows each student calling to remain on the open line for five minutes, over 200 students could participate in the discussions, while all the other students registered in the class would benefit from these discussions by radio. Under this concept, large numbers of students could receive a major part of their instruction at home. They would take whatever tests might be required on the campus and use laboratories and libraries on campus specifically designed for this type of learning activity.

Facility Planning for Interactive Television Systems.   In addition to the television and radio broadcasting equipment, a fairly sophisticated broadcasting studio should be provided at the location where the instructional program originates. This studio should be flexible, able to simulate any instructional setting normally associated with the subject being taught. For example, at times it might resemble a classroom; at other times, a science laboratory. It should also be capable of creating an atmosphere that is compatible for instruction in both the fine and performing arts. Ancillary spaces are needed for storing props, instructional materials, and supplies, as well as films, tapes, and conventional audiovisual equipment.

COMPUTERS IN EDUCATION

Little did George Boole, a mathematics professor in Ireland, realize that his "Investigation in the Laws of Thought" in 1854, establishing formal logic and creating a new algebra known as Boolean algebra, would ever have any practical application in the real world.[6] He and other mathematicians of that era were primarily engaged in developing abstract algebra. It was not until the middle of the twentieth century that Boolean algebra attained great prominence in the development of computers. His work was rediscovered and applied by scientists and engineers in designing complex logic circuits for modern digital computers.

Computer Hardware

It is interesting to note that computers have introduced a number of new words into our everyday language. We now speak of "input" and "interface" in situations that are not related with computers. We are beginning to associate the word "software," as opposed to computer hardware, with films and tapes normally used with some of the more conventional types of audiovisual equipment. Among educators, the term "courseware" is emerging as a substitute for "software." And leaders in education have introduced the expression "computer literacy," which, according to Komoski, is still "vague and undefined."[7]

The computer is well recognized as one of the most sophisticated electronic marvels of the twentieth century. Its development has been continuous, rapid, and unparalleled over a period of several decades. In the beginning, the digital computer was simply an instrument for computing numerical data at phenomenal speeds using the binary system of numbers. But, with the introduction of programmed logic circuits, the computer has become one of the most versatile instruments in the world. It is ideally suited for educational purposes. It is capable of drawing diagrams on paper or displaying them on a video screen. It can present learning material to the student. It can pose questions and supply answers orally on a video screen as well as on paper. It can generate tests, correct them, and prepare and print a diagnostic report for both the student and the teacher. It is admirably equipped to maintain a continuous and up-to-date record of student progress. And it is well-adapted for monitoring and prescribing the learning experiences of each student on an individual basis.

The computer can perform many routine educational tasks flawlessly, efficiently, and at superhuman speeds, but it is pedagogically inadequate and unsatisfactory in some respects. In its present stage of development, it is extremely unlikely that the computer of today will ever replace the teacher. After all, the computer is nothing more than a machine, albeit a sophisticated one. It has no judgment, no feelings, and no heart. It simply responds slavishly to instructions programmed into it by a human being. The computer itself is stupid. It is never more creative nor more knowledgeable than the human being who gave it its instructions. It becomes an invaluable instructional aid only when it is properly and imaginatively programmed by a person who is not only a master teacher in his or her field but also very knowledgeable about the learning process, the learners for whom the program is designed, and the capabilities of the computer itself.

Size and Capacity of Computers.   The early computers were generally large. As the state of the art developed, smaller and less versatile computers were developed for a wide variety of specialized uses. Large and small computers have an important place in education. The uses of each type will be discussed in the latter part of this chapter.

The large or macrocomputer is the ultimate in digital computers. It can accomplish tasks that transcend human capability from the standpoint of speed, memory, information retrieval, sequential thought processes, and control systems. The macrocomputer has tremendous memory capabilities and a reaction time that is measured in millionths of seconds. The macrocomputer is so fast that it can outrun its output capabilities. For example, it can process huge amounts of data in short periods of time. Since its output is much slower than the computer unit, the output from the computer unit is stored on memory banks and subsequently released to the output devices over a period of several hours or days depending upon the speed of the computer, its storage capacity, and the volume of the material. For educational purposes, the phenomenal speed of the computer makes it possible for the same computer to be serving a large number of students at what appears to be the same time through a process known as "time sharing." The computer is so fast that students are seldom aware that the computer is putting them on a "temporary hold" while it is serving other students.

The smaller computers known as microcomputers are attracting the attention of many educators. Their potential for individualized instruction is very promising. The software associated with these computers is becoming extremely user friendly and the variety of computerized instructional programs has increased enormously. The widespread use of the microcomputer as an educational tool is discussed in the next section.

Microcomputers for Instructional Purposes.   The microcomputer is undoubtedly one of the most impressive developments in computer technology. Such computers are compact, portable, fast and multifunctional.

The instructional potential of microcomputers is increasing by leaps and bounds. Not long ago microcomputers had a RAM (Random Access Memory) capacity of only 128K. Microcomputer memories have increased to over 4 mega (million) bytes, over 30 times the size of memories in earlier models, and the end is not yet in sight. There are also provisions for expanding the internal RAM memory capacity of microcomputers even further by inserting additional circuit boards in slots designed for that purpose. It should be noted that the ROM (Read Only Memory) capacity of microcomputers is concurrently expanding geometrically.

Microcomputers have become very affordable. Due to the emergence of fierce competition among computer manufacturers, the price of microcomputers has dropped sharply. Consequently, an increasing number of parents are purchasing microcomputers for home use and more and more students have access to a microcomputer after school.

Computer disk drives are highly recommended for microcomputers used for educational purposes. Computer disks, which are inserted into a disk drive, greatly expand the external RAM memory of the computer. They are capable of storing prodigious amounts of information that can be processed by the computer whenever needed for instructional purposes.

Printers should be selected judiciously. Some of them are very expensive. It is not a wise expenditure of educational funds to purchase printers which exceed the level of performance required by the instructional use of the computer. Incidentally, there are learning situations where printers are not needed at all. For example, they are generally not required when the microcomputer is used for developing and practicing mathematical and language skills. In terms of cost, the least expensive printers use a dot matrix system which is usually acceptable for student use. The ink jet printer is more expensive and produces an excellent copy. The laser printer is quite expensive, but it is fast and prints text and diagrams of super quality.

Finally, the mouse and joystick are desirable computer accessories. While many games can be played on computers with or without the use of a joystick, the manipulation of a joystick is extremely appealing to students. They often become deeply engrossed in what appears to be a computer game, but in reality is a vehicle of learning. There is a wide selection of game-based, pedagogically designed computer software that teaches principles, logic and concepts.

Computer Software

Computer software for educational purposes is developing by leaps and bounds. The quality is improving day by day as more and more of the larger computer companies allocate sizable sums of money to develop computer-oriented curricular materials. Research centers are beginning to focus "in particular on the *process* that yields sizable amounts of these high quality learning materials."[8] Bork says, "Every useful computer-based learning material begins, I would argue, with a clear pedagogical purpose. Approaches to the development that begin with the computer may produce some jazzy materials, but these materials are not likely to be very effective in the classroom."[9]

The computer has great potential for individualized instruction. However, not until more pedagogically sound and tested software become available can this application of the computer make a significant impact on the educational process. Educators in some school districts feel that their own instructional staff can prepare tailor-made programmed instruction for the students of the school district. This point of view is natural, but the level of sophistication required to develop unit-centered programs is a competency for which only a handful of teachers are trained.

Such persons must possess a mastery of psychology of learning, an understanding of microinstruction, a skill in the art of asking questions, and, most important, a full command of the subject being programmed. Unless these conditions are recognized, "homemade" programs will not achieve the desired results. Obviously, a large school district with adequate financial resources could well employ such persons. But the greatest hope in the production of software for the computer lies in private enterprise, which is set up to do the task on an economically sound basis. This situation is analogous to the idea that every school district should prepare and publish its own textbooks. Hopefully, we can look to private industry for software as we have for textbooks, films, slides, and tapes.

Computers are costly, and so using them for individualized instruction is still a matter of concern. However, with the advent of microcomputers and the reduced cost of mainframes, the application of computers now falls within the financial reach of many school districts. Under the shared-time approach mentioned earlier, a single computer can simultaneously serve many students.

Recent literature reveals that the software—or "courseware," as some educators are beginning to call it—being produced today is pedagogically sound. Furthermore, major computer manufacturers are intensely interested in developing high-quality courseware. That, and the increased affordability of computer hardware, point to a future that holds much promise for the application of computers for personalized instruction.

Application of the Computer in a School Setting

The computer is well suited for both administrative and instructional use. Some of these uses are discussed in the following paragraphs. Thus far, the major application of this modern marvel has been in the area of administration. However, there is a growing national interest in computer literacy, so there will undoubtedly be a significant shift toward its educational use.

The design of the educational facility will vary from one use of the computer to another. Specific suggestions on the space and environmental requirements of computers for instruction are offered in the next section.

Administrative Uses. The computer is used for word processing and for the compiling and retrieval of student information and statistical data. It is extremely valuable in the administration of a school district. Some of this information is also useful to guidance counselors and principals.

The amount of data available immediately to school officials through the use of computers is copious and timely in the decision-making process. The computer can store enormous amounts of information that can be retrieved on a highly selective basis. It can then locate and reproduce those millions of bits of stored information almost instantaneously. If desired, it can not only locate but also process such stored data in any way that it is programmed to do so, before the data appear as output either on the video monitor or on the printer. And it performs this tedious task on command and with lightning speed.

This computer capability can be exploited advantageously by educators in many ways, limited only by the ingenuity, knowledge, and creativity of the programmer. The computer is ideal for assembling information for student guidance and job placement and analyzing student achievement. It is an excellent device for scoring standardized tests and printing out a diagnostic summary for each student. It is helpful in making longitudinal studies on student progress in the basic skills. It is well suited for assembling health information for use by the school nurse, guidance counselors, and coach. And finally, such computers are most useful for such tasks as accounting, payroll-making, inventory control, purchasing, maintenance scheduling, and budgetary estimates. There are also a few less common administrative applications, such as projecting future school enrollments and determining whether it is more advantageous to modernize an existing school building or to abandon it. These and other applications are left to the discretion of local school administrators and their respective computer programmers.

While all of the above-mentioned administrative functions sound impressive, it might be surprising to learn that the capacity of the central processing unit (CPU) required to perform them is far less than that required for computers used for instructional purposes (see section entitled "Microcomputers for Instructional Purposes"). Computers for administrative applications utilize software that requires only a modest amount of internal computer memory for processing information retrieved from high-capacity disks.

A word of caution is in order regarding the skyrocketing computer memory capacity discussed earlier in connection with microcomputers. Educators are faced with the problem of determining how much computer memory is necessary and sufficient for specific educational purposes. Faster and more powerful computers are usually more expensive. It is difficult to justify the purchase of costly computers whose capabilities exceed the needs of any school administrative center. Owning a powerful computer may be prestigious, but it is not necessarily economically efficient. It is suggested, therefore, that school districts purchase computers with only the *necessary and sufficient* capacity to perform the functions desired by the school district. It is recommended that an *independent* computer consultant be employed by the school district when the purchase of computers is contemplated in order to make certain that the memory capacity of the computer will be neither too large nor too small for the needs of the school district.

Instructional Uses. The computer is extremely well suited for several instructional uses as well. It is an excellent electronic tool for remediation and reinforcement of learning. It can provide supplementary learning experiences for the gifted. It has the capability of motivating students. It works effectively with students on a one-to-one basis and has the capacity to deliver a personalized program for each one of them.

Thus far, computer-oriented educators have developed two reliable methods of utilizing the computer for instructional purposes. The computer can be programmed to "teach" a student a complete lesson in selected areas of learning, or it can be programmed to simply "manage" the instruction of the student as he or she advances from one learning situation to another. The two are called computer-assisted instruction (CAI) and computer-managed instruction (CMI) respectively. According to Sherry, "There will be a shift from the early forms of CAI to more sophisticated systems known as IIS (Integrated Instructional Systems)."[10]

Computer-assisted instruction utilizes a valid pedagogical procedure. The computer presents subject matter to be learned in very small segments. From time to time, it tests students on the material covered to that point. If the student fails to pass the test, the computer automatically places him or her on a branch sequence covering the same subject matter. On the other hand, if the student passes the test, the computer simply continues on the main track of the learning sequences. Under CAI, the computer serves both a teaching and a diagnostic function. After several branchings without success, however, even the computer gets frustrated and advises the student, "Please confer with your teacher."

Computer-managed instruction, on the other hand, does not "teach." It simply "guides" the student along the path of sequential learning experiences. In essence, it enables the student to advance more rapidly toward a predetermined educational goal. Let's review the major features of CMI.

The student sits at a carrel containing a computer terminal similar to that used in computer-assisted instruction. Upon proper activation, the computer may instruct the student to go to the library, read a specified section of a given book, and return to the computer upon completion of the assignment. When the student returns, he or she is asked a number of questions by the computer, based on the assignment. If the student responds correctly, the computer may instruct the student to study a series of audiovisual tapes and return to the computer for testing and further directions. In the event that a student does not answer the question correctly, the computer gives the student alternative assignments on the same general topic and retests. Traditional class instruction may be an important part of the assignment. Clearly, under this concept, the computer serves only as a control mechanism for individualized instruction. The primary responsibility for the instruction rests entirely with the teacher.

Unlike in computer-assisted instruction, most teachers can prepare the instructions to be programmed into the computer. Such directions could be taken directly from traditional lesson plans. Testing, however, requires both skill and ingenuity on the part of the teacher. There is a definite change of emphasis in the preparation of tests. Ordinarily, testing is focused on student achievement. Under computer-managed instruction, however, the focus is on the diagnostic potential of the test. Unless this potential is painstakingly built into the test, the effectiveness of computer-managed instruction is substantially reduced.

Facilities for Computer-Related Educational Functions

Recent research clearly indicates that meticulously planned spaces are required for computers and their use by students or staff.[11] The conversion of a regular classroom into a computer laboratory by simply providing a few moveable tables and chairs and installing an electrical outlet strip along the wall will no longer suffice. The well-planned computer room includes special design features that satisfy both the technical requirements of the computer and the physical requirements of the human body. The study of ergonomics in relation to the facilities for computer-related activities has made a significant impact on their design.

When planning spaces for computer-oriented facilities, either in a new building or in the rehabilitation of an existing one, review the sections describing the educational uses of computers presented earlier. The most recent literature on the latest advances in both hardware and software should be examined at the same time. Computer technology is so fluid that dramatic developments in both equipment and courseware are constantly emerging from research centers. For this reason, it is extremely important that planners review the state of the art regarding the application of computer technology to educational functions when designing educational facilities.

Administrative Uses. The basic spatial requirements here are quite modest. A small space adjoining the secretarial work area is usually sufficient. Functionally, this facility should be located in the administrative center of the school district. In some instances, however, a computer is extremely useful in high schools with large enrollments. As detailed earlier, it is admirably suited for a number of the administrative tasks in high schools.

The minimal space needed does not necessarily mean the construction of a separate room. An area of about 120 square feet is sufficient to accommodate a minicomputer and store computer supplies, computer disks, and other related materials. If a separate room is desired, the shape should approximate that of a square rather than an elongated rectangle. This shape provides greater flexibility in the placement of equipment and storage cabinets and facilitates servicing the equipment.

Research conducted by Lopez provides a starting point regarding computer needs for administrative purposes.[12] He found that a microcomputer capacity of 64K RAM with two disk drives and printer with 500K storage is generally sufficient for administrative uses, including word processing. When we recall that school administrative functions have hardly changed at all since he did the study, his findings provide a sound point of departure in assessing computer needs for administrative uses. Since Lopez conducted his research, the price of computers has dropped sharply. For this reason, it may be fiscally justifiable to consider computers with a slightly higher memory capacity. In discussing with a consultant the purchase of a computer for administrative purposes, school officials may wish to bear in mind that a computer with a RAM capacity in the vicinity of one megabyte and a printer memory of about 1,000K is generally sufficient for most school administrative offices. Higher capacities are not ruled out, however. In such instances, they should be justified by the consultant to the full satisfaction of school officials, particularly when greater capacity involves higher costs.

If the central administrative office has a large staff, it might be prudent to consider purchasing a minicomputer with greater RAM capacity and a printer with a larger buffer than suggested above, together with one terminal for each secretary and one each for those professional employees who require the use of computerized data as part of their work. Under this arrangement, one central minicomputer and a single fast printer could have sufficient capacity for the entire secretarial and professional staff. The prices of these systems have also declined, and the purchase of a minicomputer may be cost-effective for certain administrative applications.

The use of computers as word processors is not limited to central administrative offices. Microcomputers are also used as word processors in many primary and secondary school offices. Since microcomputers have become more affordable, more and more elementary schools are able to take advantage of this multipurpose marvel of modern technology.

Planning Computer Facilities for People.   Another aspect of planning computer-oriented facilities is focused squarely on the special needs of the people operating them. There are certain environmental and physical conditions that can adversely affect the health and welfare of the people working with computers for long periods of time. They are discussed in detail in the last section of this chapter.

Instructional Uses.   The painstaking planning of spaces for computers is highly rewarding in terms of the educational benefits that can be generated or supported by the computer. For example, the computer can help in developing "computer literacy" for students in elementary and middle schools. It can be a vehicle for teaching word processing to students enrolled in the secretarial science programs offered by the school district. It can serve as a teaching aid for students in mathematics and science. And it can be a powerful educational tool for individualized programs using either the CAI or the CMI method of instruction.

The number of hours per week that computers are available for students is closely related to the impact that the computers will have on the learning process. Theoretically, one microcomputer could be assigned to each student for his or her exclusive use. This arrangement would make a computer available to a student at all times during the school day. While this approach sounds ideal, it is neither educationally efficient nor financially affordable for most school districts. Furthermore, it is not very cost-effective from the standpoint of capital outlay, because many of the microcomputers would lie idle for most of the school day. For these reasons, computers are generally concentrated in one or more computer laboratories, where groups of students can be scheduled at the same time or where students can have access to computers at their convenience. This practice is economically sound, operationally efficient, and educationally productive.

The Basic Computer Cluster

In order to simplify the architectural planning of a computer laboratory, computer-oriented specialists often find it advantageous to conceive such a laboratory as a multiple of basic computer clusters, each containing a certain number of carrels. The number of computer-oriented carrels within each cluster is not fixed. It varies from case to case. For example, the number of carrels in a cluster may be as high as 16 in a situation where the central minicomputer is of sufficient capacity to supply information to 16 computer terminals.

Definition of the Basic Computer Cluster. The basic computer cluster is arbitrarily defined as a group of eight computer-oriented carrels, served by eight computer terminals tied into a minicomputer, or by eight individual microcomputers, or by any combination of the two whose total is eight. This definition is not intended to establish a standard size for a cluster but rather to simplify the planning process associated with computer laboratories. The reason for defining a basic computer cluster will become evident in the next section on planning computer laboratories.

Space Requirements for a Single Computer Carrel. Each carrel is viewed as a student station that is equipped with one computer or computer terminal. Thus, the number of computers or terminals needed determines the number of carrels required. Spacewise, each computer carrel should have a floor area of about 25 square feet. An L-shaped countertop having an area of about 12 square feet should be built along two adjacent walls of the carrel. The height of the countertop should vary from 30 inches for adults and upper-level high school students to an appropriate lower height for students attending middle and elementary schools.

Space Requirements for a Basic Computer Cluster. The basic unit cluster requires an area of about 400 square feet for the eight carrels and related storage space, either lockable cabinets or a lockable room with shelving. About 100 linear feet of shelving should be included in each unit cluster for storing computer supplies, instruction books, computer disks, and commercially prepared computer programs. Furthermore, approximately one additional linear foot of shelving should be provided for each student assigned to the unit cluster during a scheduling cycle, usually one week.

Power Requirements for a Basic Computer Cluster. The power requirement of a basic computer cluster equipped with eight microcomputers demands special attention. Each microcomputer draws about 2 amperes of current. Thus, an independent circuit having a capacity of 30 amperes should be sufficient for each cluster of eight carrels.

The current load imposed by a minicomputer cannot be specified precisely unless the memory capacity of the computer, the number of desk terminals, and the scope of its function is known. For this reason, it is important to make certain that there is an independent circuit of sufficient capacity servicing each cluster. It is also recommended that a main switch be provided to shut off the power feeding all the computers.

Computer Laboratories

The grouping of several computer-oriented carrels in specially designed laboratories provides the setting for the efficient and effective use of computers for individualized instruction. Under this arrangement, computer-related activities can be centralized in one section of the building where they can be more easily supervised. Also, the centralization of the laboratories in one part of the building facilitates the installation of security devices designed to prevent pilfering, which has become a serious problem. It is usually less expensive to install an electronic burglar alarm system, for example, when computer laboratories are brought together in one part of the building.

Location.   The location of a computer laboratory depends on its purpose. Some are located near the classrooms for business education. Others may be placed near the mathematics and science areas. But the major concentration of computer laboratories in both elementary and secondary schools is usually in the vicinity of the learning resources center (the library complex).

Space Requirements.   The size of a computer laboratory is directly related to the number of basic computer clusters included in the laboratory. The number usually ranges from one to three basic computer clusters, each containing eight microcomputers or a minicomputer system of equivalent capacity.

As a general rule, the area required for a computer laboratory is roughly a multiple of 400 square feet, the space required for the basic cluster described earlier. Thus, the area can vary from as little as about 400 square feet to as much as 1,200 square feet. Computer laboratories larger than three basic clusters are not educationally sound. Smaller units are easier to supervise and control. And, as will be seen later in this discussion, additional space for professional staff must be provided for each computer laboratory in relation to the number of students served. Therefore, in most situations, several smaller computer laboratories provide greater flexibility. The overall area specifications for computer laboratories stated above apply to the use of microcomputers in each carrel. If a minicomputer system is adopted, however, whereby computer terminals are included in each carrel, an additional 80 square feet of space should be included for the centralized computer unit and accessory equipment. This additional space need not be a separate room, but there may be some advantage in combining it with some of the storage spaces mentioned in relation to planning basic computer clusters.

Number of Computer Laboratories Needed.   The number of computer laboratories required in a given educational facility is directly related to (1) the number of students enrolled in the computerized instructional program and (2) the number of minutes or periods each student will work with computers during the week, as set by school policy. School officials must be cognizant of the direct relationship between these two figures and the amount of capital outlay required for computer laboratories. With this information in hand, the following rules of thumb can be helpful in calculating the number of computer laboratories that should be planned for a given educational facility.

1. Students engaged in a CAI program are advised to work with computers for about 20 minutes at a sitting three times a week. Thus, one computer carrel can serve approximately 30 students per week, assuming a 100-percent student utilization factor and a six-hour school day. In practice, a 70-percent utilization factor is more realistic. Consequently, it is advisable to plan one carrel for each 25 students of anticipated enrollment in computer-assisted instruction.
2. On the other hand, students enrolled in a CMI program can remain in the computer laboratory for an entire period without experiencing significant fatigue, because they are not working strenuously and continuously with the computer for the entire period. However, if the scope of the CMI program were to be limited to testing and diagnostic functions, it would be possible to schedule a class together with its instructor in the computer laboratory for as little as a half period at a time. This policy would obviously have a direct bearing on the total number of computer laboratories that would be needed in such an educational facility. See paragraph 5, below, for information on the number of basic computer clusters that would be needed in a given situation.
3. Another policy matter affecting the number of computer laboratories is related to the extent to which they are used by student groups not normally assigned to them. For example, the computer laboratory that is primarily reserved for regular classes in word processing could also be used for students enrolled in the CMI program, when it is not being used by students in secretarial science classes. Computer laboratories planned for students in science and mathematics could also be utilized for other educational endeavors when not in use for their primary purposes.
4. If multiuse of computer laboratories is contemplated, it might be advantageous to design the access to these laboratories so that classes conducted in adjoining spaces are not subject to interference by students entering and leaving the computer area.
5. A basic computer cluster of eight computers can serve a maximum of 240 students, each using the computer one hour per week, 120 students using it two hours per week, or 80 students using the computer three hours each week. These figures are based on a 100-percent student utilization factor in a six-hour school day. It should be emphasized, however, that these are *maximum* student capacities.

Realistically, as indicated earlier, the space utilization factor more nearly approaches 70 percent for such specialized spaces. Consequently, the planning figures for student capacity of each basic computer cluster of eight carrels should be in the vicinity of 70 percent of those stated above, unless there is reason to believe that a higher space utilization factor can be attained.

6. Once the required number of unit clusters is determined, their location should be established in accordance with their major function. For example, if a total of four clusters were needed, one computer laboratory containing one cluster could be located near the spaces where secretarial science is taught, and the other three could be in a single computer laboratory near the learning resources center. Or two computer laboratories, each containing two unit clusters, could be located in the learning resources center.

7. The preferred arrangement of carrels in a computer laboratory is in the shape of a U for a single cluster and a rectangle for more than one cluster. In an existing classroom 22 feet wide and 32 feet long, it is possible to squeeze in 16 carrels around the periphery of the room with access to storage rooms in at least three of the corners. There would be about 300 square feet of space in the middle of the room, where a teacher could instruct a group of 16 students whenever the need arises. This plan is functional, but it lacks some flexibility with respect to the location of the storage spaces. Nevertheless, a room of this size was selected to show that a functional two-cluster computer laboratory could indeed fit into a regular classroom commonly found in an existing secondary school. If space is available, it would be preferable to select a space of about 800 square feet for a two-cluster computer laboratory and a space of approximately 1,200 square feet for a three-cluster computer laboratory.

8. Computer laboratories of certain sizes are particularly suitable for selected instructional uses. One unit cluster containing eight carrels is usually adequate for mathematics and science laboratories. The carrels are usually placed in the shape of a U along the rear wall and part of the two side walls. A computer laboratory containing two unit clusters is fairly well suited for use in elementary and middle schools, where its primary purpose is to familiarize students with computers. In this case, a teacher can work effectively with students individually or with an entire group of 16 students who are assigned to the laboratory. If this laboratory is located near the learning resources center, it can also be used for individualized instruction under the supervision of the person in charge of the center or by the teacher responsible for the instructional use of the computers.

In summary, the following steps comprise the procedure for determining the number of computer laboratories needed:

1. Estimate the number of students anticipated in the CAI, CMI, and other programs.
2. Determine the number of periods or minutes per week each group (CAI, CMI, business, science, etc.) will be working with the computers.

3. Using a class size of eight (capacity of a basic computer cluster) and the formula on page 295, calculate the number of basic computer clusters needed. Since this figure is based on 80-percent student station utilization, add about 10 percent to that figure.
4. Form computer laboratories consisting of one, two, or three basic computer clusters until all of the required clusters are taken into account. For example, if five basic computer clusters are required, one computer laboratory consisting of one unit could be located in the science-math area, a second computer laboratory comprising three basic clusters could be placed in the learning resources center, and one computer laboratory of one cluster could be located in the business education complex.

Supplementary Spaces Related to Computer Laboratories. The computer laboratories discussed earlier provide space primarily for student use. Additional space is required for the professional staff who work with the students. In this connection, it is suggested that an area of about 150 square feet be provided for an office for the instructor and for the storage of related instructional materials. This additional space is essential for both the CAI and CMI modes of instruction, but not necessarily in the same ratio of offices to computer-oriented carrels.

One teacher can supervise about 50 students engaged in the CAI mode of instruction. This is because the computer does most of the teaching in specific areas of learning. Thus, one office is needed for each group of 48 carrels. Since the maximum recommended size of a computer laboratory contains 24 carrels, the equivalent of three basic computer clusters, one teacher office can serve two such laboratories under CAI. This office should be placed between the two laboratories to facilitate the supervisory and supportive functions of the teacher. It should be provided with vision strips in the walls separating the office from the laboratories. While a single office would satisfy the supervisory needs under CAI, there is no certainty that the two computer laboratories will be used *only* for CAI. It might be prudent, therefore, to temporarily postpone the decision on the number of offices until the number of students for the CMI program has been determined.

Under the CMI method of instruction, a group of students and their regular teacher are usually assigned to the computer laboratory to work on the same subject matter area. The computer-oriented instruction is individualized to the extent that each student proceeds at his or her own rate within the limits of the course objectives. Under this concept, a reasonable group size for one instructor is about 24 students. Thus, under CMI, one teacher office must be provided for each full-size computer laboratory containing three basic computer clusters.

As mentioned earlier, under the CMI mode of instruction, the computer serves to guide the student along a predetermined learning sequence. Consequently, the computer may direct a student to read a book in the library, to review a film strip, to watch a video program recorded on a tape or disc, or to confer with his or her teacher stationed in the nearby office. Therefore, it is imperative that the computer laboratory serving the CMI program be located adjacent to the learning resources center. Students must have ready access to library materials and audiovisual equipment.

Number of Offices Needed for the "Open Laboratory" Concept.   Under an "open laboratory" policy, students are allowed to use the computer laboratory at their convenience for any mode of computerized instruction. Without going into much detail, the entire computer complex would require constant professional staffing by four or five teachers possessing expertise in as many subject matter areas.

The implications for supplementary office spaces under this concept are quite clear. Five or six teacher offices would be required in the computer laboratory complex regardless of the number of such laboratories that are provided. Consequently, if only one computer laboratory were needed based on the computations explained earlier, five or six faculty offices would still be required under the open laboratory concept.

This concept has been mentioned primarily as a matter of interest. A priori, it can be assumed that it is not very cost effective. In addition to the cost of salaries normally required for faculty, the salary of six other teachers would be needed to staff the computer laboratories. However, if it is proven at some time in the future that computers can replace teachers in the learning process, then the required six teachers for the computer laboratory would be taken from the pool of teachers already employed by the school district. At that time, the open laboratory concept might become financially justifiable. At the moment, it is difficult to imagine that the computer can replace the teacher.

At this time, the open laboratory concept is not envisioned as a viable mode of operation. It is neither expedient nor cost effective. However, a policy that requires students to be scheduled in the computer laboratory under CMI at specific times for certain subject matter areas when an instructor with expertise in that subject area is on duty is more practical. Computer-assisted instruction, on the other hand, may be offered to selected students on a more limited scale. A student working in this program would do so under the guidance of his or her regular classroom teacher. The computer laboratory, in this instance, could be used to provide remedial instruction for some students and supplementary instruction for the gifted students.

Specialized Spaces for Storing Computer Disks and Tapes

Computer software is very sensitive to fluctuating magnetic fields and to extremes in temperature. Thus, special precautions must be taken in planning storage spaces.

A temperature range between 50 and 125 degrees Fahrenheit (10 and 52 degrees Celsius) is well within safe limits for storing computer disks and tapes. However, significant deviations should be avoided. These specifications are similar to those for the storage of videotapes and present no real problem in a school situation. Be sure no heating pipes run through the storage spaces and that the storage spaces are relatively free of dust and dirt. Air containing dirt or dust must not be allowed to circulate through space intended for the storage of computer disks and tapes.

Alternating magnetic fields weaken or destroy the magnetic recordings imposed on computer disks and tapes. Relatively strong magnetic fields always surround an electric conductor (wire) carrying a large current. An electric distribution center is usually the culprit. Storage spaces or shelving for computer disks should not be located near an electric distribution center or in the vicinity of a conductor that is carrying several amperes of current. Bear in mind that partitions, unless electrically shielded and grounded, do not insulate the disks from the magnetic field. Also, make certain that no wires carrying large currents are located within the partitions.

Special Planning for People Operating Computers

Recent research on the human needs of people working with computers is most revealing.[13] Studies in ergonomics have identified a number of problems related to the health and well-being of people operating computers. These problems are just as serious for a person working at a single computer station, such as a secretary assigned to an administrative area, as they are for scores of students performing computer-oriented instructional tasks in a computer laboratory.

The findings from these studies require the immediate attention of educational facility planners. It was discovered that screen flickering, glare, and poor contrast on the screen (CRT) caused blurred vision, itching and burning eyes, and headaches. It was also observed that an incorrect screen angle created vision difficulties and that fatigue and neck and backaches could be caused by visual discomfort or by the unchangeable position of the keyboard or screen.

These physical hardships can be significantly lessened by making a number of changes in the physical design of the space in the area immediately surrounding the computer and by improving the visual environment of the total space where computers are used. An improved lighting system, special furniture, and proper positioning of keyboard, screen, and printer in relation to the person operating the computer are imperative. A few guidelines are offered in connection with these research findings. These suggestions will not solve all problems of human engineering. It is hoped, however, that they will significantly minimize the human hardships associated with computer operations.

Special Visual Environment. All light, artificial or natural, should be in the form of indirect lighting. More specifically, it is suggested that:

1. a strip of shielded fluorescent lighting be installed on the rear wall (on the wall facing the operator) of the carrel about 3 feet above the work surface and about 12 inches from the wall.
2. a suspended luminous ceiling be installed at least in the area above the carrels.

3. all natural light be so controlled that it is reflected *down* from a reflective ceiling. Direct sunlight through windows should be directed toward the ceiling, using venetian blinds or their equivalent, so that the sunlight is diffused throughout the room.
4. computers *not* be installed along window walls.
5. painted walls be light colored and possess a high reflective coefficient.
6. dark floors be avoided in spaces where computers are located.

Special Furniture Features. In a computer room, the primary item of furniture of concern to educational facility planners is the chair. It should have a five-strut pedestal base so that it does not have a tendency to tip forward. More important, the chair should have a back that is easily adjustable, particularly if the same chair is to be used by different people, which is usually the case. And finally, the chair should permit a wide range of movement. The seat should swivel. The pedestal should be mounted on casters so the chair can be moved about without difficulty. Casters of a larger diameter are better. Ordinary casters are usually not adequate, particularly when there is carpeting.

Special Working Surface Flexibility. The countertop or table upon which the computer and related equipment are placed should be large enough so that the major components of the computer system used by the operator can be moved about. The size of the work surface should permit the positioning and repositioning of the keyboard, the monitor (if it is moveable), and the printer, in order to minimize eye strain and fatigue. More explicitly, the proper arrangement of these three components should allow the operator to keep his or her head in a normal and comfortable position. The operator should not be forced to turn unnecessarily from one component to the other.

There is no single solution to a flexible arrangement. An L-shaped counter with ample knee space will often minimize the problem, provided a sufficient number of electrical outlets are available within the carrel. In this connection, it is suggested that electrical strips be installed along the three walls of the carrel. This makes it easier to move the components and eliminates the often tangled maze of loose wires behind the computer equipment.

AUXILIARY ELECTRONIC SYSTEMS

Faster information retrieval and effective large-group instruction have been of interest to educators for decades. With the emergence of the electronic revolution, engineers and educators have been working together in developing equipment designed to achieve these goals. As indicated earlier, several educationally oriented technological applications are competing with each other. Thus, it is conceivable that the systems described in this section might be supplanted by other educational technologies in the future, using minicomputers and wireless-feedback equipment. For the purposes of this presentation, however, it is important to bear in mind that several forms of information retrieval systems are currently available and that electronic equipment for large-group instruction is in a state of fluidity.

The Information Retrieval Laboratory

This facility consists of a fully automatic electronic device which activates a given tape upon demand and sends the audio signal to a carrel where the student is waiting for the information. By simply dialing a number or utilizing a computer terminal, the student can listen to tapes of a lecture recorded in the classroom earlier, a play recorded by professionals, music for pleasure, foreign language recordings, and any special instructional material supplementing basic instruction conducted by the teacher.

The information retrieval laboratory can also be used as a language laboratory by simply adding a teacher console to the system. When the console is under the control of the teacher, the independent access feature at each carrel may be temporarily deactivated. A word of caution. If the educational program calls for the full-time use of a language laboratory, it is less costly and educationally more efficient to plan a separate language laboratory convenient to the foreign language classroom.

Facility Planning for an Information Retrieval Laboratory. Although it has been suggested that the information retrieval laboratory be placed in the learning resources center complex, it is often feasible and practical to locate listening carrels in any appropriate alcove in the building or in other buildings on the campus. There is a definite trend to provide study areas for students outside of the library or the study halls. Semiquiet areas are strategically located throughout the building or campus. In some situations it makes sense to install carrels with a dial and earphone plug in study alcoves or study areas in various parts of the building. A student could be loaned an earphone for an indefinite period of time and use it for all of his or her audiovisual work in the school—in the laboratories, in the learning resources center, and in the semiquiet areas. In order to minimize vandalism, these alcoves should be surrounded by faculty offices or be supervised by a video camera with signs clearly indicating that such video equipment is in operation. The physical features of a dial access laboratory should be built into the design of the building. Space will be needed for student carrels, for the automated switching equipment, for the storage of cassettes, and for the repair and maintenance of software. The size of the total space for the carrels obviously depends upon the number of students to be served. Allow at least 25 square feet per carrel. If the school district has had no previous experience with a dial access laboratory, it is suggested that the capacity of the dial access laboratory be about 5 percent of the school enrollment. In secondary schools, the American Library Association has suggested that the seating capacity of the library be at least 15 percent of the school enrollment. If we define "library work" as any activity whereby the student retrieves information from stored sources, all tapes, slides, motion picture films, and transparencies assume the same position as books and other printed materials. Thus, the capacity of the dial access laboratory can be included within the 15 percent recommendation. A space of approximately 300 square feet should be allocated for the switching equipment, and a storage room containing about 350 square feet should adjoin the space for the equipment. If the laboratory serves more than 50 students, an office, preferably with vision strips, should be included for a staff member who can provide assistance and supervision.

Student Response Systems

The term "large-group instruction" is relative. For the purpose of this discussion, it refers to groups of 50 or more students. Actually, the concept is not particularly sensitive to group size, whether it be 15, 30, 90, or 900.

The programmed student response system is primarily suited for instructing several hundred students, particularly in a college setting. The hardware has been on the market for a number of years. However, because the equipment is rather costly, student response systems are not widely used. The fundamental concept, however, is basically sound, and its potential educational effectiveness is high.

The simplest form of the student response system consists of four buttons installed at each seat in an auditorium. The instructor functions as in the past, with one exception. From time to time, at strategic points, he or she asks a multiple-choice question. The students respond by depressing button A, B, C, or D. A rapid, specially designed calculator instantly informs the instructor of the percent of students answering correctly. Also, the actual responses are recorded by seat number for future analysis by the teacher. This simplified system keeps the teacher continually informed of the extent to which he or she is reaching the students during the presentation, provides for active participation by the students, and records individual student progress for diagnostic purposes by the instructor.

Student response systems more sophisticated in design and function are currently on the market. The electronic heart of this equipment controls the lights, two movie projectors, one slide projector, and one tape recorder. In addition, it can record individual student response and give the instructor instantaneous feedback on the percent of students answering each test question correctly, similar to the simple student response system. The teacher can preprogram the entire presentation utilizing movie projectors, slide projectors, and tapes sequentially. For example, the presentation may begin with a slide containing the title of the subject and a tape recording of the introductory remarks of the instructor. This can be followed by a five-minute sound movie film, followed by a question and student response. If the response is acceptable to the teacher, the programmed presentation continues. On the other hand, if an excessive percent of students answer incorrectly, the teacher temporarily interrupts the programmed presentation and makes a new "live" presentation on the point missed by the students. The teacher then asks a second test question equivalent to the original. If the teacher has made his or her point, as indicated by the student response, he or she reactivates the automatic operation of the system, which resumes the programmed presentation prepared by the teacher.

In planning for a student response system, it is essential that the architect be informed well in advance. A small cable must be installed at each seat during construction. Sometimes conduits are installed in anticipation of providing the wiring and equipment at a later date. The best time, economically, to install a student response system is during the original construction of a large-group facility. It is suggested that one or two manufacturers of equipment be contacted early so that specifications for wiring can be included in the official specification prepared by the architect.

TRADITIONAL AUDIOVISUAL EQUIPMENT

Most school districts are fairly well equipped with audiotape recorders and players, overhead projectors, movie projectors, and projectors for filmstrips and slides. These are quite familiar to educators and further description would be pointless. However, the space requirements associated with special applications of this equipment is worthy of further discussion.

The early teaching machines devised by Pressey in Ohio and Skinner at Harvard have long since been replaced by modern audiovisual equipment, which is often automated and highly sophisticated. The educational use of traditional audiovisual equipment for individualized instruction is limited only by the availability of the desired software. Today, this limit is of little concern. There is an abundance of software on the market in all of the basic disciplines, such as reading, mathematics, and language arts. There is also a wide variety of software in science, social studies, the practical arts, and the fine and performing arts. The material comes in two major forms. The most common form is descriptive, resembling a well-organized type of lecture. This form is extremely useful as a supplement to classroom instruction. The second type is highly structured and serves as a sort of "teacher aide." The material is programmed and divided into self-contained learning units, similar to computer-assisted instruction, described earlier. The software, under this concept, includes testing material at various points in the series of independent learning units. This approach does not replace the teacher in any way. It simply provides a little extra time for the teacher to plan the instructional activities of each student, over and above his or her regular teaching duties. Under an individually oriented instructional setting, the teacher manages all of the instructional activities and provides the necessary basic instruction wherever and whenever it is needed.

Practical Applications

The application of audiovisual equipment for individualized instruction is limited only by the creativity of the teacher and, as mentioned above, the availability of the software. In some instances, the teacher can prepare magnetic tapes for certain uses of the equipment. A few examples illustrating some of the ways in which audiovisual equipment may be utilized in certain learning situations are presented below.

Audiovisual Tapes in Science Laboratories. Audiotapes prepared by the classroom teacher can be used advantageously in a science laboratory. For example, a class of 24 students in a physics laboratory may be conducting five or six different experiments in electricity at the same time. This is often necessary to minimize the amount of test instruments and expensive equipment required for certain experiments. Thus, by subdividing the class into, let us say, six groups of four students each, only one-sixth of the equipment would be needed. Each student group would rotate from experiment to experiment every week until all of the experiments are completed by all of the students.

Under this arrangement, the teacher could prepare a tape giving complete instructions and appropriate cautions for each experiment. A group of four students would check out a tape cassette for, say, experiment A. They would listen to it at their laboratory station. If sound is a problem, earphones could be used. The students would follow the instructions on the tape, which could be as follows: "Ask one student in your group to check out one 6-volt battery, a 1,000-Ohm resistance box, 10 feet of single-conductor #22 wire, one ammeter and one volt meter. Stop the player until the person returns with the material." Upon the return of the student with the necessary supplies and equipment, the tape recorder would again be activated for further instruction until experiment A is completed and the report on the experiment is prepared.

The preceding detailed description was meant to focus attention on the need for designing adequate storage and work areas. Easily accessible storage cubicles should be provided for about 25 tape recorders and about 150 tapes. Workbenches should include additional surface or shelves above the countertops, where tape recorders could be placed while the student is using them during the laboratory period. Unless battery-operated audiotape recorders are used exclusively, it is suggested that electrical outlets be installed at each work station.

Supplementary Instruction for Gifted Students. The descriptive-type software mentioned earlier is well suited for supplementary instruction for gifted students. This information could be provided by short subject reels of motion picture film or by audiotape cassettes. The equipment would probably be located in the instructional resources center where it would be available to all students in the school.

Assistance to Slow Learners. The use of audiovisual equipment for slow learners can be most rewarding. Routine exercises could be practiced by the student on an individual basis using the appropriate type of software. For example, if a student has not fully mastered the skill of subtraction in arithmetic, he or she could sit at a carrel in the classroom or in the instructional resources center and practice doing a large and varied number of subtractions with instructions from a tape recorder and using pencil and paper to perform the calculations.

Reinforcement of Learning. For a large number of students, the use of audiovisual equipment at a time of their choosing could strongly reinforce the regular classroom instruction, particularly those students who have just mastered certain skills or who have been introduced to new concepts for the first time. These students would be permitted to use the equipment at certain times of the school day when they have some free time, such as study periods or their equivalent in the lower grade levels.

A Full Program of Personalized Instruction.   A word of caution is in order at this point. Individualized instruction is not for all students. Many students feel much more comfortable in a group instruction setting. There are others who can profit from an individualized instructional program under certain conditions.[14] All of the audiovisual equipment and associated software can be used most advantageously under the guidance of a creative teacher, providing the students are receptive to this individualized form of instruction.

If such a program is instituted, it would be housed in a specially designed learning laboratory, which might be located adjacent to the instructional resources center, but not under its control or supervision. This laboratory is envisioned as a specialized classroom similar to any other instructional space, such as a science laboratory, homemaking laboratory, business machine laboratory, music room, or art studio. Consequently, it would be an integral part of the teaching program of the school, under the direct supervision of the respective instructional units.

The required audiovisual equipment and materials are obtained from the person in charge. If sound equipment is to be used, make certain there is provision for the use of earphones. Additional details with respect to planning student carrels are included in Chapter 13. The expanded use of carrels for personalized instruction offers a practical solution in meeting the needs of the gifted student, the slow learner, and those requiring some form of reinforcement in the learning process.

NOTES

1. Dan Watson and Lyle Rangel, "Can Cooperative Learning Be Evaluated?," *The School Administrator* (June 1989), p. 8.

2. Royal Van Horn, "Educational Power Tools: New Instructional Delivery Systems," *Phi Delta Kappan* (March 1991), p. 527.

3. Ibid., p. 530.

4. Idem.

5. Tom Pate, "Interactive Television Reaches More Students," *The School Administrator* (May 1985), p. 22–24.

6. Carl B. Boyer, *A History of Mathematics* (New York: John Wiley and Sons, 1968), pp. 634–635.

7. P. Kenneth Komoski, "Educational Computing: The Burden of Insuring Quality," *Phi Delta Kappan* (December 1984), p. 244.

8. Alfred Bork, "Computers in Education Today—And Some Possible Futures," *Phi Delta Kappan* (December 1984), p. 241.

9. Idem.

10. Mark Sherry, "Implementing an Integrated Instructional System: Critical Issues," *Phi Delta Kappan* (October 1990), p. 118.

11. James Rydeen, AIA, "New Light on Computers," *American School and University* (June 1984), p. 24ff.

12. Antonio Lopez, Jr., "Facilities for Microcomputers," *American School and University* (December 1981), p. 34.

13. Rydeen, op. cit., p. 24ff.

14. Basil Castaldi, "Personalized Instruction and Programs," *CEFP Journal* (January 1981), p. 8.

School Surveys

Education is a product of the dynamic culture in which we live. Like the changing society in which it thrives, education must continually change in response to the educational demands of our people. School districts are confronted periodically with the question of whether or not their schools are satisfying the current needs of society, a question that is often difficult to answer. The school survey method offers educators a promising technique for determining the extent to which our schools are meeting our nation's needs.

School surveys vary in profundity, in subject matter, and in method of execution, but they all have a number of elements in common. All surveys require relevant information about the school district, gathered and assembled in an orderly manner. School surveys usually include an interpretation and analysis of all pertinent data. They all contain a number of conclusions and a set of suggestions for the consideration of the board of education, and some suggest a step-by-step plan of action.

THE NATURE AND CHARACTER OF SCHOOL SURVEYS

A school survey is the *sine qua non* of educational planning. No school district can plan intelligently for its future without first making a survey of its school system. A school district cannot be assured that it is spending public funds wisely, nor can it really know with certainty whether or not its students are being properly educated, without making a school survey. And no school district can know whether it is receiving a reasonable educational return for the tax dollars it expends without some form of professional study. In fact, a school district that fails periodically to review its educational program, operating procedures, and future needs never really knows whether or not the educational goals set forth by the board of education are being achieved.

Enlightened school administrators and forward-looking members of boards of education are beginning to recognize that the school survey represents an intelligent and sound approach to educational planning. In fact, the school survey could be viewed as an essential element of the decision-making process in education. Long-range planning that stems from a school survey is more likely to be soundly based than are decisions made without the benefit of a systematic study of the school district and the education it offers. According to Huxley, "Irrationally held truths may be more harmful than reasoned errors."[1] The survey technique provides a powerful means of removing many irrational notions from consideration in the development of a long-range plan. Yet it does not restrict action on matters that seem reasonable and logical, although some of these actions will inevitably fall into the category of "reasoned errors."

The school survey is not uniformly perceived by all educators. Some view it as a study in depth of any or all matters related to education. Some regard it simply as an educational inventory of the school district. Others may use it to evaluate present practices within the school district for the purpose of effecting educational improvement. Some educators utilize the school survey as an objective and systematic approach to future planning; indeed, as an application of the scientific method to the development of long-range educational plans. To still others it is a public relations device whereby the attention of members of boards of education, citizens, faculty, and staff becomes focused upon the goals of the school and the degree to which they are being attained by the school district. Educators generally agree, however, that a well-designed school survey reveals as objectively as possible the educational status of the school district and specifies the action required if the educational objectives of the school district are to be realized.

The principal purpose of most school surveys is to develop a long-range plan of action based upon an objective and systematic study of needs, resources, and educational goals of the school district. The findings, conclusions, and recommendations resulting from a school survey are presented in a written report to the board of education. A realistic plan of action should be part of this report. According to Moser, "The purpose of many surveys is simply to provide someone with information."[2] In a school survey, that someone may be a school official, a board of education, or a citizen.

DISTINCTIVE FEATURES OF SCHOOL SURVEYS

There are a number of compelling arguments for making a school survey. Many of the benefits of school studies are not immediately apparent to school officials or members of boards of education. Nevertheless, the case for the school survey is quite impressive from the standpoint of improved education and the more efficient use of tax dollars. The survey method is a logical approach to the ever-present task of devising a well-reasoned plan of action that serves the best interest of the students, the public, and the taxpayers of a school district. A few of the fundamental considerations related to school surveys are presented below.

1. *The school survey creates a favorable psychological climate for making an objective study of the educational affairs of a school district.* A school study is generally perceived as a scientific and impartial approach to the examination and evaluation of matters related to education. Such studies should contain objective, professional judgments and a well-reasoned analysis of the educational operation. The psychological climate for educational progress is most favorable during a school survey. Local school officials and members of the board of education usually maintain an open mind during a school survey. Action on major educational issues is often postponed pending the outcome of a survey, and decisions are more likely to be made on the basis of fact than emotion in school districts where school surveys have been conducted by competent people.

2. *The school survey offers an effective process for systematically assembling and analyzing data.* The survey process demands that meticulous attention be given to the gathering and analysis of all data. The validity and soundness of the survey recommendations are directly related to the care with which all of the basic data are assembled, compiled, analyzed, and evaluated. This methodical approach is an important aspect of the survey process.

3. *The school survey is an application of the scientific method of inquiry to educational problems.* In most school surveys, the data are gathered, analyzed, and evaluated. Then conclusions are drawn, and recommendations are formulated on the basis of these conclusions. Purposes and goals of the school system are clearly specified. In the school survey, existing educational practices in a school district are compared with those considered acceptable and desirable nationally. Recommendations developed in the survey are designed to correct any differences between observed and desired educational performance and to provide for any special educational needs of the community.

4. *The recommended long-range program resulting from a school survey is built almost entirely upon facts and logic.* In a school survey emotional forces are kept to a minimum. Expert-type surveys can be conducted without being unduly influenced by emotional attitudes related to local issues. Consultants working on expert-type surveys usually treat emotionally oriented information simply as one factor that must be taken into account in formulating a logical and realistic long-range plan for the school district.

5. *The school survey looks toward the future.* All too often, school districts live in a glory of their past. Some are interested in the present, and a few focus their attention on the immediate future, but only rarely do school districts plan, in detail, five to ten years in advance. Though the survey relies heavily on past experience and performance in the school district, it is concerned with both immediate and long-range needs. Through the process of extrapolation, it is possible to identify the educational needs five or ten years hence. The school survey rests solidly on the past, is shaped by the present, and projects logically into the future.

6. *The school survey puts all parts of the educational enterprise into proper perspective.* A school survey looks at all pertinent aspects of the educational undertaking. It includes an analysis and evaluation of all relevant information. A school study can disclose the status and quality of the educational program at the elementary, junior high school, and senior high school level at a given time. It can also reveal the articulation and relationships existing among these schools. Since a survey examines all facts that shape the overall effectiveness of the school system, each part of the educational enterprise may be viewed by itself and in relation to other parts of the school operation.

7. *The school survey may reveal inequalities of educational opportunity within a school district.* The comprehensive school survey, described later, includes an examination of every classroom, every subject, and every course in the school district. In such a study, the differences between similar activities in different parts of the school district are readily apparent. For example, there may be two second-grade classrooms in two different buildings. One class may be taught in a small, poorly ventilated classroom in the basement, while the other is housed in a well-designed classroom that provides a wide variety of student experiences. The differences in the quality of educational opportunity are quickly revealed when such facts are presented in a survey report.

8. *The school survey enables boards of education to plan on the basis of facts.* As mentioned earlier, the recommendations contained in school surveys stem from a professional analysis of the facts, not from opinions, hearsay, or public perceptions.

9. *The school survey represents a sound, businesslike approach to school operation.* In 1988, over 189 billion dollars were spent in the United States to educate about 45 million pupils.[3] Any enterprise that costs almost 200 billion dollars a year to manage and operate fits into the category of big business. Because of the decentralization of education in the United States, however, the enormity of school business is not always recognized. Although not a profit-making enterprise, school business does, indeed, represent a large investment of our national resources.

THE SCHOOL SURVEY PROCESS

The school survey process has been significantly improved since the end of World War II. The construction deferred during the war years and the rapid increase in pupil population after the war created a substantial disparity between building capacity and anticipated enrollments. Local boards of education were confronted with overwhelming problems caused by obsolescence of school plants, increased enrollments, and rising costs. As a result, the accelerating demand for school surveys soon outstripped the supply of school surveyors.

State departments of education and state universities responded to this need by establishing service divisions within their administrative structures. By and large, the state universities, where service bureaus were instituted, made the greatest contribution to the development of a sound school survey process. The various offices of field services in the state universities have contributed significantly to the development of the school survey techniques that are in use today. The work of John Herrick and Marion Conrad at Ohio State University and the efforts of Harold Church at Indiana University have made a noticeable impact on the survey process. For example, the percentage of survival technique, which is discussed further on in this chapter, is frequently called "The Ohio State Method." This technique is commonly used in making enrollment projections. Merle Sumption and Basil Castaldi concentrated mainly on the development of citizens' school surveys at the University of Illinois. Don Leu and Floyd Parker at Michigan State University have added survey techniques that are peculiar to studies made in very large school districts. Some of the private schools of education have also played an important part in furthering the knowledge and application of survey techniques. Cyril Sargent and Donald Mitchell, formerly of the Center of Field Studies at Harvard University, developed noteworthy techniques in projecting pupil enrollments, in assessing community characteristics and growth, and in viewing school problems from the standpoint of the community planner and the sociologist. At Stanford University, James MacConnell made a great contribution to the survey process, before he began a promising program in school research under the sponsorship of the Ford Foundation.

The survey process can be divided into four distinct sequential operations. The initial step of the survey method involves the systematic gathering and organization of *basic data.* All pertinent information is then subjected to *professional interpretation and evaluation.* The analysis, synthesis, and evaluation of the basic data lead to the *development of professionally sound conclusions.* And finally, the conclusions form the basis for the *preparation of recommendations* designed to chart the future course of the school district. Each phase of the survey process is discussed in the order that it would normally appear in any school survey.

THE DATA-GATHERING PHASE

The validity, quality, and usefulness of any school survey depend entirely upon the sufficiency, accuracy, and appropriateness of the basic data assembled during the study. No survey recommendations can be considered valid if the data upon which they are based are faulty in any way. A few simple guides for the data-gathering process should be kept in mind.

Selection of Necessary Data

Survey data should be relevant, necessary, and sufficient. The selection of appropriate data for a school survey is crucial to the success of the study. Before embarking on the data-gathering phase of the survey, each member of the study group should spend some time determining exactly what information is needed. Experienced school survey consultants often begin by mentally reviewing every detail associated with the purpose, content, and scope of the school survey to be undertaken. They carefully analyze the objectives of the survey and list the nature of the basic data required for the study. They imagine, as accurately as possible, the field of inquiry that must be pursued in view of the topics that may be included in the recommendations, which are related in turn to the concerns expressed by the board of education and the nature of the problem itself. They also envision the *topical* aspects of the conclusions likely to be included in the survey report. At this point, the surveyors are not concerned at all about the content or specific nature of the possible conclusions and recommendations. They are interested only in the subjects or topics about which recommendations are likely to be developed. This plan of action enables the consultants to prepare a list of the kind of specific data required for the study before they actually begin the data-compiling process.

It should be emphasized that school surveyors do *not* begin a school study by setting forth the desired theoretical solutions for which they later develop the rationale to substantiate their biases. Rather, they should anticipate the *topics* that may be included in the recommendations but *should* not concern themselves with specific answers to problems at this stage of the survey process. To illustrate this point, let us cite a typical situation. A board of education has requested a building survey of a school district. The surveyors review the topics that might be included in such a study. In so doing, they would probably ask themselves a number of questions. Which buildings should be abandoned immediately? Which schools should be expanded? Which buildings should be remodeled? Which structures should be modernized? What is the maximum amount of money that should be spent in each school being remodeled? How much capacity should be added to the expanded schools? Where will new schools be located? What should be their capacity? What safety hazards should be avoided in locating new schools? What grade organization is best for the school district, in view of the desired educational program and the adequacy of the present buildings? Where should mentally handicapped students and special education be housed? Where should the central administration be located? Should there be centralized warehousing and centralized kitchens? These and many other questions could be raised. As can easily be seen, these questions are not recommendations or answers to problems. They are simply topics that might be included in the recommendations. By studying questions such as those listed above, the school surveyors can begin to list the specific types of information that should be gathered. This preliminary overview of the study will enable the surveyors to prepare forms and checklists that will assist them in gathering the data systematically and efficiently, and help them to avoid gathering superfluous and irrelevant information.

Information about Community Mores and Attitudes

Survey data should include information on local attitudes and underlying community forces.   Some educators and professional persons conducting surveys would argue that the mores of a community and the way people of a school district feel about educational matters may be ignored in a school survey, but such forces, though intangible, are real and must be taken into account. This point of view, however, does not suggest that the emotional forces within the school district should be allowed to dominate survey recommendations. Instead, it views the emotional forces and the mores of a community as the setting within which sound educational action may be planned. With a knowledge of these intangible forces, a new dimension is added to long-range planning strategy and timing.

Organized Data-Gathering Procedure

The data-gathering process should be efficient and well structured.   After a list of needed data is prepared, the logical source of information for each item should be determined. Efficiency in data-gathering demands that the number of visits to the same source be kept at a minimum, not only to conserve time, but also to promote goodwill. Persons in a position to dispense information may become annoyed if they are subjected to repeated visits. Also, when surveys are made by a group of citizens, the goodwill of those supplying information often is shattered when different survey people repeatedly ask them for the same data. Not only do such practices adversely affect human relations, but they also reveal inefficiency in the data-gathering process.

DATA ANALYSIS, INTERPRETATION, AND EVALUATION

The second phase of the survey process involves analyzing, interpreting, and evaluating the data. It is critical in any study.

Data Organization and Analysis

Accurate data must be organized logically and set forth in a meaningful and useful form. Figures should be arranged in tables. Material related to the educational program should be organized around subject matter, courses, or activities. All ideas and explanations of the facts should be clearly stated. There should be a well-substantiated *descriptive* analysis of all matters related to the educational aspects of the school district. In a sense, this phase of the study consists of a detailed description of the present status of the school facilities, the educational program, and the operational aspects of the school districts.

Data Evaluation

Once the data are organized into a logical pattern, they must be evaluated and interpreted before they can contribute to the conclusions derived from a study. The process of evaluation involves judgment; judgment that depends upon the values, experience, knowledge, and background of the person making the judgment. The appraisal and interpretation of data should be made only by persons competent to do so. While this statement may seem superfluous, educators often allow technical decisions to be made by citizens in the name of democratic action, on the assumption that everyone has a right to express an opinion. This overlooks the fact that there is a vast difference in validity between an opinion and a professional judgment.

All data related to *operational* and *instructional* aspects of education should be analyzed and evaluated by professionally trained persons. The strengths and weaknesses of the educational program and of the administrative organization should be identified and lucidly stated. The educational adequacy of all facilities should be covered in detail. All matters that work a hardship on the teacher-learning situation should be clearly noted. Any feature of the school that endangers the safety and health of those occupying the building should be strongly emphasized. In view of the wide array of topics that may be covered in a school survey, it is often necessary to employ a professional team whose members are capable of rendering professional judgments on matters related to structural engineering, community planning, fire safety, educational program, school plants, educational finance, school operation, and architecture.

TYPES OF SCHOOL SURVEYS

Although there appears to be a wide variety of school surveys, each is a specialized version of the comprehensive school survey. Specialized school surveys are generally conducted within a specified area of study for two main reasons. The first is related to cost. Specialized surveys are less costly and usually require less time for completion. The second reason for selecting a specialized survey is need. Often, the greatest need for a survey lies in one area of investigation only. For example, a school district confronted with a declining enrollment may wish to make a study of community growth and pupil population in order to plan its personnel needs for the future. It may have a lesser need for studying the educational program at such time. Each type of survey will be discussed in some detail in the subsequent sections of this text.

THE COMPREHENSIVE SCHOOL SURVEY

The comprehensive survey contains all of the specialized surveys described below. This type of survey could also include an energy audit like the one presented in Chapter 9. As its name implies, the comprehensive survey of a school district is quite broad. It includes a study of the community and its population, business procedures, budgets and capital costs, educational programs, staffing and in-service training, board policies, and educational facilities. Only the types of school surveys that are most likely to be encountered in a school district are discussed in the next section. The school building survey, which is an essential element of educational facility planning, is described in detail in Chapter 4. While a comprehensive survey is an ideal process for achieving overall educational improvement, very few school districts select this type of survey. Thus, educational surveys are usually conducted in limited areas of inquiry based on the felt needs of the school district.

SPECIALIZED SCHOOL SURVEYS

Although a wide variety of specialized school surveys are available, four major categories include practically all types of surveys likely to be conducted in a school district. There may be instances where a school survey includes more than one type of the specialized surveys described in this section. Regardless of the scope of the survey, the same general principles apply to all types of school studies.

The Community and Pupil Population Survey

Studies in this category are concerned primarily with changes in pupil population and with the growth potential of the school district. This type of survey includes an examination of the geographical growth potential of the school district, a study of the population growth pattern of the community, a careful analysis of past pupil enrollments, and the computation of a statistically sound, grade-by-grade, year-by-year, enrollment projection.

Projection of Anticipated Pupil Population.   The preparation of an enrollment projection is indispensable to long-range educational planning. Although several techniques for making enrollment projections are currently in use, the perfect method for accurately predicting future enrollments has not yet been invented. Nevertheless, current methods are extremely helpful in planning for the future, even though the results are only reasonable approximations of anticipated future enrollments. As crude as our present methods seem to be, however, it can be reasonably expected that deviations from actual enrollments later should not exceed plus or minus 10 percent under normal circumstances. On the other hand, school surveyors also point out that if the projected enrollment agrees with the actual number of pupils four or five years hence, such agreement should be attributed more to coincidence than to skill.

The most widely used technique for projecting pupil population is the percentage of survival technique. The basic concept of this method is very simple. For each year and each grade in the past five to ten years, the percent of retention is computed. (The number of years selected, which is based upon the type of growth pattern, requires professional judgment.) For example, what percent of the number of pupils in the first grade this year will appear in the second grade next year? The average percent for each grade, properly adjusted for factors foreseeable in the future, becomes the percent figure used in computing future enrollments. If, on the average, 98 pupils appear in the second grade in any given year for each 100 pupils in the first grade during the previous year, then this 98 percent plus an adjustment for foreseeable factors will determine the enrollment in each second grade if we know the enrollment of the first grade in the preceding year. This procedure is followed for each grade. A more detailed version of this method is described in *The Road to Better Schools*.[4] Work sheets and instructions are provided for the numerical computations associated with this type of enrollment projection.

The Finance Survey

The finance survey includes a study of the business practices of the school district, a review of the disbursements and income, and a determination of the expenditure trends of the school district. The finance survey analyzes in detail the cost of operating the school district, using nationally accepted classifications of expenditures such as administration, instruction, operation of plant, attendance and health services, pupil transportation, maintenance of plant, and fixed charges. Financial figures should also be presented on a cost or income per student basis, so that it is possible not only to compare the cost or income per student with that in other school districts, but also to make comparisons among the various educational centers within the school district.

Survey experts also probe other aspects of school finance. They conduct an intensive search for all possible sources of school revenue and try to determine whether or not the school district is receiving all of the revenue to which it is legally entitled from local, county, state, federal, and private sources. The finance survey also contains an analysis of present indebtedness and bonding potential, as well as a projection of the bonding capacity of a school district for the foreseeable future. Such a survey includes future trends of wealth, pupil load, and financial ability of the school district, as well as a look at assessment procedures and their effect on school revenue.

The finance survey may also contain a study in depth of the school business affairs of the district. The organization of the business services and the efficient use of all nonacademic personnel in the school district are scrutinized. The planning and procedures related to budget-making are evaluated in terms of educational soundness and financial efficiency. The accounting system and record-keeping functions are examined and studied. Purchasing procedures are judged in relation to sound business practices. The existence of adequate safeguards in the school system is also explored—safeguards to protect honest people from being falsely accused for malfeasance of duty and safeguards for the school district to protect it from being deceived or defrauded by persons or groups who are not acting in the public interest.

Educational Program Survey

Ideally, every school survey should include a comprehensive expert study of the educational program offered by the school district. The educational program of a district, after all, is the heart of the educational system in the United States. Unfortunately, school surveys often do not include an expert study in depth of the educational program. Perhaps the two principal reasons for the frequent omission of such studies are: (1) the cost of the program study is often higher than the school district is willing to pay, and (2) the need to employ outside experts for such a study is not readily acknowledged. The belief that a local staff survey of equal value can be conducted without outside assistance and at no additional cost to the school district tends to neutralize the desire of boards of education to have experts make a study of the educational program.

Regardless of who conducts the study, the educational program survey examines a wide variety of instructional materials and techniques. The program study also reviews and analyzes the specific educational goals of the school district and appraises the extent to which these goals are being met. The survey is designed to discover and identify shortcomings in the educational program and to include suggestions that will overcome such deficiencies. Properly conducted, a program study is a systematic and penetrating study of each element of the existing program in relation to the most advanced and effective instructional practices.

The program survey covers all of the instructional experiences that pupils undergo in a school. The course content, its sequence, and its depth are closely examined. The methodology and instructional techniques are scrutinized and the textbooks and instructional materials used in the schools are examined from the standpoint of appropriateness and educational effectiveness. Finally, the overall program and related activities in each area of learning are judged in terms of the practices of today and the probable techniques of tomorrow. It should be pointed out that the degree of excellence of an educational program is difficult to determine objectively. Most of our evaluations are subjective, and many of our judgments must, of necessity, be inferential. For example, if we observe a practice that appears to be outstanding, we infer, often without proof, that good learning is taking place as a result of this practice. This conclusion is not necessarily valid in all situations.

Ideally, outside experts from the various areas of instruction should be employed to work with teachers and school staff in making a program study, but for financial reasons this cooperative venture is not always possible. Consequently, the success of the teacher-staff study must rely heavily upon the competence of the school administrators and the resourcefulness of the teachers involved. With vision, cooperation, and mutual respect between the teachers and members of the administrative staff, it is possible to conduct a staff school program survey that can result in modernization of the curriculum in any school district.

The School Building Survey

One of the school surveys that is most often demanded and conducted is the building study. In many school districts, the need for a building survey often supplies the required spark that results in a much broader study. The building survey, in such cases, starts a sort of chain reaction in the thinking of members of boards of education regarding the educational areas that should be covered in a survey of the school district. While a program study, a community study, and a finance study can be made independently, since the facts needed are self-contained in the study, a building study cannot be made intelligently without a knowledge of future enrollments (community study), educational program (program study), and the financial ability of the school district (finance study). Consequently, whenever a valid building survey is made for a school district, the surveyors must take into account the findings resulting from other types of school surveys. The school building survey is discussed in detail in Chapter 4.

THE PRODUCERS OF SCHOOL SURVEYS

In exploring the educational benefits that might be derived through the survey process, a board of education must make two basic and crucial decisions. First, it must select the type of survey that best meets the needs of the school district. Second, it must determine how and by whom the survey will be conducted. The *"how and by whom a survey will be performed"* is vital to the successful implementation of the survey recommendations. Thus, school officials must make certain that the method of conducting the school survey is acceptable to the community and workable in relation to staff participation. The method selected must also take into account the nature and scope of the study, the attitude of the taxpayers toward education, the willingness of citizens to become involved in finding solutions to educational problems, the expertise available on the staff, and the readiness of the community to accept expert advice from sources outside the school district.

At the risk of being iterative, it should be pointed out that the degree to which survey recommendations are implemented in a school district is directly related to the public acceptance of survey results. In turn, the level of public acceptance of survey findings is often determined by the confidence the public has in the people who conducted the study and the methods employed in arriving at the recommendations contained therein. For this reason, it is strongly recommended that school officials and boards of education carefully review each method of conducting a survey described in the following paragraphs and select the approach that is most likely to produce the results that are most appropriate for the school district.

In this connection, it is revealing to learn of the wide variety of groups that are commonly engaged in making educational recommendations that may have long-lasting effects on the quality of education in a school district. Boards of education are often confronted with a number of questions concerning the people who should conduct the school survey. Are professional persons the only people who make school surveys? Can citizens conduct school surveys without expert assistance? Is the school staff generally best qualified to make school surveys? Are surveys performed by experts more likely to be accepted by the community than those conducted by the administration and local professional staff? The answer to all of these questions is generally "No." There are advantages and disadvantages associated with surveys done by different groups of people. Each school district must decide for itself how it wishes to proceed in conducting a school survey. It is hoped that the information presented in this chapter will be helpful to school officials and boards of education in deciding on who should become involved in making a school survey. The choice depends entirely on the local situation at the time a school survey is considered. For example, if community attitudes on certain aspects of education are diversified, and some issues have become controversial and emotional, the citizens school survey becomes a very attractive option. Each alternative will be described in detail.

School Survey by Experts

The expert survey is directed and executed by experts in education who are usually from outside of the school district. Such surveys may be conducted by organized teams employed by state departments of education or universities or they may be undertaken by private firms that conduct expert surveys.

Qualified survey groups are generally well trained, highly experienced, and very well organized. After a preliminary review of the survey objectives, they are able to determine quite specifically most of the basic data required and where they are most likely to be available.

The expert-type survey is sometimes judged in terms of the amount of time the experts spend in the field. The critics of expert studies may erroneously conclude that the validity of such studies is lower than that of locally conducted studies, because the experts have had only a brief contact with the local situation. A study conducted by the former Office of Field Services at the University of Illinois revealed no foundation for such a conclusion. The study concluded that the recommendations of the expert studies were more consistently sound educationally than those resulting from locally conducted studies. The experts have a wealth of experience and background upon which to draw, while persons conducting local surveys are more apt to have limited experience. The expert devotes full time to the study, including periods when he or she is energetic and creative, while local persons usually work on a survey after school when they are normally tired.

The expert survey has much in its favor. It makes use of an efficient and reliable method. It contains, for the most part, an impartial appraisal of the school district. It can be objective, because the experts can "call them as they see them" without fear of personal consequences, since they do not usually live in the school district. Another advantage of the expert survey is that it can usually be completed in a shorter period of time than the local staff or citizens school survey.

The expert-type survey also possesses a number of disadvantages. As a school official once said, "An expert is one who blows in, blows off, and blows out." The statement contains a number of important implications. One weakness of the expert study is that the "expertness" is not and does not become part of the school district. All that the expert leaves in the school district at the completion of a study is a survey report. Since *practically* no local citizens participate in the expert survey, there may be no feeling of ownership or strong support for the recommended plans of action on the part of local citizens including the members of the board of education. Consequently, implementation of the recommendations made by experts is somewhat more difficult to achieve than implementation of the results from other types of surveys. In spite of these weaknesses, however, the expert-type survey can be most effective if it is followed by some form of citizen participation as soon as it is completed. And it can have an even greater impact on the community if some of the members of the expert survey team can work with citizens during the transitional period between the time when the study is completed and the time when community action is planned by local citizens.

The survey, of course, is only as good as the degree of expertness of the experts. While this might appear to be self-evident, it often escapes school officials and the boards of education who employ the experts. Even if the experts are on the staff of a university or a state department of education, boards of education should not confuse the prestige of the institution with the desired expertness of the individuals. When survey services are rendered on a fee basis, and they usually are, the board of education should assure itself that the experts possess the necessary competencies for the task at hand. When a prospective educational consultant or survey group is being interviewed, it is good business to require a statement, in writing, of the training, background, and experience of each member of the survey team.

School Survey by Local Professional Staff

A school survey may be conducted by the local superintendent of schools and his or her administrative and instructional staff. In this case, the outside experts mentioned in the preceding section are simply replaced by local talent. This type of survey is often called a self-study or referred to as a form of "do-it-yourself" survey.

The advantages accruing from this type of study are limited. The major benefit is financial. Since the personnel are already employed by the school district, only the additional cost of supplies and reference materials is involved. Another significant advantage of the local school staff survey is the participation of many local professional persons. The facts uncovered by the study, the conclusions drawn from them, and the recommendations set forth in the report represent the combined effort and thinking of local people. There is full understanding of the report and a strong feeling of interest in and support for the findings among a number of people living or working in the community. This group could become a nucleus for the planning of community action designed to implement the recommendations in the report.

Before a local staff survey is authorized, however, it is essential that its disadvantages be carefully weighed. It is important to realize that local staff does not usually possess the same level of competence as do outside experts, nor does it always have the technical competencies required for a school survey. For example, demographers, or people competent to make enrollment projections, are frequently not available at the local level. In all probability, there is no one at the local level who can make a professional evaluation of the adequacy of school facilities, in terms of future changes in instructional methods or equipment. It is also very rare that someone on the local staff has had the experience of extrapolating assessed valuations, revenues, and school operating costs for five to ten years. On the other hand, in studies involving the educational program, it is possible to identify a number of outstanding local teachers who can make a significant contribution in this type of school survey. But even in this area of investigation, some of the local staff may not be as up to date or as competent in some respects as outside experts. A second disadvantage is that local personnel would very likely be asked to conduct a staff survey on an overload basis, i.e., the survey would be one more responsibility added to an already full schedule. Obviously, the amount of energy that could be devoted to such a study would be quite limited. Third, the prestige of local people is usually not as great as that of an outsider. For some unknown reason, local people are seldom considered experts by the community. Therefore, the recommendations in a local survey report do not always carry as much influence as those found in the expert survey. Fourth, the local school staff is often accused, rightly or wrongly, of empire-building. Citizens may view local school surveys with suspicion; after all, they reason, the school staff has an educational axe to grind. Also, a local school staff survey is colored by the built-in biases of the various staff members in relation to the power structure and mores of the community. And finally, the local staff survey is more time consuming than the expert survey.

Admittedly, studies of the educational program undertaken as a joint responsibility by teachers and staff have significantly improved education in many school districts. While the quality of such studies is usually good, the attention of the teachers and staff is concentrated primarily on the best-accepted practices of today without the benefit of the knowledge of changes that are likely to occur in the future.

It must not be concluded that surveys of the school program conducted by the local staff do not have a place in our educational scheme of things. It is well known that, whenever studies of the educational program are conducted jointly by staff and teachers, curriculum improvement usually occurs. These studies are largely responsible for the updating of existing programs. There is often a lag between the time when educational innovations are accepted as good practices and the time when they appear in most of the schools. The work of teachers and staff on educational program development is indispensable to the introduction of accepted practices in the schools and the improvement of pupil experiences in the classrooms.

School Survey by Citizens

For the purpose of this discussion, a citizens school survey is a comprehensive study of the school district and educational matters conducted by a group of selected citizens *under the guidance of experienced professional personnel*. This definition excludes school studies made by a self-appointed group of citizens or surveys conducted by citizen pressure groups. A well-conducted citizens school survey can be a powerful, constructive educational force in any school district. Citizens school surveys should be welcomed rather than feared by local school officials, provided the board of education and local school administrators are thoroughly familiar with the scope of such surveys, proper selection of members of the citizens committee, organization of the groups, procedures, and operating principles associated with this type of study, and the specific roles played by professional personnel as resource persons. Citizens can and should delve deeply into educational matters concerning *what the schools should accomplish* and into educational problems that *reflect the values and mores* of the community. On the other hand, they should not be asked to undertake studies of educational matters requiring technical and professional competence. Briefly, it is the responsibility of a citizens school survey committee to examine and evaluate *what* the schools should do but *not* to define *how* it shall be done. In a good school system, it is the duty of professional educators to determine *how* the results desired by the citizens shall be best achieved. Educational Facilities Laboratories, under the directorship of Ben Graves, has developed a "Community Planning Assistance Kit," which is distributed by the Council of Educational Facility Planners. Graves presents a concise outline on the involvement of citizens in planning educational facilities.[5]

The citizens school survey is often responsible for significant changes in attitudes. In a citizens survey of school district reorganization in central Illinois, the change in attitude that occurred over a nine-month period was quite pronounced. During the first meeting of the study committee, fewer than 25 percent of the committee members were in favor of consolidating the two school districts in question. Nine months and 22 meetings later, the survey committee unanimously recommended that the two school districts form a single educational unit. According to social psychologists, such changes in attitudes are not at all surprising. They can be explained on the basis of sociopsychological principles. In discussing attitudinal mutability, Newcomb attributes such changes in attitude to "increased familiarity with the problem or object."[6] Attitudinal changes are more likely to occur "when existing attitudes about it [the problem] are relatively weak" or when increased familiarity with the problem is brought about "by first-hand experiences." In a school survey, both of these principles are operating. There are usually a few persons on a citizens survey committee whose attitudes about the issues to be examined are weak when the study is initiated. Also, the citizens school survey encourages citizens to gather basic data first hand whenever possible.

In citizens school surveys, when the line of demarcation between the responsibilities of lay citizens and those of professional personnel has not been clear, confusion often results. There have been instances where professional persons have dominated citizens groups to the point that the citizens merely "rubber stamped" the plans of the educators. On the other hand, there have also been situations where citizens have improperly involved themselves in technical matters related to education, such as methods for teaching reading and writing, or whether laboratory experiences are needed for effective instruction of science in junior high school. Citizens committees have on some occasions expressed their views on whether a three-year or a two-year junior high school should be established in a school district. This problem is complex and highly technical, requiring a knowledge of child development, educational psychology, and educational administration. It is not one that can be intelligently solved by lay citizens without technical guidance from professional educators. An analogy illustrates the line of demarcation between the responsibilities of citizens and those of professionals. Let us suppose that a bridge must be built over a river. It is the responsibility of the citizens to decide where such a bridge shall be located and to specify its load, its capacity, etc. Once this determination is made, it becomes the responsibility of engineers to decide upon the length of the spans and the technical specifications of materials and design. Again, the citizens state *what* is needed and the professionals decide *how* best to achieve the desired results.

It should be emphasized, however, that citizens have much to contribute to a citizens school survey. They have the right and duty to describe what kind of educated individual they hope the school will produce. Citizens have every right to demand that certain areas of learning or skills be included in the school program. Citizens have the right to request the schools to impart attitudes and values to the students consistent with our culture and with our democratic way of life. These matters are not for the professionals to decide. In practice, school officials have made decisions in these matters under the guidance and direction of the board of education. Citizens committees can play a major role in shaping the education of the future in any school district, through the use of a well-conducted citizens school survey.

Principles Underlying the Organization and Function of Citizens School Surveys

The results of citizens school surveys will be most gratifying for boards of education, school personnel, and citizens if each person concerned can feel that he or she has made a worthwhile contribution to the study. The quality of a citizens school survey is directly related to the degree of participation of each member of the committee. The considerations listed below are drawn from the results of research on citizens school surveys conducted by the former Office of Field Services at the University of Illinois. Since a detailed description of procedural matters relating to citizens school surveys has been published by Sumption, information regarding the details of organization, operation, and techniques will not be covered in this text.[7]

1. *Citizens school survey committees should be established on an ad hoc basis.* A citizens committee should be organized to assist the board of education with a specific set of problems. The purpose of the citizens group should be stated clearly and precisely and, when that purpose has been achieved, the group should be dissolved. The practice in some school districts of establishing a citizens advisory committee as a continuing group is not in the best interest of the school district or the citizens. Standing committees seldom experience the satisfaction of completing a job and receiving due recognition for it. The advantages of the ad hoc citizens committee far outweigh its disadvantages in regard to a citizens school survey.

2. *The members of the citizens survey committee should represent the total educational community.*[8] It is essential that the study group selected be a valid sample of the community and that the individuals in the group, insofar as possible, be those whose opinions and views are respected. Contrary to common belief, influential people are not necessarily those from the elite group. It might well be that the waitress at the hotel dining room is just as influential in her segment of the voting public in matters related to education as the bank president who lunches there is among his contacts on similar matters.

3. *The citizens committee should be directly commissioned by the board of education and report directly to it.* Citizens who are expected to give generously of their time, energy, and skills in conducting a school survey should be invited to participate in such a study by the highest educational authority in the school district. Also, the board of education should impress upon the citizens that their advice and assistance are genuinely desired. Citizens school survey committees should not be used to promote a point of view or a plan of action that has been developed outside of the committee. On the contrary, the committee is responsible for the development of a plan of action which is transmitted directly to the board of education for its study and consideration.

4. *The citizens survey committee should be organized so that competent resource persons from outside of the school district are assigned to each area of study.* The success of a citizens school survey depends almost entirely upon the ingenuity and

creativity of the citizens and the quality of professional assistance and guidance available during the study. From the direct observation of many citizens groups in action, it has been found that a citizens survey committee is more likely to make a significant contribution to the educational program of the school district when it is assisted directly by competent resource persons. It has also been observed that citizens school surveys may have a negative or regressive influence upon the quality of education in a school district when professional resource personnel are completely lacking.

5. *The overall span of time for a citizens school survey should not exceed one year.* Experiments in which the overall time span of a survey was varied from three months to two years revealed clearly that citizens studies that extended over the long summer vacation into another school year lost their initial impact and that the enthusiasm of the citizens waned noticeably with the passage of time. These experiments also indicated that the optimum time span from the time the study group is selected to the completion of the survey report is between eight months and a year. Too short a time span apparently does not allow sufficient time for the committee to reach its peak performance as a group, and too long a time span causes frustration among the more impatient members of the group, increases dropouts, and increases the number of absences from the survey committee meetings.

6. *Citizens survey committees should meet once or twice a month.* Experimentation on the frequency of regular meetings of citizens survey groups also revealed that, if the full committee met more often than once every two weeks, the subgroups did not have enough time to complete their work between these regular meetings. It was also observed that, if regular meetings were held less frequently than once a month, the continuity of the study was adversely affected. There was also an observable tendency to devote too much time to recapitulation at subsequent meetings when the time interval between survey committee meetings exceeded one month.

7. *The formulation of recommendations in a citizens school survey should be the result of a joint effort by citizens and resource persons.* The development of recommendations is one of the most important tasks of a citizens survey committee. The proposed recommendations should *not* be formulated by the professional resource persons and imposed upon the citizens. Nor should the citizens formulate recommendations without the guidance of professional personnel. The procedure suggested for the development of survey recommendations is discussed later in this chapter. It is sufficient to state here that the quality of the recommendation contained in a citizens survey report is directly related to the degree of cooperation between the citizens and the professional consultants when the recommendations are formulated.

8. *The citizens survey committee should be organized to provide opportunities for maximum participation on the part of all its members.* As noted earlier, the quality of a citizens school study is related to the degree of participation of the citizens. The organization and the procedures of a citizens school survey should be designed to facilitate maximum participation by committee members. Whenever possible, additional citizens should be involved in the study at appropriate points. For example, the PTA could participate by taking a census under the guidance of the Pupil Population Subcommittee. Or additional citizens could rate school buildings under the direction of the Building Subcommittee. A strong feeling of interest in the study is generated through such participation. With more people actively interested in the results of the study, a larger nucleus of informed citizens will be available in the school district when the time of community action approaches.

9. *The board of education should give prompt recognition to the citizens who worked on a school survey.* The board of education should formally accept a citizens survey at a public function. A letter or certificate from the board may be used as a form of recognition. It is important, too, that the board of education seriously consider each recommendation made by the citizens group. In the event that certain recommendations are not favorably received by the board, it must, as a representative of the people, explain to the satisfaction of the citizens group why it cannot act favorably on them. The board of education should not dismiss lightly any results of a study on which citizens spent many months.

Any delay by the board of education in giving recognition to the citizen survey committee for its work or in accepting the survey report can produce a potentially explosive situation. It should be realized the citizens have spent considerable energy in completing the study and that they are apt to have paternalistic feelings toward the results of their study. In a sense, the survey may appear to be a masterpiece to the citizens. It is easy to understand, therefore, that any delay on the part of the board in accepting the report can be, and often is, interpreted as board disapproval of the study. Two basic principles should be borne in mind by the board of education: (a) *The more promptly a citizens report is accepted, the greater the goodwill generated by the school board among the citizens participating in the survey.* (b) *The greater the number of citizens recommendations that can be favorably acted upon by the board of education, the greater will be the citizens support for the improvement of the schools in the district.* Application of the latter principle makes it imperative that the board of education state clearly why it cannot follow citizen recommendations, if such is the case.

Organization, Process, and Procedures in Citizen School Surveys

A citizens school survey should not be employed by local school officials or boards of education until they have gained a complete understanding of the citizens survey process. Unless tested procedures and techniques are employed, the results of a citizens school survey may be disappointing and even disastrous. It should be pointed out that a citizens school survey is not always the best type of survey. In general, the more technical the area to be studied, the less desirable it is to organize a citizens survey. For example, it would be inappropriate to ask a group of citizens to offer recommendations as to the best method of teaching set theory in high school mathematics, but it would be quite proper to seek their help in determining the character of the Christmas program in the public schools. The citizens school survey is highly suited to situations involving community attitudes, values, and aspirations. Also, in school districts that have repeatedly lost school referenda, the citizens school survey becomes an excellent method of developing citizenry that is informed on educational matters. The school survey in such cases also provides the mechanism for valuable feedback to local school officials.

The Committee on Recommendations

As stated earlier, it is extremely important in citizens school surveys that the citizens themselves play a major role in the formulation of recommendations. According to Sumption, the survey committee is subdivided into study groups.[9] The four major divisions are:

a. the community and its people
b. the school finances
c. the present school plant
d. the educational program.

These work groups are responsible for gathering, analyzing, and interpreting data in their respective areas. Each group acts almost independently during the first few meetings of the survey. As the survey progresses, each subcommittee in turn presents its report to the entire survey committee. The creation of a committee on recommendations (CORE committee) during the subcommittee reporting stage greatly facilitates the formulation of recommendations.

The CORE committee consists of a representative from each subgroup, the consultant to each subgroup, the chairman and secretary of the overall school survey committee, and the survey director. The superintendent of schools and other school officials serve as resource persons for the CORE committee. This committee is not conceived as an executive body but as a work group that prepares a set of tentative recommendations and presents them to the full committee for its consideration. The full committee may accept individual recommendations, reject them, or modify them. In some studies, the operating rules of the study may require that all modifications of the recommendations submitted by the CORE committee be approved by the appropriate subcommittee before such recommendations are adopted by the survey group as a whole.

Although citizen participation in educational affairs has been generally supported by both school administrators and boards of education over the past few decades, the need for such participation has been greatly intensified recently through the efforts of the National Community Education Association with headquarters in Washington, DC. A number of centers for community education have been established throughout the United States, including the Council of Education Facility Center in Ohio. Dwayne Gardner, former executive director of the Council of Educational Facility Planners, set the tone in an issue of the *Community Education Journal* featuring various aspects of educational facility planning.[10] With dwindling school enrollments and an increased interest in reducing taxes, community education activities are assuming a new and constructive role in society.

Guides for Deciding Whether to Make Citizens School Surveys

As indicated earlier, the citizens school survey is not always the best solution for all situations. While it is true that all citizens are familiar with education because they have all attended school, it does not follow that all citizens have the competence to deal with technical matters related to education. A citizens school survey does hold an important and esteemed place in education in the United States and can serve as a powerful and constructive means of improving education.

A citizens school survey is most appropriate in situations where

1. the perceived educational problems involve community values and local attitudes.
2. there is a lack of community understanding of what the schools should accomplish.
3. repeated defeats of school referenda indicate that the public is not fully informed about the educational needs of the school district.
4. public apathy has been responsible for a stagnant educational program.
5. the board of education is desirous of developing a sound long-range building program.
6. school district reorganization is being explored.

A citizens school survey is unsuitable in situations involving

1. the planning of specific school buildings.
2. a study of content and methodology in any subject matter field.
3. studies of grade-level organization.
4. studies of administrative procedures, organizations, and operational school policies.
5. studies where less than six months can be devoted to a survey.
6. studies requiring technical competence in the field of education and educational psychology.

School Survey by Citizens Assisted by Experts

This type of survey differs from the full-scale citizens school survey in that outside experts are not part of the study group but are invited by the chairman of the citizens committee when they are needed. This type of study has impressive advantages and formidable shortcomings and involves a calculated risk. Unless the local superintendent of schools has had previous experience with the citizens school survey and is prepared to assume full responsibility for directing the study, it is very unwise to undertake a modified citizens school survey. In some situations, such a survey has jeopardized the position of school administrators and reduced the effectiveness of the educational program in the school district; hence it should be undertaken with extreme caution.

Strengths and Weaknesses. The modified citizens school survey technique is one that should be approached very cautiously. School officials and members of boards of education should become familiar with the risks inherent in this type of study. Unless strong, positive leadership exists among the local school administrators and in the board of education, the risks in the use of the modified citizens school survey are greater than the potential value of such a study.

Advantages. The primary advantage of the modified citizens school survey over the full-scale citizens survey is lower cost. The modified survey utilizes local school people as resource persons, and thus entails no additional cost for personnel. The full-scale citizens survey, discussed earlier, would require between 50 and 60 workdays of professional service paid for by the school district on a per diem or contract basis. It can be seen, therefore, that a medium-sized school district having an enrollment of about 5,000 pupils could save several thousands of dollars by conducting a modified citizens survey rather than a full-scale citizens survey.

Other arguments frequently offered in favor of this type of study are not conclusive. Some educators maintain that the employment of local school personnel as resource persons to citizens subcommittees makes available to the study groups information that is directly related and applicable to the local situation. It is further argued that local professional persons are also locally oriented and are, therefore, more sensitive to the local problems than outside consultants would be. These arguments, of course, cannot be refuted. What is often overlooked in comparing the modified and full-scale citizens survey is that local resource persons are also used in the full-scale survey to supplement the services of the outside consultants. Consequently, it cannot be claimed that the use of local professional persons is an argument *for* the modified study and *against* the full-scale citizens survey.

Disadvantages. The modified citizens school survey has a number of serious weaknesses that should be carefully considered before such a study is undertaken. The major disadvantages of the modified study school survey are listed below.

1. *Citizens rarely request expert assistance, even though it is made available to them.* In studies of this type, citizens are not always aware that they need professional assistance. As a result, they act or make decisions on the basis of ignorance rather than knowledge. The writer hastens to add, however, that to the best of his own knowledge in such instances, the citizens acted in good conscience. In each situation it was evident that the citizens simply were not cognizant of the complexities of the problem or issue at hand and hence did not realize that technical assistance was required.

More specifically, citizens do not always realize their limitations in coping with problems related to modern education. For this reason, they are likely to draw erroneous conclusions and make unsound recommendations. In all fairness to citizens who give generously of their time, energy, and effort on such committees, it should be pointed out that they are sincere, conscientious, and well-intentioned. The only question that can be raised is whether or not citizens groups possess the necessary technical competence to conduct a school survey and to make recommendations that are educationally sound, financially possible, and administratively feasible.

2. *Citizens seldom receive proper guidance in the organization, procedures, and content of citizens surveys.* In a do-it-yourself survey such as this, there is, in all probability, no local person, professional or otherwise, who has the know-how for organizing and conducting a citizens school survey. Only in rare situations does a school district have among its professional personnel a person who has had broad experience in school surveys, in the use of group dynamics, and in applying the principles of social psychology to educational improvement.

3. *There is a real danger that citizens will make decisions more on the basis of emotion, tradition, and loyalties than on the basis of facts.* While this danger exists in any type of citizens school survey, the lack of experience among the local consultants assigned to the modified citizens school survey makes it difficult for them to cope with the problem. Also, since the local consultants live in the community, they tend to carry less influence and status than a resource person from outside the community. Experienced consultants working with citizens are extremely sensitive to group feeling and perceive the direction of thought in the group long before ideas begin to crystallize. It is during this crucial period that a consultant can be extremely effective as a resource person by raising fundamental questions at the appropriate time. This high-quality guidance is usually lacking in a do-it-yourself survey.

4. *The modified survey may be quite provincial.* Since the modified survey utilizes local personnel, local problems are viewed in a rather narrow perspective. Promising ideas and practices in use in other parts of the country are not always considered by such a group, simply because they know nothing about them. In all fairness to local resource persons, it should be pointed out that most of them probably have full-time duties as teachers or administrators and must carry the committee assignment as an overload. Also, many promising educational innovations initiated in local school districts are not widely publicized and educational research findings are not systematically disseminated. It is not at all surprising, therefore, to find that local professional people do not have as broad a perspective as experienced consultants, whose primary responsibility is to be up-to-date on educational matters.

5. *The modified citizens survey could create a negative educational force in the community.* There are a few instances where a do-it-yourself survey has had no impact, positive or negative, on the education of the school district. There are also a few cases in which the modified citizens school survey became a liability to the board of education and to school officials. A modified citizens survey was completed in an Ohio city. The citizens committee spent two years on the study. During that time they requested no expert assistance, other than to have a demographer make an enrollment projection, and they did not communicate either with the board of education or with school officials. The citizens simply studied the educational problems of the school district independently and rejected the services of local resource persons when such assistance was offered. When the study was finally completed and submitted to the board of education, its recommendations were found to be neither financially nor educationally sound. The recommended grade organization was quite impractical for the school district in question. The board of education, in good conscience, could not accept the citizen recommendations, whereupon the members of the committee took it upon themselves to make speeches throughout the city promoting their own point of view. The board of education and superintendent of schools became the target of public criticism, even though their position was educationally sound and financially efficient.

The writer does not intend to demonstrate that there is no place for the modified citizens school survey in education in the United States but rather to emphasize that the do-it-yourself survey is *risky*, unless strong, positive leadership is exercised by the local board of education or school administrators in conducting it. To be sure, there have been successful surveys of this type. But, without exception, strong local leadership and conscientious citizens were associated with these successful surveys. When a spirit of cooperation and understanding exists between the citizens group and the school officials and board of education, a modified citizens school survey can be undertaken with some degree of confidence, provided the local school officials are prepared to furnish competent and positive leadership in conducting such a study.

PRODUCT OUTCOME

In pursuing the scientific method of inquiry, no recommendations are possible unless they are preceded by the development of well-founded conclusions. Although the process of forming conclusions from data assembled in school surveys is complex and sometimes difficult, by examining many small pieces of related educational information it is often possible to arrive at valid conclusions. This approach demands logic, common sense, and professional judgments, together with objectivity and understanding of the situation. Admittedly, conclusions in school surveys cannot always be derived from completely objective information and from a precise mathematical analysis of the available data. But there is no justification for substituting clichés or biases, opinions, and hearsay for logic and sound reasoning. To ignore well-considered professional judgments in arriving at conclusions in school surveys in the absence of more exact information is to destroy the very foundation of the survey process.

CONCLUSIONS

Conclusions Supported by Facts and Sound Professional Judgment

Conclusions included in a school survey must be substantiated by irrefutable evidence or sound professional judgment. It is extremely important that the relationship between the conclusions and the facts or judgments be clearly established and easily recognized by the reader of the survey report.

The care with which conclusions are formulated can also have an impact on school-community relations. Citizens are less likely to disagree with professional conclusions when such conclusions stem directly from valid professional judgments, objective data, and intelligent reasoning. If school officials can present conclusions that many citizens can understand on the basis of information included in the survey, the superintendent of schools and the board of education will encounter less opposition to the implementation of recommendations.

Conclusions in a school survey suggest a plan of action. Any study that leaves the reader with the feeling of "so what" defeats its purpose and represents a waste of both effort and money on the part of the school district. On the other hand, a survey containing sound recommendations can be invaluable to the educational growth and development of the school district. The essential characteristics of survey conclusions and recommendations are discussed in the following paragraphs.

Conclusions Avoid Educational Clichés and Shibboleths

Again, if a conclusion cannot be made on the basis of the evaluation and interpretation of the facts or professional judgments, it might better not be made at all. One weak conclusion that is questioned by citizens can cast doubt on other conclusions that are perfectly sound. The use of educational jargon to substantiate a conclusion does not particularly impress the citizens of a school district.

Analogies may be introduced to emphasize a conclusion, but they should not be used to substitute for the factual basis supporting it. Citizens may get the impression that educators must resort to analogies because the facts of the situation are not strong enough to support the conclusions.

Conclusions Focused on Strengths and Weaknesses of a School District

Many school officials and school board members have the erroneous impression that the purpose of a survey is solely to find out what is wrong with a school district. This version of a school survey is correct as far as it goes, but it is too limited. The survey should also recognize and give due credit for the strengths and superior characteristics of the school program.

No school district is all bad or all good. The writer has found, without exception, that several positive statements can always be truthfully made about any school district. The positive approach to school surveys demands that evidence of excellence be given the same emphasis as evidence of inadequacy, inefficiency, and inferiority. Obviously, very little, if any, improvement can be expected from a survey report that accentuates the positive and eliminates a discussion of the negative. On the other hand, the shotgun approach that tears mercilessly into the negative aspects of the school district is also damaging. It tends to build up resentment among those affected by the study and often places school officials and boards of education on the defensive. What is really needed, of course, is a well-reasoned, factual, and firm presentation of the shortcomings discovered during the study which, if possible, implicates neither individuals nor groups. In any effective school survey, it is essential that both praiseworthy and uncomplimentary features be given equal consideration.

Conclusions Tactfully Stated

Conclusions that reflect unfavorably on the people of a school district are always unpopular. Many citizens may already recognize the deficiencies of their school district, but for some reason no one dares to raise questions about them. In this respect, the school survey can serve a most useful function by bringing the truth out into the open for wide discussion. Without distorting the truth or minimizing the shortcomings of a school district, conclusions can be carefully prepared to make the needed impact in language that does not arouse readers in the immediate defense of personal pride or the school district. There is sometimes a tendency for school officials and school surveyors to deemphasize the deficiencies observed in a school district. This is not justifiable, because boards of education pay substantial fees for school studies, from which they hope to gain a complete picture of their districts so that improvements can be effected. It is a disservice to the boards of education to withhold or minimize the negative aspects of a school district. On the other hand, there is no point in antagonizing members of boards of education, school officials, and citizens by stating conclusions in an offensive or tactless manner. A judicious choice of words is appropriate in expressing conclusions that are not complimentary.

Conclusions and Recommendations Clear and Concise

Conclusions, as well as recommendations that are discussed in the next section, should be clear, concise, and to the point. Conclusions may reflect a positive, negative, or neutral position. It is not uncommon to encounter conclusions that tend to confuse the reader. In their attempt to be fair, educators sometimes present more than one position related to a single point in one concluding statement. This technique should be avoided, if possible, since it only bewilders the citizens. If no definite conclusion can be drawn from the facts on a point of interest to the citizens, it should be stated in the conclusions.

It should be emphasized, in this connection, that every conclusion will not necessarily include a positive or negative statement on the issue. A neutral conclusion is possible and sometimes desirable. While a neutral conclusion does not usually lead to recommended action, other than perhaps suggesting further study on the issue in question, the inclusion or exclusion of a neutral conclusion in a survey depends upon the importance and nature of the issue under consideration.

Complex recommendations frequently confuse the readers and are likely to result in misunderstanding. It is true that many recommendations are inherently complex, but these can often be broken down in such a manner that two or three simple recommendations can replace a single complex statement.

RECOMMENDATIONS

Recommendations consist of a series of statements designed to achieve the goals and purposes of the school survey. Recommendations serve many purposes. They are instrumental in correcting deficiencies uncovered during the study. They promote improvements in the educational program. They focus on economic efficiency. And they suggest viable solutions to educational problems confronting the school district. Regardless of the intent of a recommendation, it should not be proposed unless it is the direct outcome of a well-documented conclusion. A valid recommendation, therefore, is one that can be traced back to one or more conclusions that can, in turn, be substantiated by the facts stated in the report. As indicated above, recommendations should be unambiguous, concise, and clear-cut. They should be expressed in tactful language. On the other hand, recommendations should not be worded so evasively or so conditionally that they lose their effectiveness. Each recommendation should focus on a specific type of action and each set of recommendations should apply to one option. It is possible for a survey report to include several options, but each option should be educationally sound. If the team conducting the survey believes that the alternative recommendations, though educationally sound, vary in quality from one another, it is within the prerogative of the survey team to list the alternatives in priority order and to give reasons for its choice of priority. This information is helpful to the school officials and boards of education who will be making final decisions after they have had an opportunity to study the survey report.

Recommendations—Realistic, Educationally Practicable, and Financially Feasible

Unless a recommendation appears logical, reasonable, practicable, and feasible to those responsible for taking action, it is doomed to failure. Educational soundness and financial feasibility are two fundamental considerations in the formulation of recommendations in school surveys.

Recommendations—Evolutionary in Nature

The application of the principle of gradualism is essential in recommendations that involve changes or the introduction of innovations. Fundamental changes often demand changes within and outside of people. When recommendations provide for evolutionary changes, the desired results are more likely to be achieved because gradual change seems to be more acceptable to most people.

Recommendations—Sensitive to the Values and Attitudes of the Community

In school surveys, recommendations are designed to correct educational deficiencies, to effect essential improvements, and to provide for future needs. But any recommendation that contains ideas contrary to the feelings and attitudes of the people responsible for taking action will probably receive little, if any, consideration. The school surveyor thus finds herself or himself in a dilemma. Should recommendations be designed to improve the educational ills of the school district or to please those empowered to act on the recommendations? It would be ideal if all recommendations could accomplish both purposes, but with regard to recommendations dealing with highly controversial educational topics, it is unlikely. In such instances, only knowledge and understanding of the values and attitudes of the people enable the school surveyor to express sensitive recommendations tactfully.

NOTES

1. Thomas Huxley, "The Coming of Age of the Origin of the Species," *Science and Culture,* v. 12.

2. C. A. Moser, *Survey Methods in Social Investigations* (Toronto: Heinemann, 1958), p. 2.

3. U. S. Bureau of Census, *Statistical Abstract of the U.S.: 1991,* 111 Edition, Washington, D.C., 1991.

4. Basil Castaldi, *The Road to Better Schools* (Cambridge, MA: New England School Development Council, 1955).

5. Ben E. Graves, "Community Involvement in the Planning Process," *Council of Educational Facilities Planners Journal* (January–February 1980), p. 5.

6. Theodore M. Newcomb, *Social Psychology* (New York: Dryden Press, 1950), p. 202.

7. Merle R. Sumption, *How to Conduct a Citizens School Survey* (New York: Prentice-Hall, 1952).

8. Ibid., p. 6.

9. Sumption, op. cit., p. 23.

10. Dwayne Gardner, "Facility Planning for Community Education," *Community Education Journal* (January 1980), p. 2.

▶ 4

The School Building Survey

The school building survey report contains an evaluation of existing buildings in relation to the educational functions desired by the school district, including a calculation of building capacities, a statement of unmet educational needs, and a recommended long-range building program.

FACT FINDING

Knowledge of the Educational Program and Curriculum

While building surveyors do not necessarily evaluate an educational program, nor do they formulate it, they must, nevertheless, be well acquainted with all of the programs, activities, and student experiences that should exist in a given school.

Formal Educational Offerings. As a first step in appraising the educational adequacy of a school building, the surveyor must develop a detailed mental image of a model school plant against which to compare existing buildings. In creating the mental image of the model school facility, he or she should have a detailed description of the educational program. It is not enough, for example, for local school officials to indicate that "art" will be taught in a high school. The course organization and content should be described briefly. The major types of student activities included in each course and the approximate number of students participating in each type of learning experience should be noted.

Informal Educational Offerings. The cocurricular opportunities available to students in a well-conceived educational program are designed to satisfy their individual interests and to supplement the formal instructional program. Accordingly, the building survey should evaluate the suitability and adequacy of existing school buildings for these instructional activities. Again, it is imperative that the school surveyor have a complete description of these supplementary activities to assist in developing the image of the model school facility for the district.

Supplementary Instructional Activities. Not all instructional activities occur in classrooms or laboratories. Self-instruction, for example, is carried on in the library, in the study halls, in the carrels where teaching devices are used, and in the sound laboratory through the medium of tapes. The school surveyor should build into the mental image of the model school building those features that facilitate additional activities, such as assembly, remedial instruction, group library work, dramatics, music, and art exhibition. He or she should also envision a school facility that can house other programs desired by the school district, such as adult education, special education, and summer education.

Noninstructional Activities. All schools provide some type of service activities such as administration, health, and guidance. The major functional features of all noninstructional services supplied in the various types of school buildings should be noted by the school building surveyor. Other services that might be considered in a building survey include hot lunch, book rentals, secretarial, curriculum material preparation, audiovisual, and public relations.

Board of Education Policies Affecting School Plant. The school surveyor should be aware of all board policies governing the manner in which school buildings are to be utilized. Knowledge of board policies serves two purposes. It permits the school building surveyor to determine the extent to which existing school facilities limit the implementation of established board policies and guides him or her in developing recommendations designed to facilitate implementation of board policies on matters such as grade organization, maximum class size, nursery school, kindergarten, post-high school training, adult classes, night school, and summer school. Board policies related to the maximum distance students are required to walk to school, the maximum time they may ride on school buses, and the optimum size of the various types of schools are also of primary concern to the building surveyor.

Educational Adequacy of the Building Design

After the pertinent facts about a school building have been studied, the surveyor must answer the question, "Is the building under consideration designed to satisfactorily house the desired educational program?" To answer it, he or she turns to the mental image of the model school and then compares the actual school with it. School buildings do not always possess every feature contained in the model, of course. Consequently, the building surveyor specifies whatever excellent features the real building may have and also lists its deficiencies. This evaluation enables the surveyor to arrive at a well-reasoned conclusion regarding the educational adequacy of the school.

It might be advantageous for the building surveyor to translate into words the mental image of the model building. He or she might prepare a checklist of such characteristics as size, shape, location of instructional spaces, and environmental conditions, and also describe any special features related to the school as a whole or to any space contained in it. Special work areas, unusual equipment, storage requirements, and certain display facilities might also be specified. Circulation patterns within the school and desirable space relationships could be mentioned. The checklist should be the product of an analysis of the desired educational program, imaginatively translated into reasonable and necessary space requirements.

Sufficiency of Instructional Spaces

The educational adequacy of a school can be adversely affected by any deficiency in either the number or size of available teaching spaces. Theoretically, capacity represents the largest number of students that can be instructed in a school building without curtailing the desired educational program. In practice, however, school capacity has different meanings to different people. To some educators, the capacity of a building is simply the number of students that can be accommodated for "homeroom" purposes. To others, it is the number of students for which the architect originally designed the building. To many, the capacity of a school is the sum of the capacity of individual spaces multiplied by a student station utilization factor of 0.80 for secondary schools and 0.90 for elementary schools. Note, however, that in none of these conceptions of capacity is any mention made of the school curriculum, administrative policy, or organization of the school day.

The adequacy of instructional spaces with respect to size, number, and type was a major concern of some professional school plant planners following the end of World War II. They, along with the author, became particularly alarmed at the continuing downward trend in classroom sizes since the Great Depression of the 1930s. The problem was somewhat more complicated than they had anticipated. They found that the size of a classroom could vary from school district to school district depending on the nature of the respective instructional programs. Thus, specifying a fixed number of square feet for a classroom was not the answer. Perhaps the formulation of a set of guidelines would be a more useful approach. Under this plan of action, it was necessary to determine the amount of space needed to accommodate the desired educational program. This proved to be impossible because there was no standard educational program. Thus, they were forced to find some other way of relating instructional space to educational function.

Conrad,[1] Knezevich,[2] and Castaldi[3] independently proposed a general principle that could be implemented by local school administrators. While this solution lacks numerical specificity, it does, indeed, provide a firm basis for local educational facility planning. The three educational facility specialists mentioned above are in agreement that ideally the size, the number, and the type of instructional spaces contained in a school building should be those necessary and sufficient to accommodate the desired educational program for the total number of students enrolled in the school. A properly computed capacity of a school provides a measure of the spatial adequacy of the building in relation to the program housed in it. Consequently, if the capacity of a school is substantially lower than its student enrollment, the building is restricting the educational programs in some respects. Under these conditions, often characterized as "overcrowding," it is the quality of the educational experiences that usually suffers. The extent of educational deficiency is directly proportional to the difference between capacity and enrollment.

In any school building survey, the calculation of student capacity for each serviceable building is a prerequisite to long-range planning. To specify the type and size of additional school buildings needed in the foreseeable future, the capacity of all usable existing buildings must be accurately determined. Thus, the computation of building capacity provides information that is fundamental in the evaluation of the educational adequacy of a building and in the development of a long-range building program.

Secondary School Capacity

The most logical and meaningful approach to secondary school capacity to date was developed by Conrad in 1952.[4] The Conrad technique directly relates capacity to educational program. His procedure is based on the principle that the building should fit rather than determine the program. Accordingly, the effective capacity of a building for a given educational program is determined by the number of students that can be properly accommodated in the subject-matter area where overcrowding would first occur.[5] For those who may wish to compute secondary school capacity using this method, a manual describing the application of the Conrad technique is available.[6]

Although the Conrad technique is undoubtedly the most precise procedure for determining the operating capacity of secondary schools, the method of successive approximations employing the "concept of dynamic capacity" will also produce satisfactory results.[7] In using this method, the number of each type of space *needed* to house the desired educational program for any selected school enrollment is compared with the number of corresponding spaces *available* in an existing building. The trial-and-error method may be employed to determine the capacity of a school building by repeatedly comparing needed spaces with available spaces. A computation of the number of the various types of spaces needed for the current school enrollment adjusted for the *desired* rather than the present educational program may be a logical starting point. According to the method of successive approximations, the spaces needed for the desired educational program are computed for each selected total enrollment. The selected enrollment figure is repeatedly revised and space needs are recomputed until there is a fairly good match between spaces needed for the program and spaces available in the building. The total enrollment producing the best fit between needed and available spaces becomes the capacity of the building. Only in rare situations will there be a perfect match between available spaces and those needed for a given educational program and total enrollment. At best, the stated capacity will be a compromise in which there will be a deficiency in some types of spaces and an excess in others, and thus the stated capacity is usually qualified.

As an example, let us assume that the number of the various types of space in a given building is in close agreement with the corresponding spaces required by the desired educational program for a selected enrollment of 500 students. Let us assume that the existing building lacks one room for general science, one-half room for instruction in art, and contains three regular classrooms more than are needed for a total enrollment of 500 students. The capacity of this building, therefore, would be 500 students with an excess of three regular classrooms and a deficiency of one-half teaching station for instruction in art and one teaching station for instruction in science. Additional information on secondary school capacity is presented in Chapter 13.

A rule of thumb is sometimes utilized in making an approximate estimate of the capacity of a secondary school, but this approach is neither exact nor meaningful. On the other hand, it is sometimes necessary to make a rapid capacity computation for nontechnical purposes. The capacity of a conventionally organized secondary school can be roughly approximated by multiplying the number of *teaching stations* by 23. A teaching station is defined as any space where one teacher (conventional school) instructs a group of students. Thus libraries, study halls, cafeterias, and auditoriums would be excluded from the enumeration of teaching stations, but a gymnasium designed so that four classes can be taught in it simultaneously would be recorded as four teaching stations.

Elementary School Capacity

The capacity of an elementary school (K–6) organized in accordance with the self-contained classroom concept is relatively simple to compute. The acceptable class size at the elementary-level ranges between 20 and 25 in kindergarten and between 22 and 27 in grades 1–6, provided the floor area of the classroom exceeds a minimum size of 1,100 square feet for kindergarten and 850 square feet for the remaining grades. The minimum figures have been reduced slightly from earlier accepted sizes for economic and energy conservation reasons.

This matter is discussed more fully in Chapter 12. Two factors affect the capacity of conventionally organized elementary schools. One is related to school district policy regarding maximum class size and the other to limitations imposed upon the desired class size by the lack of space in the classroom. In determining the capacity of an elementary school, the school surveyor simply uses either the maximum class size established by the board of education or the maximum class size that may be effectively instructed in a space of limited size or improper shape, whichever class size is lower. Since there are no standards, as such, the school surveyor must use professional judgment in determining the number of pupils that can profitably participate in the learning experiences intended for the space in question. For purposes of long-range planning, the capacity of an elementary school may be taken as the sum of the capacity of the individual spaces less 10 percent. Some educators simply regard the sum of the capacity of the individual self-contained classrooms as the capacity of the school. Deducting 10 percent, however, allows some leeway for the annual variations in grade enrollments. Of course, it is often extremely difficult to balance class sizes in school districts where only one or two sections per grade may be in operation. Class load equalization can be a troublesome problem in school districts of any size.

In the less conventional elementary schools, where team teaching, large- and small-group instruction, and departmentalization are used, capacity computations are made in accordance with techniques described earlier under the heading "Secondary School Capacity." A simple method of approximating the capacity of nontraditionally organized elementary schools consists of converting existing spaces into "equivalent self-contained classrooms" and applying the technique described in the preceding paragraph.

Safety and Health

Every school building survey must include a close examination of all features of the school that affect the safety and health of its occupants. Any school that endangers the safety or health of those using the building should be closed, unless the deficiencies can be corrected.

Although school surveyors are not expected to possess all of the technical competencies required to evaluate the safety and health characteristics of a schoolhouse, they should, at least, be sufficiently familiar with such problems to recognize the need for further study by experts. A few of the major aspects of safety and health are mentioned below.

Fire Safety. The danger resulting from fire is of primary concern to school officials, boards of education, and school surveyors. Points to be considered in evaluating the fire safety of a school include heating plants, escape of combustible gases, the rapidity with which fire may spread through the structure, electrical wiring and overloaded circuits, storage of combustible materials, fire alarm systems, condition and serviceability of fire extinguishers, and safety of emergency egress from the building. Whenever feasible, a school surveyor should engage the services of an authority in fire hazards to assist in assessing the fire safety of a school.

Structural Soundness. The evaluation of the structural safety of a school lies strictly within the province of structural engineering. Unless the school surveyor is a structural engineer, he or she would be well advised simply to report all observable structural deterioration without an evaluation of its possible consequences. If, in the judgment of the school building surveyor, the structural deterioration has reached the point of endangering lives, he or she should urge that the building be examined by a structural engineer without delay.

Environmental Conditions. Healthfulness is closely related to a number of environmental factors that are of primary interest to the school building surveyor. For example, lack of cleanliness; improper disposition of garbage, trash, and ashes; insufficient control of rodents, flies, and insects; and improper storage of foods are all matters of concern. Also it is essential that the school surveyor examine the visual environment of the school, including the quality of illumination, brightness balances in the instructional areas, and freedom from glare in the visual sphere of the students. The building survey also includes a study of the performance of heating and ventilating systems and an appraisal of the acoustical environment, particularly in very quiet or extremely noisy areas.

Other Safety Considerations. The school survey should take careful note of safety conditions both inside and outside of the school. The improper location of doors, worn stair treads, loose plaster, slippery floors, and unprotected plate glass represent only a few examples of possible hazards within the building. Outside of the building, safety considerations may be concentrated on matters such as the layout of driveways, the location of student bus-loading zones, the type and condition of play equipment, the various play surfaces, and the presence of unprotected high-voltage electrical transformers.

Development of the Long-Range Building Program

Long-range planning is the process whereby the actions of the past and present are logically and sensibly related to those planned for the future. Because of the permanent and fixed nature of both school buildings and instructional equipment, it is essential that future planning be based upon sound reasoning and desirable educational objectives.

Before a sound long-range plan can be developed, the conclusions related to educational program, existing buildings, student population, and finance must be examined and carefully considered. A valid long-range building program is the product of many factors. Logically, conclusions pertaining to the desired educational program and anticipated student enrollments establish the overall housing need of a school district. Conclusions about the adequacy of present facilities indicate the extent to which present buildings can meet the overall need. And conclusions concerning finance and rate of population growth determine the rate at which new facilities will be needed and the extent to which construction of new buildings can be financed.

Principles of Long-Range Planning

Sometimes, of course, a board of education must deviate from a well-conceived long-range plan because of public sentiment or the necessity for gaining public support. However, before yielding to a less-desirable solution, the board of education should do all within its power to raise the educational expectation level of the citizens through some form of participatory action, such as the citizens school survey discussed in Chapter 3. A sound long-range building program

1. *is based on fact and sound professional judgments.* A good long-range plan of action should stem from conclusions derived from facts and professional judgments, not hearsay, unsubstantiated opinions, personal biases, and superficial explanations. Facts, together with common sense and practicality, are likely to produce a plan that is financially prudent, educationally defensible, and logically justifiable to the public.

2. *makes the most effective use of serviceable facilities.* Present school buildings represent a substantial amount of capital outlay and should not be cast away lightly. Obviously, any building that is hopelessly obsolete should not be continued in operation, but every bit of useful life should be extracted from a school, even though it may mean that some compromises must be made temporarily. Furthermore, no school should be abandoned simply because it is old, if it is still structurally and educationally sound.

3. *does not freeze the action of future boards of education.* Any building program that commits future boards to a single plan is not desirable. A "one-way street" feature of a long-range plan ignores the unforeseeable changes that may take place in the future and may prevent future boards from making choices advantageous to the students and the school district at a later date. For example, a board of education may decide to add to an existing junior high school instead of constructing the nucleus of a new one on a separate site. Adding to the existing building may well mean that a future board of education is committed to further additions to that school because the amount of space needed might not justify building the nucleus of a new junior high school at a later date. The one-way street action is quite insidious, because it has every appearance of an ideal solution at the time it is taken. It is important, therefore, that the board of education be constantly on the alert to recognize the one-way street approach and avoid it.

4. *avoids the "tack-on" policy.* The practice of adding space to a school a little at a time, or of planning a series of small additions to existing buildings, is costly and may provide capacity where it is not needed a few years hence. A sound long-range plan, therefore, can best satisfy the principles of economy and efficiency when construction consists of sizeable units on adequate sites *where schools will be needed in the foreseeable future.*

5. *specifies the most suitable grade organization.* There may be several solutions regarding grade organization and attendance areas in a school district, depending upon the character of the educational program, distribution of homes, and the capacity, location, and use of existing schools. Any grade organization should be carefully considered in terms of educational, psychological, and operational factors. The fact that a given grade organization works well in one school district is no guarantee that it will work in or even be applicable to any other. To some degree, the capacity, location, and type of available facilities will favor one grade organization over another, but the focus should be primarily on the educational soundness of the plan, rather than simply on providing space for desks. The recommended grade organization should help to provide high quality of education and effective utilization of present buildings with a minimum of pupil inconvenience.

6. *is educationally effective.* A good long-range plan should produce the maximum educational impact upon the students enrolled in the schools by promoting high staff utilization in schools that are designed for efficient instructional practices. Spatial adequacy and suitability are of paramount importance in providing meaningful learning experiences. Thus, the use of school buildings possessing these two characteristics should be maximized.

7. *is economical.* A good long-range plan is geared to long-term economy in capital outlay, maintenance, and operation. Such a plan provides for maximum space utilization and keeps costs of operation, maintenance, transportation, supervision, and administration to a minimum. Buildings with a high maintenance cost per pupil should be scheduled for abandonment. Schools that are too small to offer a broad program of modern education should not be continued in operation except on an emergency basis.

8. *is flexible.* Any long-range plan must provide for the foreseeable and make allowances for the unforeseeable. The plan should be devised to leave open as many alternatives as possible to future boards of education. For example, if a board of education has a choice of providing two high school buildings or one, it would be far more advantageous, from the standpoint of future planning and community growth, to include two high schools in the long-range plan. The flexibility of such a plan is quite clear. Any future board of education could add to one or both schools, or in the event of a large growth in a given area, could simply plan a third unit and still retain a balance in the size of the high schools in the district.

9. *takes into account the accepted minimum and maximum range in the size of enrollment.* Current educational practice in the United States suggests certain limits in the size of the various types of schools. Table 4-1 indicates the generally accepted minimum and maximum capacities for elementary, junior high, and high schools.

TABLE 4-1 **Generally Accepted Range of Enrollment of Various Types of Schools**

Type of School	Minimum Enrollment	Maximum Enrollment
Elementary	200	600–650
Middle School (7–8 or 7–9)	500–600	900–1,000
High School (9–12 or 10–12)	600–700	1,200–1,500
High School (9–12 or 10–12) using school-within-a-school concept	2,000	5,000–6,000

Admittedly, there are a few high schools in the nation exceeding the limits stated in Table 4-1, but such large enrollments in a single school are due primarily to circumstances, such as an extremely high student population density, which is fairly common only in major cities. It can be demonstrated mathematically that there is no significant economic advantage in increasing the size of a secondary school beyond a capacity of about 1,400 students. While no validated research findings exist on the relationship between school size and educational effectiveness, advanced educational programs can be found both in schools whose enrollments are within the accepted range and in those exceeding it. It can be concluded, therefore, that size beyond a certain minimum enrollment does not, per se, contribute to improved education. In considering the size of a school, it is also necessary to take into account the added cost of transportation often associated with large schools. Many educators maintain that very large high schools have no significant advantage over schools with a capacity of about 1,200, and that there is an appreciable loss psychologically and instructionally in such schools owing to their size.

10. *takes into account the size of the school site needed.* Table 4-2 indicates minimum standards for size of school sites. Within the past decade, the trend has been toward acquiring the largest possible school site. Many school districts have acquired large tracts of land only to discover that neither the architect nor school personnel could devise ways of using so much space. Excessively large sites cannot be justified in urban and suburban areas where land costs are exceedingly high. On the other hand, we cannot be satisfied with the "postage-stamp" sites prevalent during the Depression years. It can be demonstrated through the use of a scaled

TABLE 4-2 **Reasonable Minimum Standards for School Sites**

Type of School	Basic Number of Acres	Additional Acres per 100 Students
Elementary (K–6)	5	1
Middle School (7–8 or 7–9)	10–15	1
High School (9–12 or 10–12)	15–20	1

drawing of the site layout that the size of the sites suggested in Table 4-2 will provide sufficient space for all of the activities and outdoor instructional programs *normally* associated with the respective schools. (See Chapters 6, 12, and 13).

Ideally, school sites should be located at the center of the attendance area served by a given school building. Thus, a properly situated school site is logically found in the middle of a relatively well developed residential area. Unless the school site is already owned by the school district, however, boards of education often learn—to their regret—that the price of the land has skyrocketed. They find themselves in a dilemma. Land is scarce at locations where school sites are needed and the price of the land is frightening. For this reason, many educators are rethinking the old cliché that "The cost of a school site is negligible compared to the cost of the building" and are beginning to explore more precise methods of determining the proper size of a school site. The Rule of Thumb approach (see Chapter 6) employed for the past half century may soon be outdated.

One way to overcome the problem of skyrocketing land prices, of course, is to develop a sound long-range plan well in advance of the need for school sites, when undeveloped land can still be purchased at reasonable prices at locations where schools will likely be needed. This goal sounds simple and straightforward but often requires clairvoyance far beyond the power of the human mind. In some situations, of course, the center of future population growth in a community is foreseeable well ahead of the need. But, in many others, school sites are often purchased after a significant portion of the residential development has occurred, simply because the location of the residential development was unforeseeable. Consequently, in these instances, it can no longer be assumed that the cost of a school site is negligible compared to the cost of the building itself.

A more rational, pragmatic approach is needed in determining the size of a school site. Some states have adopted a new method. In these states, the size of a school site is no longer specified in terms of school enrollment and acres required. The new approach requires that the total area be determined on the basis of the educational functions to be accommodated on the site, with proper allowances for future expansion and potential changes in the educational program. This is a much more practical approach in determining the size of a school site, especially at a time when taxpayers are more sensitive to capital outlay expenditures. This functional method of determining the size of a school site is described in Chapter 6 and the size of school sites for specific purposes is discussed in Chapters 12, 13, and 14 in connection with the planning of elementary and middle schools, secondary schools, and colleges and universities, respectively.

For the purpose of making a judgment relative to the adequacy of an existing school site during the survey process, however, it is suggested that the figures in Table 4-2 be used as a point of reference. Generally, it is not economically feasible to expand an existing school site located in a densely populated area. Nevertheless, it is important to give some indication in a survey report as to the degree of deficiency of a school site in a given situation.

11. *is related to the financial ability of the district.* A long-range building program should be geared to the financial ability of the school district. It should be realistic and practical from the standpoint of public acceptance but should not compromise desirable goals and sound principles. Fortunately, most citizens are willing to support good education if they are fully informed of current needs and the soundness of proposed methods of meeting these needs.

12. *provides for safety, welfare, and convenience.* Schools should be located so that students do not have to cross principal highways when walking to school. Other barriers such as railroads and rivers should be taken into account. Elementary-grade students should not have to walk more than three-fourths of a mile to school, and it is preferable that the walking distance from home to school does not exceed one-half mile "as the student walks." The use of half-mile radius circles is not realistic in areas such as the Midwest where the grid system is used in laying out streets. It is suggested that a square, three-fourths of a mile on each side, be used as the unit for the placement of schools in urban or suburban areas where the layout of streets forms a grid pattern.

13. *provides new facilities in strategic locations.* The long-range building program relates the location of new schools to those that are to be continued in operation indefinitely. Also, the location of new schools should take into account the ultimate abandonment of some of the existing buildings, insofar as possible. This goal is sometimes difficult to attain when school sites are not available at a reasonable cost where they are needed. Nevertheless, every effort should be made to locate new schools so that they can absorb the capacity of schools scheduled for abandonment, without causing unnecessary inconvenience or hardship for the students involved.

THE EDUCATIONAL PROGRAM AND THE LONG-RANGE PLAN

School buildings are often regarded as educational tools designed to facilitate, promote, and stimulate the educational program. Actually, school buildings sometimes possess physical characteristics that impose severe restrictions on the educational program. Inadequate or unsuitable instructional facilities can reshape, limit, or modify the school curriculum beyond tolerable limits. Consequently, the school surveyor should clearly envision the complete educational task to be accomplished *before* making any attempt to devise a long-range building program.

It is assumed that the school surveyor has either devised a systematic procedure of his or her own or has employed one of those described elsewhere for the review, study, and synthesis of the desired educational program. (Some of the pioneer educational facility planners mentioned in Chapter 1 were prolific writers and made long-lasting contributions to the school survey process. The basic techniques described in their publications are just as sound today as they were then.[8]) It is further assumed that

1. the school surveyor has the major characteristics and features of the recommended educational program clearly in mind.
2. the school surveyor has listed all of the program conclusions and recommendations in the survey report affecting the type, location, or design of school buildings.
3. the school surveyor has established an order of priority for each program conclusion and recommendation related to school facilities.
4. the school surveyor has specified, insofar as possible, the manner in which each program recommendation affects the overall or specific planning of school facilities.

Future Uses of Present School Buildings

Before a long-range building program can be developed, the most effective use or uses of existing facilities must be determined. To do this, the school surveyor should review the evaluation of each building discussed in the survey report, study carefully all of the conclusions derived from the basic data, and examine the preliminary estimate of the overall housing needs of the school district. With this knowledge clearly in mind, he or she is prepared to make an intelligent decision regarding the future use of each building. Any of four fundamental decisions may be made in regard to each school. The use of the building for instructional purposes may be discontinued. It may continue to be used on a temporary or emergency basis. It may be remodeled and used for an indefinite period of time. Or it may be continued in use indefinitely "as is." Also, serviceable buildings may be utilized in the future to house the same or different grade-level groupings. Once the specific future use of an existing school is determined, a capacity should be computed, as described earlier, in terms of its new use and the program to be housed in it.

While citizens seem to take the continued use of existing school buildings almost for granted, the experienced school building surveyor insists that under certain conditions school buildings should not be continued in operation. A few of the conditions are listed below. The continuing use of a school building is considered questionable if

1. the building is educationally obsolete and cannot be modernized at a reasonable cost.
2. the building is structurally unsound and endangers the safety of its occupants.
3. the building is no longer needed at its present location, and it is financially unwise to transport students to it.
4. the building is unsafe from the standpoint of fire hazards and cannot be made safe and sound at a reasonable cost.

Schools to Be Abandoned. When a school is no longer suitable or desired for instructional purposes, it can either be relinquished by the school district and utilized for other purposes or disposed of by the board of education according to law. In the event that a building is scheduled for abandonment, the survey should indicate the method of its disposition. It may be advantageous for a school district to sell its obsolete school buildings. Thus, a school district receives a monetary return from the sale of capital items and simultaneously increases the value of the taxable property from which, in turn, the district may derive additional annual income. Sometimes, obsolete school buildings may still be of service to the school district as maintenance, supply, or administrative centers. It may be argued that if a school is inadequate for instructional purposes, it should not be used for other educational activities such as administration. What is erroneously assumed in this viewpoint is that the spatial requirements of, let us say, administrative functions are the same as those demanded by the educational program. A building may be definitely unsuitable for instructional uses, and still be utilized to the advantage of the school district for other purposes. When a building is retained for other purposes, however, the survey report should indicate the manner in which it will be utilized in the long-range plan.

Schools to Continue in Use on an Emergency Basis. Sometimes it is financially impossible to replace obsolete and inadequate schoolhouses with new facilities. In these instances, such schools should be operated on an emergency basis. The long-range plans should provide for their ultimate and speedy abandonment. As long as they are in service, however, these schools should be kept safe and healthful. No major expenses for capital outlay are warranted for buildings in this category.

Schools to Be Remodeled and Continue in Use. Expansion or remodeling may be justified in some schools because the building has high educational potential or because a change in use is contemplated. Not all schools with educational potential should be remodeled. Several important considerations should be carefully weighed before major remodeling is planned. The urge to remodel is often stronger than the will to rebuild. Consequently, long-range planners should resist the temptation to remodel when rebuilding might represent a wiser expenditure of public funds.

The expansion of existing schools is often more readily accepted by the public than other solutions, but additions are sometimes difficult to justify from the standpoint of economy, student convenience, and need for additional capacity in that area. The question of making additions to existing schools should be considered very carefully. The topics of remodeling and expansion of existing buildings are treated in detail in Chapter 17.

Schools to Continue in Use "As Is." Except in rare cases, most schools that are less than 10 years old fall into this category. In these instances, the buildings would be utilized in the future in the same manner as in the past. Only buildings or parts of buildings that are structurally safe, educationally sound, and operationally efficient should be continued without alteration.

Community Growth and the Location of New Construction

Timing—the Key Year. The overall need for school facilities depends on two distinct variables—the educational program and future enrollments. In the preceding section, it was pointed out that, before a long-range building program is developed, a well-defined educational program must be specified. While the nature of the educational program strongly influences the type, design, and function of school buildings, a study of community growth and student population provides the facts that determine the future number, size, and location of school facilities within the school district.

In formulating a long-range building program, it is desirable to select a key year for planning purposes. In general, the key year is determined by adding two years to the estimated date of completion of the first stage of the recommended building program. For example, if anticipated enrollments indicate that additional facilities for a given capacity are needed by year "X," the planning capacity should be geared to the enrollments expected in year "X + 2." This suggestion stems from practical considerations with respect to public relations. It is advisable to allow about two years to elapse between the time that one building project is completed and the time at which citizens are asked to vote on another school building referendum. Admittedly, this leeway cannot always be provided in school districts where the bonding capacity is not increasing at the same rate as the school enrollment. All too common is the situation in which a new school is overcrowded on the day it opens. Consequently, a two-year leeway between project completion and referendum on a subsequent project should be built into a long-range building program, if possible.

In selecting the key year in the building program, it is important to estimate the time required for planning and construction. About two years should be allowed for the planning and construction of schools having a floor area of less than roughly 50,000 square feet, and about three years for the planning and construction of schools not exceeding about 200,000 square feet in usable floor area. For example, if the survey findings indicate that a 1,000-student high school is needed immediately, at least one year would be required for the educational and architectural planning of the school and the passage of a bond referendum. If the planning and construction of this urgently needed school proceeded with dispatch, the building would probably be ready for occupancy at the end of the third year. If two years are to be allowed for leeway purposes, the key year in this instance is five years beyond the time at which the planning process for the proposed school is initiated.

Location and Capacity of New Construction. The location and capacity of new school buildings are directly related to the direction and extent of community growth. In school districts where an annual census is taken in fixed geographical units, rather than by school attendance areas, community growth can be predicted with reasonable accuracy using the percent of survival technique. Since, as a rule, most school districts do not systematically collect and update census data, the problem of defining the geographical area where a specified capacity is required is somewhat complicated and requires a special technique. (See Appendix.)

Relationship of New Construction to Obsolete Schools. In determining the precise location of new schools, it is extremely important to take into account existing buildings with a limited educational life. New schools should be located so that they can absorb all or some of the load from existing schools that are likely to be abandoned because of obsolescence. The future configuration of school buildings should facilitate the abandonment of schools that are unsafe, unhealthful, or educationally unsound without causing undue hardships or unnecessary inconvenience to the displaced students.

Additions to Existing Buildings. The expansion of existing schools often appears to be an attractive solution to the inexperienced long-range planner. Oftentimes, an addition which makes good sense in the short-range view would be a serious mistake in a long-range building program. The urge to expand existing buildings is very strong among citizens, but school planners should not adopt this solution to building needs without careful study.

The following guidelines should be observed in making decisions regarding school additions. An addition to an existing school is financially or educationally questionable if

1. the school under consideration is no longer needed in its present location.
2. the building has structural defects that cannot be corrected at a reasonable cost.
3. the school is educationally obsolete and cannot be modernized at a reasonable cost.
4. the building is unsafe or unhealthful and cannot be made safe and sound at a reasonable cost.
5. the site is inadequate and cannot be expanded or improved at a reasonable cost.
6. the addition would not be part of *both* a short- and a long-range building program.
7. the cost of adding to the school is unreasonable in relation to the probable useful life of the existing building.

School Site Acquisition

The selection of school sites that will be required in the foreseeable future is an important aspect of long-range planning. Ideally, new schools should be located where they provide maximum convenience and safety for the students. New schools should be located in areas that are free from excessive noise, obnoxious gases and fumes, and approaches to airports. Simply stated, a school district should provide proper facilities with sufficient capacity at locations where they are needed at the time when they are needed. To achieve these objectives, a well-conceived site acquisition plan should be included in the long-range building program.

The characteristics of school sites depend upon many factors, including the type of school proposed for the site, its initial and projected ultimate enrollment, the breadth of educational program, the cost and availability of sites, the grade levels to be housed, and the aesthetic values possessed by the community. The specific characteristics and general location of the school sites needed in the future should be clearly stated and discussed in the rationale supporting the site program (see Chapters 6, 12, and 13).

For several reasons, school sites should be acquired several years before a building is actually needed at a given location. Cost usually rises when land is converted from farming or general purposes to residential use. The availability of school sites at locations where they will be needed later is substantially reduced if the selection of a site does not precede the population growth in any part of the school district. And finally, the desired acreage for the site may have to be sacrificed if school sites are not acquired very early, sometimes as much as five years before the actual need arises.

School site acquisition may be handled in at least three ways.

1. The desired site may be acquired outright as soon as the future need for it is established.
2. The desired site may be selected but not purchased immediately. The school district may take an option on a parcel of land.
3. The desired school site may be carefully watched by the board of education. Oftentimes, when it is not known exactly in which direction the population growth in a school district will occur, a board of education may simply "pinpoint" a site or sites and not act until it feels that it would be wise to acquire the needed land.

Finance

No long-range building program would be complete without some discussion of financial matters relating to capital outlay for new construction, remodeling, and modernization. In most states, the bonding potential of a school district is set by a state finance commission or by statute. In any case, the school surveyor must ascertain from state sources the maximum bonding capacity of a given school district before he or she can develop a realistic long-range building program. Where finances are limited, the long-range plan must be organized in stages. As the school district recovers bonding potential, it can construct additional facilities that may be required.

As soon as the total need for additional facilities has been specified, cost estimates can be made to determine the magnitude of the building program required.

If the total amount of capital outlay is within the bonding capacity of the school district, the long-range building program can proceed without restriction. On the other hand, if there is a deficiency in bonding capacity, the school surveyor must plan the long-range program as a series of steps based upon priorities of need and upon rate of recovery of bonding capacity.

The impact of the recommended building program on the tax rate is of paramount importance in the minds of taxpayers who are, in most cases, also voters. Once the magnitude of the required capital outlay is determined and a bonding period and repayment plan are established, it is possible to compute the tax rate for the foreseeable future, provided a projection of assessed valuations has been made in the basic finance study of the school survey. It would not be realistic, in a growing community, to base future tax rates on present assessed valuations. On the other hand, future assessed valuations can fluctuate within wide limits, depending upon assessment procedures and policies. The rate of increase of assessed valuation due to new construction in the school district is also subject to considerable fluctuation. Nevertheless, it is desirable to make a conservative estimate of future increases in assessed valuation in order to give voters as true a picture of the future as possible.

Multistage Planning

The long-range building program is often organized in sequential phases. Each stage of the plan is determined largely by the rate of increase of needed capacity or by financial limitations. In school districts where the rate of growth of student population is not rapid, the various stages of the long-range building program are influenced primarily by the rate at which additional capacity is needed.

In rapidly growing school districts, however, financial ability often lags behind the demand for additional capacity. In these districts the solution to the building problem must be ingeniously contrived in order to extract the maximum capacity and educational return per dollar of capital expended. Each stage in the building program will be determined literally by dollars and cents, and the facilities provided under these circumstances require buildings that are designed with extraordinary educational vision. They must possess design features that will satisfy temporary needs without requiring costly remodeling later when their ultimate purposes are to be fulfilled.

THE LONG-RANGE BUILDING PROGRAM—A PLAN OF ACTION

A well-conceived long-range plan contains several essential elements. In the preceding paragraphs, it was suggested that the long-range school planner assemble facts, conclusions, and inferences from conclusions. He or she was urged to initiate the task of long-range planning only after all the salient facts were written down or carefully noted. In the process of formulating the recommended long-range building program, it might be helpful to view the entire school facility problem, first in relation to its component parts and then as a whole. The long-range plan may include the acquisition of school sites, construction of new facilities, abandonment of existing schools, the remodeling and expansion of present buildings, a multistage plan of action based upon priority of need or financial limitation, financial implications of the recommended plan, and a rationale supporting the proposed long-range plan. It is realized, of course, that not all of these elements are necessarily included in all long-range building programs, but certainly each of them should be seriously considered in the formulation of any sound long-range building program.

Rationale for the Long-Range Building Program

Every long-range plan should contain a detailed rationale supporting the recommendations. It is unrealistic to expect the public or board of education to accept a plan without a clear understanding of the reasoning that underlies it. The rationale should convince the reader that the recommended plan possesses most of the characteristics described in the following paragraphs.

1. *The rationale should demonstrate that the recommended plan is logical.* The rationale should deal at length with each major recommendation, tracing its evolution from facts through well-reasoned conclusions. Clichés should be avoided insofar as possible, and the voice of authorities should be used sparingly. Facts, professional judgments, reasoning, and common sense are often more convincing to citizens than opinions uttered by some national authority.

2. *The rationale should emphasize the flexibility of the recommended plan.* Boards of education are often quite impressed by the variety of possibilities that the recommended plan offers to their successors, the future boards of education. It is worthwhile, therefore, to accentuate all characteristics of the plan that make provision for unforeseeable developments.

3. *The rationale should stress the educational soundness of the recommended plan.* Citizens, by and large, desire the best educational program their school district can provide. School districts that are recognized statewide or nationally for excellence of educational program generate a deep sense of civic pride among citizens. In preparing the rationale, every effort should be made to point out exactly how the various recommendations contribute to high-quality education for the school district.

4. *The rationale should clearly explain the economic and financial advantages of the recommended plan.* People seek the assurance that they are getting a high return for their money. A sound and well-conceived building program is usually designed for maximum financial efficiency and its economic advantages should be stressed.

Citizens are usually more willing to support education when they are convinced of receiving reasonably good value for their tax dollars.

5. *The rationale should emphasize any part of the recommended plan that reflects the feelings and attitudes of the people in the school district.* Any recommendation or any part of the long-range plan that is in harmony with the thinking and attitudes of the community should be highlighted in the rationale, because citizens are more likely to accept a plan they feel is designed with them in mind.

6. *The rationale should stress that the recommended plan is advanced in character but conservative in action.* People are interested in the new and yet often loyal to the old. The rationale should assure the citizens that the recommended plan is solidly based on the best practices of the past, but firmly oriented toward the promising instructional patterns of the future. It might also be desirable to explain the evolutionary nature of the plan and to indicate the manner in which a series of gradual changes provides a smooth transition from the good practices of today to the improved teaching techniques of tomorrow. The rationale should convince the citizens that a well-reasoned and properly controlled dynamism for educational improvement is incorporated in the recommended long-range building program.

NOTES

1. Marion J. Conrad, "Technique for Determining the Operating Capacity of Secondary School Buildings," Doctoral dissertation, Ohio State University, 1952.

2. Stephen Knezevich, "When Are Schools Overcrowded?" *American School Board Journal*, v. 134 (January 1957), p. 46–48.

3. Basil Castaldi, "The Concept of Dynamic Capacity," *School Executive* (August 1959), p. 44–45.

4. Conrad, op. cit.

5. John H. Herrick, Ralph McLeary, Wilfred Clapp, and Walter Bogner, *From School Program to School Plant* (New York: Holt, 1956), p. 70.

6. Marion J. Conrad, *A Manual for Determining the Operating Capacity of Secondary School Buildings* (Columbus: The Bureau of Educational Research, Ohio State University, 1954).

7. Castaldi, op. cit.

8. Merle R. Sumption and Jack L. Landes, *Planning Functional School Buildings* (New York: Harper and Brothers, 1957), pp. 43–61; Wallace Strevell and Arvid Burke, *Administration of the School Building Program* (New York: McGraw-Hill, 1959), pp. 80–82; John Herrick, Ralph McLeary, Wilfred Clapp, and Walter Bogner, *From School Program to School Plant* (New York: Holt, 1956), pp. 35–47; Basil Castaldi, *The Road to Better Schools* (Cambridge: New England School Development Council, 1955), pp. 52–57; Harold L. Hawkins, *Appraisal Guide for School Facilities* (Midland, MI: Pendell, 1976).

▶ 5

Summary of Planning Procedures: Step by Step

The purpose of this chapter is to suggest a systematic sequential plan of action for identifying school plant needs, exploring alternative solutions, and developing suitable options. The process starts at a point when there is an intuitive feeling on the part of someone associated with the schools that some kind of school facility is needed, and culminates in the fulfillment of that need if such need is justified. This discussion is primarily concerned with process. From time to time, the procedures presented in this chapter reflect many of the fundamental principles described earlier in this text. When appropriate, these principles will be summarized for the convenience of the reader. It is suggested, however, that the reader review those sections of the book that discuss these principles and theory in greater detail.

TASK ONE: DEVELOPING A LONG-RANGE PLAN

No substantial capital outlay funds should be expended by a school district unless such expenditures are a part of a valid long-range plan. This rule should apply to funds used for major maintenance, remodeling or expanding existing school buildings, or for new construction. Before a sizeable amount of money is committed for a given project, it is in the best financial interest of the school district to assure itself that such monies are not used for vaguely conceived purposes.

Step One: Make an Enrollment Projection

There are currently several standard methods of projecting future student enrollments. Perhaps the simplest method is the percentage of survival technique that was discussed in Chapter 3. Avoid using the absolute number of students gained or lost from grade to grade each year. This seemingly logical approach leads to gross errors in making estimates of future enrollments. Always use ratios. Once the average grade-by-grade ratios are computed, it is necessary to refine these ratios by applying reasoned professional judgment. The validity of this enrollment projection depends greatly upon the wise adjustment of such computed ratios. In this connection, it might be advantageous for a school district to employ an experienced educational consultant to make an enrollment projection. If sufficient funds for this purpose are not available, a consultant might be retained on a per diem basis (one or two days) to refine the ratios and complete an enrollment projection that was partly prepared by the school district.

In a large school district, it is necessary to make an enrollment projection for each residential area. Such residential areas should be established approximately along elementary school attendance areas. Once fixed, such residential areas should not be changed, even though students living in such areas may be assigned to schools located in other residential areas. The reason for retaining residential lines over a number of years is to accumulate sufficient data to establish a growth or loss pattern for each residential area. Information related to residential tracts is extremely useful in selecting sites for new school buildings and in determining future costs of student transportation.

Step Two: Conduct a School Building Survey

Chapter 4 contains the basic information for conducting a school building survey. The nature and degree of precision of the desired data are also specified. It is suggested that the various methods of conducting school surveys discussed in Chapter 3 be reviewed and that one of those methods or their equivalent be selected. If time is of the essence, the professional survey is perhaps the best approach. If "selling" a solution to the public is seen as a problem, the citizens school survey is undoubtedly the best choice.

Step Three: Adopt a Long-Range Building Plan

Educators and boards of education are frequently placed on the defensive during a campaign to support the passage of a school referendum simply because they lack a well-defined long-range plan. Opponents of educational referenda often use this technique to discredit school officials and school boards and, in so doing, succeed in defeating a school bond issue.

Aside from the public relations aspect, however, the adoption of a sound long-range plan is simply good business. A proposed action concerning educational facilities should be an integral part of a well-conceived long-range school building plan for the school district. This approach assures the school district that each proposed action within the plan moves the school closer to the achievement of the educational goals set forth in the long-range plan. As mentioned in Chapter 4, any long-range plan should be flexible. It serves as a tool for the school district, not as its master. Thus, as circumstances and situations change in a school district, the long-range plan should be modified to reflect these changes. On the other hand, the long-range plan should not be so provisional or contingent that it loses its meaning. At any given time, a school district should have a clear, well-stated, defensible long-range plan within which it is operating. When the need for changes in the long-range plan arises, such modification should produce another long-range plan that is as precise and as justifiable as the original.

The principles underlying the formulation of a sound long-range plan are discussed in depth in Chapter 4. It is suggested that any long-range plan considered for adoption be tested against the thirteen criteria listed in Chapter 4. If the proposed plan violates three or more of the criteria stated there, a serious question would exist as to whether or not the long-range plan should be adopted as proposed.

In essence, the adopted long-range plan is the blueprint that charts the future course of the school district. Not only does the adopted plan specify the nature of this action but it also assigns a priority to each element within it.

Step Four: Take Official Action

After the long-range plan has been adopted, school officials and the board of education would normally begin to implement the plan in accordance with the order of priorities specified in it. Since there may be a lapse of time between the adoption of the long-range plan and the implementation of individual elements contained in it, the board of education should always review the proposed action called for in the long-range plan in relation to the circumstances existing at the time when the action is contemplated. Unless the time lapse mentioned above is extremely long (over two years), it is more than likely that the actions stated in the long-range plan are still valid.

On the other hand, if the situation in the school district is substantially different from what it was when the long-range plan was prepared, no further action should be taken on any other element of the long-range plan. Under these conditions, it is strongly recommended that Steps Two and Three be repeated and a new long-range plan be adopted by the board of education. However, if the proposed action is still part of a sound long-range plan, the board of education should take positive action to move the proposal forward.

Step Five: Enlist Citizen Participation

The advantages of enlisting citizen participation have already been discussed in Chapter 3. Many boards of education involve lay citizens in matters requiring a school referendum or a town meeting vote. In all but the New England states, boards of education are responsible for providing educational facilities. Thus they have a choice as to whether or not citizens should be involved in the planning of school facilities. In New England, however, school committees are not authorized to construct school facilities. In these six states, it is required that a school building committee be appointed to plan and construct school buildings, except in certain cities that operate under special charters. Consequently, school building committees rather than school boards determine whether or not to use citizen groups.

In arriving at a decision as to whether to enlist citizen participation in the planning of a school building, the board of education, except in New England, may wish to consider the attitude of the citizens with respect to education in general and the construction of school buildings in particular. If the climate appears to be favorable to the action proposed by the board of education, the involvement of lay citizens is strictly optional depending upon the philosophy of the members of the board in this regard. On the other hand, if the citizen attitude is neutral and even a bit negative toward the proposal, citizen participation should be encouraged by school officials and the board of education. Specific details and suggestions concerning citizen participation in educational matters are presented in Chapter 3.

TASK TWO: GENERATING PUBLIC SUPPORT

The best-developed plans of a much-needed school building are useless unless the public or its elected representatives provide the necessary funds for its construction, furnishings, and equipment. There seems to be a natural tendency among many school officials and boards of education to postpone informing the public until the plans and specifications are completed. There is, indeed, some basis for this approach. Educators and members of boards of education may feel that the public is not interested in partial information. The question is often raised, "Why bother taxpayers until we have something to show them?" This position is justifiable in some situations. If the electorate has always exhibited a generous and supportive attitude toward education, this approach could result in the passage of the school referendum for the acquisition of additional facilities. Attitudes change rapidly. Past history may no longer be a reliable indicator of public support. More and more taxpayers are offering increasingly greater resistance to school referenda. Thus, it is important that serious consideration be given to the public attitude toward education very early in the planning of school facilities.

Step Six: Assess Public Attitude

As soon as the board of education has adopted the long-range plan (Step Four), it should make an assessment of public attitude. This task need not be time-consuming or complicated in most cases. It can take the form of an open discussion called by the board of education with parents, teachers, school administrators, students, and classified staff. While no specific plans could be discussed at such a time, it would be possible for the board of education to get a sense of the feeling of the group. For example, if the proposed action called for the construction of an elementary school at a possible cost of a million dollars, the following questions might be asked of the group:

1. "How do you think the people whom you know living in the school district would react to an expenditure of this magnitude if it meant 'X' dollars on the tax rate?"
2. "How would they feel about locating it in the south side of the district?"
3. "What arguments do you think opponents of the proposal would raise against it?"
4. "What arguments could be used to counteract those of the opposition?"

In a relatively small and cohesive school district, the technique described above might suffice.

In a larger school district, it might be more productive to use a well-designed questionnaire prepared by a professional group with expertise in polls. In this case, some form of sampling technique should be adopted. It might be more economical for a school district to make a small investment in a scientific survey of public attitude before spending large sums of money for architectural plans that may never be used by the school district due to repeated rejections by the citizens.

Step Seven: Develop a Strategy for Gaining Public Support

There are a number of techniques that are likely to improve public support on a school bond issue. Each will be described briefly. The list is by no means complete. Other approaches should be explored by school officials and the board of education. Each community has its own character and cultural makeup. Thus, a technique that is effective in one school district may be a disappointment in another. For this reason, some of the techniques listed below may not be applicable to all school districts. In some situations local school officials may well find it necessary to modify these suggested approaches or develop new ones. Regardless of the techniques used, however, there are two basic considerations to bear in mind in connection with public support. First, it is important to know the level of public support for a potential bond referendum. And second, it is equally important to select a technique that is motivating rather than coercive, and one that is in harmony with public sentiment. It might be helpful to study the suggestions listed below with these thoughts in mind and choose the approach that best fits the situation.

1. *Establish a citizens advisory committee.* This technique has already been discussed under Step Five earlier in this chapter. Specific information regarding the creation and organization of the citizens committee is presented in Chapter 3. Properly staffed and well organized, a citizens study committee provides the opportunity for many lay members of the community to become involved in educational matters. This technique can build mutual trust and understanding between school officials and board members on the one hand, and citizens groups on the other. This positive attitude, if it can be achieved in a school district through this process, could provide substantial support for the passage of a bond referendum.

2. *Consider the use of the installment plan.* In some school districts, the economic climate may not be conducive to the passage of a bond referendum for the entire foreseeable school needs. Under the circumstances, it might be possible to consider completing the project "by parts." At first glance, this approach may seem fragmentary and impractical, but, with careful planning, it can be used effectively in many instances. A study should be made to determine the feasibility of this approach. After all of the facts related to the economic status of the school district are assembled, an assessment of how much the school district can afford to spend on capital outlay expenditures must be made. In a few cases, the determination may not be what the school district *can* afford to spend, but rather, how much it is *willing* to spend for public schools. In either case, it is necessary to determine what that figure is. The next step in this technique is to make a study of all the options that could be considered within that expenditure level. If, after a careful study, it is found that the adoption of the installment plan concept is not feasible, the board of education can simply discontinue any further consideration of this approach.

On the other hand, if the proposed school can be built in two or three planned stages, consistent with the bonding capacity of the school district, the architect should fully explore these alternatives during the schematic design phase of the planning. The installment plan approach can also be developed as an option and be held in abeyance in the event that citizens reject the entire project. The board of education should make an assessment of the public attitude just prior to the date of the bonding referendum. At that time, it may decide on one of three options. The board may wish to ask the electorate to vote on the entire facility; it may choose to present only the first installment of the proposed school; or it may give the citizens an opportunity to vote on either proposal.

3. *Start the public information program early.* The public information program should start as early as possible. The superintendent of schools or a designee should be assigned the responsibility for public information in the local newspapers, on the radio, and on television. Additionally, information should be transmitted by word of mouth as much as possible. A speakers bureau should be established, consisting of administrators, teachers, students, interested and supportive citizens, and members of the board of education. Such speakers should be available to present the school story and specific details on the status of the project at meetings of local groups whenever such groups request such reports.

4. *Organize coffee groups.* One of the most effective methods of word-of-mouth transmission of information takes place in a small neighborhood group meeting in the home of one of the neighborhood residents. Groups of 10 to 15 people are assembled in one home and a member of the speakers bureau mentioned above can act as a resource person.

It should be reemphasized that this activity should start early. Many school administrators view this approach as proper during the "hard-sell" phase of the campaign. Actually, it is far more effective if it is started at the time a building is still a gleam in the eyes of school officials and members of the board of education. To be sure, meetings of this nature in various parts of the district will not be too frequent in the early stages of the planning. The first meeting should be held no later than Step Eight and the second may take place immediately after Step Eleven. A series of meetings in different places of the district at these times could produce an enormous amount of feedback that would be valuable to the planners of the school building.

5. *Develop a greater awareness of public opinion.* While it is true that most elected officials are very sensitive to the pressures and demands of their constituents, they are not always conscious of the less apparent and subtle feelings that exist just below the surface. School officials and members of the board of education should make a conscious effort to keep their fingers on the pulse of public opinion. This informal and incidental source of information often provides hints and clues that can be followed up through the more formal lines of communication. By keeping their ears close to the ground, school planners can take positive and constructive action in developing a supportive attitude toward the public schools on the part of the voters of the district.

6. *Become thoroughly familiar with every detail on the proposed building, why it is the best answer and why it is being located at the proposed site.* Every school official and each member of the board of education (and the school building committee, where one exists) should become intimately familiar with every aspect of a school facility proposal. One of the major weapons wielded by the opposition is that of discrediting the persons identified with the proposal. It takes only one incorrect or partially correct statement by anyone of the official family to seriously damage the credibility of the proponents of a project. Once such misstatements are made, opponents of a project take the offensive and the entire proposal is placed in jeopardy. When this happens, it is best to "stop, look, and listen."

Care must be exercised in responding to the opponent on matters affecting the credibility of the official family. The persons on the defensive are at a distinct disadvantage. Under these unfortunate circumstances, it is suggested that the person making the incorrect statement *not* answer the charge. The group, as a whole, should determine the best strategy to follow, and some other official, preferably the superintendent of schools or the chairman of the board, should serve as the spokesperson. If one of these persons was involved, the other should act. If both are inadvertently involved in voicing incorrect or vague statements, some member of the board should assume the role of clarifier.

Another common practice utilized by the opponents of school referenda is attacking the logic or reasoning underlying the need for the proposal as a whole, or any part of it. For example, opponents may agree, on the surface at least, that the project is needed, but may zero in on what they unilaterally label as costly frills. Such frills could be almost anything in the building that can be called too big, too costly, or too luxurious. Or the proposal may be attacked because it is inadequate, too little, or an unwise expenditure of public funds. Regardless of the attack, the objective is identical—to kill the proposal.

The only countermeasure for such attacks is to make certain that all persons associated with a proposal are familiar with every detail of the reasons underlying all aspects of the project. Obviously, it is unrealistic for every member of the official family to know everything about the entire project. It is important, however, that someone in that group be an expert on any question that may be raised. It is also prudent for members of the group who are less familiar with a given question or issue to defer to the expert. It is better not to answer a question at all than to give an answer that may turn out to be incorrect or partly correct. This is especially true when questions are directed at certain details of the project. Everyone in the official group, however, should be well versed in the reasoning and logic underlying the proposal itself. All should be able to defend its location, its capacity, and its function.

Everyone should be able to justify the major activities planned for the building. For example, why is a swimming pool needed in the building? Why are not more provisions made for vocational education? Do we need such a large auditorium? Why can't we use the cafeteria as an auditorium by locating a stage on one end of it and eliminate the auditorium? Again, any member of the official group who does not have the answer should refer such questions to the expert on the board or on the staff.

7. *Know the real issue underlying the opposition points of view.* There are always two categories of reasons associated with the opponents of school referenda. The expressed arguments reflect the overt reasons for opposing a proposal. These are important, of course. But it is even more crucial to know the covert reasons for opposing the referendum. The proponents of a school issue can play the same game on the opponents as the opponents play on the proponents. The major thrust of the proponents of a school facility should be aimed at neutralizing the *covert* reasons. Thus, every attempt should be made to differentiate between the stated reasons for

opposing a bond issue and the real ones. Once the real reasons are identified, they should be kept clearly in view as the public information and citizen participation programs are developed.

There are, to be sure, a thousand and one reasons why citizens oppose school bond issues. Some of these stated reasons, of course, are real. Others are perhaps just as effective but do not reveal the true motivating force of the opponents. For example, a citizen may privately feel that taxes are already too high in a school district. He is opposed to anything that will increase his tax bill regardless of the nature of the expenditure. This conviction, on his part, is the real reason for his opposition to a school bond issue. Publicly, however, he may not wish to take a position opposing education by arguing against a bond issue. Thus, he may use subtle approaches in opposing the school bond referendum, without revealing his unwillingness to support additional taxes for school purposes.

A study made by the writer revealed that the reasons most often expressed publicly in opposition to school bond issues can be divided into three distinct groups. The first category includes reasons related to the argument that "we can't afford it." The common element among these reasons is cost. Whatever it is that is being questioned, it costs too much. These reasons could encompass the entire project or parts of it. For example, we can't afford this frill or that space. The second group of reasons overtly offered by opponents of school bond issues is related to the argument that "we don't need it." These reasons are all too familiar, such as "we don't need a new school," "we don't need the field house," "we don't need the swimming pool," and "we don't need an auditorium." And finally, the third category of expressed reasons for opposing a school bond issue assumes a more conciliatory attitude but one that is equally devastating to the passage of a bond referendum. These reasons are related to the argument that "we need something, but not that."

This is an interesting approach in that citizens offering reasons that fit into this third category are not questioning the need. They are openly opposed to the solution, but they are nonetheless not opposed to the project. There is little solace to be gained from this type of opposition, however. The objective is the same—*defeat the bond issue*. If the reasons offered by this group of citizens are genuine, and this may not always be true, it might be possible to gain some support from this group in the next attempt to pass a bond issue, if the first fails to pass. Some of these citizens could be asked to serve on a citizens committee to revise the solution that was defeated and to develop one that still meets the educational needs of the school district and is more acceptable to the public than the original proposal.

In view of the foregoing discussion, it can be seen that it is very important to look beyond what appears on the surface. It is vital to the success of a bond issue to identify the true nature of the public resistance, which is often at variance with the reasons stated publicly by such opponents. In a few cases, very little can be done to counteract these unrevealed arguments. For the most part, however, a knowledge and understanding of these underlying reasons can be extremely helpful in developing an effective campaign for the passage of a bond issue.

TASK THREE: PLANNING A SCHOOL BUILDING

Step Eight: Obtain Planning Funds

In general, boards of education include planning funds in their budget in anticipation of future expenditure related to capital outlay. It is often difficult to determine how much money should be earmarked for planning purposes. There is a wide variety of practices among school districts in this regard. Some school districts set aside $5,000 to $10,000 to be used for preliminary planning purposes. This amount allows them to engage an architect and an educational consultant to explore several alternatives, one or more of which may be presented to the electorate for its consideration. Under this procedure, the proposals submitted to the public contain very few details other than the estimated cost and the general nature of the proposal. The major advantage of this approach is that, if the proposal or proposals are rejected by the citizens, the school district has lost only a nominal amount of money in such an aborted venture.

There are also a few disadvantages associated with this approach. Under this plan, many of the best architects would not be attracted to the speculative nature of such a proposition. A second deterrent on the part of architects and consultants is that they both would be required to provide more services than the funds could reasonably purchase. Thus, their normal and legitimate fees could be realized only if the proposal materialized. Consequently, under normal economic conditions, such a school district could not easily attract the best professional services when token funds are appropriated initially. Only those not employed at the time could afford to apply.

A second approach is, by far, the most defensible of the three that will be discussed in this section. Under this plan, the school district would earmark for planning purposes an amount equivalent to 1–1.5 percent of the estimated total cost of a potential project. A rough idea of the possible cost of a given proposal can usually be obtained from the school facilities division of the state department of education. With this estimate in hand, the board of education can begin planning intelligently. Let us illustrate how such an estimate could be used. If the total cost of a proposed high school were estimated at $5,000,000, the school district would be well advised to earmark about $60,000 for the preliminary plans and associated fees. Under this plan, the educational consultant and the architect, together with the school officials and the board of education, could complete all work up to the design development stage of the proposed high school.

The advantages of this approach are many. In contrast with the first method, the school district can attract the best available professional services because it has the funds to pay legitimate fees in full. Secondly, the proposal presented to the electorate can be described in precise terms and in considerable detail. Thirdly, the plans of the proposed building are developed to the point where the architect can make a fairly accurate cost estimate of the project. And finally, school officials and members of the board of education are in a better position to defend the proposal on the strength of its educational merits, which are clearly reflected in the detailed plans of the proposed school building. The major disadvantage of this procedure is, of course, that a larger amount of money is at stake in the event that the proposal is rejected by the electorate.

A few school districts move confidently ahead in planning for a needed school facility by setting aside sufficient funds for the complete planning process including the cost of going to bid. This method, of course, enjoys all of the advantages of the second approach discussed above. It does, however, have one colossal advantage and one conspicuous disadvantage versus the other two procedures. The major advantage is that the taxpayers of the school district will know exactly what the construction cost of the building is before they are asked to vote any capital outlay funds for the project, since the bidding process is completed. The obvious disadvantage of this procedure is that a very substantial amount of district funds would be lost if the project were to be turned down by the voters.

In states where school building committees are required, it is suggested that the school committee, in preparing an article for the town warrant creating a school building committee, also request that an amount of money be appropriated for the use of the committee equivalent to about 1 percent of the estimated total cost of the project. If this request is approved by the voters, the appointed building committee may, at its discretion, follow the first or second procedure described earlier. In fact, it has the option of following the third procedure by asking the voters to appropriate sufficient additional planning funds to carry the work of the committee through the bidding stage at a subsequent town meeting.

Step Nine: Secure Professional Services

Once funds are available for planning purposes, the board of education should engage a capable and skillful architect. Chapter 6 contains a detailed procedure for the selection of an architect, one of the most important decisions a board of education must make in planning a school building. Every board member should clearly understand that the architect strongly affects both the function and the cost of a school building. The author has had first-hand experience in this regard. Two architects were given identical educational specifications in the same school district, yet there was a significant difference between them of approximately 12 percent in the cost per student.

An analysis of the plans clearly disclosed the reason for this difference. In one instance the architect kept circulation space at a minimum by the ingenious grouping of rooms and the careful placement of doors, and designed the building in a delightful combination of cubical spaces in order to keep the volume of the building low. The second architect favored a more open concept, with spacious glass-walled peripheral corridors, open lobbies, and a generous amount of circulation space. He also introduced two-storied glassed-in courts for both natural light and architectural effect. In this particular school district, the additional cost amounted to almost a million dollars. It is not intended to discuss the merits of one plan over another. Both schools satisfied the educational requirements. Both schools were pleasant and educationally stimulating. And both schools had a distinct architectural character of their own. The point being made, however, is that the basic philosophy of the architect can greatly influence the design of a school building and thus control the cost and sometimes the function of the building. Before making the final selection of an architect, a board of education would be well advised to visit some of the schools designed by the architects under consideration and talk to the school officials with whom each worked.

If cost is of prime concern, the board should ask the state department of education what the average cost per student was at the time when the bids were awarded for a school designed by each architect, and then compare the cost per student of each architect with the state average, taking into account changes in construction cost for differences in time of construction. This information could be quite revealing. In fairness to the architects, however, the superintendent should review the educational specifications for each of the buildings compared. If the educational requirements are comparable, and the cost per student is high, the architect was generous in providing noneducational space. If the educational specifications are generous and the cost per student is high, the architect cannot be held solely responsible for the high cost. If low cost is coupled with austere educational specifications, then part of the responsibility for the low cost is attributable to the frugal allocation of educational space and part of it to ingenious architectural design. And finally, if the educational specifications call for a generous allocation of space, and the cost per student is low, the architect has accomplished an extremely rare feat.

If the school district is in the process of planning a middle school or high school building, it is strongly recommended that an educational consultant be employed to prepare educational specifications and review the development of architectural drawings as the plans progress from one stage to another. Chapter 6 describes the selection procedure and qualifications of an educational consultant. The employment of an educational consultant in planning an elementary school is optional. Such facilities are not as sophisticated as those for the upper grades, and one of the local school administrators can often work with the architect, from time to time, as an educational advisor. This person is often the principal-designee of a proposed new elementary school building, or the principal of an existing elementary school.

Step Ten: Select the School Site

The selection of a school site is one of the major responsibilities of the board of education. It is an involved, complicated, and time-consuming endeavor. For this reason, the school board should seek the advice of a number of professional persons in making its final determination. These persons should include the superintendent of schools, his or her chief administrator, and other members of the professional staff. The architect and the educational consultant should also make their recommendations to the school board. If the location of the school site becomes controversial, as it sometimes does, it might be helpful for the school board to establish a citizens advisory committee to assist it in this task.

The nature and function of a school site are discussed in Chapters 4 and 6. It is suggested that this list be used as the starting point. Some of the items included in the list may be deleted if they are not applicable and others should be added in order to satisfy certain local needs not reflected in the initial list. Once the set of criteria has been established, the task of pinpointing a number of potential school sites becomes a matter of evaluating a number of possible sites in terms of these criteria. Some site evaluators find it helpful to use a score sheet listing all of the criteria. As each site is considered, a number ranging from 0 to 10 is placed beside each item—0 for poor and 10 for superior. The sum of the individual scores then becomes the total score for a given site. If more than one person scores all of the sites, the average score for each site is used in ranking the potential school sites.

Step Eleven: Prepare a Comprehensive Set of Educational Specifications

A good set of educational specifications is the *sine qua non* of planning functional school buildings. This task is the responsibility of the superintendent of schools or his or her designee in the absence of an educational consultant. When a consultant is employed, it becomes his or her responsibility to receive a wide variety of input from many sources, including school administrators, teachers, students, classified personnel, and citizens. The consultant submits the completed set of educational specifications to the superintendent of schools, who receives reactions to them from all concerned persons or groups. The consultant will then modify the specifications to reflect these reactions insofar as possible. At this point, the educational specifications are submitted to the board of education for its final review and approval.

As soon as the educational specifications are approved by the board of education, they are transmitted to the architect, who will follow them in designing the building. It should be mentioned at this time, however, that the architect should also be given an opportunity for input at the time when the consultant is preparing the educational specifications. Thus, when the architect receives an approved copy from the board, they should come as no surprise, since he or she was involved earlier in their development.

In the event that the school board chooses not to employ an educational consultant, it is suggested that the person assigned this task review Chapter 6. It is further suggested that he or she become very familiar with Chapters 12 and 13. These chapters contain specific requirements that should be included in the specifications. It might also be helpful if he or she would scan the table of contents for any topics or features that should become a part of the specifications. For example, Chapter 2, which is quite theoretical in content, might offer or suggest a number of ideas that should be incorporated in the specifications.

Step Twelve: Stage I—Preliminary Drawings—Schematic Design Phase

The most crucial time in the planning of a school building that is functional, outstanding, and distinctive occurs during the schematic design phase of the architectural drawings. It is at this time that the educational consultant can make the greatest impact on the function of the building. It is the time when teachers and school administrators can get positive responses to changes from the architect. The reason is obvious. At this point the proposed school building is no more than lines on a piece of paper. The architect can easily accommodate most of the changes requested by his or her clients, because the plans at this stage do not represent a large investment by the architect on the structural and mechanical design of the building.

In Chapter 8, it is clearly demonstrated that boards of education or school building committees soon reach the point of insignificant savings in their discussion of changes in materials or surfaces specified in the architectural specifications. The facts presented in that section quickly disclose that, in spite of good intentions on the part of all persons involved in the planning, such a time-consuming exercise can, at best, result in a saving of 2 or 3 percent in the total cost of a school building under the best conditions with respect to the timing, bidding, and economic situation when the bids are advertised. The point being made is that the savings are so miniscule that other factors beyond the control of the committee can easily wipe them out. Such an effort to save money in the construction cost of a building by substituting less expensive materials is highly commendable, but it is made at the wrong time and on items that are not likely to result in significant savings.

On the other hand, boards of education, school officials, and school building committees would find it far more profitable to start their economy studies when it can make a substantial difference in the ultimate cost of a building—at the schematic design phase. It is not suggested that the choice of materials described in the architectural specifications be overlooked, but rather, that the time spent on this activity be kept to a reasonable amount, since the law of diminishing savings per hour of discussion time expended soon reaches the point of insignificant returns. On the other hand, the design of a school building, which becomes fixed after the schematic design phase of the planning, does have an *enormous* effect on the cost of the building and on its efficiency as an educational tool.

It is suggested that the principles discussed in Chapters 6 and 8 be reviewed. It is further suggested that additional items of economy of design generated by those involved in the planning be considered and reflected in the design of the building whenever possible. It can be stated categorically that the amount of time spent by all concerned at this stage will be quite rewarding from the standpoint of significantly reduced costs and substantially increased educational function.

Step Thirteen: Stage II—Progress Prints—Design Development Plan

At this point in the planning of a school building, the outside perimeter of the proposed building becomes more or less fixed. The functional design features of the school are beginning to display their ultimate form, and the major economy measures influenced by the design of the school have been taken. During this phase, most of the changes occur within the perimeter of the building and are concentrated primarily on the functional aspects of the building. The nature of the changes, at this time, appear as refinements in the overall educational configuration of the school building developed during the first phase of the planning. The consultant, school officials, and teachers can still make suggestions during this phase, provided they are submitted within a week or two of the onset of this phase and provided that the changes can be accommodated within the perimeter of the building approved by the board of education at the completion of the first phase.

In fairness to the architect, there is a practical reason for the restrictive conditions imposed on the extent of changes that can be made in Stage II. These limitations have nothing whatsoever to do with the attitude, philosophy, or personal feelings of the architect. They reflect the stark reality of architectural planning. It is imperative that the planning of a building move forward in a systematic and orderly fashion if the architect is to meet the deadlines imposed upon him or her by the school district. Also, the architect must employ, at considerable cost to her or to him, a battery of highly trained persons: designers, structural engineers, heating engineers, electrical engineers, communication and electronic engineers, plus a host of consultants in specialized fields such as acoustics, food services, auditorium lighting and controls, and the installation of specialized teaching equipment and devices. These individuals are brought into the planning in a predetermined sequence and at the proper time.

At the end of Phase I, the person primarily involved in the planning is the design architect. To be sure, the design architect consults from time to time with each of the specialists when suggestions and ideas are submitted to him or her and reacts to suggestions, oftentimes, upon the advice rendered by such persons who are primarily concerned with the feasibility of the suggestion. Outside of this kind of dialogue between the design architect and the specialist, no substantial investment in time or work has been made on the plans by these experts in Stage I. It is clear, therefore, that the architect is understandably more receptive to a wide variety of changes in the drawings in the schematic design phase of the planning.

During Phase II, the various engineers and consultants begin working on the project in a tangible way. They begin to make studies, calculations, and drawings that supplement the architectural planning. Their work assumes that the approved schematic design is final with respect to perimeter, total area, total volume, and stated functions appearing in the educational specifications. As mentioned earlier, if a few outstanding suggestions are presented to the architect in the *early phases* of this stage, they might still be incorporated in the plans, provided the various experts have not progressed beyond the point at which the change can be made without redoing the plans. Very soon in the design development phase, however, the engineers and consultants have invested a substantial amount of time, energy, and effort on the project. Thus, it is quite likely that certain changes suggested at this point could result in the scrapping of whatever work has been done by these engineers and starting all over again. Under these conditions, the forward momentum of the planning is retarded and may even retrogress. In addition to being unnecessarily costly, a number of such changes could seriously affect the deadlines and delay the occupancy of the proposed school building.

While requests for changes should be discouraged after a certain time suggested by the architect for the reason stated above, there may be a few situations when changes can be justified at any stage—sometimes even after construction has started. Any glaring error that deleteriously affects the educational functions of the building should be corrected at any time and at all costs. Hopefully, the team of educational and architectural planners would have corrected any oversight during the early stages of the planning. In spite of the best of intentions on the part of all concerned, any rule allowing no changes after a given date should be broken wisely and with demonstrated cause.

Step Fourteen: Stage III—Final Working Drawings and Specifications

Stage III is the final phase in the architectural design of a school building. At this point about 95 percent of the educational planning is completed. During this phase of the planning, the architect is deeply involved in a multitude of client-oriented details such as the choice of surface materials, the selection of doors, the development of an integrated lock system, the selection of appropriate fixed educational equipment in the laboratories and Learning Resources Center, and the choice of communication systems.

It is during this phase of the planning that the architect will ask the client for his or her preferences. These questions may be concerned with floor surfaces in various parts of the school, such as carpeting, terrazzo, sealed concrete, exposed aggregate, and tile. They may be focused upon certain aspects of the interior decoration of the building. They may include a discussion of various types of wall and ceiling surfaces in certain spaces within the building. They may relate to the nature and extent of the site development around the building. These are only a few examples of questions that may arise during this stage of the planning. Behind the scenes, however, the engineers and consultants are hard at work putting the final touches on the working drawings and preparing a comprehensive set of specifications that clearly define the materials, installation, and functional performance of all equipment and the nature of the workmanship expected from the builders of the proposed school building.

Step Fifteen: Procedures After the Approval of Drawings and Specifications

After the board of education has approved the final working drawings and specifications, these documents are made available in sufficient quantities to all contractors wishing to submit bids for the construction of the school. Chapter 16 contains a detailed discussion of post-planning procedure. For the most part, the architect is responsible for all of the technical work associated with bidding and the awarding of bids to the lowest responsible bidder, as required by law for the construction of buildings financed by public funds.

▶ 6

Foundations and Principles of Educational Facility Planning

A great deal of preliminary work must be completed before an architect can begin to design an educational facility. The board of education must develop and publicize its plan of action. Local school officials must be ready to execute these plans. The professional expertise of the staff must be mobilized. Faculty groups must be organized so they can systematically convey their thoughts to planners. Outside professional experts must be interviewed and hired. And a sound public information program must be developed and activated. The end product of all these activities is a set of educational specifications that will guide the architect in designing the proposed facility. All are time consuming. The completion of these prearchitectural tasks can take as little as six months and as long as a year from the day the board of education announces the need for new or additional educational facilities.

Once the architect is ready to begin the conceptual process, he or she should have a complete list of the concepts to be embodied in the design of the building. In this connection, it might be helpful to the planners to review the principles and concepts of educational facility planning presented in this chapter, as well as others that are brought to their attention. It is important to bear in mind that the school building of today must be adequate to house the educational program of tomorrow. It should also include design features that will facilitate the incorporation of future changes not yet clearly defined. Chapter 7 deals with this aspect of educational facility planning in considerable detail.

PREARCHITECTURAL PLANNING—THE EDUCATIONAL PROGRAM

The educational program should strongly influence the design of any school building. No educational facility that imposes unwanted restrictions upon the educational program is well planned. Faulty design or overcrowding adversely affects the function of a school. Overcrowding is sometimes unavoidable because of limited financial resources or unexpectedly rapid population growth in the school district. In designing educationally effective school buildings, it is essential that the curriculum be clearly defined before architectural planning is initiated.

Statement of the Educational Program

No architect can design a functional school building for a given educational need without a lucid description of the educational program. The term "educational program" is often used loosely to signify curriculum and vice versa. It is not enough to inform an architect that history, physics, and music are parts of the program. What the architect must know is exactly what the students do in a physics laboratory or in a music room. He or she must know what equipment is needed and how much space the educators feel a student needs to perform each type of educational experience.

Curriculum Development. Considerable time should be spent by the faculty in developing the curriculum before an architect is asked to put a single line on paper. If possible, the architect should be invited to attend some of the meetings, particularly during the last stages.

It is not within the scope of this book to discuss effective practices and procedures in curriculum development. However, as suggested earlier, the group process should be employed in working out clearly specified educational goals and the means of attaining them. These means can then be translated into a logical and pedagogically sound series of student experiences.

As noted above, the architect must be familiar with each different student activity, the number of students participating in it, and the nature of the activity itself. For example, he or she must know that senior English is taught to groups of 250 students who may subdivide into smaller groups of 10 or 15 or work individually or in pairs part of the time. The architect should be informed that students are also involved in individual and group conferences with the teacher and that they may use learning devices for the purpose of program enrichment about 10 percent of the time. It is essential that the school designer be aware of the use of special equipment, such as centrally stored tapes from which audio signals may be transmitted to booths located in strategic points within the school. Briefly, every type of student experience should be described for the architect, including the space and equipment required as well as the approximate proportion of time devoted to a given type of activity. This latter information may become quite important if compromises in a school must be made because of circumstances beyond the control of school planners, especially when it is either impossible or impractical to provide for every type of student experience within a given school building.

Curriculum development is a crucial aspect of school plant planning. Without it, an architect is deprived of the basic knowledge needed to design an educational facility that meets the need of the client, the school district. Lacking such information, he or she must look elsewhere. This places an unfair burden upon the architect that may well result in a design that is inappropriate.

Many educators are pressured by architects and boards of education to get the building in blueprint form before the curriculum is developed. There is often a dire need to erect a new school building without delay. Under such circumstances, both the architect and the board of education are acting expediently and in good faith. But the fact remains that a functional school building meeting the needs of a given educational program cannot be planned until such needs are clearly identified through curriculum development. School buildings have a useful life exceeding half a century and therefore should be planned to meet both immediate and long-range needs.

Promising Educational Practices. In developing the curriculum, faculty members should explore the possibility of introducing new practices that seem to hold promise for educational advancement. Certainly, the faculty should strive to improve existing practices as well. Faculty members can learn about other developments by attending conferences and national conventions.

A propitious time to consider incorporation of new educational practices into the curriculum is during the planning of a new school building. At this time architectural changes can be made with ease and often without additional cost.

PLANNING FOR COMMUNITY USES

Public school facilities belong to the people of the school district. They are provided primarily for the education of the children, youth, and adults of the school district. Unfortunately, these facilities are often used for this purpose less than 50 percent of the available time during the week and less than 60 percent during the year. Many school districts use school facilities for continuing education programs for adults, evenings and weekends, and offer summer courses for the children and youth of the district. Obviously, this supplementary use of public school facilities improves their utilization to some extent, but much more could be done to better serve the community that supports the public schools. Due consideration should be given to the use of school facilities for recreational and cultural community functions. It is therefore important for school planners to actively explore a wide variety of community uses for possible inclusion in the design of educational facilities.

Consequently, every effort should be made to design school facilities for both existing and anticipated community uses. Such uses can be identified through some form of citizen participation. Often, with only minor changes in the plans, play fields, gymnasiums, swimming pools, and large-group spaces can be functionally designed for numerous community activities. The benefits are quite diverse. The pool, gymnasium, and play fields contribute to better health. The auditorium serves to enrich the cultural activities of the school district. The cafeteria can be utilized for civic activities designed to improve the community through collective action. The learning resources center is ideal for taxpayers interested in individual self-improvement. And the classrooms can become meeting places for small groups engaged in constructive community activities. It is important, therefore, that school plant planners consider all of the supplementary community uses of a proposed school facility when it is in the "educational specification" stage of the planning. The architect should know as early as possible what special needs the building is to house and what specific features should be incorporated in the design of the building.

Educational facilities planned for community use are often viewed by taxpayers as a school building with a plus feature. This positive public attitude may have an important bearing on the outcome of a school bond issue. Planning school facilities for community use is, per se, a sound and wise investment of public funds, regardless of other considerations. But when it is coupled with the positive impact that such planning may have on the passage of a bond issue, the case for planning school buildings for wide community use is significantly strengthened. Two excellent publications deal in depth with the planning and function of educational facilities for community uses. The *Community Education Journal*[1] and the Educational Facilities Laboratories in New York[2] have published exhaustive and authentic information on the use and operation of school facilities for community purposes.

If school buildings are to be used for educational and community-oriented functions, they should be planned specifically for this dual purpose. School plant planners should also take into account whether or not the community will use the building while classes are in session. At the present time, for example, there is an ever-increasing demand by community groups to establish daytime child-care centers in school buildings. With more and more mothers joining the work force, this trend will increase dramatically in the near future.

A crucial consideration in school plant planning is the potential conflict between the educational function and the community use. When school facilities are used during the school day for day-care centers, programs for the elderly, and special community health services, there may be conflict with the educational function. Community-oriented school facilities are also used by the public after school hours during the academic year and/or during the summer months. The need for this use is quite pronounced and will grow substantially in the future as working hours are shortened and recreational time is increased.

Under these conditions, school plant planners are presented with a real challenge in designing multipurpose educational facilities. Ideally, there should be no interference whatsoever between educational and community uses of a school building. There should be no noise pollution attributable to community functions conducted in a school building. Such public use should not pose any safety hazards to the students in the building or on the school site. The community use of the school building should not restrict or impede the normal flow of student traffic within the building.

There are other design characteristics that must be given high priority in the planning of school-community centers. School plant planners should provide effective solutions to several questions.

Does the design of the building provide adequate safeguards against vandalism or pilferage when the facility is used after school or during the summer? Are spaces designed for community use self-contained from the standpoint of exits, zoned heating, toilet facilities, and storage spaces needed for each public use? Are the spaces planned for community use judiciously clustered in one segment of the school building in order to facilitate control over areas open to the public? Does the plan of the building minimize conflicts between public and school use and does the layout promote harmonious school-community relations? Is the site plan designed for the safety of both students and members of the community who are authorized to use the facility? Is public access to educational spaces effectively restricted by appropriate barriers?

PLANNING FOR SPECIAL EDUCATIONAL NEEDS

There is currently an ever-increasing emphasis on the individual needs of students. The public is demanding a higher level of performance in the basic skills. The massive influx of non-English-speaking students into the public school systems has accelerated the need for transitional bilingual education (TBE). And the widespread focus on individuals with educational and physical handicaps has placed additional demands on the design of modern school facilities.

One of the most comprehensive and well-researched studies on meeting the school facility needs of exceptional students is entitled *Facilities for Special Education Services.*[3] This publication should be read from cover to cover by all educational facility planners, including school architects and local school officials engaged in the planning of new or modernized school facilities.

Implications for Planning School Facilities for Supplementary Programs in the Basic Skills

In order to satisfy the public clamor for improved student performance in the basic skills of reading, mathematics, and language, school officials have responded by providing supplementary instruction for students who are extremely deficient in these skills. Many of these programs have been established in existing buildings that were not planned for supplementary instruction. Consequently, small groups of three to five students are often found working with special teachers in small unventilated book storage rooms, on an auditorium stage where groups are separated only by movable storage or vision barriers, in corridors where partial partitions are installed, and in libraries where no barriers are used. It is not surprising that teachers and students often report that these spaces hinder the educational program for supplementary instruction.

It is suggested that the well-designed school facility make adequate provision for supplementary instruction. The number of clusters of specialized spaces for this purpose depends upon the size of the enrollment in supplementary instruction in the basic skills. There should be one cluster of related spaces for each team of one special education teacher and one or two teacher aides. This cluster should contain one miniteaching room of an area between 300 and 400 square feet for testing and teaching individual students or small groups of five or six students for each teacher-teacher aide team in the program. A space containing approximately 600 square feet should be provided as a resource center for each skill area included in the program. All miniteaching rooms should be clustered around the resource center with direct access to this central resource room. Thus, if a school district is providing supplementary instruction in reading, mathematics, and language arts simultaneously, three related groups of spaces should be included in the school facility. Conceivably, these spaces would consist of a cluster of one or more miniteaching rooms for each skill area, and one or more teacher planning rooms with an area of about 300 square feet each surrounding a common resource room, whose size should range from a minimum area of 600 square feet for single-skill programs to about 1,500 square feet when three or more basic skills are involved. If funds are available, it is strongly recommended that an office having an area of about 150 square feet be provided for the principal teachers in each area of supplementary instruction. These offices are invaluable in providing such teachers with a space for conferences with students and teacher aides and for individualized testing and instruction of students whenever the need arises.

Implications for Planning Facilities for Bilingual Programs

The space needs of bilingual education are similar to those of supplemental instruction but less demanding in relation to miniteaching rooms. Students enrolled in full-service or intensive bilingual programs generally utilize regular classrooms for their education in their native tongue. In addition, they are enrolled in "English as a Second Language" classes (ESL) where they are taught to communicate in English in a normal class setting. Another group of students, however, is often given "Support Services." Bilingual students in this category have some understanding of the English language but need supplementary instruction under the guidance of bilingual teachers. The space needs for this group are the same as those for supplementary education. For bilingual education, each cluster of spaces (miniteaching rooms and resource center) is designed to accommodate instruction in one foreign language. If, for example, both Portuguese and Spanish are in the bilingual program, two clusters should be planned.

Implications for Planning School Facilities for Special Education Programs

Within the past few years, tremendous strides have been made in the field of special education. Originally, special education was primarily concerned with students suffering from physical handicaps, such as in vision and hearing. But special education is now a comprehensive service that is often mandated by state laws and supported by state and federal agencies. The scope of the service is very broad, ranging from psychological and educational handicaps to physical disabilities.

The spaces required for this extensive program of individualized service are varied and specialized. The actual number of spaces needed for each facility depends upon the number of students enrolled in the program. Every facility should provide at least one soundproof conference room having an area between 350 and 450 square feet for the use of the professional team and parents. These people, sometimes known as the core group, are required by statute in some states to assess the needs of each student. This space should be carpeted and tastefully furnished with drapes and appropriate furniture. One miniteaching room, similar to the one suggested for supplementary instruction, should be provided for each special education teacher. One or more resource centers of an area between 600 and 700 square feet should be planned for this program. Additionally, there should be specialized spaces to accommodate four or five students at a time for each type of activity prescribed for the students. These special needs may require space for special education students with dyslexia or other reading difficulties, those with hearing and vision problems, those requiring individually prescribed exercises caused by physical handicaps, and those under group therapy. There are numerous additional features related to special education that should be incorporated into the design of a school facility. Since such a detailed discussion is not within the scope of this book; it is strongly suggested that *Facilities for Special Education Services,* cited earlier, be reviewed for such details. Suffice it to say at this point that the design of the educational facility should facilitate and promote the freedom of movement of all handicapped students and provide for their participation in as many of the regular activities of the school as possible.

The need for planning educational facilities for students with physical disabilities is far greater than is normally believed. Schwartz points out that, "there are well over 5,000,000 handicapped children in the United States." As indicated earlier, physical handicaps appear in different forms ranging from deafness to lack of mobility. Special features must be built into educational facilities to satisfy the needs of exceptional children, youth, and adults who attend school in the daytime and evenings. In addition to the specialized spaces required for some types of physical handicaps, particular attention should be given to students in wheelchairs. There should be no barriers between the parking lot and every part of the school facility normally occupied by such students.

Types of School Plants and Planned Enrollment

Although the long-range plan describes in general terms the type of facility needed, its approximate size, and the general area in which it should be located, the school survey or campus master plan should be reviewed carefully when the building is actually being planned. There are two reasons for this review. First, if the facts on which the recommendations were based have changed appreciably since the study was completed, corresponding changes would be needed in the original recommendations. And second, the school survey report or campus plan contains vital information that is directly related to the planning of school facilities.

Common Types of Educational Buildings. Educational facilities may be classified in many ways. For the purpose of this discussion, school facilities are classified according to primary function; that is, according to the grade groupings to be housed in them or the level of education they will serve. A few types of school facilities are described below.

1. An elementary school plant is an educational facility that usually accommodates students from kindergarten or grade 1 to grades 4, 5, or 6. Buildings housing students from kindergarten or first grade to grade 3 are also called primary schools.
2. The middle school is a building that serves students from grades 4, 5, or 6 through grade 8.
3. The junior high school usually serves students in grades 7 and 8 (the two-year junior high school) or in grades 7 through 9.
4. The high school houses students in grades 9 or 10 through 12.
5. The community or junior college offers two years of post-high school education in technical and semiprofessional curricula and programs that approximate the courses found in the first two years of four-year colleges.
6. A college is a four-year post-high school institution of higher education offering students a bachelor's degree upon the completion of a prescribed course of study. Technological institutes are included in this category.
7. The university is an institution that consists of two or more colleges offering degrees that range from the baccalaureate to the doctorate.

Prep School ?

In the lower educational domain, facilities are usually conceived in terms of the grade groupings described above. Some of the smaller school districts may operate junior-senior high schools housing students in grades 7 through 12. Many eloquent arguments have been posed for and against each type of school listed. There is at present no validated research proving that one grade grouping is superior to another. To be sure, there are many opinions on the matter and a sound rationale is often presented to favor one type of school over another. But, unfortunately, there are no tested and proven guides to indicate just what type of school should be planned under any given circumstances. There is, however, a rule of thumb that might be helpful. The type of school selected should be that which provides the greatest educational efficiency in a given school district. Whether or not, for example, the ninth grade is included in the high school or in the junior high school is of little consequence. The important question is, "Under what organization does the ninth-grade student receive the highest level of education per tax dollar expended?" In other words, it is not what one *calls* a school that matters. What really counts is *what the student gets educationally* when he or she attends such a school. Altogether too much emphasis has been placed upon peripheral notions about the various types of schools. In a citizens school survey conducted by the writer, several citizens became disturbed when a junior-senior high school was recommended. Some maintained that senior boys would be able to make dates with seventh-grade girls, and that this situation was highly undesirable. The hypothesis posed by the citizens had not been tested. In fact, this particular school district transported students at all grade levels in the same bus. Boy-girl relationships had not been a problem in unsupervised buses in the past, but suddenly it assumed great proportions in a junior-senior high school where the supervision was far greater than in the school bus. Such are the extraneous arguments that are sometimes posed when innovations are proposed. Again, it should be emphasized that there is no best type of school or grade grouping. The type of school that makes the best sense in terms of educational efficiency is the one that should be selected.

Planned Enrollment for a Given Facility.   What should be the size or capacity of a proposed educational facility? There is a dearth of research on optimum sizes of educational facilities. Obviously, the lower limit is determined by the lowest number of learners needed to justify a broad educational program at a reasonable cost per learner. The upper limit is reached when the facilities required by fields of learning enrolling the lowest number of students can no longer be accommodated in a single teaching station. For example, if a special laboratory is required to house advanced programs in physics and chemistry, and if these two courses have the smallest enrollments, then the total school enrollment at which a second laboratory would be needed for these advanced courses would represent the upper level of the enrollment range. According to this concept, the lower and upper limits of the capacity of a school would depend upon the desired educational programs. For the school planner who is interested in applying this theoretical concept at the secondary school level, the Program Index Approach developed by Marion Conrad is suggested.[4]

The National Council on Schoolhouse Construction has developed a number of criteria for the size of public schools.[5] According to this source, elementary school capacities should range between 300 and 500 students. At the secondary level, the minimum size is set at about 300 students and the maximum at about 1,200. These enrollment ranges reflect the views of many educators.

Of course, it is sometimes necessary to deviate from desirable enrollment ranges. At the elementary level, every effort should be made to provide at least one room per grade, and therefore the minimum size for an elementary school (K–6) should be seven classrooms, or six classrooms if a kindergarten program is not provided. In the judgment of the author, elementary schools (K–6) should not exceed three rooms per grade or 21 classrooms (see Table 4.1 in Chapter 4). At the secondary level, the enrollment should not fall below 500 or about 150 students in the freshman class of a four-year high school. The upper limit should not exceed 1,500 (see Table 4.1). Much has been written about the advantages of a large high school, but the position taken by the Council of Educational Facility Planners is sensible and defensible.

Contrary to popular opinion, large secondary schools are not less costly to operate nor are they free of duplication. A study of any 4,000-student high school quickly reveals not only duplication but the multiplication of similar spaces including those in the library, which is not duplicated in the ordinary sense. It is simply made larger and more complex and must contain several copies of numerous books because of the great demand for them. Large high schools can be justified only in cities where the population density is very high, such as New York, Chicago, St. Louis, Philadelphia, Los Angeles, and Boston. In other situations, the single large high school simply channels tax dollars into transportation costs which do not directly contribute to the education of the students. In a sense, unnecessary transportation costs represent a waste of public funds.

Big is not always better

PREPARATION OF EDUCATIONAL SPECIFICATIONS

No architect should be asked to plan a school before a complete set of educational specifications has been developed by the educational planners. It is unfair and unwise to ask architects to do both the educational and the architectural planning. An architect is not an educator nor pretends to be one. While an architect may have planned many schools already, he or she should not be forced to produce plans that are carbon copies of buildings designed for other school districts, simply because educators have failed to prepare educational specifications as a guide.

Purpose of Educational Specifications

Educational specifications serve as the link between the educational program and school facilities. They consist of a series of interrelated statements that translate the physical requirements of the educational program into educational facilities.

The basic purpose of educational specifications is to describe clearly and concisely the various learning activities to be housed in the school, their spatial requirements, and special features. The statements should not be couched in general terms such as "appropriate size," "sufficiently large," or "properly related." These terms are meaningless to an architect. On the other hand, educators should not submit drawings showing dimensions, shape, and relationships to an architect. The primary purpose of preparing educational specifications is to enable the architect to clearly imagine every detail of educational activity to be conducted in a proposed educational facility. From a study of such specifications, he or she should be able to develop a number of architectural concepts that fit the situation.

Organization of Educational Specifications

There is no best way to organize a set of educational specifications. In practice, school planners often find it convenient to develop educational specifications in three distinct sections. The first is usually devoted to matters related to the educational program, including a detailed description of instructional and learning activities. Expressions of educational philosophy are of little consequence to the architect, for they do not say much about the form or design that a proposed school building should assume.

The second group of educational specifications deals with the numerical aspects of the architectural problem. How many students must be housed? How many of the various types of instructional spaces are needed for the desired educational program? Approximately how large should each type of space be, and where should it be located in relation to other spaces?

The last section of the specifications describes in detail all special features that should be incorporated in the school building. These statements deal with matters such as special shape, ceiling heights, temperature and humidity control, acoustical treatment, and unusual lighting requirements.

Content of Educational Specifications

Some of the broad topics included in a set of educational specifications have already been mentioned. A more detailed account of such topics is presented here.

The greater the detail and clarity of the educational instructions prepared, the greater the likelihood that a school district will acquire the school building it really needs. Architects frequently refer to educational specifications as the "program" or "educational program." They often speak of "programming a building." The architectural expressions for educational specifications are quite proper, but they have not been adopted in educational terminology because the word "program" has a distinct meaning of its own in pedagogy, and the expression "educational program" conveys a meaning to the architect that is completely different from that intended when it is used in educational specifications.

Part I: Description of the Educational Function

The architect must fully understand the function of a proposed school before he or she can design it. Unless a clear description of specific student and teacher activities is provided, the architect will be forced to design a structure that reflects his or her own educational concepts rather than those of the school district, college, or university. Broad, general statements should be kept at a minimum but included when they may give the architect valuable background information.

Perhaps the best approach in preparing Part I of the educational specifications is to describe the educational function of each space, activity by activity. For example, what tasks are performed by teachers and students in a room used for instruction in physics? How will the lobby be used? What specific equipment will be located or used in a certain space? What are the weight and dimensions of such equipment? How will it be used? The architect must also be given a clear description of each type of teacher and student activity for each space. How large a group of students does what, with which equipment, and for what percent of the time in a semester? At first glance, the amount of time that a particular activity occupies in a semester may seem irrelevant. Actually, at some point in the planning, the architect may find that for some reason provision cannot be made for every single activity in a given space. If compromises must be made, the architect will try to eliminate special features for those activities that students undergo for the least amount of time.

The description of the operational and educational function to be housed in every part of the building should be so detailed that the architect will be able to visualize the entire school in operation before making a single sketch. For example, if the large group-small group concept is envisioned for the school, the architect should be able to imagine exactly what takes place instructionally under each circumstance and what special features, if any, are involved. For instance, the architect should be told about the processes involved in handling and using materials, tools, and fixed equipment. Details must also be furnished regarding the work of administrators, secretarial personnel, health officials, custodians, and maintenance crews.

Sample Description of Educational Function

The program to be housed initially in the proposed building will probably be traditional in many respects. Class size will vary between 25 and 30 students in science, social studies, English, foreign languages, and mathematics. Homemaking and shop class sizes will range between 20 and 24 students. It is also expected that classes will be instructed more or less conventionally at the time the school building is first occupied after its completion. It is believed, however, that the existing traditional instructional practices will be short lived. As teachers and administrators become more involved in developing promising teaching techniques, the building will be utilized more effectively as a modern educational tool.

The educational practices envisioned for this building within the next decade are quite different from those that will be housed in it initially. It is postulated that within the next eight to ten years, one teacher will instruct one student in his or her office. He or she will work with six or eight students in a small room, meet 15 students in a seminar situation, work with a few groups of 25 or 30 students in a class, and conduct large classroom instruction in groups of 150 students.

Within the next decade it is also anticipated that approximately three-quarters of the total enrollment will spend about 20 percent of its time in groups of 150–300, about 40 percent of its time in groups of 15–20, about 20 percent of its time in seminar sessions, 10 percent in groups of 5–6, and 10 percent in a 1:1 ratio in the teacher's office. The remaining 25 percent of the student body will be taught in classes of 25 students using current methods. This group will probably include many students in classes devoted to instruction primarily in art, music, homemaking, business, industrial arts, and vocational programs.

Part II: Physical Specifics of the Desired School Facility

From the standpoint of the architect, the data included in this section are the *sine qua non* of school plant planning.

Number and Types of Spaces. The architect must know exactly how many of the various types of spaces are desired. Such spaces include classrooms, laboratories, offices, storage spaces, libraries, cafeterias, gymnasiums, custodial closets, lobbies, and the like.

Suggested Size of Each Space. The architect should not be expected to do the research required to determine the proper size for each type of space. Educators should supply the approximate square footages needed for such spaces. In general, such information can be determined with relative ease by school officials in an ongoing school system. New concepts can be "tried for size" in existing structures and the approximate area needed for each type of space can be specified. If the architect fully understands the educational program, he or she can often raise a question about sizes that seem to be too large or too small.

Space Relationships. The efficient operation of an educational institution depends partly upon the proper location of related spaces. Perhaps no one knows more than the school administrator about the relationship that exists between one type of space and another. It is obvious, for example, that a storage room for chemicals

TABLE 6-1 **Sample Statement of Physical Specifics**

Teaching Stations Required		Proposed Area of Each Space	Storage Space (Area)	Relationship to Other Teaching Stations
General Art				
Art	3	1,050	150	
General				Near Homemaking
Typing-Bus.	1	900	50	or Shop
Homemaking				
General	1	1,200		
Clothing	1	1,100	150	
Foods	1	1,200	150	
Office	1	150		Near Multipurpose Room
Multipurpose				Between Foods
Area	1	400	50	and Clothing

should be adjacent to the chemistry laboratory, but it is not quite so apparent that the entrance to the guidance suite should be removed from the entrance to the general office, or that the office of the guidance counselor should be adjacent to those of the principal and school nurse. A few architects, incidentally, have satisfied these relationships quite ingeniously.

Circles or ellipses could be drawn to represent each type of space. The large spaces could be indicated by large circles or ellipses. One, two, or three straight lines could be drawn between them to indicate a weak, close, or very close relationship, respectively. The use of straight lines to indicate spaces should be avoided whenever possible, because by using them educators would be entering the province of the architect. Furthermore, educational specifications should allow the architect as much freedom in design as possible.

Part III: Description of Special Physical Features

In some instances, the educational program demands the incorporation of certain special features in the design of a school plant. These special features may be dictated by the need for special equipment or by the requirements of certain teaching or learning activities.

It is essential that all exceptional or special features of a school building be clearly set forth space by space. Special features are most often concerned with shape, ceiling height, intensity of lighting, acoustical conditioning or insulation from other spaces, humidity and temperature control, orientation, color, ability of the floor to support more than average weight, type of flooring, arrangement of built-in equipment, and utilities.

Sample Descriptions of Special Features

The Art Room. The art spaces should possess the features listed below:

1. Long dowels resting on built-in racks should be provided to hold rolls of paper at least 36" wide.
2. Two work sinks and work counters should be installed in the art room. Long gooseneck spigots should be provided.
3. If possible, the art room should have a northern exposure with as much natural lighting as possible.
4. About 200 square feet of the art room should be planned for ceramics and a wet area. The floor should be durable and capable of being easily cleaned in this area where water, clay, paints, and abrasive materials are used.
5. Electrical power 220 V for kiln should be available in the ceramic art area.
6. Artificial lighting should simulate the daylight spectrum as closely as possible.
7. About 12 linear feet of tackboard from floor to ceiling should be provided in the art room.
8. This room should be capable of being blacked out in order that all details can be seen on color slides and films.
9. If the art room has a beautiful vista at a second-floor location, window sills should be dropped as close to the floor as possible to facilitate painting of landscapes.
10. The art room should convey the feeling of being an art studio where creative activity is stimulated.

The Homemaking Spaces. This category includes the clothing laboratory:

1. Provide a three-way mirror in the fitting area.
2. Include about 20 linear feet of shelving for reference books.
3. Include cabinets with at least 150 tote trays for sewing supplies and equipment.
4. At least two cabinets to be used as wardrobes should be provided. Each cabinet should be about 4 feet in length. Unfinished garments are stored in such cabinets while work is in progress.
5. A work sink and counter should be provided in the clothing laboratory near the grooming center.
6. In addition to high-intensity general lighting, provision should be made for local lighting.
7. At least 24 double electrical outlets should be provided, two for each student.
8. About four outlets should be located in the demonstration area used by the teacher.
9. At least two ironing boards should be provided in the clothing laboratory. Provision for storage of irons and other small equipment should be made in the storage space specified for the clothing lab.

10. At least two cutting tables, 32 inches and 6 feet long, should be provided in addition to tables holding sewing machines.
11. At least 12 electric sewing machines should be provided in the clothing laboratory.

EDUCATIONAL FACILITIES PLANNERS

Many people participate in the planning of a school building in one capacity or another. The planning process should tap the creative potential of the faculty, professional persons, administrators, nonprofessional personnel, and students. To realize this potential, these people must be organized. Two basic planning groups are needed, one group to serve as the executive planning team and the other to act in an advisory capacity to the executive planning team.

The Executive Planning Team

The executive planning team assumes the primary responsibility for planning an educational facility. It has full authority to develop plans of a proposed school building, subject to the review and approval of a higher board, such as the board of education or board of trustees in a college or university.

The executive planning team should consist of the chief school administrator, one of his or her assistants, the architect, the educational consultant, and a faculty member who is also a member of the institutional planning team discussed below.

The executive planning team reviews educational specifications prepared by the educational consultant and works closely with the architect in the development of architectural plans. While the architect has the primary responsibility for designing the building, the team as a whole continually reviews the plans in terms of educational adequacy. The chief school administrator is the representative of the board of higher authority and, therefore, assumes the role of the client in dealing with the architect. In planning school buildings, however, the final approval of plans and specifications generally rests with a board of higher authority, such as the board of education, board of trustees, state building commission, or school building committee.

The Institutional Planning Team

The institutional planning team is not a new concept in school planning, but its role has not been clearly defined and its unlimited creative potential has not been fully utilized by school planners. The value of planning teams is well known. Properly organized in an administrative climate that is conducive to creative thinking, the institutional planning team can make a major contribution to the planning of educational facilities.

The institutional planning team is viewed as a central advisory committee. It is usually composed of a cross-sectional representation of faculty and nonprofessional persons employed by the institution. The group may also include one or two students whenever it is felt that their thinking will contribute to imaginative planning.

The team should include about 15 persons, a group that is large enough to stimulate the creative process but small enough to avoid awkwardness and loss of group cohesion and informality. In large institutions, subgroups may be organized so that everyone in the employ of the school may make a tangible contribution to the planning of a school plant. The subgroups send representatives to the institutional planning team. Provision should be made in the organizational structure of these groups for ideas and feedback to move from the executive planning team through the institutional planning team to the subgroups and vice versa. Perhaps nothing kills initiative and creativity more quickly than the lack of assurance that an idea will be given full consideration. Feedback may be used to provide this needed assurance.

The institutional planning team is essentially the stimulator and clearinghouse for all ideas regarding the educational planning of a school building. The group may make studies of educational matters or recommend that such studies be made. They serve as a coordinating council for the various subgroups developing concepts, innovations, and ideas to be considered in planning the new facility. While the authority to implement or reject ideas, suggestions, or recommendations rests with the executive planning team, the institutional planning team is entitled to a full explanation when ideas are rejected by the executive planning team. Arbitrary action by the executive planning team would destroy the climate that fosters creativity and encourages participation by both the faculty and nonprofessional personnel. The institutional planning team reviews educational specifications and all architectural plans. It submits reactions and recommendations to the executive planning team and it serves as a liaison group between the executive planning team and faculty, students, and interested parents.

The Educational Consultant

The educational consultant is another key member of the executive planning team. The services of a qualified educational consultant are invaluable in planning an economical and functional school building. A competent educational consultant can usually offer suggestions that may result in savings amounting to several times the fee, coupled with improvements in educational efficiency that cannot be readily converted into dollars and cents.

Since, unfortunately, there is no state certification or board of registration for educational consultants, school officials must exercise great care in selecting one. Boards of education must be sure that the qualifications of the educational consultant are higher than those of persons already employed by the board. Otherwise money expended for a consultant would be a waste of public funds.

The Qualifications of the Educational Consultant. The educational consultant should be a person of wide and varied experience. He or she should have:

1. an advanced degree in general educational administration (the superintendency), preferably at the doctoral level, from an accredited university.
2. formal training in school plant planning at the graduate level.
3. broad experience. Work over a wide geographical area, including several states, is an indication that the consultant is unhampered by provincial or regional thinking.
4. teaching experience in the public schools and, preferably, also at the college level.
5. experience in at least two levels of educational government, such as local, state, or federal.
6. evidence of competence confirmed through reports, studies, and services rendered to other school districts.

The Role of the Educational Consultant. The educational consultant has the prime responsibility for the educational planning of a proposed school building. As a member of the executive planning team, he or she is in an excellent position to assist the architect in converting educational concepts into school facilities.

The consultant can be of assistance to school officials in a number of ways.

1. Advise school officials in the selection of an architect.
2. Be of assistance in the selection of a school site.
3. Review any existing long-range educational plan and make recommendations in the light of new developments.
4. Prepare educational specifications that reflect the thinking of the institutional planning team and the concepts expressed by school officials and the board of higher authority.
5. Review architectural plans and judge them in terms of their ability to satisfy educational needs.
6. Evaluate all ideas submitted by the institutional planning team and make recommendations regarding the disposition of each suggestion.

The Selection of the Educational Consultant. Since the supply of competent educational consultants is very limited, boards of education would be well advised to ask the school building authority in the state for suggestions. Schools of education sometimes have competent school plant consultants. Care should be exercised, however, not to confuse the prestige of the school with which a person is associated with professional competence. Only those professors of education who have had training in school plant planning and educational administration and who possess the qualifications listed above should be considered.

Persons who have had university or state department of education experience in school plant planning and are engaged in private practice are often highly competent and reliable. Even in this case, however, the hiring board should make certain that the educational consultant meets the qualifications listed earlier.

The Architect

As mentioned earlier, the architect is a key member of the executive planning team. The architect has the primary responsibility for translating educational concepts and functions into educational facilities that are conducive to effective learning.

Qualifications of the Architect. In most states, minimum qualifications for school architects are prescribed by law. In and of itself, however, the employment of an architect does not automatically assure a board of higher authority that the school design will satisfy their institutional needs. The architect should be creative, competent, flexible, understanding, perceptive of educational needs, open-minded, aesthetically oriented but cost-conscious, imaginative, practical, and cooperative in spirit. The architect should:

1. possess a thorough knowledge of building design, economical construction methods, and efficient use of building materials.
2. be endowed with creative ability and artistic talent. This characteristic can be judged by reviewing past works, which need not have been school buildings.
3. work harmoniously with individuals or groups of people.
4. be open-minded and willing to explore new ideas. The architect should refrain from imposing his or her will upon the executive planning team with respect to educational matters or architectural design that may adversely affect the educational program.
5. be willing and able to follow detailed educational specifications for the design of a school.
6. be capable of producing final working drawings that are clear and precise.
7. conduct himself or herself professionally with dignity, integrity, and honesty.
8. demonstrate an ability to provide for aesthetics in school design without sacrificing function or ignoring cost.

Procedure for Selecting an Architect. As soon as funds are available for the employment of an architect, the institutional board of authority should widely publicize its intention to employ an architect for a given project. Architects may learn of the project through the news media and through the local chapter of A.I.A. (American Institute of Architects). The group entrusted with the planning of a school should seek names of architects whom they may wish to consider.

In this age of rapid travel, no special preference should be given to local architects. They should, indeed, be considered, but deserve no favored treatment simply because they live in the community and pay local taxes. The most important considerations in the selection of an architect are competence, creativity, and willingness to design a school that can accommodate the desired educational program—*not* the place of business. A number of clichés are often used in support of the employment of a local architect, such as "he is easy to contact," "she can supervise the job more thoroughly," "he is more conscious of our problems," and "as a local taxpayer, she will be more eager to save us money." Obviously, these arguments can be nullified one by one. Any architect is as close as the telephone. As far as supervision is concerned, on large projects, an architectural firm employs a resident architect, and it really does not matter where the office of the principal architect is located. On small projects, most architects can afford to provide only the supervision called for in the contract, perhaps an afternoon per week. Therefore, the location of the architectural firm is of little consequence from the standpoint of supervision. In one case, a local architectural firm in Illinois admitted publicly that the reason for the collapse of an entire ceiling 200 feet long in a school 10 months after occupancy was due to the use of improper clips by the contractor during construction. This statement was not an indictment of the architect. Under the usual contract, the architect is not required to supervise the construction on a full construction-time basis. And finally, the argument is frequently voiced that, as a local taxpayer, the architect is more likely to try to save money through efficient design. The local architect does not possess a magic cost formula. All competent architects can design inexpensive buildings if they so desire. Reputable architects differentiate between cheap buildings and inexpensive ones. If the local architect favors the cheap concept, the local board of education can expect just one thing—a cheap building.

The employment of an architect by a board of education, board of trustees, or its equivalent is one of the most important duties performed by such a board in the construction of educational facilities. Steps to be followed in selecting and employing an architect are listed below.

1. Widespread publicity should be given to the board's intention to plan and construct educational facilities.
2. A list of architects should be prepared by the board of higher authority. All available sources of names should be consulted, including other boards who have recently built new schools or colleges.
3. A brochure explaining the project in detail and a questionnaire requesting pertinent information should be mailed to those on the list.[6]
4. Returns should be screened as objectively as possible and then ranked. Some form of rating sheet should be used.
5. The 10 highest-ranking architects should then be mailed questionnaires requesting additional information, including names of persons for whom they have worked.

6. The 10 remaining architects should be reranked on the basis of data contained in the second questionnaire and information gathered from direct contacts with their former clients. The number of firms under consideration should be reduced to about five at this point.
7. The architects under final consideration should be invited to appear before the board (1) to make presentations of their own choice, (2) to answer specific questions prepared in advance and placed on a rating sheet,[7] and (3) to exchange ideas with members of the board.
8. Visits should be made by board members to some of the buildings designed by the architects, and discussions should be held with other boards for whom each architect worked in the past.
9. A selection can be made after all ratings and scores applying to each architectural firm have been recorded on a rating sheet.

The Contract with the Architect.   Because school officials frequently have certain misconceptions regarding the responsibilities and duties of an architect, it may be helpful to list what is and is not within the area of responsibility of the architect in a normal contract.

1. The architect *is* responsible for architectural programming. He is *not* responsible for educational specifications.
2. She *is* responsible for preplanning studies. She *is not* responsible for making the final choices among the alternatives she may present as possible solutions to the educational problem.
3. He *is* responsible for preliminary plans, large-scale drawings, and final plans and specifications to be approved by school officials. He *is not* responsible for making architectural changes, at his expense, after final working drawings have been approved by the board.
4. She *is* responsible for bidding and contract award. She *is not* responsible for the legality of the contracts as to form or content.
5. He *is* responsible for the periodic supervision of the construction. He *is not* responsible for continuous "on-the-job" supervision, unless it is so specified in the contract.
6. She *is* responsible for all architectural matters related to the acceptance and occupancy of a school.
7. He *is* responsible for overseeing the correction of defects in construction during the warranty period and acts in the interest of the owner.
8. She *is* responsible for the selection and installation of all fixed equipment. She *is not* responsible for the selection and purchase of movable equipment when she is paid only the normal architect's fee.
9. He *is* responsible for certifying the amount of monthly payments due to contractors, but he *is not* responsible for the availability of funds at the time when payments are due.

School Officials as Members of the Executive Planning Team

The remainder of the executive planning team consists of a legal adviser and school officials. Most institutions employ a legal counselor on a full- or part-time basis. As a member of the school planning team, he or she makes certain that all actions, contracts, and procedures comply with the law. The adviser assists in the bonding and business aspects of school plant planning.

The role of the superintendent of schools or college president is crucial. As the chief school officer, he or she is the status leader of the school district or institution of higher learning. The chief school officer represents the board and is the client whom the architect serves. The final decision in the executive planning team rests with the chief school officer. He or she has the power to reject or veto any idea or concept proposed by the executive planning team or any member thereof, or by the institutional planning team. As a practical matter, however, the chief school officer should consider each rejection carefully before exercising veto power. On the other hand, he or she should not hesitate to reject any suggestion that is felt to be detrimental to the institution, and should explain the reason for this action to the individual or group submitting it.

THE SITE

The school site is, of course, an essential part of any educational plant. In addition to providing the space and setting for the school building, the site must include space for a large number of essential educational functions and supporting services.

1. *The size of a school site should be sufficient to accommodate all educational functions and supporting services plus an additional 25% in area for unforeseeable future needs.*

The Rule-of-Thumb Approach. Several approaches may be used to determine the required size of a site. The simplest method, by far, is to apply one of the many rules of thumb that are in vogue. Applicable rules of thumb (Table 4.2) are detailed for each type of school plant under the chapters dealing with elementary and secondary institutions (Chapters 12 and 13).

The Functional Approach. The functional approach of determining the desired size of a school site is based on an estimate of the amount of area required for each type of outdoor function demanded by modern educational facilities and contemporary educational programs. The sum of the individual areas needed plus 10 percent for unforeseeable needs represents the total size of the required site. A number of the functions served by the site are listed below.

The school site must contain space for

1. the proposed educational building. A high school building for 1,000 students, for example, requires about three acres of land. An elementary school serving 600 students occupies about one and a half acres of land.
2. future additions to the building and increases in the other functions of the site listed below.
3. main drives and walks.
4. lawn, trees, and landscaping.
5. parking of automobiles (300 sq. ft. per vehicle).
6. service drives and unloading zones.
7. bus loading and unloading, including covered areas and turnaround drives.
8. secondary access to the school site or central campus.
9. practice fields for organized athletics such as football and baseball.
10. hard-surfaced areas for tennis, volleyball, handball, and the like.
11. informal games.
12. gardens and other instructional areas.
13. social activities and large-group programs, perhaps an outdoor amphitheater.
14. bus garages and physical plant equipment.
15. landscaping accents, such as pools, fountains, and shrubbery.
16. football bleachers and athletics.
17. public and student picnic areas.

2. *The school site should be safe, healthful, attractive, and properly located with respect to student homes.*

Location. The general location of an educational facility is usually set forth in the long-range plan (Chapter 4). Before a specific educational building can be planned, however, it is necessary that a definite site be selected for it. For facilities at the precollege level, the school site should be properly related to future school buildings and to those to be abandoned in the foreseeable future. A well-selected school site, therefore, can conveniently absorb the remaining load of schools scheduled for abandonment. The school or campus site should also be located in an area that is free from air pollution and noxious gases, and far from sources of noise or danger, such as heavily traveled highways, airports, and heavy industry.

Topography and Soil Conditions. A good site possesses several physical characteristics. Its topography should be slightly convex and its level somewhat higher than the area immediately surrounding it. It is not necessary that the entire area be flat, provided there is sufficient space in which play areas may be developed at a reasonable cost for grading. In fact, buildings are sometimes built into the natural topography of the site in ingenious ways. Borings must be taken in prospective school or campus sites to determine the adequacy of the drainage and bearing of the soil. The presence of ledge cropping through the surface at a few isolated spots should not eliminate an otherwise desirable site from consideration. Modern buildings are generally constructed without basements, and therefore ledge does not generally constitute a major problem.

Aesthetics. Aesthetic considerations should be stressed in the selection of a site. The building and the site should provide an environment conducive to effective learning. Trees, brooks, parks, or golf courses, on or near a potential school site, do much to beautify the area surrounding an educational facility. Such features can be used to produce dramatic results by an imaginative landscape architect.

Safety. Finally, it is imperative that matters related to safety be given high priority in the selection of a school or campus site. If possible, it should not border a heavily traveled highway, railroad, or high-tension electric wires. Drives and walks approaching the buildings should be designed to keep the crossing of pedestrians and vehicular traffic to a minimum. Special care should be exercised in the design of a bus-loading area. Driveways should not be located between the unloading zone and an educational facility. Neither should it be necessary for buses to travel in reverse in order to turn around on a school site or college campus.

Placement of the Building or Buildings on the Site. Educational facilities should be located about 160 feet from any well-traveled thoroughfare in order to minimize the interference from traffic noise. Instructional facilities should be strategically situated on the site with respect to convenience and function. The gymnasium, for example, should be located near the play fields and away from quiet areas, such as the library and classrooms. On the other hand, the auditorium and recreational facilities should be convenient to the parking areas. Aesthetic considerations should also figure in determining placement and orientation of each building on the school site, but not at the expense of function.

The Development of the School Site. It is strongly suggested that a landscape architect be engaged to prepare a master plan of the site development. All too frequently, the area immediately surrounding school buildings is carefully planned and developed while the development of the remainder of the site is left to chance. When school planners recommend school and campus sites of the size mentioned in this text, they envision a site that is carefully developed and laid out to accommodate the outdoor functions associated with a modern educational program.

The layout of a school site should be geared to both safety and function. Driveways, for example, should not encircle a building. Such a plan endangers students using the building. Walks should be located along *natural* paths. One school district delayed the installation of sidewalks until after the school had been occupied for a few months. Sidewalks were then placed where foot paths had been made by students attending the school. While this is a practical approach to side-walk location, aesthetics should also be considered in laying out sidewalks.

Landscaping is an extremely important part of site development. Trees, shrubs, flower beds, and the arrangement of walks and drives contribute to the general environment of a school building. The design of the building and the layout and development of the site are important ingredients in the creation of an atmosphere that is educationally stimulating. The building should blend pleasingly into the terrain and the site should accentuate the beauty of the structure.

BROADLY BASED CONCEPTS RELATED TO EDUCATIONAL FACILITY PLANNING

1. *The concept of balance.* Educational planners should place each educational goal of the institution in proper perspective. The curriculum should reflect a well-balanced array of student learning experiences that further the basic purposes of the institution. There should be balance among the courses offered and in the depth of penetration required in each course. There should be a balance of focus on different types of student experiences. Not all courses should receive equal attention, but at the same time, emphasis in one area of learning should not be accomplished at the exclusion or expense of another area that is equally important in the attainment of the goals of the school. For example, school planners should guard against empha-sizing the physical sciences at the expense of the humanities or emphasizing the gymnasium and competitive athletics at the expense of the library.

School planners should test the proposed curriculum for balance before trans-lating it into building specifications. They might ask: Is there a direct relationship between the emphasis to be given a learning experience and the goal it is intended to achieve? If the goals of an institution are well balanced, then this test leads to a balanced curriculum.

2. *The concept of educational efficiency.* Curriculum planners are deeply con-cerned with the type, sequence, and effectiveness of the multitude of learning experiences necessary to achieve educational goals. In selecting the experiences that should be included in the curriculum, priority should be given to those that are more likely to produce effective, high-quality learning. The type, organization, and sequence of the learning experiences, therefore, should be educationally efficient; i.e., they should produce maximum learning for the minimum expenditure of en-ergy, time, and money. Admittedly, it is extremely difficult, if not impossible, to measure educational return. In this application of the principle of educational efficiency, however, it is intended that the educational planner simply recognize the objectives underlying the concept without becoming too concerned about its mathe-matical implications.

At some point in the process of developing the curriculum, educational plan-ners should test the various learning experiences under consideration against the principle of educational efficiency. In applying this concept, they should select those learning experiences and educational practices that are likely to yield more effective and desirable educational results and reject those that tend to produce limited or questionable educational outcomes.

3. *The concept of gradualism.* Evolutionary changes in educational methodology are more likely to be effected than revolutionary revisions in school practices. Since the readiness principle applies to teachers as well as to students, it cannot be assumed that all teachers will be ready for proposed changes in instructional methods simultaneously. School buildings must be designed, therefore, for a smooth and gradual progression from existing teaching methods to those that may be proposed. Furthermore, it should be possible to vary the rate of such changes within the same area of instruction in accordance with the readiness of the teachers and students for proposed modifications in teaching methods. The application of the principle of gradualism in school plant planning has many implications for school design which transcend those of the well-established principle of flexibility.

The need for gradualism, however, should not in any way interfere with or interrupt the introduction of promising innovations into the school program. On the contrary, the concept of gradualism is viewed as an accelerator of desired change. Recognizing the existence of at least one major deterrent for change, it provides for it in a constructive and positive manner. Thus, the architect should plan a given school facility as though a desired new practice or practices were to be instituted on the day on which it is occupied, but design it so that the contemplated innovations may be introduced slowly over a period of time. Accordingly, a board of education and superintendent of schools should plan a school plant that can accommodate many bold and promising educational innovations without disturbing the security of its occupants or the serenity of the taxpayers or alumni financing it.

4. *The concept of reversibility.* The principle of reversibility is another new dimension in school plant planning. Educational practices that seem to hold much promise when a school is designed may prove to be ineffective or inappropriate later. There must be ample provision to move gradually in a desired direction, as mentioned in the previous paragraph, but there must also be an equally efficient procedure for reversing the direction of the change at any time. Although no school can be planned for reversibility of every change, the principle of reversibility should be applied in planning school buildings whenever possible.

5. *The concept of contractibility.* In the late 1960s, contractibility was given little or no consideration in the planning of school facilities. The emphasis was mostly on expansibility since school enrollments were increasing from year to year. The enrollment trends have reversed since that time and many school districts are confronted with excess building capacity.

In those school districts where new or expanded school facilities are needed, serious consideration should be given to contractibility of educational use. Under this principle, a school building should be designed so that a predetermined part of the facility could be used for other than educational purposes. In the event of a substantial decrease in school enrollment, the school district would be in a position to allow part of the school facility to be used by other public agencies or nonpublic enterprises whose activities are compatible with the educational function conducted in the remainder of the building. Thus, when planning new construction, school plant planners should ask the question, "How can this proposed school facility be used, if only about one-half of the capacity is needed at some future time?"

6. *The concept of equity of educational opportunity within a school district.* In formulating a long-range educational facility plan, special care must be exercised to make certain that there is equality of educational opportunity within all of the school buildings of the school district. In some situations, for example, new elementary schools are built in the growing sections of a school district while the older school buildings, often with substandard educational facilities, remain unchanged. It is realized of course, that parity cannot usually be achieved when large capital outlay expenditures are being made to satisfy the demands of increased enrollments. It is important, however, that the long-range plan provide for the modernization of existing school buildings (see Chapter 17) within the period covered by the long-range plan.

7. *Conceptual school planning.* It is difficult to express the full meaning of conceptual school planning. It is an intellectual activity that scans the universe of human thought in order to retrieve groups of related ideas for further study. It may be viewed, at times, as the end product of a search into the depths of knowledge for new and promising concepts related to the educative process.

Conceptual planning is perhaps one of the most important ingredients in the design of *educationally imaginative* school buildings. Conceptual school planning may be defined, in this connection, as the creative intellectual activity that precedes and contributes to the preparation of the educational specifications. It is the process whereby fundamental educational concepts are formulated, developed, expressed, evaluated, and incorporated in the design of the school. The steps associated with conceptual school planning lead from the intellectual to physical. Once the concept is developed to the point at which it can be verbalized, it must be carefully evaluated in relation to psychological principles of learning, principles of administration, and local and state educational policies before it can then be included in the educational specifications.

8. *Planning functional school buildings.* In 1880 Louis Sullivan, an eminent American architect, enunciated a fundamental principle of modern architecture: "Form follows function." This new principle, coupled with the influence of Richard Morris Hunt and Henry Hobson Richardson, men thoroughly trained by European study in architecture, hastened the revival of an architectural style that was destined to have a significant impact on the design of school buildings in the United States.

The future holds much promise for the planning of educationally creative and functional schools. A number of emerging educational concepts seem destined to make radical changes in the design of schools in the United States. The remaining sections of this chapter will be devoted to new dimensions in school plant planning. Each major concept will be introduced in this chapter.

9. *Image-building through education.* Little thought has been given to the image-building aspect of education. The image that the community projects to the world is important to the social and economic growth of that community. Although "Good schools build better communities," many local school districts make little effort to improve their overall image through education. A high-quality educational program is a vital feature of a favorable community image, and so are well-planned school buildings that contribute to the attainment of that program.

The school building enhances the community image in two ways—through its contribution to the educational program and through its visual appeal. Architects are very conscious of this feature of school design, but unfortunately boards of education and school officials sometimes override their judgment.

Silently, but forcefully, school buildings create favorable or unfavorable impressions upon those who view them. To someone exploring the community as a prospective industrial site, an attractive building on a well-landscaped site may speak more eloquently than thousands of words spoken by the local chamber of commerce.

10. *Curriculum-oriented school planning.* If educationally effective school buildings are to be planned in the future, educators must explore and develop school planning in an entirely new dimension—curriculum development. To be sure, curriculum development is neither new nor unfamiliar to educators. Before an architect designs a school building, the local school officials should acquaint him or her with specific information related to the curriculum, the actual experiences that students undergo under the guidance of the school. For example, it means very little to an architect to say that a space is desired for general science. But if he or she is told that for about 30 percent of the time 25 students watch demonstrations by the teacher, about 20 percent of the time a group of 25 perform simple experiments using water, gas, and electricity at work benches, about 10 percent of the time a group of 14 work on the chalkboard, about 30 percent of the time the instructor lectures and discusses material with 25 students, and that special projects are done in a separate room by about five talented students, the architect can begin to relate student activities or experiences to spatial requirements.

Information about the curriculum is indispensable to the architect. It might be helpful to place ourselves in the position of the architect. What would we do, as architects, if we were asked to design a general science room? We might think back 20 years to the one we used in junior high school and design one like it. We might read about the desired features of a general science room listed by the National Association of Science Teachers. We might travel to many schools and look at many science rooms in order to design a science room that contains what we think are the best features of all of them. If we were architects, we would be forced to design a science room of some kind, but we would never know whether or not we had designed the type of room our client needed unless we had a detailed description of the curriculum for general science.

11. *Planning schools for people.* The human aspects of school plant planning, known as ergonomics, are beginning to receive attention from educators and architects alike. Currently, primary emphasis is on functional planning of schools, that is, on designing the building to serve its intended functions effectively. Admittedly, functional planning is important, but it is equally important to plan for the needs of people. These needs transcend those that are met when a proper thermal, visual, and acoustical environment is created.

The concept of planning schools for people introduces a new dimension in school plant planning. This concept calls for design of a school that meets the physical, psychological, and social needs of people, and protects their health, safety, and well-being. Basically, of course, the school must be planned to accommodate and facilitate the activities of students, teachers, clerical workers, custodians, and administrators. Naturally, these matters are consciously or subconsciously considered in the design of some of our most advanced schools, but little effort has been made to conceptualize these needs in a systematic and logical fashion.

12. *Planning schools for effective learning.* No competent school planner would, in good conscience, permit the design of a school that would not promote effective learning. And yet, Roth, an international authority on schools, felt prompted to say that the development of school buildings up to 1957 had been "faulty" because their design had not been based upon "sound and valid pedagogic principles."[8] According to some architects currently engaged in planning schools, the situation has not changed significantly since Roth made this statement. A survey of the literature on school buildings published during the past few years seems to support this view. Many educators are planning schools for team teaching, for variable grouping, for television, and for teaching machines, but relatively few are consciously concerned with the direct application of accepted learning principles that should affect the design of entire buildings. The glamor surrounding educational technology seems to obscure the fundamental principles of learning that should underlie the planning of every instructional element of a school building.

NOTES

1. *Community Education Journal,* v. VII–2 (January 1980). Published by the National Community Education Association, Washington, DC.

2. *Community School Centers* (New York: Education Facilities Laboratories, series of 6 booklets, October 1978 through February 1979).

3. Allen C. Abend, Michael J. Bednar, Vera J. Froehlinger, and Yale Stenzler, *Facilities for Special Education Services* (Reston, VA: The Council for Exceptional Children, 1979).

4. Marion J. Conrad, *A Manual for Determining the Operating Capacity of Secondary School Buildings* (Columbus: Bureau of Educational Research and Service, Ohio State University, 1954).

5. Council of Educational Facility Planners, *Guide for Planning School Plants* (East Lansing: Michigan State University, 1964), p. 12.

6. Forms available from American Institute of Architects, 1735 New York Avenue, NW, Washington, DC 20006.

7. Basil Castaldi, *The Road to Better Schools* (Cambridge, MA: New School Development Council, 1955), pp. 99–100.

8. Alfred Roth, *The New School* (New York: Frederick Prager, 1957), p. 26.

► 7

Leeway for Change

Education reflects the world in which we are living. Our civilization is in the midst of a technological and scientific revolution. The world has shrunk as the time needed to traverse the globe has dwindled. The boundaries of our world itself are rapidly expanding into the outer limits of earth space. We are engaged in the conquest of the universe and in the discovery of the secrets of life itself. As part of this wave of change, it is natural to anticipate changes in thought, in attitude, in modes of living, in occupations, and in education. Thus, the plans of any educational facility on the drawing board must provide not only for the instructional practices of today but for those that will be conceived by and for generations yet unborn.

The world is continually changing—climatically, economically, and sociologically. It is in a state of confused equilibrium. Cultural values remain fluid and are poised for unpredictable change. The economic structure supporting the several societies of the world are uncertain. Under these circumstances, Rogers prophesied, "But the changes of the past 20 years will seem insignificant compared to the changes in the next 20 years."[1]

PREPARING FOR THE UNFORESEEABLE

Planning a school building for educational practices still unknown seems an impossible assignment. Of all the aspects of school plant planning, designing a school for not-yet-apparent instructional needs requires the highest level of thought from planners. The brainstorming technique might be quite fruitful in achieving this objective. The task is extremely difficult, however. Rogers states the problem quite concisely. "We know there will be change, but our crystal ball becomes mirky when we try to anticipate exactly what those changes will be."[2] Thus, our most fruitful approach is to plan a school building that is so flexible and adaptable that it can accommodate the unanticipated needs of future educational practices.

Projection of Present Trends

Obviously, we cannot plan for the future in a vacuum. We must grasp certain clues in the concepts and practices of today in order to imagine those of tomorrow. It should be remembered, furthermore, that the ridiculous notion of today may be the accepted and desired practice of tomorrow. To plan for the unforeseeable, school planners must answer the question, "How can this seemingly fantastic innovation be accommodated in this building in the event that the citizens 50 years hence desire it?" A word of caution is in order, however. Cost limits the extent to which a building can be planned for the unforeseeable. Obviously, design features that do not add substantially to the cost of a school plant should be incorporated, but those that require appreciable additional capital outlay should be adopted only after careful study.

School planners can prepare themselves for the task of planning for the unforeseeable by carefully analyzing present trends in educational innovations, their types, and objectives. For example, do current trends seem to indicate greater or less attention to the individual learner? Do they seem to give greater emphasis to program enrichment? to self-instruction? to supervised study? to reorganization of learning experiences? to new forms of administrative and instructional organization? to increased student services? to a greater use of automated aids to education? to increased or decreased student participation in learning experiences? These are only a few of the questions that might be raised in a faculty brainstorming session. Indeed, school planners should consider both national and international developments in their review of existing educational trends.

Once the trends have been identified and clearly stated, school planners should try to project them. As a bonus, projecting trends tends to bring to light many practices that can be incorporated into the plans of a building. It is important, however, that the thinking of the planning team not stop at this point. It must proceed further, much further into the future, into the realm of the unknown. Clues gleaned from a study of the present trends should be amplified and imaginatively projected, so that the school building of today can be designed with special features that will facilitate the incorporation of unforeseeable educational practices some time in the distant future.

Clearly, it makes no sense to plan for ideas or concepts that are unlikely to be realized during the life of the proposed school building. On the other hand, there are numerous design features that can simplify future modifications. The revision of plans of conventional buildings to accommodate future innovations is a matter for considerable study in terms of long-range economy. As noted previously, the type and magnitude of such revisions depend upon the nature of the future practices inferred or suggested by a systematic study of current trends. For example, if private tutoring were envisioned for the future, present classrooms could be planned for easy conversion to teacher-offices by introducing a system of bolt-type prefabricated partitions into the plans. It is realized, of course, that new and improved construction materials and methods will appear on the market in the years to come. But it must also be remembered that, while new products will be developed, the building constructed today will not change substantially in material or products incorporated in it for at least half a century. Consequently, the architect must ingeniously utilize the building materials of today in meeting the educational needs of tomorrow.

Enrollment Growth

Increases in enrollment are not always predictable. The problem in large communities is complicated by changes in population density. For example, a zoning change from single- to multiple-dwelling units may mean a substantial increase in student enrollment in an area once thought to be stable.

In view of the unpredictability of enrollment growth, it would be prudent and reasonable to assume that any school should be designed with a potential increase in capacity of about 25 percent in mind. Planning for this hypothetical growth is easy when plans are in the pencil stage. Buildings can be designed so that a given space can be changed from one function to another without difficulty and without unreasonable cost. The principle of expansibility is not new. In fact, it has been foremost in the minds of architects and educators for many decades in planning functional school buildings. Until recently, however, the full potential of this concept had not been explored. It is now generally accepted that the principle of expansibility can be employed in planning for both the foreseeable and the unforeseeable aspects of educational change.

Leeway for unforeseeable enrollment growth can be gained by incorporating in the initial plans features that tend to facilitate expansion at a later date. The area of the school site should be sufficient, and utilities and other services should accommodate the additional student load. Obviously, there are sometimes circumstances under which these conditions cannot be met, but such circumstances should be compelling before the planning team accepts a school site that cannot accommodate even a modest hypothetical increase of 25 percent in enrollment.

It would be ideal if the exact nature of the hypothetical addition to the building were known, but such is not often the case. Ideally, educators would assess all educational trends and extrapolate their implications for the future. But it is not practical to expect this of superintendents of schools, college presidents, and their staffs, who, generally speaking, are already overworked in the day-to-day operation of schools. They have neither the time nor the funds, except in rare situations, to divert human resources for the research necessary to discover trends in the exact nature of the school of the future. In time, state departments of education might perform this type of research service. From a practical standpoint, however, educators must assume that current fundamental areas of learning will persist for the next decade or two and might concentrate on the major areas of learning rather than on specific student experiences or instructional techniques.

Planning for an enrollment growth of about 25 percent should be made on a space-by-space basis. For example, if four science rooms are required now, how could one or two more be added if they were needed? Would they be functionally related to the existing spaces? How could spaces for fine and applied arts be expanded by 25 percent? The answers to these questions should be more detailed than, "We have the space along this corridor or at the end of this wing." (The figure of 25 percent was selected arbitrarily. Any other percent could be used. In some instances the figure could be zero if it were almost a certainty that no expansion could occur.)

In planning schools for enrollment growth, it is imperative that proper functional *space relationships* be preserved. The importance of maintaining good space relationships is well recognized among educators and school plant planners. Expansion does not mean numerous open-ended corridors. The ultimate circulation pattern is a vital concern in planning. The architect should demonstrate not only the physical expansion but also the operational relationships of spaces serving related functions. For example, it is not enough to show that a wing can be expanded to accommodate a given number of rooms. The architect should also be able to show a board of education or board of trustees that the unified clustering of the science spaces, shops, art rooms, and the like can be maintained in the expanded building. He or she should prepare a single line drawing of the expanded school for the appraisal of school officials.

Enrollment Decline

School enrollments are subject to many sociological and economic forces. There are periods of large increases in school enrollments in certain school districts followed by periods of decline. Some communities mature while others age. Some are created and some are on the wane. In the preceding section, the focus was on unforeseeable enrollment increases. It is equally important to provide for possible enrollment decreases.

School plant planners would be well advised to ask themselves the question, "How could the proposed building be utilized fully if the enrollment were to drop by 50 percent?" For many school districts, this question has become a reality. And, unfortunately, the school buildings of the past were never designed for this eventuality.

During the design stages, school officials should make every effort to identify as many noneducational uses for a proposed school as possible and, with the architect, incorporate special features that would facilitate such uses. Examples are clustering of related spaces, isolation of one part of the building from the other, and separation of utility lines so that heat, light, and power distribution can be controlled for certain segments of the building.

Educational facilities that are not used to capacity for their planned grade groupings may sometimes be used by different grade levels. For example, a middle school designed for grades 6, 7, and 8 could also accommodate students in grades 2 through 5, if designed with this possibility in mind. Oftentimes, when school enrollments in a school district drop drastically, it may be possible to abandon obsolete school buildings and transfer students from these schools to those that are more functional. This practice is widespread and well justified. But the school facility to which students are transferred is not always properly planned for these students. For example, if first-grade students are transferred to a relatively new middle school, the chalk trays may be too high, the locker combination locks difficult to operate, and the urinals too high from the floor. All could have been easily designed for, if this potential use had been envisioned when the middle school was in the design stages.

Educational Practices

It seems hopeless—and yet fascinating—to try to design a structure for functions yet unknown. Our school buildings will far outlast most present educational practices and must, therefore, be designed with this in mind.

School plant planners should design buildings that are easily adaptable to future practices, as shown in Figure 7-1. This concept is not new, by any means, but it needs to be taken more seriously by school designers. To be sure, a small number of outstanding school architects are already designing truly adaptable school buildings. Unfortunately, a larger number are still planning traditional school buildings, in accordance with the dictates of conventional boards of education. Boards of education want to avoid antagonizing or arousing citizens by introducing radical changes in school design. This is, of course, understandable. But such boards ought to realize that adhering strictly to conventional design can lead only to mediocrity. Designing *adaptable* school buildings requires boldness and imagination. This adventurous spirit is contagious, and can be transmitted from the board to the electorate through a good community relations program.

A few general principles of modifiability have been discussed in this section. Concrete examples of their application are presented in the latter part of this chapter. In general,

1. all instructional spaces should be capable of being altered in size and shape at a reasonable cost.
2. all utilities should be easily accessible to all parts of a school building.
3. mechanical and electrical elements should be installed so as not to impede the relocation of interior partitions.

4. ceilings should be designed so as to facilitate changes within a school building.
5. the type of luminaries employed should not restrict the placement of interior walls within the building to any major extent.
6. the design of the building should facilitate the installation of electronic devices in all parts of the structure.

Economic Considerations

As mentioned earlier, preparing for unpredictable instructional practices should be done judiciously. Obviously, when design features do not add appreciably to the cost, they should be incorporated. On the other hand, if they increase the cost by more than 10 percent, the individual features should be studied and evaluated very carefully and reintroduced into the plans one at a time. Oftentimes, the original capital outlay can be significantly reduced by simply making *provision* for later construction. In general, whenever it is less costly to provide for future change during construction than at a later date, it should be done, provided it does not increase the construction cost by more than 10 percent.

It is not known whether or not the 10-percent figure is proper. It is reasonable to assume, however, that an investment greater than 10 percent of the cost of a building might be difficult to justify. Many features that promote adaptability and flexibility can be incorporated without appreciably increasing the cost of a school building. Therefore, the 10-percent figure seems reasonable and sufficient.

Fads versus Function

Fads often impede leeway for change. A school administrator or a faculty group can impose certain features on the design of a school that make it difficult to make sensible changes in the curriculum later. Fads come and go, but the teaching function persists. Whenever the planning team is confronted by a technique or student grouping whose value is not validated or widely recognized, it should analyze the educational needs on a functional basis and design the school accordingly. It is not sound planning to design a school building around the wishes of the principal or faculty committee unless their wishes are based on educationally functional concepts.

In one case involving the design of a middle school in a New England school district, the junior high school principal had grouped students in four rooms under four teachers for instruction in language arts, social sciences, mathematics, and science. The students moved from room to room and attended centrally located classes for physical education, music, art, and shop or homemaking. In designing the middle school, the principal simply grouped the basic four rooms in a cluster with two clusters on the first floor and two on the second. When it was pointed out that all of his science rooms were decentralized, thus necessitating a quadrupling of equipment, he simply shrugged his shoulders and insisted that the group of four rooms be kept together at all cost. The science teachers objected to the decentralization on at least three scores. They pointed out that the demonstration concept was quite important at the seventh- and eighth-grade level. They stated that it was not likely that the school district would purchase four units of every piece of science equipment, even though the principal insisted that it was theoretically possible to do so. And they felt that the inconvenience of moving equipment up and down stairs was great enough to deter the use of a single piece of equipment in all science rooms. The teachers, in this case, were not allowed to plead their case before the planning team, and so the principal succeeded in locating two science rooms on the first floor, two on the second, and, incidentally, a fifth science room at the opposite end of the building. The short-sightedness of this kind of planning is clear. Long after the principal retires, the building will remain functionally restricted for the teaching of science.

Practical Considerations

It would be almost impossible to list, even in elementary fashion, the many ways to provide for the unforeseeable in planning a school. A few examples of flexibility and adaptability of school buildings are presented in the hope that they may generate many others.

Sumption and Landes properly refer to "modifiability" in the planning of school buildings.[3] They discuss the principles of adaptability, flexibility, expansibility, and contractibility. Schools designed with these features in mind can provide amply for unforeseeable changes in methodology, student grouping, course offerings, type of instructional machinery and equipment, teaching aids and materials, size of enrollment, and the like. It can be seen, therefore, that planning for the unforeseeable could involve much more than the ability to change the size and shapes of spaces within the exterior walls of the structure and to expand it in one or more directions.

Ideally, a school building should be capable of modifications in many forms. It should be planned for both horizontal and vertical expansion. It should contain internal partitions and supporting columns that facilitate the reshaping and resizing of interior spaces without functional limitations. It should be designed so that electrical power, utilities, communication cables, electromagnetic wave guides, optical systems for lasers and masers, and other technological devices yet to be invented can be brought to or utilized in any part of the building. Obviously, it would probably be far more expensive to attain this ideal than to adopt a more realistic approach to the problem.

Expansion

The continued trend toward urbanization, with its rapid increase in population densities in metropolitan areas, means that land will be at a premium in the future. As a result, school buildings should be conceived for vertical expansion in order to conserve expensive urban land. The structure and footings of a single-story building should be designed so that additional supports could be incorporated for the addition of a second or third floor.

Horizontal expansibility has long been recognized as a desirable feature in a school building. When the function of the expanded building has been determined, the architect customarily plans the ultimate structure and then cuts it back to the spaces needed for the first stage of construction. When future need has not been determined, the building should still be planned for expansion, but in a more general fashion. Circulation areas should not hinder future expansion. Utility lines should be designed with future expansion in mind. The planning team should always ask itself the question, "Where and what would we be likely to add to this building if we were asked to increase its capacity by 25 percent?" even when the likelihood of expansion appears remote.

Attention should be focused on the general layout and circulation pattern of a building as well as on specific design features. Ideally, a school building should be designed so that it is capable of being expanded sensibly and functionally in five directions—on four sides and upward. Realistically, school buildings should be able to expand in at least three directions.

Contraction

For several decades following the baby boom immediately after World War II, the principle of contractibility escaped the attention of most educational facility planners. With school enrollments increasing rapidly from year to year, architects and school officials were primarily concerned with expansibility. Beginning in the 1960s, however, the birth rate in the United States declined dramatically, and the number of students entering kindergarten and first grade dropped far beyond expectations. Within a few years, the cumulative effect of this sociological change brought about a substantial reduction in total school enrollments. In a number of school districts, total school enrollments dropped by as much as 30 percent. Consequently, a fairly large number of school districts throughout the country found themselves with a surplus of educational facilities. Under these circumstances, many school officials and boards of education were caught unprepared. They had to face difficult and sensitive decisions on what to do with superfluous and unneeded classrooms or entire school buildings.

Planning for an unforeseeable decline in school enrollment is much more difficult than planning for expansibility, but can be accomplished in two ways. The simplest is to devise a long-range plan so that obsolete buildings can be phased out easily if school enrollments drop. In this connection, location of new facilities is a major consideration. This approach is particularly adaptable for school facilities over 50 or 60 years old. In a relatively young school district, however, planning for contractibility is much more complicated. If all of the existing school buildings are relatively modern and highly functional, the need for less space cannot be solved easily by simply closing out excellent buildings. A more realistic approach would be to continue using a school facility for educational purposes but allow part of it to be used for noneducational activities. However, this solution is not always practical or feasible because the building was not designed with contractibility in mind.

Reversible Contractibility

Enrollment trends are in a constant state of flux. They respond to a number of concurrent influences, such as changes in economic conditions, variations in quality of life, and changes in societal attitudes to family size. The principle of reversible contractibility is designed to assist school officials in coping with problems of capacity, particularly when school enrollments are declining. When excess capacity develops, school officials would be well advised to examine birth rates, along with other pertinent information.

Although the birth rate has stabilized at a level that is much lower than immediately following World War II, the number of women of childbearing age—the baby boomers of yesteryear—has increased substantially. Thus, demographers predict a sort of "boomlet" in student enrollment over the next 15 years or so. This period will be followed by relatively small changes in school enrollment during the first part of the next century as the population begins to stabilize. This conclusion, however, is based on the premise that both the birth rate and the total childbearing population remain fairly constant.

Under these circumstances, it would be prudent for school officials and boards of education to look twice at future enrollment projections and birth rate patterns when contemplating closing or reducing educational space. If a decline in enrollment is anticipated, special attention should be paid to the principle of reversible contractibility. This principle stipulates that surplus educational spaces assigned to noneducational functions should be capable of being readily restored for instructional uses when so needed again. In applying this principle, bear in mind that the noneducational functions should be either temporary or easily moved to other locations on short notice.

Adaptability

Adaptability refers primarily to the ease with which spaces designed for a given function can be transformed to accommodate changes in methodology, student grouping, teaching aids, and the like. For example, by installing uniformly spaced standards on the walls of a classroom, it is possible to convert a regular classroom with chalkboards and tackboards on two walls to a general physical science room with peripheral counters and wall storage simply by hanging counters, shelves, storage cabinets, sinks, and other needed accessories on the standards. Rubber hoses could be used to connect the hung science sinks to the various utilities. Such a room is highly adaptable. Generally speaking, the concept of adaptability is confined to internal conversion. School planners also refer to the adaptability of a school building as a whole. In this sense, the term is related to the ability to utilize a building designed for a specific purpose for another purpose. For example, can a given junior high school be readily converted to a middle school? If it can, then the building is said to be adaptable. In a broad sense, the concept is closely associated with multipurpose spaces, such as cafeterias, play areas, general science rooms, student union buildings, and lobbies.

In planning for the unforeseeable, every effort should be made to include all features that facilitate internal changes in all instructional areas: the multipurpose use of all walls, the ease of locating power and utilities in various parts of the room, the possibility that equipment may be hung from the ceiling, the control of internal lighting within a given instructional area, and the quick and simple rearrangement of furniture and equipment on the floor. How far to pursue this depends on the amount of funds the planning team feels it should invest in the unforeseeable.

Flexibility

Flexibility is closely related to adaptability but is somewhat broader in scope. Flexibility is conceived as a feature of a school building that facilitates extensive changes in the sizes and shapes of teaching areas without endangering the structural system of the building. Adaptability makes it possible to accommodate new functions in given spaces, while flexibility makes it possible to redesign old spaces to satisfy new needs.

The basic ingredient of flexibility is fluidity. Accordingly, all walls of a school building, with the exception perhaps of the outside envelope, should be conceived as temporary space dividers. Ideally it should be possible, in a flexibly designed school, to relocate all internal partitions without jeopardizing the structural system of the building. No conduits, pipes, ducts, or other service elements should be located in interior walls. Also, no interior walls should be load bearing. Heating, cooling, and lighting systems should be concentrated in the floors and ceilings. It is not usually financially justifiable to provide all of these features throughout an entire school building. Furthermore, many walls may never be moved. Consequently, good school planning calls for the judicious application of the principle of flexibility. If movable walls are desired, it is imperative that supporting columns be strategically placed so as not to interfere with sight lines when the positions of the internal partitions are changed to meet the demands of a changing curriculum.

The principle of flexibility should be applied to the equipment as well as to the building. The design of a school should facilitate the relocation of instructional equipment. For example, flat floors, rather than risers, are preferable in instructional areas because they permit flexibility of seating arrangements. Many colleges and universities still adhere to the traditional rise-type classroom, which destroys flexibility in the placement and arrangement of furniture and equipment.

Practical Features of Modifiable School Plants

Some specific suggestions are presented in this section. These suggestions are focused upon those elements of school planning, discussed above, that promote expansibility, contractibility, adaptability, and flexibility.

1. *Placement of a building on the site.* First and foremost, it is essential that school planners select a site of adequate size in accordance with the standards suggested earlier. Assuming that the area of the school site is great enough, the building should be placed so that additions can be made to it on all four sides if possible. If not, additions should be possible on three sides of the school.

2. *The traffic pattern and location of corridors.* Corridors, stairways, and exits should be located so that the traffic pattern may flow naturally into any space added to the original structure. Also, the initial design of a school building should be aimed at keeping the costs of expansion at a minimum through the proper placement of corridors and stairways.

3. *The central utility core concept.* The establishment of a service core in the central part of a building is one method of providing for the unforeseeable. Wires, pipes, ducts, and cables can be easily extended to any part of the building from a centrally located service core.

4. *Anticipation of new instructional aids.* The imaginative school plant planning team endeavors to anticipate technological advances in instructional aids. There are currently a number of promising technological developments that should be taken into account in planning a school building. Open- and closed-circuit television are now quite commonplace in school design. The use of teaching devices is spreading at all levels of learning. Self-instructional devices, including automated, centralized tape recordings involving the use of scores of listening booths throughout a school building are beginning to appear. Computerized teaching devices using at least three branching stages are in the operational stage. A single computer can give individual personalized instruction to several hundred students at a time. In order to exploit this computer capability, any futuristic educational facility should be designed so that it can accommodate integrated instructional systems (IIS) such as those developed by Wicat Systems, Computer Curriculum Corporation, and the Education Systems Corporation.

5. *Destructible partitions.* Destructible partitions are often used in lieu of movable partitions where the need for removing a partition is not immediate. The destructible partition is preferable to other types of walls from the standpoint of capital outlay when a movable or operable partition is not clearly required. A destructible partition is designed so that it can be destroyed without affecting the structure of the building and without the problems of relocating pipes, ducts, wires, or cables that are often imbedded in ordinary partitions.

The destructible partition has an important place in school design. Operable partitions that are only rarely oper~ ` costly and unnecessary. Conventionally designed permanent partitions th~ ~ ~ ducts, wiring, and plumbing are very costly to eliminate and may eve~ a formidable barrier to change. The destructible partition, on the other ´ provide an excellent acoustical barrier at a reasonable cost, one that can be ~ ~moved at a later date without difficulty at a reasonable cost. Thus, the inclusion ~ a large number of destructible partitions in the design of a school building provides additional insurance that the building can cope with the unforeseeable.

6. *The movable partition.* The movable partition serves fundamentally the same purpose as the destructible partition, but the movable partition is salvageable, and it can be relocated without much difficulty. Several types are currently available. One type utilizes a nut-and-bolt assembly system which enables two men to move a 35-foot partition from one location to another in about eight hours. Another type of movable partition is quite ingenious in design. It utilizes a pneumatic rubber boot along the top. A section of the partition, with the boot deflated, can be moved easily by two men. When the new position is reached, the boot is simply inflated and the panel is automatically sealed at both top and bottom. From the standpoint of cost, the nut-and-bolt system still has an economic advantage over other types. The pneumatic type of partition, however, holds much promise for the future.

7. *Suspended ceilings.* Suspended ceilings provide great flexibility at a reasonable cost. In certain circumstances, suspended ceilings using tile may actually be less costly than some of the common nonsuspended types.

8. *Ideas that look toward the future.* Planning for the unforeseeable must focus on those design features that facilitate and encourage both minor and major changes in an educational facility. To conceive and create a design that readily lends itself to change, school planners must ask themselves, "What provisions in the design of the school should be made now so that certain changes can be made later at a reasonable cost?" "What special features should be incorporated in the plans at this time?" More specifically, they might ask themselves, "What would we do

a. if the heating capacity were to be increased by 50 percent?
b. if air-conditioning were to be installed?
c. if utilities were needed in any part of the school where they are now lacking?
d. if electrical power of various voltages were required in any part of the school?
e. if computer terminals were to be installed in selected classrooms?
f. if radio wave guides were to be installed in the science and engineering areas?
g. if self-instructional teaching devices with a centralized control point were to be installed in any part of the building?

h. if carrels were to be provided for students in the ratio of one per two students? One for each student?

i. if offices were to be provided for all secondary school teachers?

j. if effective germicidal lamps were to be installed in instructional areas?

k. if luminescent chalkboards using ultraviolet light were to be introduced in all classrooms?

l. if the building were required to have instructional spaces for tutoring (teacher with one student), for groups of 3, for groups of 6, for groups of 15, for groups of 30, for groups of 90, for groups of 150, for groups of 300, for groups of 450 in the same building?

m. if instructional spaces for over 50 students were to require the installation of automated feedback instructional equipment?

n. if 25 percent of the instructional materials were to be produced by a staff of artists at the school?

o. if 20 percent of the instructional staff were composed of trained teacher aides who need offices, equipment, and space for in-service training?

p. if the school were to be expanded vertically?

q. if instructional programs could originate thousands of miles away from the school and be conveyed to the students in any classroom via picturetelephone?

r. if the library and communications center of the school were, at the request of the student, to send audio and visual information automatically to the student's home at any time during the day or night? (This idea is now economically feasible.)

s. if the school were to provide its own air pollution filtering plant?

t. if a systematic plan whereby students were to learn from their peers were to be instituted?

u. if large, flat television screens were to be hung on an appropriate wall for viewing educational programs?"

This list purposely contains a number of suggestions that would seem revolutionary to the conservative and even somewhat advanced for the liberal. But it is hoped these thoughts indicate the character of the ideas that should emanate from the planning team when it endeavors to cope with the problem of planning for the unforeseeable.

NOTES

1. Werner Rogers, "Education for the Future of America," *The Educational Facility Planner*, v. 30-1 (Jan.–Feb. 1992), p. 6.

2. Ibid., p. 7.

3. Merle R. Sumption and Jack W. Landes, *Planning Functional School Buildings* (New York: Harper and Brothers, 1957), p. 201.

▶ 8

Adequacy, Efficiency, and Economy

Adequacy, efficiency, and economy are three related fundamental concepts in the planning of educational facilities. The adequacy of a school plant is measured by the degree to which it satisfies the quantitative and qualitative requirements of the educational program. Efficiency is related to the functional characteristics incorporated in the design of the facility. And economy is calculated by an estimate of the potential educational return per dollar expended for school facilities, although, of course, one cannot measure the absolute educational return per dollar expended. At any rate, there is greater economy in school plant planning when the expenditure of funds is more likely to produce increased educational returns or greater utilization of space and materials over a long period of time.

ADEQUACY AND SUITABILITY OF SCHOOL SPACES

The concept of adequacy is primarily concerned with the number, size, shape, and quality of educational spaces. Adequacy alone does not ensure a well-planned school facility. Suitability of instructional spaces with respect to function and operation of a school is a correlated consideration. In more specific terms, spaces for learning should be suitable from the standpoint of environmental controllability, shape, atmosphere, location, ease of maintenance, long-range economy, and the like.

Adequacy of Number

Educational specifications should state the number of the various types of spaces estimated to be both necessary and sufficient for the desired educational program. Any reduction in the number of proposed spaces from the number appearing in the specifications results in a corresponding cutback in the educational program.

In addition to instructional spaces, a certain number of supporting spaces must be included, such as storage areas, preparation rooms, faculty offices, research areas, washrooms, locker spaces, toilets, lounges, and the like. The number depends primarily upon the type and size of the school planned and upon the scope of the educational program to be housed in it. These needs will be discussed in detail in later chapters. Suffice it to say at this point that a necessary and sufficient number of both instructional and supplementary spaces should be provided. The term "sufficient" suggests that spaces in excess of the number called for by the educational program should not be included.

Adequacy of Size

The size of an instructional space directly influences its proper functioning, particularly if the number of square feet falls below the minimum needed for the function. Suggested sizes for selected educational spaces are presented in Chapters 12 and 13 for each type of school plan. These figures are based on accepted practices.

The functional analysis technique may also be employed. The space required for each activity should be determined by actual measurement, under experimental conditions if necessary. It is surprising that the functional analysis technique, despite its relative simplicity, is not universally adopted. For example, it may be necessary to determine the space required for 10 student carrels. It is quite easy to compute the space needed for a table 3 feet wide and 2 feet deep. The dimensions required for a chair and circulation space can be estimated as 3 feet long and 3 feet wide. The total square footage per carrel and circulation space then becomes 15 square feet. For 10 carrels, at least 150 square feet would be needed. If we add an estimated 50 square feet for circulation, the size of a room for 10 student carrels would be approximately 200 square feet. This procedure can be applied to any instructional space, provided the number of students involved and the estimated space requirement of each type of learning activity are known. In situations where new experiences are being introduced in the curriculum, experimental situations may be set up to determine the approximate amount of space needed. The author has found this technique to be quite fruitful. In some instances, the use of this method has revealed that spaces smaller than those suggested by rules of thumb were adequate for the function under consideration.

Adequacy of Environmental Controls

Adequate environmental controllability is vital to effective learning and to healthfulness. Thermal, acoustical, and visual controls are directly related to the needs of the human body. Instructional spaces should be designed with ample thermal capacity, including controls for both heating and cooling. In addition, they must have adequate illumination and optimum acoustical characteristics.

Details regarding the specific requirements associated with environmental control will be discussed in subsequent chapters. It is intended, at this point, simply to note the need for adequate heating, cooling, humidity, lighting, and acoustics.

Suitability of Shape

The shape of an instructional space should be suited to the function it is designed to serve. In general, rectangular, almost square classrooms are quite suitable for classes of about 30 students engaged in nonlaboratory-type instruction. Shape may be critical in some instructional spaces. For example, a combination lecture room-laboratory, where peripheral laboratory tables are desired, should be almost square. A music room should not be long and narrow. Elementary-grade classrooms can be supervised more effectively if the space is "squarish." On the other hand, a storage room should be long and narrow to make the most efficient use of floor space. In fact, a width of about 7 feet is preferable from the standpoint of economy. Characteristics of the various spaces are discussed in the chapters pertaining to the planning of elementary school, secondary school, and college buildings.

Suitability of Atmosphere

The environment created by an architect in the design of a school building should be psychologically stimulating to the students. Color, proportions, shape, lighting, fenestration, texture of interior surfaces, and furniture and furnishings all contribute to the atmosphere produced within an instructional space. Obviously, the total effect should both please and stimulate the student, who must sense that she or he is an integral part of the space and welcome in it. Instructional spaces should be warm, cozy, and attractive.

Color can be used most effectively in creating a proper psychological environment. Birren has spent a lifetime studying color and its effect on human beings. He has written an informative and well-documented treatise on the subject.[1] Color psychology is a topic of major concern to school planners as they seek to create an environment suitable for learning.

Adequacy of Space Relationships

A school building should be designed so that it functions as a single organism. All of its parts should be located in proper relationship to each other in order that the activities in the building can be conducted efficiently, conveniently, economically, healthfully, and safely.

Clustering of Functionally Related Spaces. From the standpoint of economy, efficiency, and ease of communication between faculty and staff, it is highly desirable that spaces housing similar or closely related instructional activities be clustered together. For example, all science spaces, such as those for biology, chemistry, physics, and general science, could be located in a single cluster in a high school building. In a college or university, for example, a chemistry building, a physics building, and a biology building could be clustered, perhaps, around a science library. In general, it is recommended that an educational facility be conceived and designed as a series of clusters of related spaces. The relationship of one cluster to another and other matters will be treated in chapters dealing with the planning of each type of school.

Separation of Incompatible and Unrelated Spaces. Incompatible spaces should be well separated. For acoustical reasons, for example, it is necessary to separate spaces planned for noisy activities from those whose activities are quiet; e.g., shop areas should not be near the library. For psychological reasons, it is highly desirable to separate the entrance to the guidance office from that of the principal's office, but for functional reasons, the interior areas of the guidance suite should be adjacent to those of the principal. For aesthetic reasons, large masses may be separated somewhat. For reasons of economy, air-conditioned spaces would be separated from the power plant or boiler room. From the standpoint of natural lighting, it might be necessary to separate adjoining wings by substantial distances, if natural lighting were to be the primary source of illumination. The principle of separation should be applied judiciously in school plant planning, for example, by spacing the clusters or related spaces properly rather than isolating an individual space from the cluster to which it is closely related. The time necessary for students to travel from one space to another should be taken into account, too. If distances between classroom buildings become too great, it may be necessary to increase the time allowed between periods and, perhaps, lengthen the school day.

Location in Relation to Safety and Health. In placing each function within the building or on the school site, planners should pay careful heed to the safety and health of the students and staff. For example, the location of storage space in lofts in shop areas presents a serious safety hazard. Spaces requiring service drives should be laid out with great care to insure the safety of students and school personnel. Unloading zones should be properly situated in relationship to both sidewalks and main driveways. Students should not be required to cross driveways in traveling from the bus unloading area to the building or in walking from the play areas to the gymnasium. On a college campus, it is desirable simply to eliminate all vehicles from the central core of each group of buildings.

THE EFFICIENCY OF A SCHOOL BUILDING

At first glance, it would appear that efficiency and economy are virtually the same. Actually, they are similar only to the extent that both principles are designed to achieve the highest and best return for each dollar expended by the school district. For the purpose of this discussion, efficiency refers to architectural design that is likely to improve the instructional effectiveness or operational characteristics of the building. Economy, on the other hand, has reference to actual savings in capital outlay that can be effected through architectural design. In a broad sense, therefore, efficiency is related to greater functional return per dollar expended, while economy is associated with the attainment of a given educational result at the lowest possible cost.

Greater educational return can be achieved in a host of ways through the creative design of a school building. School planners and faculty should keep efficiency of instruction in mind as they consider and discuss various proposals. The question that one should ask in relation to efficiency is, "Is this particular solution to the problem likely to yield the greatest educational return?" To arrive at a proper answer, one should further ask such questions as, "Does the solution promote the convenience of both teacher and students?" "Will most teachers find it simple to implement?" "Can the proposed solution be adapted to most of the situations that are likely to be encountered?" "Will the solution facilitate instructional or learning activities?" "Is the proposed solution too complex or elaborate in terms of the foreseeable need?"

Efficiency of Function

All school planners want to design a building that is tailor-made for the educational function of the school. Therefore, it is paramount that the functional aspects of the proposed school building be stated and described clearly in the educational specifications. Then the architect has no difficulty or uncertainty preparing sketches that are reasonably close to the desired design in terms of function.

As mentioned earlier, it is not possible to list functional features that apply to all educational facilities. A creative planning team and an imaginative faculty can supply the architect with hundreds of functional suggestions. In fact, it is not unusual to gather several hundred promising ideas from a faculty of 50 teachers, when the techniques of group dynamics are employed.

In planning for functional efficiency, school planners must also take into account the type of teaching materials and instructional equipment to be used. Functional efficiency demands that both the building and its equipment be conceived as a single, unified educational tool.

Many ideas related to functional efficiency will evolve as the faculty works with the planning team. One idea suggests another. It might be helpful to describe two situations in which this approach was used. After a group of teachers had become thoroughly acquainted with the concept of functional flexibility, it was suggested that faculty offices and classrooms be supplied with uniformly spaced vertical standards, such as those used for bookshelves, so that chalkboards, shelves, cabinets, or coat hangers could be hung on the walls. A faculty member could prepare charts and graphs on a small unit chalkboard hung in her office. She might then unhook it and carry it to the lecture room where she could hang it on the standards for instructional use. In designing a gymnasium-natatorium, a faculty member posed the idea of locating the pool about 50 feet away from the gymnasium floor and parallel to it. The intervening space above the lockers and showers could contain folding bleachers that could face either the pool or the gymnasium. When the pool was being used for swimming meets, the bleachers could seat spectators in the natatorium. When the bleachers were reversed, spectators could face the gymnasium play area during basketball games. When the bleachers were folded, the space between the two facilities could be used for instruction in physical education. The first example was submitted by faculty members who were planning a junior high school, and the second originated in a group of professors who were planning a college physical education facility. These examples illustrate to some extent the variety of ideas that may be offered by the school planning team and the faculty and staff associated with it.

Efficiency in Maintenance and Operation of a Building

School plants should be planned and designed to keep the cost of maintenance and operation at a minimum. Operational costs are directly related to the cost of services, fuels, expendable supplies, utilities, and the like. Maintenance costs refer primarily to the expenditure required to maintain the building and its equipment in its original state of utility.

Operational Efficiency.   School planners should give a penetrating look to all matters related to the operation of a school. Services represent relatively large operational costs. Consequently, the building should be designed, the materials chosen, and the equipment selected on the basis of maximum human efficiency. For example, easily and quickly cleaned surfaces should be chosen over those that involve a lower initial cost but are more costly to maintain. Features that save the time of employees who operate or occupy the structure are important. For example, the placement of doors and the location of service spaces with respect to entrances, driveways, unloading zones, and each other should be carefully studied to minimize unnecessary loss of time or motion. Fuels and utilities should be conserved as much as possible. Heat losses and gains must be taken into account, not only to provide sufficient heating or cooling capacity but also to achieve economies in the operation of the system. Additional insulation or low-conductivity windowpanes mean greater initial costs, but the savings in operational costs over the life of the building will generally more than compensate for them. The design of the building should reduce waste of electrical power, gas, and water as much as possible. For example, the use of low-voltage light controls would permit the custodian to control all of the lights in a building from a single panel. By pressing a few buttons in the custodial area after a given hour, he or she could activate relays that extinguish some or all of the lights in a building, or the lights could be controlled automatically by use of a time clock. Water conservation is also desirable, but not at the expense of function. The use of spring faucets is a case in point. In order to wash one's hands at a public lavatory hygienically, it is necessary to use tempered running water. Spring faucets, one carrying hot and the other cold water, simply cannot be operated hygienically. On the other hand, a knee- or foot-operated single-spigot faucet having tempered water is an excellent solution, because it both achieves economy and meets sanitary requirements. The initial cost may be somewhat higher, but the operation is both functional and economical.

Efficiency Related to Maintenance. Efficiency of maintenance is concerned with durability and cost of upkeep. Materials that are relatively maintenance free should be given preference over less costly materials requiring greater care. The life expectancy of both materials and equipment is a basic consideration in the selection of such items. Those that have the lowest depreciation cost per year should be given first consideration, unless such choices adversely affect the educational function.

Efficiency in Storage and Handling of Materials

All materials should be stored as close as possible to the place where they are used. Storage rooms, therefore, should be strategically placed in a building with reference to *delivery, distribution,* and *utilization.* Sound business practice demands that storage spaces be controlled. Consequently, storage rooms should be designed and situated so that control is facilitated. It is also necessary to plan storage spaces to prevent spoilage or damage to materials stored in them. Unfortunately, architectural engineers often utilize storage rooms for ducts, transformers, distribution boxes, and the like. Besides reducing the effective size of storage spaces, the secondary use of these spaces may damage the supplies or materials placed in storage.

Efficiency in the Design of Circulation Patterns within a School

The architectural design of student circulation space has a pronounced influence on the educational function of a school building. Circulation patterns must allow student traffic to flow rapidly from one part of the building to the other; however, extreme care must be exercised to insure that the space provided for circulation is not only necessary but sufficient. Excessive circulation space is wasteful from the standpoint of both initial investment and operation. There seems to be a slight tendency among a few school planners to overdesign circulation spaces. In one instance, for example, there was a single loaded corridor 10 feet wide surrounding three sides of a large cafeteria-dining area. In another plant, two corridors were provided to serve three rows of classrooms. In both of these cases the excess corridor space added somewhat to student convenience, but in neither case did the circulation pattern indicate an efficient use of space.

Secondary corridors and lobbies should be carefully studied in any school facility plan. Circulation space should be completely adequate, but, in planning the size of lobbies, corridors, and other circulation spaces in a school building, it should be remembered that efficiency in circulation space yields two bonuses—savings in initial capital outlay and reductions in operational costs.

ECONOMY

Every effort should be made by school planners to achieve maximum economy in both capital outlay and operation of a proposed school building. Economy, however, should be differentiated from cheapness. A building should be economical but not cheap. Economy, as used in this text, is not the acquisition of a school facility for a given enrollment at the lowest possible cost. Rather, it is defined as the achievement of maximum educational and utilitarian value per dollar expended. According to this concept, the lowest-cost building is not necessarily the most economical. For example, a school district in northern Illinois constructed a brick and masonry school at a phenomenally low cost per square foot. When it was viewed by the author after it was barely five years old, the mortar had crumbled so badly that a pencil could be pushed through an outside wall. The building had settled so badly that light could be seen through the walls of one of the toilet rooms. And water damage had caused the window frames to rot, permitting cold air to enter the building. The superintendent of schools conceded that the school district had a serious problem on its hands, because the building was too new to abandon and yet too costly to continue in operation.

How Much Economy Can Be Achieved by Educational Boards?

Conscientious members of boards of education or boards of trustees spend months poring over plans and specifications in an effort to achieve real economies in school buildings. Their worthy efforts are concentrated on items of construction that represent only a small percent of the total cost of the project.

Human Effort and Potential Savings. Let us demonstrate the low potential savings that may be effected by educational boards in selecting less costly materials for walls, flooring, hardware, ceiling, lighting, acoustics, and the like. On the average, the total cost of a building is distributed as follows:

- 20 percent for fees, furniture, furnishings and equipment, and site development.
- 80 percent for construction, of which 30 percent is attributable to heating, ventilating, electrical, and mechanical equipment.

If we subtract 30 percent from the construction cost for heating, mechanicals, and the like, the remainder is 50 percent of the total cost. Assuming further that labor represents about one-half the cost of construction, and also that a board of education or trustees has practically no control over it, the cost of all remaining construction materials in a school plant is thus reduced to about 25 percent of the total cost. Let us assume further that about one-half of the materials cost is predetermined by the physical requirements, such as steel beams for framework, slabs of concrete, and the like. Consequently, a board is left with about 12 percent of the cost of building materials over which it has some choice. If we also assume that it will cost at least one-half of the 12 percent to acquire basic materials over which the board has a choice, the maximum possible saving that could be effected by a board of education or trustees appears to be 6 percent of the total cost of the school. Since most members of boards of education or trustees are not professional engineers or architects, it is reasonable to assume that, at best, a saving of 2 or 3 percent in the total cost of a building might be effected at a personal cost to the board members in time and effort that is inordinately high in relation to such savings.

The time invested in discussions, research, and study to effect economies is not always commensurate with the savings realized. All boards must review plans and specifications in terms of function, efficiency, and economy. It is suggested, however, that economy not be belabored. After initial corrections have been made, the return is disappointingly small when compared with the additional effort that must be expended. More substantial economies are possible through creative building design, long-range planning, use of new concepts, and the like, which are discussed subsequently.

True and False Economies. School planners must differentiate clearly between real and false economies. A true economy must meet the following two tests:

1. The reduced cost in capital outlay does not adversely affect the curriculum or educational efficiency of the school.
2. The reduced initial cost does not result in *increased* maintenance and operational costs.

The first test deals with intangible educational outcomes that are difficult to evaluate. Nevertheless, school planners should be fully convinced that an economy does not hinder or restrict the desired educational program. The second test, on the other hand, is quite objective and relatively simple to apply. For example, Pierce concludes that "the fluorescent system (of school lighting) will probably cost slightly more initially, but the annual cleaning, relamping, and operating costs will more than offset this slight difference in less than a year's time."[2] While Pierce's conclusion may seem startling to the proponents of incandescent lighting, it was supported by a study conducted by a school district in the Boston area on the comparative cost of purchase, installation, and operation of both types of lighting under controlled conditions. It was found that the initial higher cost of the fluorescent fixtures was compensated for in less than seven years because of their lower cost of operation and maintenance. Since the average life of a school building is over half a century, the fluorescent fixtures were actually producing income for the school district after the initial difference in cost between the two types of fixtures was equalized.

While this illustration is striking, many others are not so dramatic, nor so obvious. For example, the use of costly glazed tile on the lower part of corridor walls and in toilet rooms is a real economy. The installation of expensive ceramic tile on toilet room floors represents another real economy. The plastering of both sides of lightweight concrete blocks on walls between two classrooms is a real economy, because it significantly decreases noise interference between two adjoining instructional spaces. The installation of suspended acoustical ceilings on a mechanical track system is another real economy from the standpoint of maintenance, replacement of tile, and adaptability of the space as a learning laboratory. The installation of wall-to-wall carpeting in certain areas of a school building also represents real economy from the standpoint of money saved and improved educational function.

Economy Related to the Design of a School Building

The design of a building strongly influences its cost. In discussing cost reduction by educational boards, it was assumed that the design of the building was approved and fixed before board members sought to effect economies by selecting less costly equipment, furniture, and interior surfaces. Not only does the design of the building have a profound influence on the initial cost of a school plant, it also affects its cost of operation.

The Compact Design. The School Planning Laboratory has found a close relationship between "compactness of a school building and both subsequent maintenance and operation expense," in elementary and secondary schools.[3] There was also a strong negative correlation between initial cost of a building and compactness. In these studies, the index of compactness was obtained by dividing the perimeter footage by the square footage within the walls. The compactness effect was more pronounced in the larger buildings than in the smaller structures, as might be expected. In designing economical buildings, therefore, it is desirable to keep the linear feet of perimeter per square foot of enclosure as small as possible. The architectural profession has applied this principle of economy to school design for many years. Many architects have turned to the cube, the circle, and more recently to the sphere, as exemplified by the introduction of the geodesic dome by R. Buckminster Fuller, in their efforts to achieve maximum compactness.

In designing educational facilities, however, school planners should bear in mind that the primary purpose of a school building is to educate students. No predetermined design should be adopted unless it satisfies the requirements of the desired educational program. If the compact plan satisfies the educational need just as well as the rambling type of school building, then the principle of economy would dictate that the compact design be selected. On the other hand, there may be circumstances, particularly in the design of elementary schools, where the rambling single-story, finger plan is particularly suitable. The author believes that school planners should give a strong preference to the compact plan but should not insist upon it in all situations. It is also felt that a rambling school cannot be justified in terms of economy unless its design meets a specific educational need.

The compact design does not mean that the entire school must be designed as a single large cube or hemisphere. Indeed, architects have utilized this principle in many ingenious ways. They have used a series of cubes varying in size. They have planned circular school buildings. They have employed combinations of spheres, cubes, and cylinders. Of course, the influence of compactness on economy of school construction is less pronounced in school buildings having areas under 15,000 square feet. For secondary schools containing less than 50,000 square feet, the correlation between cost of construction and compactness was –0.78, while schools with areas in excess of 100,000 square feet yielded a coefficient of correlation of –0.90.[4] A similar research project was conducted at the School Planning Laboratory using data related to elementary schools, which are generally substantially smaller in area than secondary schools. Even in these cases, the economy due to compactness was quite pronounced. The coefficient of correlation between compactness and the cost of elementary schools was –0.41.[5]

The principle of compactness suggests that greater economy of initial capital outlay and operational cost with respect to heating and cooling is obtained when the perimeter of a building is kept as short as possible. For this reason, jogs should be avoided. Long, narrow wings are less desirable than structures in which wings are combined to form a more compact building. For example, arranging classrooms so that the narrow end faces the corridor tends to promote compactness and economy. The geodesic plan is another illustration of compact design in school plant planning.

Planned Economy for Capital Outlay Programs

Economy can be the result of educational planning that takes place long before a building is conceived or proposed. In fact, economy is an important aspect of long-range planning. The strategic location of new buildings, the judicious rehabilitation of facilities with educational potential, and the abandonment of obsolete school buildings contribute to educational economy.

A few highlights of economy related to long-range educational planning are reviewed. A more detailed account appears in Chapters 4 and 5, where many elements of long-range planning are discussed. Economy in long-range planning is promoted by acquiring school sites in advance of need. It is not always necessary to purchase the site early. On the other hand, an educational board should obtain an option on property that may be required for expansion as many as five years prior to the anticipated need, if possible. New schools should be located properly in relation to the area of future population growth of the school district and to existing buildings that are likely to be abandoned in the foreseeable future. Economy may be improved through the development of a long-range financial plan designed to keep the credit rating of the school district as high as possible. Such a plan can provide for advantageous timing of financial transactions. Economy can be achieved by selecting the proper type of grade organization for the educational program offered and in relation to existing school buildings with educational potential for future use. And finally, economy is substantially improved when new facilities are designed for real, as contrasted with pseudo-, expansion. In the experience of the writer, there has rarely been an occasion when an architect was unable to show that provision was made for future expansion of the school. In fact, a few dotted lines showed exactly where expansion could occur, but there was little or no consideration, in most cases, as to exactly what educational functions would be housed within the space enclosed by the dotted lines, or how they would be related to existing functions. All the architect did, in such cases, was to point out that there was sufficient land to expand at the end of a corridor. Educators must help architects envision specific educational uses for the space contained within such dotted lines. Such planning fosters economy.

Another aspect of economy that precedes the planning of a building is the employment of an architect who can prepare a proper set of final working drawings and specifications. Economy is substantially improved if the architect prepares plans and specifications that are complete, detailed, and easy to understand. A board of trustees or board of education never really knows how many additional dollars contractors add to bids simply because they want to be on the safe side in translating ambiguous specifications into the cost of labor and materials. Also, drawings and specifications that lack sufficient detail may lead to change orders and misunderstanding during construction, both of which are costly.

Suggestions for Improving Economy in School Plant Planning

It would be a monumental, if not impossible, task to list every conceivable method of achieving economy in planning school buildings. A few suggestions are presented here with the expectation that many other money-saving ideas will evolve during the planning process.

1. *Economy is improved when instructional spaces can be designed to serve several functions.* In such cases, the room utilization factor is likely to be increased and, under certain conditions, fewer spaces may be needed.

2. *Classroom ceilings can be lowered to 9 feet or 9 feet 6 inches without any harm to the educational program.* Such a change would result in savings of both initial capital outlay and in heating and cooling costs.

3. *A reduction in the amount of glass in a school building decreases the cost of both maintenance and operation.* The use of fixed glass is more economical than the installation of movable window sash.

4. *The quantity of ventilation should be kept as low as possible but consistent with minimum needs,* about 10 cubic feet of fresh air per student per minute or less in some states.

5. *Construction materials should be selected on the basis of ease of maintenance and durability.* As mentioned earlier, substituting materials that reduce the cost of initial capital outlay does not necessarily achieve economy.

6. *Stock plans should be avoided since they do not save educational institutions money in the long run.* According to Pierce, " . . . the cost of a project can be reduced by using stock plans only when the school is willing to settle for inadequate and incomplete planning; and, therefore, willing to settle for less than the most appropriate functional provisions in the building."[6]

Where stock plans have been used, the results have been less than encouraging. The amount that can be saved is insignificant. For example, if the architect's fee is 6 percent, one-quarter of the fee, or 1.5 percent, is reserved for supervision. Consequently, a school district can effect savings on only the remaining 4.5 percent of construction cost. Since sites and soil conditions vary greatly, some revision will be required in the structural aspects of stock plans. If we assume that it would cost a school district about 1 percent for the adaptation of stock plans to a given site and orientation, then the school district would have a potential savings of 3.5 percent, providing its school program is exactly the same as the one for which the original stock plans were designed. Changes in stock plans will probably be needed, because the educational needs in any given district are likely to differ. Perhaps another 2 percent of construction cost would be needed to employ an architect to modify the stock plans to satisfy the educational needs of the school district. At this point, it would appear at first that a school district can save about 1.5 percent of the construction cost of the proposed school after all changes are made. However, stock plans must be designed and continuously kept up-to-date at the standard cost of architectural services. This cost must be shared and borne by the school districts using such stock plans. Consequently, potential savings of about 2 percent are virtually wiped out by charges made to the state or school districts for the original stock plans. When it is realized further that the modifications required to meet local needs represent at best a series of compromises between the changes that *need* to be made and those that *can* be made, because of the necessity of adhering to the basic concepts of design in the original stock plans, the appeal of stock plans almost disappears.

7. *A rather impressive case for prefabrication can be made on the basis of the savings possible through mass production of major sections of a school building.* Prefabrication has a great deal of appeal when the construction cost of a school is compared with that of custom-built facilities. Savings attributable to prefabrication techniques, however, should be weighed against the cost of depreciation and maintenance of prefabs. Great positive strides have been made by the building industry over the past decade. Prefabricated buildings are meeting with public acceptance and local codes are being revised to allow the placement of prefabricated buildings within most municipalities.

It is often not realized that even conventionally planned buildings are prefabricated to a large extent. The major difference between the so-called prefabricated buildings and those of modular design lies in the extent to which the parts of a building are preassembled at the factory. Under prefabrication procedures, relatively large sections of walls and ceiling structures are preassembled. In both conventional and prefabricated buildings, practically all of the component parts are prefabricated. For example, bricks, steel framing, doors, window sash, tiles of various types, etc., are prefabricated in any type of construction. Consequently, the potential savings often claimed for prefabricated buildings become relatively insignificant compared with the cost of construction of buildings of modular design, which take advantage of both prefabrication and preassembly.

In all fairness, it should be stated that the process of prefabrication possesses at least three important advantages over other types of construction. First, large parts of a structure can be assembled in a shop under ideal conditions. Second, a minimum amount of labor is needed on the site. Third, the time required to erect a prefabricated structure on the site is dramatically reduced (by over 50 percent) using mass-production techniques.

The technology underlying prefabricated buildings has advanced by leaps and bounds over the past few years. Predesigned plans can now be changed at once and at will to meet the special needs of any school district. No longer are architects and engineers required to spend hours and hours over drawing boards. They are using CAD (Computer-Assisted Design) software to assist them in preparing architectural and engineering drawings. For this reason, they are now able to design and redesign plans of prefabricated structures more quickly and inexpensively. Since computers are also used to control robots that fabricate the components of prefabricated structures, these two technological advances combine their computer power to produce prefabricated units that can be readily designed to meet the specific requirements of any educational program.

According to Clark, prefab schools can be flexible, stylish, and functional.[7] He describes a prefabricated elementary school building consisting of 102 components manufactured offsite. The facility features 22 classrooms for students in grades 1 through 6, four kindergarten rooms, and ancillary spaces for special education, preschool education, and early childhood care. Clark calls attention to portability of prefabs. He explains that this building can be disassembled and moved to other sites where additional capacity may be needed in the future.

The writer recently had an opportunity to closely examine several prefab houses in a subdivision in southern California and was deeply impressed with the creative design of such homes. The environment and structural appearance of the interior of these homes gave no indication that they were prefabs. One owner indicated that she was able to modify the basic plan of the house to meet her specific needs without any difficulty whatsoever. Furthermore, the changes were integrated into the building as though they were part of the original plans.

The acquisition of prefabricated school buildings should be done judiciously. Under certain conditions, prefabs are indeed a viable solution, particularly when capital outlay funds are severely restricted or when there is an immediate need for additional student housing.

The question is still raised, however. "Are prefabricated buildings a sound investment for a school district?" As indicated earlier, there are pros and cons regarding this type of structure. The initial capital outlay is generally lower than that of a conventional building. The buildings can be tailor-made to satisfy the needs of the school district. They can be erected quickly. And, last but not least, they can be disassembled and moved from one location to another. On the negative side, one must answer two crucial questions: How does the useful life of the prefab compare with that of a conventional building?, and How do the operational and maintenance costs of the prefab compare with a conventional-type building? There is a dearth of documented research regarding these two questions. Nevertheless, educational planners must carefully consider the advantages and disadvantages of prefabricated school buildings and arrive at a well-reasoned assessment of whether or not it would be fiscally prudent for the school district to proceed with the acquisition of prefabricated school buildings.

OPERATIONAL ECONOMY

The rapidly increasing costs of labor, materials, and energy over the past two decades have placed a high premium on certain aspects of school plant planning. Formerly, these matters were inconsequential. Labor was so cheap that a school building could tolerate a number of items that were low in initial cost but relatively costly to maintain. School plant planners were able to overlook possible savings in heat, light, and power, because the cost of energy was insignificant in relation to the operational costs of a school building. Today, the situation is quite different. The high cost of labor and the dwindling availability of energy places an extremely high value on the cost of maintenance and on the selection of energy-saving equipment. There is also a greater emphasis on the ways and means of conserving energy losses. See Chapter 9 for energy saving measures.

Planning for Minimal Expenditures for Maintenance

The design of school buildings that are not costly to maintain entails much more than selecting materials that are easy to clean. To be sure, the choice of such materials is an important consideration, but that is just the beginning. There are many other important aspects of planning that can produce dramatic savings in the cost of maintaining a school facility.

Let us look, for a moment, at the placement of equipment, lighting, plumbing, shrubbery, or lawns. With high labor costs, time represents money. School planners would be richly rewarded in the form of substantial savings in maintenance costs if the architect were required to design a building in which each item requiring routine maintenance is installed so that the time required to maintain it is at a minimum. There are hundreds of such items in a school building, including light fixtures located in the high ceilings of an auditorium, boiler tubes in a confined heating plant, and shrubs that hinder lawn mowing. These undesirable design elements consume hours of valuable time. Every effort should be made to eliminate all design features that increase the time required for maintaining the facility or the equipment associated with it.

It is not practical in this publication to describe the many ways by which savings in maintenance cost can be achieved. If the principle stated above is kept in mind in designing a school building, the appropriate solutions will evolve naturally in the course of the planning. The application undoubtedly suggested by the above principle—i.e., design features that promote efficiency—reduces the time required for maintenance and bolsters the operational economy of the educational facility.

The Principle of Least Probable Maintenance

It often pays high dividends to determine the potential cost of maintenance over a long period of time. Indeed, the practice of selecting materials that are durable in quality and economical in maintenance is an application of this principle. But the potential savings or losses over the life of the building are not always known. For example, many materials that are enduring and easily preserved are also more costly in initial capital outlay. The added initial cost, however, should be balanced against the estimated savings in cost of maintenance over a period of at least 20 to 30 years. Once these two figures are determined, the answer becomes self-evident.

Until recently, very little thought was given to the potential cost of maintaining building equipment, such as boilers, circulators, pumps, electronic controls, plumbing control devices, and electrical relays. The functional specifications of such equipment were prepared by the architect, and the contractor was obligated to conform to the specifications. Accordingly, the contractor simply selected the specified equipment that was the lowest in cost. Potential maintenance cost was of little or no concern to the contractor. In the interest of greater long-range economy, it is suggested that all persons involved in planning educational facilities consider the overall maintenance cost of equipment. It might be quite profitable for a school district to include some statement concerning the "frequency-of-repair" characteristics of potential maintenance costs, in addition to the usual functional specifications of all equipment to be installed in a school building. This practice may encourage some manufacturers to include long-term maintenance guarantees on their equipment. Thus, in selecting the equipment for a school facility, the contractor would be responsible for selecting equipment that is both low in maintenance and functional in design. In general, the cost of maintaining equipment is directly related to the level of sophistication of the equipment. The more complicated the equipment, both mechanically and electronically, the more important it is to determine the potential cost of maintaining such equipment in accordance with the principle of least probable maintenance.

NOTES

1. Faber Birren, *Color and Human Responses* (New York: Van Nostrand Reinhold, 1978).

2. David A. Pierce, *Saving Dollars in Building Schools* (New York: Reinhold, 1959), p. 88.

3. *School Planning Laboratory Research,* Reports 3 and 4 (Stanford, CA: Educational Facilities Laboratories, Inc., Stanford University, 1961).

4. Ibid.

5. Ibid.

6. Pierce, op. cit., p. 32.

7. Thomas Clark, "Flexible, Stylish Prefab Schools," *The School Administrator* (June 1989), p. 21.

► 9

Planning for Energy Conservation and Management

Prior to the Middle East embargo on oil shipments to the United States in 1973, architects, educational facility planners, and school officials were not fully aware of the eventual depletion of world sources of energy derived from fossil fuels. At that time, energy was of no particular concern to the public or school officials. There was an overabundance of fuel and the cost was relatively low. Accordingly, there was no reason for anyone to become apprehensive about energy consumption. Under these conditions, architects and school plant planners were only concerned with the form of energy that would be supplied to a proposed school building—coal, oil, gas, or electricity. Boards of education often asked architects and utility companies to make studies in depth to determine the cost-effectiveness of each form of energy for a particular school facility in a given location. In this connection, it is interesting to note that the electric companies were very aggressive and often successful in promoting "all electric" school facilities. They spared no effort and were ingenious in their attempts to convince local school officials that electricity was the clean, cost-effective heating energy of the future—at a time when the cost of electricity per British Thermal Unit (Btu) of energy was about 1.5 times that for oil heat.

Since 1973, however, the future outlook on energy has changed completely. The recognition by the public and leaders of the world that the supply of fossil fuels is finite has been shocking. The dwindling supply of energy from fossil fuels such as coal, oil, or gas has become a major concern of the industrialized nations. A few far-sighted scientists issued warnings of an impending depletion of fossil fuels about a half century ago. But no one seemed to take these warnings too seriously. These scientists predicted that there would be a serious energy shortage before the year 2000 and that the world supplies of fossil fuels would be completely exhausted about the middle of the twenty-first century, assuming that the demand for energy continues to grow in the future at the same rate it did in the past. And still, no one believed them! And why should they? After all, more and more reserves were being discovered. The supply of oil far outstripped the demand, and fuel prices were quite low. Automobile makers were producing high-powered vehicles with very low efficiency. It was not until the beginning of the 1980s that the world began to realize that the supply of fossil fuel energy stored in the crust of the earth was very limited and finite, and that it was being depleted at an alarmingly high rate. The predictions of when the present known reserves of coal, oil, and gas will be completely depleted varies from the beginning of the twenty-first century to about the year 2100. These predictions are based on the increased demand for energy caused by the growth in world population and by the foreseeable industrialization of underdeveloped countries. Under these circumstances, the energy outlook for the future is bleak.

Solar energy, biomass energy, wind energy, geothermal energy, and energy from the sea are all viable alternatives for the future. But there has not yet been a major scientific breakthrough in any of these potential approaches. For this reason, the world needs more time for scientists to solve the world energy crisis. If the industrialized nations of the world are to avoid reverting to the level of the economy and the way of life that was prevalent two or three centuries ago, energy conservation is the most viable alternative for the next two or three decades. For school districts, however, energy conservation is much more than planning for the future. For them, energy conservation is imperative, if they are to cope successfully with the relatively high price of fuels.

In concluding this introductory narrative on energy consumption and conservation, it might be enlightening to take a brief look at the unbelievable rate at which energy is consumed, compared to the time required to produce it. A real situation will be cited to illustrate this point. A family in New England is using an efficient, airtight Fisher wood stove to heat a Cape Cod-style house with an area of about 1,000 square feet on the first floor and 600 square feet of space developed in the attic. The total floor area of the house is about 1,600 square feet. During the coldest part of the winter, this wood stove maintains the temperature of the house at about 70° Fahrenheit and consumes one cord of hardwood in four weeks. Foresters have found that it takes an average of five trees between 35 and 40 feet high to produce one cord of fire wood. The time required for an oak seedling to become a tree of this size is between 15 and 20 years depending upon soil conditions. For the purpose of this discussion, let us assume that the growing time for such a tree is about 17 years, or 200 months. Thus, it takes 200 months to produce five trees that will heat one average-size house in New England for one month! In this case, energy is consumed 200 times as fast as nature can produce it through the process of photosynthesis.

Hopefully, the energy picture of the future will be brighter. For the present, conservation is the best insurance against economic disruption and an unsatisfying way of life. For school officials and boards of education, conservation of energy has both external and internal implications. Conserving energy contributes to the well-being of the industrial nations throughout the world. But, internally, conservation of energy becomes an absolute necessity in terms of fiscal considerations. The dramatic increases in energy prices make energy conservation an unconditional imperative of modern educational management.

THE ESSENCE OF ENERGY

A few short years ago, the word "energy" was primarily restricted to the routine vocabulary of the scientist and the engineer. Today, "energy" has become a household word for something that is of vital concern to everyone in the industrialized nations of the world. Energy is something whose cost has doubled and redoubled over a very short period of time. Energy is also that elusive something that appears and disappears at the whim of circumstances beyond our control. And it is becoming more and more evident that energy, whatever meanings and forms it may take, is something that is seriously threatening the way of life of everyone living in the industrialized nations.

Scientifically, "Energy is that which is capable of doing work." But, to boards of education, school officials and school plant planners, energy is coal, oil, gas, electricity, and solar power. It is also lighting, heating, cooling, and power for communications devices and mechanical equipment. Few people realize that our own sun is and has been the only primary source of energy for our earth ever since the world was formed millions of years ago. The sun is a nuclear furnace that continually radiates a substantial amount of energy in the form of light and heat onto the surface of the earth. It must be remembered that the supplies of fossil fuels found in the crust of the earth in the form of coal, oil, or gas are the products of solar energy which took thousands and thousands of years to accumulate. And it is frightening to face the stark reality that, at the anticipated rate of consumption, all of these accumulated reserves will be completely exhausted in the foreseeable future. A number of geological scientists have already predicted that this will occur during the twenty-first century. The exact time at which our fossil fuels will be totally consumed is still open to question. But, despite the glut of fuel that appears on the market from time to time, there is absolutely no question whatsoever that the time will come, perhaps sooner rather than later, when there will be no more coal, no more gas, and no more oil that can be economically extracted from the crust of the earth.

While the energy outlook of the world is not particularly bright at this time, there is every reason for looking toward the future with optimism and renewed hope. We still have the nuclear furnace on the sun that is producing energy at an enormous rate. The world is indeed blessed by the abundance of energy that the sun continually showers upon its surface every day. In fact, the sun is daily supplying the earth with an amount of energy that is many more times the amount of energy that the world is likely to need in the foreseeable future. This energy arrives in the form of light and heat, and some of it reappears in the form of vegetation, wind, weather, ocean waves, ocean currents, and temperature differentials both in the oceans and in the atmosphere. With these forms of energy in mind, the future is really exciting and challenging. There is indeed an abundant source of energy—the sun. In due time, human creativity and ingenuity will discover the ways and means of converting this vast source of energy into forms that can best serve the inhabitants of the earth.

ENERGY MANAGEMENT

The management of energy has emerged as a crucial and multifarious operation in the administration of educational facilities. Before the energy revolution of 1973, the conservation of energy was of no particular interest to school officials or educational facility planners. There was really no reason to be concerned. The cost of energy was low and the supply was plentiful. At that time, architects rarely considered the use of insulation materials, for example, in the walls and roofs of school buildings. In many instances, they summarily rejected them by stating categorically that the addition of insulation materials was not cost-effective. While that may have been true, no research findings were produced by such architects substantiating their contention that the pay-back period for the added cost of insulation would exceed the usable life of the educational facility.

The energy crisis, however, produced fundamental changes in the planning and modification of educational facilities. It also had a salubrious and stimulating effect on educational facility planners concerning matters related to energy. They were no longer apathetic and indifferent about design features that had the potential of reducing energy consumption. They became deeply involved in the selection of building materials, equipment, and control devices that contributed to the conservation of energy. They were receptive and responsive to any feasible concept or innovation that promoted energy conservation. They vigorously searched for promising solutions to the energy problem. Their concerted and sustained efforts were quite successful. In a relatively short time, they were able to bring the total cost of energy down to tolerable levels in many school districts.

Architects and engineers considered and evaluated a wide variety of feasible and achievable solutions to the energy problem confronting school officials and boards of education. During this process, they identified two major categories of energy-conserving measures. The first group included items related to changes in building design or materials and to the replacement or alteration of selected parts of the heating, cooling, ventilation, and electrical equipment. The second category, on the other hand, was focused primarily on energy management techniques that were designed to reduce energy consumption by *controlling* the use of available energy. This control was accomplished through carefully selected changes in some of the operational policies of the institution and through the use of a variety of promising energy control systems.

It might be helpful, at this point, to clarify certain terms that are currently associated with matters related to energy. Whenever fundamental changes occur in any field, new terms and expressions are likely to emerge. The energy conservation movement is no exception. Retrofitting refers to any change in an *existing* building or equipment that saves energy. The term *energy management* has been widely adopted by educators. It refers to *any* measure or procedure that effectively reduces the energy budget of the school district. Strictly speaking, of course, any measure that saves energy is generically a form of energy conservation, regardless of whether it is accomplished by major changes in the building and its equipment, by implementing policies designed to save energy, or by the installation of energy control devices. For the purpose of this text, however, the terms "energy management" and "conservation of energy" are used synonymously. The end result is the same—lower energy costs for the school district.

There are many sound and reliable procedures, techniques, and practices that are frequently employed in counteracting the high cost of energy. These are discussed in considerable detail in the latter sections of this chapter. School officials would be well advised, however, not to implement any of the suggested solutions before completing an energy audit, such as the one described later in this text. Special attention is directed to *step one* of the energy audit. As will be discussed later, the information derived from this preliminary study can be helpful to the local staff in many ways. Among them is the disclosure, perhaps for the first time, as to how much, where, in what form, and for what purpose energy is being used in an existing educational facility.

The information included in the next section under "Energy Needs in School Facilities" is intended to assist local personnel in conducting step one of the energy audit. While this material may seem trivial and redundant to persons familiar with educational facility planning, it is hoped that it will be practical, useful, and informative to local personnel assigned to the task of completing step one of the energy audit and for students in the planning and maintenance of educational facilities.

Energy management appears in many forms. In addition to the suggestions made under "Retrofitting" and "Planning Energy Efficient School Buildings" later in this chapter, studies have shown the application of computers in controlling the use of energy in school buildings is quite cost-effective.[1] Later studies confirm these results.[2] The use of wireless electronic timers that control the consumption of energy in various parts of the educational facility is another type of energy management. And finally, the modification of existing school policies may sometimes play an important part in the management of energy. For example, a substantial number of school districts and colleges have adopted changes in their academic calendars whereby schools open the fall semester during the last week of August instead of the traditional date in September. Through this change in policy, these institutions operate their facilities in August when there is little or no requirement for heating and close them in December when the cost of heating educational facilities in cold climates is quite high. The net result is a substantial saving in the cost of energy for heating purposes.

ENERGY NEEDS IN SCHOOL FACILITIES

In order to conserve energy intelligently in any educational facility, it is helpful to identify and locate all fixtures, appliances, and equipment that consume energy, including all types of teaching aids that need power. In general, the items that use energy fall into two major categories. Most of the energy supplied to a school building is associated with the health and comfort of the occupants. This group includes energy for heating, cooling, ventilation, and lighting. The second category consists of a multitude of items that are used in conjunction with the teaching process. Since the amount of energy consumed by each teaching aid is often relatively small, the total amount of energy required by such items is frequently underestimated. But when it is realized that instructional equipment includes power tools, shop machinery, kitchen ranges, clothes dryers, sophisticated computers, and other electronic systems, the amount of energy consumed by such equipment is no longer negligible. It must be taken into account in any plan designed to control energy.

Uses of Energy for Health and Comfort

As indicated above, the major portion of the energy required for an educational facility is devoted to the health and comfort of the occupants. The energy is used for heating, cooling, ventilation, lighting, and various types of automated control mechanisms (see Chapters 10 and 11).

Energy for Heating. Throughout the United States, a considerable portion of the energy budget is allocated to heating, which includes space heating, water heating, and heat for food preparation. Ordinarily, this energy is derived from coal, gas, oil, or electricity or from various combinations of these. In addition to the energy required to produce heat, power is required to distribute the heat to various parts of the building. This ancillary equipment consists of fans and various types of pumps and automatic valves. Power for these items is almost always electricity, which activates motors of one sort or another. And finally, controls such as thermostats, automatic valves, internal and external photoelectric devices, and various types of gas detecting systems consume electricity even when on a standby mode.

Energy for Ventilating.   Ventilating systems generally consume energy in two ways. Heat must be provided to all incoming fresh air so that cold drafts are avoided. Some designers are using a number of clever ways of recovering heat from air that is being exhausted from the building. This approach will be discussed in more detail in this chapter under the section entitled "Planning Energy Efficient School Buildings." The second major use of energy in a ventilation system is to maintain a supply of fresh air in all the classrooms and other parts of the building, such as the gymnasium and auditorium. A substantial amount of energy is consumed by scores of electric fans that move air from one point to another at predetermined rates of flow. All air movement is not by fan, however. In some of the older school buildings, gravity systems still provide ventilation in classrooms. Regardless of the functional merits of this system, it cannot be denied that it is energy efficient. Perhaps it should be resurrected and included in the design of future schools.

Energy for Artificial Lighting.   An enormous amount of electrical energy must be supplied to hundreds of lighting fixtures in school buildings. A proper visual environment is extremely important from the standpoint of health and educational function, and adequate levels of illumination should be maintained despite the energy cost involved. Until recently, the upward trend in the use of energy for artificial lighting has persisted. Only a few years ago, architects were designing school buildings with very little fenestration, in order to keep the cost of air conditioning at a minimum. In so doing, the amount of energy devoted to artificial lighting increased substantially.

Artificial lighting is found almost everywhere in a school building. It appears in closets, in storage rooms, in crawl spaces, and pipe trenches. It is seen in attics, in the corridors, above the stairways, inside of walk-in safes, and hidden behind panels for the indirect lighting of walls. Artificial lighting is also widely used for local illumination on various articles of furniture or equipment, such as sewing machines, shop tools, kitchen ranges, table and floor lamps, microscopes, and art and drafting tables. There are also many special applications of artificial lighting. Athletic fields are highly illuminated for night games. The auditorium is supplied with thousands of watts of artificial lighting. And all of the spaces occupied by students and teachers during the learning process are well illuminated by artificial lighting. This partial list of the more common applications of artificial lighting clearly indicates that its use is widespread throughout an educational facility and represents a substantial portion of the total energy supplied to the building.

Energy for Cooling.   In certain parts of the United States, the amount of energy used for cooling school buildings during the warm months accounts for a relatively large part of the energy budget. To be sure, the designers of air-conditioned school buildings are cognizant of the high energy consumption of cooling equipment. In an effort to reduce the cost, they have decreased the amount of fenestration and have installed insulating glass. Unfortunately, architects rarely insisted that all exterior walls and roofs be heavily lined with thermal insulation.

In fairness to the architects, however, it should be pointed out that they were deeply concerned about the high energy consumption of cooling equipment long before it became an expensive and precious commodity. Consequently, architects and engineers devised several ingenious methods of reducing the cost. Among them was the use of heat for cooling. This paradox was accomplished through the application of the diffusion principle using high pressure steam. On a more conventional note, engineers developed heat pumps to transport heat out of the building in the summer. During cold weather, the same pumps can be used to heat the building by simply reversing the cycle.

Energy for Instructional Uses

Some of the instructional uses of energy have already been mentioned in connection with artificial lighting. But illumination is only part of the energy requirement of the teaching equipment. To be sure, many types of electronic teaching devices consume relatively small amounts of power. But the aggregate of all these low users of power becomes quite important, particularly in a fairly large secondary school enrolling over 1,500 students. For example, one television set may use as little as 200 watts of power, but 100 such units in various parts of a school would consume 20,000 watts or 20 kilowatts of electricity per hour. One electric iron in the home-making laboratory uses about one kilowatt of electricity, but 30 of them would consume 30 kilowatts of power per hour. The same reasoning applies to tape recorders, slide and film projectors, electric typewriters, business machines, electronic equipment in the science laboratories, kilns in the arts and crafts room, and special equipment for reading. Sophisticated computers and automated devices for large group instruction also consume an appreciable amount of energy. One area of a secondary school where large amounts of power are used for instructional uses is that devoted to vocational education and industrial arts. Relatively large machines and numerous power tools are found in this area. And finally, the amount of energy required by the homemaking areas for instructional purposes is probably second to that expended by industrial shop areas. Ranges and clothes dryers consume thousands of watts of electricity per hour. Fortunately, the number of clothes dryers, ranges, dishwashers, and clothes washers provided in these spaces is relatively small. But the cost of energy required to operate them over the course of a year can easily reach several hundred dollars. The auto-tutorial teaching aids associated with the so-called "wet carrels" in the learning resources center also need energy for their normal operation. Each of these teaching devices is transistorized and consumes only small amounts of energy. But, taken as a whole, the amount of energy they use annually is not negligible.

From the standpoint of energy conservation, the primary purpose of calling attention to the wide variety of instructional equipment, teaching aids, and learning devices that consume energy in a modern school facility is to alert school officials to the hundreds of energy outlets that must be monitored and controlled in effecting energy-saving measures. The object of energy conservation is not to reduce the number of teaching aids but rather to make certain that power is not expended uselessly.

Other Uses of Energy in School Buildings

In addition to the major uses of energy in a school facility mentioned earlier, there are a few less obvious energy needs that are worthy of note. In most states, elevators are required for the physically handicapped. The custodial workshop is often equipped with various types of power tools. The physical education area may have equipment for washing and drying towels as well as electrically powered whirlpool baths and other related equipment. The entire school facility may be serviced by a public address system. Signaling devices such as bells, chimes, and fire and smoke alarms are all users of energy, albeit the amount of power consumed is quite small.

Although the transportation of students is not considered part of a school facility, the amount of energy consumed by this school service is enormous indeed. Except for the New England states, most school districts in the country own and operate their own school buses. It is not within the scope of this book to discuss this educational service. Suffice it to say, however, that school officials and boards of education can save a substantial amount of energy by streamlining bus routes, reducing the number of bus stops, improving bus maintenance, and operating each vehicle at optimum speed and capacity.

A STEP BY STEP APPROACH TO ENERGY CONSERVATION

Energy conservation will not just happen. It must be planned as a series of sequentially related steps. The techniques for conserving energy range from measures that are simple and inexpensive to those that are more extensive, more costly, and more technical. Unfortunately, the specific measures or changes that lead to energy conservation are not always obvious. Consequently, some kind of systematic examination of a given school facility is required in order to determine the exact nature of the changes that promise to conserve energy. Such a study would also include a cost analysis of such changes and what effect they are likely to have on the educational function. Several questions must be raised before any energy conservation action is taken: "Does the proposed action interfere with the educational process in any way?" "Does the proposed action create an atmosphere that is not conducive to learning?" "Is the proposed action really energy-effective?" "Is the proposed action cost-effective?" A "no" answer to one or more of the preceding questions denotes that the proposed energy-saving action may not be in the best interest of the school district from the standpoint of economic efficiency, educational impact, or the well-being of students and teachers. Energy conservation should not outweigh educational function or the healthfulness of a school building. Let us cite a typical situation to show the need for balance between energy conservation and healthfulness. In order to save energy in an elementary school built in 1912, the board of education proposed that the temperature in each of the eight classrooms be reduced from 75° Fahrenheit to 68°. An examination of the building revealed that all of the window sashes were loose and there was high infiltration of air through the wooden sheathing on the lower walls. The rooms were noticeably drafty on cold wintry days, and when the wind was blowing it was almost impossible to maintain a uniform temperature throughout the classroom. While the obvious saving in energy looked very attractive, the consequences of changing the thermostat setting from 75° to 68° were not entirely positive. Realistically, this change could threaten the health of some of the students occupying the classroom. It could induce a level of discomfort that would reduce the efficiency of learning and decrease the effectiveness of the teacher. Consequently, although the proposed change would appear to be cost-effective, it would not satisfy the basic requirements of healthfulness and educational soundness.

A step-by-step approach to energy conservation is outlined in this chapter. A detailed description of each step, together with numerous forms and checklists, can be found in the *Energy Sourcebook for Educational Facilities* published by the Council of Educational Facility Planners.[3] This publication is one of the most comprehensive and authentic sources of information about energy conservation in school facilities. It is well organized, lucid, practical in design, and extensive in coverage. For the convenience of the reader, the sequence of steps presented here follows the same order as that which appears in the *Energy Sourcebook*.

In most situations, the plan of action for energy conservation consists of four sequentially interlocking parts ranging from the simple to the more complex. The first step is a preliminary energy conservation survey which is conducted by local school maintenance and operation personnel. This study deals with energy conservation matters that are relatively uncomplicated and that can be put into effect by the local staff without further technical training. The second step is a little more technical. Local personnel assemble all of the physical data about a given building and send them to a computer center. These data are then fed into a computer that is programmed to yield various types of energy information through the use of a model building similar to the actual school building from which the data were obtained. In this step, energy gains and losses are quantified and energy costs are determined. The third step calls for a two- or three-hour inspection of a school building by various types of engineers and architects. The suggested energy-saving measures recommended by this team of experts may be quite sophisticated and quite technical. There is very little quantification of cost data and energy savings by this team. In a sense, it is somewhat similar to the preliminary energy survey, except that it is conducted by a team of experts. The fourth step is conducted by a team of experts over an extended period of time. A large amount of technical data is assembled and many types of calculations are made to support a wide variety of recommendations. Each of these four steps is discussed in detail in the following sections.

Step One–The Preliminary Energy Survey

A team of local school staff is organized to conduct a preliminary survey of a given school building. This team is usually made up of a representative from the administrative office, such as the director of building maintenance and operation, or equivalent, and the maintenance and custodial staff of the building being surveyed. Similar groups are established to survey each school building in the district. The organization and structure of the energy survey teams for each school are designed to facilitate the implementation of desirable energy conservation measures. These teams accumulate a wide variety of practical information about energy conservation. They become highly knowledgeable groups who can provide the basic data for some of the more technical energy audits that may be conducted at a later date for every school building in the school district. The primary responsibility of each school team, however, is to recommend and implement energy-saving measures that are relatively simple to execute. These measures often require little or no capital outlay funds. And finally, since each school team has been involved in the energy conservation program from the time of the program's initiation, they are well informed about the various techniques associated with energy conservation. Furthermore, they will be in a better position to implement energy-saving measures that are more complex and comprehensive in nature than those introduced in step one, if and when a more sophisticated energy audit is made by experts at a later date. In completing step one, it is suggested that the team use the comprehensive checklist for conducting a preliminary energy survey found in the *Energy Sourcebook for Educational Facilities.*

Step Two–Computer Simulation Analysis

For a nominal fee, the energy characteristics of a real school building can be analyzed by a computer under simulated conditions. The principle underlying this technique is not particularly mysterious or complicated. The characteristics of a real building are compared with the known characteristics of a model building that are programmed into the computer. Several models have been developed by the Educational Facilities Laboratory in California. These models simulate buildings that were constructed during specified periods of time, such as those built before World War II and after 1945. Within the groupings, the computer models are further classified as to shape, construction, and mechanical systems. The models are also categorized as to whether they are elementary schools or secondary schools. This technique is also called "PSECS (Public Schools Energy Conservation Service)—Computer Simulated Model." The address is available in the *Energy Sourcebook.*

The characteristics of the real building are entered into the computer, which, in turn, compares the real situation with that of the appropriate model programmed into the computer. The computer printout does not list individual energy-saving measures, nor does it specify any saving that would result from each measure. It does, however, state potential energy savings that could be expected in the real building as a percent of current costs. For example, the computer printout would *not* show that if all of the single-pane glass in a school building were replaced by insulating glass the saving would be a certain number of dollars. It would indicate that it would be possible to save a certain percentage of the cost currently expended for energy in the real building if an energy audit of the building were made and the energy conservation measures were implemented. These limitations apply only to the PSECS analysis mentioned as a second step in approaching the energy-saving problem. Stated differently, for a nominal fee, the PSECS method would indicate how close to the ideal model the real building is performing with respect to energy conservation. If the real building has been ideally retrofitted, for example, the PSECS report would simply show that the expected savings in that particular building were negligible. In practice, however, PSECS would not be applied to a retrofitted building. Rather, it would be employed as a second step in the energy conservation program. To be sure, the results of the PSECS could be instrumental in the ultimate retrofitting of a given school facility if additional studies show that retrofitting is warranted.

There are other applications of the Computer Simulated Model in making an energy analysis of a real school building. However, the data for this more sophisticated analysis are quite technical and complex. It is usually provided by several professional engineers and an architect who make studies in depth of school facilities scheduled for retrofitting. In this application, the computer provides specific information regarding expected energy savings, cost of retrofitting, and pay-back periods. This approach will be discussed in step four, "The Maxi-Audit." Suffice it to say at this point that the PSECS report is intended to show potential overall savings in energy, if any, through the use of energy conservation measures. It is *not* designed to provide any kind of detailed analysis of specific needs. The PSECS report can be invaluable to school officials because it can indicate whether or not further study and analysis of a given building is warranted, from the standpoint of energy conservation.

Step Three—The Mini-Audit

Let us review what has been accomplished in steps one and two. In the first step, a team of local staff members, knowledgeable in the maintenance and operation of school buildings, has attended workshops sponsored by the appropriate state and local agencies on energy conservation. Each team has acquired as much knowledge as possible on immediate steps that could be taken in order to conserve energy. Each team surveyed a school facility and made recommendations to school officials of the local school district on how energy could be conserved. Some, if not all, of these recommendations have been implemented for each school surveyed. Secondly, this knowledgeable team has assembled accurate and detailed information that has been recorded on the appropriate forms and submitted to the Educational Facilities Laboratories, under the PSECS program. A report has been received by the local school district that additional energy savings are possible in certain school buildings in the district. The potential magnitude of these savings has also been included in these reports. On the basis of this information, local school officials have selected a few school buildings where substantial savings in energy could still be made. These officials have also made a study of whether or not these selected school buildings are part of the long-range school facility needs of the district. As a result of a comprehensive study by school officials and the board of education, a decision has been made to take additional steps to conserve energy in certain school buildings. The local maintenance and operational staff has taken every conservation measure within its level of expertise and budgetary limitations. There is computer-generated information to indicate that sizable potential savings in energy and tax dollars can be made in certain school buildings in the district. Thus, the board of education has authorized school officials to study the matter further and return to it with recommendations. They have approved a "mini-audit" of selected school facilities in the school district.

The "mini-audit" is a sound and well-conceived third step in meeting the urgent and pressing need of saving energy as well as public funds. The mini-audit is conducted by a small number of highly trained professionals over a short period of time. This team of professionals usually consists of a structural engineer, a heating and ventilating engineer, an architect, and a representative from the utility company. This group, together with one or two school administrators, walk through a given building over a period of two or three hours, concentrating primarily on two aspects of energy conservation. They focus on measures that can be accomplished quickly and on those that are not costly, such as operational practices, eliminating unnecessary energy-consuming equipment, and reduction of light intensities in certain areas. This team also searches for ways and means of reducing energy consumption that can be accomplished easily and with relatively small amounts of capital outlay. For example, the hot water supply system may be separated from the main boiler, so that the school boilers could be shut down earlier in the school year and be fired-up at a later time. This recommendation would involve some expenditure of funds, but it would save a considerable amount of costly energy during late spring, summer (if the building is used), and early fall.

There are several reasons underlying the use of a mini-audit. First, the overall cost is reasonable and has the potential of being highly cost-effective. Secondly, the team consists of experts that are not readily available in most school districts. Thirdly, this audit is an extension of the one conducted in step one by local school personnel. In the mini-audit, the survey includes high-level technical expertise not available in step one. In both instances, however, energy-saving measures that are feasible and not too costly are recommended. It seems natural, systematic, and logical that the process related to energy conservation should be a continuum that ranges from the simple to the more complex and from the least expensive measures to those of greater magnitude and cost.

Step Four–The Maxi-Audit

The maxi-audit is the *sine qua non* of retrofitting an existing school building in cases where substantial amounts of capital outlay funds are required. Relatively inexpensive retrofitting measures such as adding insulation, caulking doors and window frames, and installing clock-controlled thermostats may be taken at any time. Extensive retrofitting may be partial or comprehensive.

In either instance such action should be the direct result of a maxi-audit. The maxi-audit is generally conducted by a competent and experienced engineering and architectural firm, which has a team of experts in the fields of architecture; structural engineering; heating, cooling and ventilating engineering; electrical engineering; and solar energy engineering. Care should be exercised in selecting a consulting firm. It is extremely important that the qualifications of each chief professional person whose expertise is required for the audit be thoroughly scrutinized. Not every architectural or engineering firm is capable of conducting a maxi-audit. The cost is relatively high, and a school district would be well advised to consider several firms. It is suggested that the same procedure described in Chapter 6 for the selection of an architect for the planning of a school facility be employed in choosing a consultant firm to conduct a maxi-audit for the school district.

The maxi-audit is a comprehensive, methodical, expert investigation of the energy characteristics of an educational facility. This in-depth energy study is extensive; detailed and cost estimates are geared to the cost of labor and materials prevalent where the building is located. Besides the building, the maxi-audit includes a close examination of the educational uses of energy, such as audiovisual equipment, auto-tutorial aids, shop machinery, homemaking appliances, typewriters, business machines, and kilns. The pattern of power usage in the entire school facility is examined very closely from the standpoint of energy conservation. Also, the possibility of using a piece of equipment more efficiently and at maximum capacity is explored in every instance, such as operating dishwashers with a full, rather than partial, load. These are only a few glimpses of the type of investigation that is required by the consulting firm that conducts a maxi-audit for a school district.

The maxi-audit differs enormously from any of the approaches to energy conservation mentioned thus far in one major respect. It is an accurately *quantified,* scientific investigation of the energy characteristics of an educational facility, including every type of energy use found in the building, on the school site, and off the school site in the transportation of students to and from school. The quantification of energy savings is an invaluable piece of information for school officials and the board of education in assessing energy conservation measures. This detailed information enables them to make intelligent decisions regarding the expenditure of capital funds for retrofitting a school building. One of the most important end products of the maxi-audit is a cost analysis of the pay-back period required to retrieve the cost of capital outlay and interest through the savings in energy brought about by a recommended capital outlay expenditure.

The energy consultant provides a wide variety of data. It includes a description of the existing pattern of energy consumption and current unit costs for each major energy use within the building. The consultant prepares and submits a considerable number of energy-conserving recommendations. Each recommendation has a price tag attached to it, together with a realistic financial analysis of each aspect of the recommendation. The information submitted with each energy-saving recommendation includes the anticipated annual reduction in energy consumption, cost savings per year, cost of capital outlay required to implement the recommendation, length of the pay-back period, and the priority of a given recommendation among the other items recommended.

The cost of a maxi-audit is not modest. It represents a substantial initial investment that has the potential of returning savings that are many times the initial cost over the remaining life of a school building. Despite the cost, there is really no other way of obtaining the information required for retrofitting an existing building. The cost of a maxi-audit is fully justified, however. First of all, the audit must be conducted by highly trained, competent, and experienced architects and engineers. Secondly, the work required by these experts is often greater than that which would be required if this same team were asked to design a new building of the same size and shape as the existing facility. In designing a new building, the team makes all of the required computations for achieving maximum energy efficiency. These computations involve all forms of energy to be consumed in the building, such as lighting, heating, cooling, mechanical equipment, appliances, and electronic devices of various and sundry types. In conducting a maxi-audit, these same computations and studies must be performed for an existing building. This aspect of the maxi-audit addresses itself to the question, "How much energy, of the various types, would be required to operate the existing structure under optimum conditions?" Obtaining the answer to this question is time-consuming and relatively complicated. But, in a maxi-audit, the answer is only the beginning. Phase two of the maxi-audit represents another segment of the study, which involves a high level of creativity and expertise and requires a great deal of time on the part of the team experts. The question to be answered in phase two is, "In what ways can the existing building, equipment, and pattern of energy use be modified in order to conserve energy?" This phase demands a concentrated study of the use and operation of the building and calls for an extended period of observation by the team of experts. As can well be imagined, phase two takes considerable time. It is time that would not be spent on the planning of a new building. The maxi-audit includes phase three which develops the data obtained in phase two and compares the information with the corresponding information prepared under phase one. The question to be answered in phase three is, "What energy-saving measures are feasible, how much will it cost to implement them, and what is the pay-back period for each one of them?" The response to this question is highly technical, fiscally oriented, and broadly based. More specifically, the consultants must look at all alternatives for each recommended measure and select the one that seems most appropriate. They must make detailed cost studies of capital outlay funds and interest needed to effect the recommended changes. And they must compute the anticipated amount of energy saved by each recommendation, convert these energy savings into dollar savings and estimate the number of years needed to compensate the school district for the funds expended to implement the proposed energy-saving measure. All of this work takes time and costs money for the services of the team of experts. In view of the extensive nature of the maxi-audit, it can be an expensive venture for a school district. But it can also be one of the most rewarding investments a school district makes. If the savings in the cost of energy to the school district are quite substantial, the pay-back period for the cost of the maxi-audit can be very short, indeed. But the school district will never know this for sure until a maxi-audit is completed!

ENERGY CONSERVATION THROUGH RETROFITTING

The word "retrofitting," mentioned earlier, has been recently added to the English language. Perhaps the best way to define it, in relation to energy conservation, is "the act of modifying an existing structure in a manner that would result in the saving of energy." From another point of view, retrofitting could be envisioned as changing an existing building that consumes energy liberally and wastefully to one that makes optimal use of energy and conserves it as much as possible. Perhaps the term retrofitting could be further clarified by asking a question. "What cost-effective changes can be made to an existing building and its equipment today that will conserve energy for the remaining useful life of the building?"

Retrofitting is often a costly and highly technical undertaking. It is strongly recommended that a maxi-audit be completed before any funds are committed to a retrofitting program. The board of education and school officials should know in advance what the pay-back period is for each measure. A 10-year pay-back period is generally considered a good investment of public funds. Longer pay-back periods are also justifiable if the savings in cost of energy is relatively high. For example, if it costs $100,000, including interest, to replace all the windows and doors with insulating glass, and if the savings in the cost of energy are $10,000 per year, the pay-back period is 10 years. This $100,000 capital outlay expenditure would be an excellent investment on the part of the school district. After 10 years, the $10,000 saving would continue to accrue to the school district if the cost of energy did not change. On the other hand, if the annual energy savings were only $5,000, the pay-back period would be 20 years. In this case, the economic benefits would not be as attractive as the 10-year pay-back period, but the national goal of conserving energy would still make such retrofitting quite desirable.

Retrofitting a school building should be done on a priority basis. A maxi-audit will recommend an order of priority. Usually, those measures that have the shortest pay-back periods are given the highest priority. In some instances, measures that require a large expenditure of capital outlay funds initially may have the shortest pay-back periods. For this reason, initial costs should not automatically override other considerations. Retrofitting should be done with the same thoroughness that is exercised in the construction of a new school building. The project should be clearly defined. The architect and engineers should be selected with care. Specifications should be prepared by the architect and engineers and the project should be bid in accordance with the procedures discussed in Chapter 16.

Retrofitting varies greatly from school building to school building. For this reason, it is felt that a maxi-audit is absolutely necessary if a school district is to expend public funds wisely in retrofitting a school facility. No attempt will be made to describe the multitude of forms that retrofitting may assume. It is suggested, however, that the *Energy Sourcebook* be reviewed in this connection. It contains several examples of school buildings that have been retrofitted. It also mentions many individual modifications that can be made to conserve energy. In some of the examples described in the *Energy Sourcebook,* not only was energy saved through system and building modification, but energy was also gained by including passive solar energy features in the retrofitting project.

Common Elements in the Art of Retrofitting

A wide variety of energy conservation techniques are employed in retrofitting school buildings. They range from simple and inexpensive measures to those that are more complex and costly. They differ from situation to situation. They vary from engineer to engineer. And they are different from one climatic region to another. Despite these differences, however, there are also similarities in the art of retrofitting that tend to simplify the task of coping with energy conservation measures. These common elements include the selection of energy-efficient equipment, the reduction of energy losses or heat gains through the exterior surfaces of the structure, the recovery of energy that would otherwise be lost to the atmosphere, and the prevention of energy waste due to lack of proper controls and monitoring procedures.

These common elements are mentioned here briefly. They are, however, described and discussed in greater detail in the next section. Since the primary goal of retrofitting is to make existing buildings more energy efficient, it follows that any technique or action that promotes energy conservation in new facilities is equally beneficial in retrofitting existing school buildings.

Heating, Cooling, and Ventilation. The efficiency of heating, cooling, and ventilating equipment is a major consideration in any retrofitting program. Each unit must be capable of extracting the maximum amount of utility, usefulness, and serviceability for each unit of energy that is supplied to the unit. Thus, every effort should be made to select heating, cooling, and ventilating equipment that is highly efficient from the standpoint of energy consumption.

Artificial Lighting. During the process of retrofitting, artificial lighting provides fertile ground for conserving energy in school buildings. Fixtures should be selected on the basis of minimum energy consumption per lumen of light produced. Also the intensity of light falling on the task of students engaged in learning activities should be kept at a reasonably high minimum. The light intensities provided in recently constructed schools is far above that which is needed for good seeing conditions.

Air Infiltration. The elimination of the infiltration of air from the outside to the inside of a school building is of paramount importance with respect to energy conservation. In some of the older buildings, not only does air infiltrate around windows and doors, but also through the walls themselves, particularly around loose mortar between bricks.

Energy Distribution and Its Control. Generally, two forms of energy are widely distributed throughout a school building. They are heat and electricity. Electric power is available everywhere in the building. Heat is also supplied to all parts of the building occupied by teachers and students and in a lesser amount to spaces where temperatures must be maintained a little above 32° Fahrenheit so that water pipes will not freeze.

In many of the more recently constructed school buildings, the distribution of heat among the various parts of the building is fairly well controlled on a room-by-room basis. Some areas are still overheated due to the proximity of these spaces to major pipe lines. In the older buildings that are more likely to be retrofitted, such controlled distribution of heat is either nonexistent or not very effective. Consequently, a considerable amount of heat energy is wasted when these buildings are in use or because heat cannot be properly controlled throughout the building. There is also a waste of heat in these buildings when they are not in use, because certain spaces receive heat regardless of the need for it.

The distribution of electrical energy throughout a building presents no problem, but its control from a central point leaves much to be desired, particularly in older school buildings. In many cases, it is almost impossible for the custodian to make certain that all outlets are not consuming energy uselessly without disconnecting power from major parts of the building. The obvious solution to this problem lies in the installation of low-voltage switching devices which readily lend themselves to centralized control. Under this system a panel of signal lights would indicate where electric power is being supplied in all parts of the school building at any given time.

PLANNING ENERGY EFFICIENT
SCHOOL BUILDINGS

As mentioned earlier, the world faces the inevitable depletion of its fossil energy reserves. Conservation is needed not only to extend our present supply of energy but also to soften the economic impact that the increasing cost of energy is having on school budgets throughout the United States. In attempting to conserve energy, however, care must be exercised to make certain that all conservation measures really save energy. Some of them may appear to be very attractive and appealing at first glance. But, upon further study and consideration, they may actually waste more energy than they purportedly save. On the other hand, there are many energy-saving measures that are sound and stand the test of scientific analysis. Both false and real energy conservation measures are discussed in this section.

Questionable Energy Conservation Practices

1. *Reducing the weekly use of a school building.* Various plans have been advanced by boards of education and school officials to reduce energy consumption by rescheduling the use of educational facilities. Under one plan, schools would be closed entirely for a four- or five-week period during the coldest part of the winter and the school year would be extended into the summer for an equal length of time. Another proposal would operate the schools four days per week and extend the time for each of the four days to compensate for the lost day. In this plan, school buildings would be closed from the end of the school day on Thursday until the following Monday morning. To be sure, the cost of energy consumed in a school building can be substantially reduced by these measures, but does it really conserve energy within the boundaries of the school district? There is reason to believe that closing school buildings may actually waste energy in some situations. If the net gain or loss in energy consumption is measured *within the boundaries of the school district* rather than within the boundaries of the school site, the conclusion may be quite surprising.[4]

A hypothetical case illustrates the questionable nature of the four-day school week from the standpoint of energy conservation. Let us assume that a school district has an enrollment of 2,000 students and that the board of education has introduced a four-day school week and increased the length of each of the four days to compensate for the time lost on Friday. Under this plan, all of the school buildings could be set on "low heat" from Thursday evening to Monday morning. Beyond any doubt, the amount of energy saved *on the school site* would be substantial and measurable. This represents an impressive plus for the school budget. Let us now look at the negative side of this alleged energy-saving measure. What happens to the 2,000 students who are not in school on Friday? It can be assumed that most of them will be home on these cold days. Many students will be at home watching television, cooking snacks, and consuming energy. Some of them will be in their room with the thermostat raised a little, the lights turned on and consuming energy. And some of the high school students will be driving their automobiles and consuming fuel. When the additional consumption of energy by these 2,000 students on their Friday holiday is compared to the amount of energy saved in the school buildings, studies reported by Denning and LeBlanc suggest that, on the whole, it is highly probable that the total increase in energy consumption within the boundaries of the school district due to the Friday holiday will exceed the amount of energy saved on the school site.[5] This would represent an *energy loss* within the boundaries of the school district as a result of the Friday holiday. The burden of the cost of energy for the Friday holiday is simply shifted from the school to the parents of the 2,000 students enrolled in the school. No useful purpose would be accomplished by this kind of "energy-saving" measure.

On the other hand, real savings could be effected if a school facility were planned initially for maximum energy conservation. Educational services could be maintained at optimum levels and the cost of supplying energy to a school building could be held at a minimum. This approach is realistic in function, promising in concept, and effective in economic efficiency.

2. *Reduction in educational services.* Some school districts have seriously considered closing the school building promptly at the end of the school day during the cold winter months. In these instances, students would be deprived of extra help from teachers and the use of library and other school facilities. Some students might not be able to participate in extracurricular and athletic activities.

Under close scrutiny, it is questionable whether or not this practice would result in any noticeable savings in the energy budget at the end of the year. And even if some savings were effected, would the amount of money saved compensate for the loss of educational opportunities suffered by the students? This energy-saving measure and others like it should be carefully examined relative to educational values lost and the number of dollars gained, if any.

Sound Energy Conservation Practices

There are several effective and well-founded techniques for keeping the amount of energy consumed in a school facility to a minimum. Each one is presented from the standpoint of energy conservation. It is realized, of course, that it may not be possible to implement all of them in all cases. It is hoped, however, that this list of techniques will serve to stimulate the creative thinking of educational facility planners in designing school buildings that are both educationally effective and energy efficient.

1. *Shaping the building.* Heat loss or gain is directly proportional to the total area of the walls, floors, and ceilings of a structure. Theoretically, the external surface area should be kept at a minimum. A sphere meets this requirement. It contains maximum volume within minimum exterior surface. For obvious reasons, a spherical school building, though possible, is not too practical. The most practical shape that provides maximum volume with a minimum of exterior surface is the cube.

In view of the foregoing considerations, the ideal shape of a school building from the standpoint of energy conservation is one consisting of a large cube or a combination of varying sizes joined together to form a single, contiguous structure. Consequently, the long and narrow, single-storied buildings of yesteryear should be avoided. The high-rise tower building is not consistent with the principle described above. Neither is it desirable to design a building with jogs or indentations. Not only is this practice wasteful in energy but it is uneconomical to construct. A building constructed in the shape of a hemisphere could be considered if there were some ingenious way of utilizing the odd-shaped spaces along the curved walls. Perhaps some creative architect may find a practical solution to this problem and design a structure that is efficient both in space utilization and in the conservation of energy.

2. *Orienting the building.* For maximum absorption of passive heating from the sun, one side of the building should face east and the other side should face west. The south wall should also be exposed to the sun. Care should be taken to control heat gain in the summer and permit maximum energy gain from the sun in the winter.

Whenever possible, passive solar heating features should be designed into the building. These characteristics are discussed later in this chapter, but the orientation of the building should be such that passive solar heating can become an important part of the heating system of the school building.

3. *Insulating the building.* It is a well-known principle of physics that the conductivity of heat varies from substance to substance. From the standpoint of energy conservation, the transmission of heat from one side of a wall or window to the other should be held to a minimum. The transfer of heat from within the building to its exterior through roofs, basements, and walls should be kept as low as possible.

Our present perceptions of brick and concrete should be reexamined. Indeed, from the standpoint of maintenance and durability these materials are economical, functional, and desirable. But in terms of thermal efficiency, looks are deceiving. Visually, it would appear that brick, mortar, and concrete are good insulators of heat. Quite the opposite is true. In fact, heat travels through concrete nine times as fast as it does through an equal thickness and area of wood. And stone conducts heat about 20 times as fast as wood. In other words, a wooden board 1 inch thick is thermally equivalent to concrete 9 inches thick and to a stone wall 20 inches thick. It is not suggested that stone and concrete be abolished in the construction of school buildings, but simply to point out that these materials are not good heat insulators despite their massive appearance. When these materials are used, they should be lined with highly insulating substances, such as fiberglass and insulating panels. Wood, on the other hand, is a good insulator and may have a wider application in school construction, particularly in areas where wood is plentiful. The penalty for using wood, however, is its relatively high cost of maintenance. The architect is in an excellent position to advise school officials as to the best balance between the use of wood and concrete.

Materials of construction should be chosen so that heat losses from the building to the atmosphere in the winter and heat gains from the atmosphere into the building in the summer are kept at a minimum. Exterior walls and ceilings exposed to cold attics should be heavily insulated. The amount of glass on the north side of the building should be reduced as much as possible but not below that required for good seeing conditions through the use of natural light. Basements should be designed so that the heat transfer between the building and the earth is as low as possible.

4. *Selecting and installing windows and doors properly.* The loss or gain of energy within a school building is greatly affected by the design, construction, and method of installation of windows, doors, and ventilation units. Unless special precautions are taken in the selection and proper installation of doors, windows, and ventilation units, the transfer of heat through these openings by conduction and by the infiltration of air could result in substantial losses of costly energy.

Conduction of Heat Energy Through Windows and Doors.   Windows and doors should be designed to severely impede the flow of heat from one side to the other. Since windows must be constructed of transparent substances such as glass or special plastics, the choice of materials is quite limited. However, great strides have been made by the glass industry in restricting the flow of heat through windows by providing alternate layers of glass and air in a sandwich-like panel of glass or plastic sheets. Ideally, a vacuum between two sheets of glass separated by one centimeter (about one-half inch) would effectively impede the flow of heat through the window by conduction. Technologically, it is impractical to construct such a window panel due to the tremendous force of the atmospheric pressure on both sides of the panel tending to shatter the glass into the evacuated space between each sheet. Thus, the glass industry has created an acceptable substitute that is relatively easy to produce but which is not as thermally efficient as the ideal situation described above. Insulating glass, as it is called, consists of two sheets of glass separated by about one centimeter of moisture-free air or nitrogen and is sealed along the edges. Such glass panels are also produced with two layers of gas separated by three sheets of glass. In this case, the window panel would consist of an outer sheet of glass followed by a layer of dried air or dried nitrogen, then another sheet of glass, followed by a second layer of gas and covered on the other side by another sheet of glass. This combination of alternate layers of glass and gas effectively impedes the flow of heat through the panel and conserves energy.

The construction of insulated doors is much simpler than that described above for windows from the standpoint of heat transmission. First of all, doors need not necessarily be transparent. Thus, the choice of materials of construction is less restrictive. Weight and thickness of doors is somewhat less stringent than that for windows. Consequently, the door industry has produced a wide variety of insulating doors from light, hollow doors filled with insulating materials, to the more massive solid doors which are fabricated from highly insulating substances. If a door requires that a person should be able to see through it for safety reasons, small panels of insulating glass can be installed at the proper height to meet this specification. Thus, from the standpoint of energy conservation, all exterior doors in a school building should have the capacity of severely impeding the flow of heat from one side to the other.

Infiltration of Air Around Windows and Doors and Ventilation Units. In any building, substantial amounts of heat are transmitted through the infiltration of air around the perimeter of windows, doors, and ventilation units. In general, there are two major sources of infiltration. One is around the window sash, the door, or the cover of ventilation units; that is, the element that opens and closes. This source can be effectively corrected by specially designed edges of windows, doors, and covers and by the use of weather-stripping. The other source of infiltration is also around the perimeter of windows, doors, and ventilation units, but it occurs at the interfacing of the frame within which the window, door, or cover is mounted, and the building itself. This source of infiltration of air can often be remedied by properly installing the frames that are specially designed to keep the infiltration of air at a minimum, and by caulking the edges where the frames interface with the building. The caulking material should be vermin-proof, long-lasting, weather-resistant, and capable of withstanding a fairly wide range of temperature changes without cracking or crumbling.

5. *Selecting efficient heating, cooling, and ventilating equipment.* The heating and cooling of school buildings is accomplished by converting one form of energy to another through the use of an appropriate contrivance. Fuel is one form of energy that can be burned on the site to produce heating and cooling for the building. Or energy produced offsite in the form of electricity can be transported to the school building and then be transformed into heating and cooling. The contrivance commonly used to convert fuel directly into heat is the boiler or furnace. Electricity, on the other hand, can be transformed into heat by the resistance method (heating coils) or by a heat pump. Cooling is usually produced either by a diffusion process utilizing high pressure steam or by a heat pump which is powered by electricity.

Some type of specially designed contrivance is necessary to convert fuel or energy from one form to another. While the heating and cooling industry is experimenting with a number of more sophisticated contrivances designed to conserve energy, the boiler and the heat pump are still the major practical contrivances for generating heat or cooling. Thus, in designing a heating and cooling system for energy conservation, special care should be exercised to specify the contrivance that has the highest energy output for a given input of energy. The more efficient the contrivance, the less fuel or electricity consumed to produce a given result and the more energy conserved in the process. The continued improvement of heat pumps holds much promise for the future with respect to energy conservation. The contrivance itself is simply a machine that moves heat from one location to another. The electricity consumed by this machine is not directly converted into heating or cooling. It simply powers the pump which moves heat from the ground or atmosphere into the building during cold weather or transports heat from within the building to the ground or atmosphere during warm weather. Consequently, the efficiency of the heat pump can be far greater than that resulting from other means of converting energy into heating or cooling.

Ventilation is another important aspect of energy conservation. The amount of fresh air required per student per hour in the past can be substantially reduced in most instances. In some states the amount of fresh air required per student is modest, realistic, and economically justifiable. These states specify 10 cubic feet per minute per occupant when the outside temperature is above 35° Fahrenheit, and no fresh air is required for temperatures below 35°. In these instances, the lower volume of air required per student reduces the amount of energy needed for ventilation.

The efficiency of heating, cooling, and ventilating equipment is a major consideration in energy conservation. Ideally, the maximum amount of usable energy should be extracted from the amount of available energy supplied to a given school facility. Hence, when the source of energy is intended to heat the building, all of it should be utilized for that purpose. Electrical heating most closely approaches this ideal. When resistance electrical heating is used, all of the energy purchased provides heat for the building, except when the transformers and meters are placed outside of the building. When various fuels are used for heating, the efficiency of the boiler and heat distribution systems can greatly affect the amount of heat that actually reaches the spaces where such heat is required. This reduction stems from two causes. A certain amount of heat is lost through the stack in the combustion process, and cold air from the outside is needed to support the combustion. During this necessary and essential chemical action, the outside air tends to cool the heating equipment. And finally, when heat is transmitted from the boiler room to the classrooms, for example, some of it is lost en route where it is not needed or wanted. Cooling, heating, and ventilating equipment does not always use energy efficiently. For this reason, care should be exercised in selecting equipment that possesses a high energy efficiency rating.

6. *Utilizing electric power efficiently.* The major part of the electrical energy consumed within a school building for purposes other than heating or cooling is attributable to artificial lighting and to the operation of mechanical equipment associated with the heating and cooling of the school building.

The proper design of an artificial lighting system provides fertile ground for conserving energy in a school building. First of all, the number of foot-candles of light intensity striking the task of students engaged in learning activities in school has been raised continually since the end of World War II. When energy was inexpensive, the increase of intensity of light in classrooms from 30 foot-candles to 70 or 80 foot-candles was not a major cause for concern. The research conducted by various groups of lighting engineers was well done, in most cases, but the nature of the tasks for which the various light intensities were applied tended to be focused on specialized activities that occupied only a small part of the curriculum of the student. And, as long as energy was still quite inexpensive, increases in the overall intensity of light in a classroom presented no real problem. Today, the situation is quite different. The question that is posed for educators and school boards due to circumstances beyond their control is, "What is the minimum intensity of classroom illumination that is healthful and provides a good visual environment for the tasks normally performed in the teaching-learning process?" With this objective in mind, it can be seen that the intensity of high-quality light at the task level of the student could be reduced to 30 foot-candles in regular classrooms. It is well known that the acuity of elementary and secondary age level students is very high. Hence, high light intensities are not needed for such students. To be sure, if the same spaces are to be used for educating the elderly, a higher intensity of light is needed. However, in view of the energy crisis, it might be well to plan certain spaces for use by both young people and adults and to design others for young people only. In spaces for both young and old, additional lighting could be switched on when adults are occupying the space. Otherwise, the 30-foot-candle intensity could be maintained when the regular school was in session.

7. *Controlling energy distribution effectively.* Both electrical and heat energy should be readily available in sufficient quantity at any location in a school building where it is needed at a given time. Conversely, energy should not be supplied and consumed in any part of the building where it is not required. These two considerations suggest that a sophisticated system of control in the distribution of electricity and heat (also cooling) be made an integral part in the design of the building. Such controls can be provided at a relatively small additional cost through the use of remote relays and controls activated by a low-voltage wiring network or by a low-powered radio transmitter within the building. The controls can be activated by the custodian from a central location, perhaps near the boiler room. Also, clock mechanisms can control energy availability at various points in the school. There is one drawback in the use of clock controls, however. Power outages also stop clock movements that are not battery operated. This, in turn, changes the real time at which such clocks turn the energy on and off. Consequently, these clocks need constant monitoring by school personnel who may find it necessary to reset them from time to time.

Control over the temperature of hot water is another way of saving energy. Rather than allowing the individual mixing of hot water with cold water at every point of usage, it might be advantageous to supply hot water to each faucet at a temperature that requires little or no mixing with cold water. In widespread, strung-out buildings, this arrangement may be somewhat more difficult to achieve, but special consideration should be given to devise ways of conserving energy by controlling waste of hot water. Such waste often occurs when the temperature of the water at the mixing faucet is higher than needed or when the hot water faucet is left partially open. Even in large buildings, it might be possible to bring relatively long hot water lines close to a point of usage and mix hot and cold water centrally at that point, so that water flowing from the hot water spigots, in toilet rooms, for example, is at the proper temperature for hand washing.

8. *Recovering normally wasted energy.* School plant planners should always be on the alert for ways and means of recapturing heat that may be lost to the atmosphere or ground. For example, a certain amount of fresh air is required to ventilate classrooms. Normally, warm air inside of the building would be exhausted in order to provide space for the fresh air. Some architects exhaust the warm air through spaces above the ceiling in order to minimize the loss of heat from the classroom through the ceiling. If the plenum chamber is used to distribute air throughout the building, the heat from the exhausted air could be exchanged with the fresh cold air being drawn into the building. In this way, the heat from the exhausted air could be recovered and transferred back to the classroom while the so-called stale air could be exhausted—minus heat.

There are often spaces within a school building that are unavoidably hot, such as boiler rooms, kitchens, pipe trenches for heating pipes, and foods laboratories. This excess heat is ultimately dissipated through the walls and by natural infiltration. It might be worthwhile to design a school facility so that this excess heat could be redistributed to other parts of the building. This feature would make it possible to reduce the temperature to comfortable levels in areas where excess heat is generated or accumulated and transfer this excess energy to other parts of the building where it is needed. Thus, energy that is normally wasted would be recovered.

9. *Exploiting humidity control to save energy.* Humidity control has been widely used to promote comfort within homes, schools, and other types of shelters. Humidification has not been used very extensively for the purpose of energy conservation. It is well known that human comfort within an enclosure is a function of both temperature and humidity. Discomfort occurs when both temperature and humidity are high. It is also recognized that the human body controls its comfort level and temperature through the process of perspiration. Discomfort sets in when the body cannot cool itself by the evaporation of perspiration due to high humidity.

The school plant planners of the future should utilize the effect of humidity on human comfort in an effort to save costly energy. During the heating season, the room temperature can be dropped and the level of humidity can be increased to the level of comfort for the occupants of the building. It is realized, of course, that the level of the humidity should be kept within limits so that furniture, doors, and equipment are not affected in any way. But even a temperature drop of three or four degrees Fahrenheit could produce substantial savings in the cost of energy in a school building over the heating season. The same principle could be applied to cooling. It might be possible to use dehumidifiers instead of air conditioners in certain areas and save the cost of energy to operate high-capacity condensers that are found in air-conditioning equipment.

PLANNING SCHOOL BUILDINGS FOR SOLAR ENERGY

The energy from the sun is free, but collecting it and putting it into practical use still costs a considerable amount of money. The outlook for solar energy is promising and very optimistic. The solar energy industry is making rapid strides in the development of more efficient and less costly solar energy systems. For this reason, all new school facilities should be designed and oriented so that solar energy systems can be incorporated into them at a later date.

A Brief Look at Solar Energy

It is indeed difficult to imagine the enormous amount of solar energy that reaches the surface of the earth every day. To be sure, the intensity of the solar energy is not uniform the world over. It varies from place to place, from day to day, and from hour to hour. But the accumulated amount of solar energy falling on one square foot of horizontal surface per day, even in February in the northern hemisphere, is surprisingly high in many parts of the world.

Looks are sometimes deceiving as we feel the pleasant and soothing warmth from the sun in a sheltered area even in the middle of the cold season. Under these circumstances, the sunshine looks gentle, pervasive, and innocuous. Actually, the light and heat produced by the nuclear furnace on the sun is very intense. In fact, it is so intense that the retina of the human eye can be burned and permanently damaged if one stares directly at the sun for any length of time.

Without getting deeply involved in the technical aspects of solar energy, it might be helpful to the reader to describe the active collecting of solar energy in more meaningful terms. Let us place one gallon of water in an insulated wooden box whose interior is painted black and is covered by a sheet of glass having an area of one square foot. Let us further assume that the box is level, has been exposed to the sun for a full day in February, has not lost any of its heat to the atmosphere, and is located out-of-doors in the northern United States. If the initial temperature of one gallon of water from a faucet was 40° Fahrenheit, the temperature of the water would have risen to 150° Fahrenheit at the end of a clear day! This idealized but realistic situation clearly shows that the amount of energy available from the sun annually is enormous. In extracting energy from the sun, however, allowances should be made for a variety of heat losses. In practice, the temperature of the gallon of water in our example would have lost a considerable amount of heat directly from the box to the atmosphere. An additional amount of heat would have been lost in transit while pumping the water from the box to the inside of the building, where it could be put to practical use. In this hypothetical situation, the temperature of the water reaching the inside of the building at the end of the day could conceivably have dropped to 78° Fahrenheit, which is still sufficiently high to heat a building.

Solar Energy Collectors.   Realistically, the efficiency of a commercially produced solar energy system is surprisingly high, but it varies with the ambient temperature of the atmosphere. Consequently, panel-type solar energy collectors are more efficient during periods of warm weather than they are in the winter months. But it must be remembered that, no matter how well solar energy systems are designed and engineered for efficiency, they cannot develop more energy than was available at our hypothetical box described above. But solar energy engineers have been very ingenious in capturing the energy from the sun. A few of the more advanced manufacturers of solar energy collectors have virtually created "solar energy traps." Once the energy enters the collector, very little escapes. The transfer of energy from the collector to some storage device within a building is accomplished with as little energy loss as possible. Sophisticated temperature devices control the rate of flow of water or air through the collector unit so that the temperature of the water or air returning to the building is as high as possible. The total area of the collectors is determined by the geographical location of the system. The area of the solar collectors may range from several hundred square feet for heating water to several thousand square feet for space heating. Although the technology underlying solar heating and cooling is well developed and scientifically sound, cost is still a formidable barrier to the widespread use of active solar energy systems. These systems are discussed in detail in the following section.

Photovoltaic Energy.   Within the past five years, the efficiency of photovoltaic cells has risen from 7 percent to 16 percent for crystalline silicon, the most widely used cell material. The still experimental gallium cells have an efficiency of 37 percent, but further research is needed to reduce their production cost.

The future of solar energy from photovoltaic cells is very promising. There are plans to develop 10-megawatt solar energy generators using photovoltaic cells before the end of this century. The efficiency of photovoltaic cells has been increasing steadily and new cell materials are being developed at several research centers. Photovoltaic energy has a great potential for reducing our dependence on energy from fossil fuels.

Windmill Farms.   Wind energy is being harnessed in many localities where strong winds are continually present. Windmill farms, which consist of hundreds of windmills operating in a given area, are both practical and commercially profitable. One of the largest windmill farms in the United States is located in the Palm Springs area of southern California. While dependable winds of the strength needed for windmills are not found everywhere, the contribution of windmill farms to the energy pool of the world can be quite sufficient.

The Core Features of an Active Solar Energy System

Any active solar energy system must perform three basic functions. It must be capable of collecting the energy of the sun efficiently and transforming that energy into a form that can be easily transported from one place to another. The system must be able to move the energy from the collector to the interior of a building. And the system must provide some means of storing the energy, once it has been conveyed from the collector to the interior of the building. Each function is discussed briefly in the following sections.

Solar Energy Collectors.   There are basically two types of solar energy collectors on the market. One of them concentrates the solar energy at a point or along a straight line through the use of lenses or reflectors. The other type is simply a flat, boxlike structure that entraps the energy that enters the box. The concentration-type collector is complex and must always be aimed directly at the sun, while the flat solar panel is relatively simple to construct and functions well in a fixed position. For this reason, solar panels are more practical for heating purposes in school buildings.

There is a wide variety of solar panels on the market. Some are very sophisticated and highly efficient. Some trap the solar energy inside evacuated glass cylinders that resemble fluorescent tubes. Others consist of copper tubing soldered onto a sheet of copper that is placed inside a box whose sides are about 6 inches high. The bottom and sides of the box are covered with insulation. The copper sheet, with the pipes facing the top of the box, is laid on the insulation. The pipes and copper sheet are sprayed with a special type of heat-absorbing black paint. And the top of the box is sealed and covered entirely with glass or sheets of plastic. In simpler terms, the box resembles a miniature greenhouse.

The working medium in a collector is either liquid or air. The heat is removed from the box by passing cold or cool liquid through the copper tubing which is soldered to the copper base. There are many variations of the arrangement described above on the market, but the principle is always the same. Black, heat-absorbing pipes or plates are sealed in a well-insulated, glass-covered box. The collected heat is removed from the enclosure by passing air or a liquid through the box. The heated air or liquid is then brought into the building. For those interested in obtaining more detailed information about the many types of solar panels on the market, it is suggested that brochures be obtained from the various manufacturers of solar energy equipment. The Department of Energy distributes lists of solar energy suppliers. Incidentally, these brochures are a rich source of information on solar energy. Not only is the reading exciting for the solar energy enthusiast but it clearly demonstrates the creativity and ingenuity of the manufacturers of solar energy equipment in a free enterprise system. In addition to brochures, there are a number of good books on the subject written by experienced authorities in the field, such as Halacy[6] and Daniels.[7]

Transference of Solar Energy. After solar energy is collected, it must be moved from the collector to the inside of the building where it can be stored or used as desired. The medium for conveying solar energy is usually air or a liquid. When air is selected, fans are used to circulate the air from the building to the collector and back to the building through a closed system of ducts. These ducts are well insulated to minimize loss of heat during the process. Water, however, is more commonly used as the medium for transporting solar energy from the collector to the building. Water is pumped through the sun-heated collector and is returned to the inside of the building after absorbing heat from the solar panel. The pipes connecting the building storage unit to the collector are heavily insulated in order to keep heat losses from the water in transit at a minimum. Antifreeze is usually mixed with the water during cold weather.

In both liquid and air systems, temperature control devices prevent the transfer of heat from the building to the collector. When the temperature of the medium in the collector is close to that in the building, the fans and pumps become inoperative. In some water systems, there are controls that drain the water from the pipes when the temperature of the water in the collector approaches the freezing point. In some systems, there is also a computer-controlled flow valve that keeps the amount of water or air flowing through the collector at an optimum volume at all times.

Storage of Solar Energy. Since solar energy is available only during daylight hours, it is necessary to store some of the collected energy for use at times when solar energy is not available or insufficient in quantity. This situation may arise when the sun is not shining brightly, during the night, or when the outside temperature is so low that the amount of energy collected is not sufficient to maintain the proper temperature within the building.

Solar energy is commonly stored in water or in stones. There are also physical-chemical methods of storing energy, but the problems associated with these methods plague those who experiment with them. Consequently, large tanks of water (ranging from 10,000 to 15,000 gallons) are used for storing solar energy for space heating if water is chosen as the transporting medium. When air is the transporting medium, several tons of loosely piled stones in or adjoining the basement of the building are used to store the solar energy. Warm air from the collectors is filtered through the stones, which absorb the heat.

The retrieval of the stored heat is a relatively simple process. The hot water is pumped to other parts of the building where the heat is required. Or air from the building is circulated over the warm stones and returned to other parts of the building where additional heat is needed.

Practical Considerations Related to Active Solar Energy Systems in School Buildings

Theoretically, solar energy is ideal. It is free. It is nonpolluting. It is constant and renewable. It is abundant. It can be used for both heating and cooling. It reduces our dependence on fossil fuels. And, ultimately, solar energy will greatly improve the quality of the air we breathe, when its use becomes widespread.

There are, however, practical limits to the extent that solar energy can be utilized in school buildings at this time. The major drawback is cost. The cost of solar panels, pumps, controls, and storage systems is still very high. To be sure, the federal government and some states are paying part of the cost, but the full purchase price for a total solar energy heating and cooling system is still beyond the budgetary reach of many school districts. But future prospects look promising. With the advent of more efficient equipment and improved design, the cost of solar energy systems should drop considerably and become more affordable for more and more school districts in the nation.

On the other hand, the possibility of utilizing solar energy at this time must not be overlooked. It should, however, be limited primarily to hot water heating. This application of solar energy is economically justifiable and very practical for a number of reasons. First of all, no special storage system is needed. The existing hot water tank also serves as the heat storage tank, assuming, of course, that the water tank is not less than 500 gallons. Secondly, the cost of purchasing the limited number of solar panels that are needed to supply energy for hot water purposes is cost-effective. And thirdly, the heat transfer system can be very simple, uncomplicated, and relatively inexpensive.

Solar energy for space heating need not be ruled out entirely, however. If space heating is planned, it should be done judiciously. It is suggested that a conventional backup heating system supplement the solar energy system. By so doing, the size of the solar energy system can be scaled down to one that is economically efficient. In this instance, a considerable amount of money can be saved by eliminating almost all of the solar energy storage. Under these circumstances the solar energy panels can supply solar heat to the building during daylight hours in varying quantities. Any deficiency in heat is automatically compensated for by the standby system. Under this arrangement, whatever energy is collected from the sun represents a saving in the cost of energy for the building. On the other hand, purchasing the number of solar panels and ancillary equipment required to heat the building on a 24-hour basis, employing extensive storage and distribution facilities, will not be economically efficient until manufacturers of solar energy equipment can find ways of reducing the cost per Btu of heat delivered to the point of need within a school building.

Planning School Buildings for Passive Solar Energy Heating

Thus far, the major focus has been on active solar energy systems. In these instances, as mentioned earlier, solar energy is collected at some location outside of the building. It is then transported into the building and stored in water or stone for distribution within the building wherever it is needed at a later time. Passive solar energy heating, on the other hand, is primarily a function of building design and requires no special equipment.

Under the concept of passive solar heating, no effort is made to pump solar energy in from the outside. However, through ingenious building design, solar energy is allowed to enter the building naturally and is trapped within it by various methods. A number of typical methods for capturing solar energy at little or no extra cost are listed below. Passive solar energy is achieved primarily by building orientation and design.

1. *The south window wall.* The admission of heat through the south wall warms objects and surfaces within the building when the sun is shining. The heat is trapped within the enclosure by the so-called greenhouse effect. In classrooms, special care should be exercised to keep the glare away from student desks through the use of venetian blinds or their equivalent. Also, reflecting shades should be closed at night to keep the heat within the building.

The architect should design the proper overhang along the south facing windows so that sunlight will not enter the building during the summer months when the sun is high in the sky. The dimensions of the overhang will depend upon the location of the building on the earth with respect to the solar plane. Solar angle tables should be consulted in determining the proper angle of the shadow line for winter and summer.

2. *Using a roof reservoir for sun heating.* Flat roofs can be made into shallow water reservoirs by forming a watertight glass- or plastic-covered box 2 or 3 inches deep over part of the roof area. The box would be filled with water. Since the roof is already coated with black asphalt, which absorbs heat, the temperature of the water would rise and store solar energy.

The specific application of this concept depends upon the climate where a given building is located. An insulated and reflective cover could slide over the box at night, during which period the accumulated heat in the water would be radiated into the building. This application assumes that outside temperatures do not fall below freezing. In colder climates, however, it may be necessary to add antifreeze to the water. If covering the reservoir with reflective material at night is not feasible, the sun-heated water would still reduce the amount of heat that would be lost through the roof during daylight hours when outside temperatures are low.

3. *Air heat collectors.* An air heat collector, consisting of a simple box about 4 feet wide, 8 feet long, and 12 inches deep, insulated on the inside, could be located on the roof of the building. Its interior surfaces would be painted black and the top would be sealed with a glass or plastic transparent covering. This box would be tilted to the proper angle depending upon the latitude of its location. Two ducts would be attached to the box. The inlet duct would receive cool air from within the building while the exhaust duct would force air warmed by the sun into the building. No fan would be needed since the air would be moved by natural convection.

4. *Skylight solar heating.* Solar energy could be admitted and stored at various points within the building through the expedient use of skylights. Ideally, the solar energy should fall on massive stone or masonry walls or on floors that are painted in dark energy-absorbing colors. During the daylight hours, heat from sunlight entering through the skylight would be absorbed by the floors, walls, and other materials. At night the stored solar energy would be released into the building.

5. *Collecting solar energy in containers of water.* Several 55-gallon drums of water could be stacked inside the building along a window wall facing south. These barrels would be painted black on all sides. At night, insulating doors covering all of the windows could be closed. The warm water would then radiate heat within the building and keep it warm. Aesthetics would be a matter of concern. However, any imaginative architect utilizing this approach to passive solar energy would find no difficulty creating a pleasant, aesthetic atmosphere.

6. *Going partially underground.* It is well known that the temperature of the soil a few feet below the surface rarely falls below freezing in most of the United States. It is also a recognized principle of physics that the flow of heat through a wall, floor, or ceiling is directly proportional to the temperature difference between the two sides of the surface. For example, if the temperature is 70° Fahrenheit inside a building, and 0° Fahrenheit outside, the amount of heat lost to the atmosphere per square foot of surface is approximately twice as much as that lost to the ground 5 or 6 feet below the surface. Consequently, the more of the building that is underground, the less will be the loss of heat from the building during cold weather.

It is not suggested, however, that school buildings be entirely underground. Two important considerations should be borne in mind when school plant planners think about underground school facilities. As more and more of the building is constructed below the surface, more and more energy will be required for artificial lighting. On the other hand, as more and more of the building is constructed below the surface of the ground, less and less heat is lost from the building in cold climates.

At some point, there is a balance between heat energy saved and electrical energy consumed for lighting.

The concept of building at least part of the structure underground has merit from several points of view. Some heat energy will be saved for reasons mentioned earlier. Passive solar energy features can be incorporated into the facility, because part of it is still above the topographical grade. In fact, light wells extending below the surface of the ground can be designed so that they may become effective solar energy traps.

It may be of interest that there have recently been a number of proponents for school facilities built completely underground. Their reasons have considerable merit. Underground schools are ideal as civil defense shelters, not only for the students but also for the residents of the community. Underground schools conserve land use, particularly for parking. Underground schools are free from noise pollution. And underground schools are purportedly less expensive to build and maintain. In warm climates, the supporters of underground schools contend that the added cost of energy for artificial lighting is more than compensated for by savings in the cost of energy for air conditioning aboveground buildings.

NOTES

1. "Report of Energy Management Information Center, Honeywell, Inc.," *CEFP Journal* (November–December 1980), p. 14.

2. Edward Churchill, "School's Energy Costs Cut Two-thirds with No Capital Investment," *CEFP Journal* (March–April 1985), p. 21.

3. *Energy Sourcebook for Educational Facilities* (Columbus, OH: Council of Educational Facility Planners, International, 1977). Order from CEFPI, 29 Woodruff Ave., Columbus, OH 43210.

4. Charles K. Denning and Edmond A. LeBlanc, "Community Education and the Energy Problems," *CEFP Journal* (January 1980), p. 10.

5. Ibid.

6. D. S. Halacy, Jr., *The Coming of Solar Age* (New York: Harper and Row, 1973).

7. Farrington Daniels, *Direct Use of the Sun's Energy* (New York: Ballantine Books, 1977).

▶ 10

Safety, Health, and Comfort

The safety of those occupying a school building is of prime concern to the architect, educators, and boards of education. Safety hazards in school plants may be due to building design, site planning, selection of floor materials, or location of obstacles such as fire extinguishers, water fountains, electrical floor stubs, and protruding pipes. No school planner or architect can justify such hazards on the basis of design or aesthetic unity. Although safety cannot always be completely assured, every effort must be made to achieve as high a safety level as possible. For example, a service driveway must be located near a school building, even though it introduces a safety hazard and it is difficult if not impossible to plan the crossings of walks and drives at grade level so that they are absolutely safe.

HAZARDS ASSOCIATED WITH THE MOVEMENT OF PEOPLE

The safety of people moving from one part of the school plant to another is discussed in the following paragraphs.

Ramps

Ramps, like stairways, are an integral part of the circulation system within and outside a school building. Their use is receiving increased attention from both architects and educational planners, especially as a means of meeting the needs of physically handicapped students, particularly on college campuses where students must travel from building to building. Ramps should be designed for wheelchair use and should be covered with nonslip materials. According to federal standards, the slope of a ramp should not exceed 8.3 percent, which is equivalent to a rise of not more than 1 foot for a horizontal run of 12 feet in length. Elevators are preferred for people with physical handicaps. However, where the change in elevation within a building is less than three risers, a ramp is preferable to stairs for the safety of *all* students traveling from one level to another.

Architects and school planners should give additional thought to the problem of wheelchairs outside the building. While elevators are adequate within the building, ramps should be provided for wheelchairs to reach the elevators from out-of-doors. Sidewalks and outside areas should be planned with the handicapped student in mind. It should be possible for such a student to travel by wheelchair from the bus-unloading zone on the campus to any other point within and outside of buildings.

Stairways

Stairways can be dangerous, so certain precautions should be taken in their design. Stair runs should not exceed 16 risers, nor should they be less than three. The riser height on all principal stairways should not exceed 6½ inches, and treads should not be less than 10½ inches deep, exclusive of nosing or overhang. Experiments conducted in one of the major department stores in Boston revealed conclusively that accidents on stairways were reduced when the riser heights in a stair run did not vary by more than ⅛ inch. The engineer conducting the experiment was convinced that uniformity in riser height was fully as important as the riser height itself. Stairways should insure a rapid and safe egress from a building when emergencies arise. Speedy evacuation from a school is imperative in the event of fire, the escape of noxious fumes, or other dangers. Stairways, therefore, should be specifically designed for such emergencies.

Multistory buildings should have at least two main stairways located well apart from each other. At least two independent and smoke-free paths to safety should be provided from any point in a school building where students work. For example, some state codes require that a door be located in every partition between classrooms adjacent to the wall opposite the corridor. In the event that hot gases filled the corridor, students could travel from room to room until they reached a smoke-free stairway in multistory buildings. Two stairways terminating on the same landing should be considered as a single stairway. Stairways should run at right angles to main corridors and should be enclosed in fire-resistant stairwells. Handrails may be composed of combustible materials. It is also important that main stairways be open to egress and that they lead to an exit on the ground floor.

Stairways should be at least two lanes in width, with 44 inches between handrails. Handrails should be installed between 26 and 30 inches above the nosing on the stair tread. Where pupils of many ages attend a school, two handrails, one at the normal height and one at a lower position, should be provided for the safety of both younger and older children.

Corridors

The mass movement of students from one point to another on the same floor level usually takes place through a corridor. Corridors should be wide enough to accommodate the traffic and free of obstructions and bottlenecks. It is generally accepted among school planners that main corridors should be at least $8\frac{1}{2}$ feet wide. In schools with enrollments exceeding 200 pupils, they should be wider. The width of secondary corridors, on the other hand, is governed by the number of classrooms served by each corridor, and by its length. In any case, secondary corridors should not be less than 7 feet wide in the clear.

There should be no projection into the corridor greater than 8 inches beyond the face of the corridor wall. Doors should be installed so that they do not project into the corridor by more than 8 inches. In addition to being a safety hazard, doors opening farther into a corridor create a bottleneck and thus appreciably reduce the effective width of the corridor. Also, radiators, fountains, fire extinguishers, and the like should be completely recessed in corridor walls.

Dead-end corridors are very dangerous and should always be avoided in planning. Corridors should always terminate at an exit or at a stairway leading to an egress. Doors that open onto a stairway or tend to block passageways create safety hazards and should, therefore, be avoided.

HEALTH HAZARDS DUE TO GASES, CHEMICAL AGENTS, RADIOACTIVITY, AND DUSTLIKE PARTICLES

The danger from commercially produced heating gas in school buildings is well recognized, but the hazards resulting from inhalation of fumes produced by some cleaning agents, insect sprays, and paint thinners are not quite so obvious. Every effort must be made to minimize the hazard from noxious fumes. Admittedly, it is often difficult to cope with the problem of poisonous vapors because it is not always possible to determine the type, origin, or location of the source of such fumes.

Heating Gases

The presence of detectable amounts of heating gas in the atmosphere creates a potentially explosive situation, particularly in the case of propane gas. Since bottled gases are heavier than air, they spill over onto the floor and are, therefore, difficult to smell until the accumulation has reached dangerous proportions. Regardless of the type of heating gas used, the selection of the equipment, the installation of the distribution system, and the attachment of equipment and appliances to the outlets supplying such fuel should be performed with the utmost care by a competent person.

Noxious Fumes

The problem of noxious fumes in schools is elusive. Architects have worked diligently to minimize the health and fire hazards from noxious or combustible vapors, particularly in areas where the need for special precautions is obvious, such as bus garages and paint-spraying shops. There are, however, a number of other spaces in an educational facility where the problem of harmful vapors is present. While hoods are provided in chemistry laboratories, special provision for the escape of noxious gases is not always made in the preparation rooms. Nor is special attention always given to the exhaust of fumes from cleaning agents and chemicals used in the physics and biology laboratories. The custodian is often required to refinish furniture, but rarely does one find a well-ventilated custodial workshop. Maintenance personnel often clean parts of light fixtures and rugs using agents that emit noxious fumes, but one does not often find a properly designed space for this function. All of the places where noxious gases should be exhausted in a school building cannot be listed. It is hoped, however, that school planners will make a mental note of the areas that might require additional ventilation. Electronic sensors should be provided.

Radioactive Substances

The wide use of radioactive materials for experimental purposes in high schools and colleges has introduced another element of danger. Radioactive materials are now available in a variety of forms. Nuclear research laboratories are an integral part of many comprehensive institutions of higher learning. The commercial producers of nuclear equipment have taken every precaution to protect students from possible harm through design and proper use of shielding materials.

The proper storage of radioactive materials vitally concerns school planners. While industry can cope with matters related to radioactive safety through the design of equipment, educational planners and architects are responsible for safe storage. It is imperative to provide for stringent control of access to radioactive storage areas. No student should be able to accidentally find herself or himself in an area where radioactive materials are stored. It is also necessary that special attention be given to the radioactive shielding surrounding such areas. The Atomic Energy Commission has published a considerable amount of information to guide architects in designing hazard-free spaces where radioactive materials may be used.

Radioactive Gas–Radon

Radon is a colorless, odorless, radioactive gas that occurs naturally in low concentrations almost everywhere on earth.[1] It is the first product generated by the normal radioactive disintegration of radium. In nontechnical terms, radon might be envisioned as the grandchild of uranium. In more precise language, however, it is the result of a chain reaction which starts with uranium. When uranium decays radioactively, one of its products is radium. Radium, in turn, decays radioactively and produces radon. Unfortunately, the process does not stop at this point. The radon gas continues to decay radioactively, and produces a new generation of radioactive materials. Thus, if a person inhales radon gas, this new generation of radioactive particles releases small amounts of radiation which can damage or kill normal living cells. Although research on the effects of long-term exposure to low-dosage radiation is not conclusive, "People exposed to significant amounts of radon for a long time run an increased risk of lung cancer."[2]

Radon can be found in major regions of the United States and Canada. Radon gas is discharged from rocks containing even infinitesimal quantities of radium. High concentrations of radon have been traced to granite or sillimanite rock. To further complicate matters, radon gas has a great affinity for water. It is readily dissolved in it. For this reason, it is often found in well water that has permeated through rock formations containing radioactive materials. The most radon-prone regions in North America are near the Atlantic coastline from the Maritime Provinces to Florida, in the Lake Superior region including south-central Canada, and in the Rocky Mountain area including parts of Washington and California. This may be disquieting to people living in those regions. However, there is no reason to be disturbed. The corrective measures are effective, reliable, and technologically sound, and the outlook is positive and reassuring. More specifically, the remedies are uncomplicated, straightforward, and doable.[3] Furthermore, the presence of radon can be easily detected and accurately measured without difficulty. And finally, even high concentrations of radon gas can be rendered harmless through a combination of increased ventilation and effective control of the points where the gas enters the building.

When educational facilities are being planned in radon-prone regions, it is imperative that the architect determine at the outset whether or not radon is present on the site. In the event that radon gas is present, corrective design features can be incorporated in the plans. In pursuing this preliminary investigation, educational facility planners will find health agencies to be of invaluable service. Local and state health officials have the staff and apparatus to detect and measure the quantity of radon present in well water or in the air at a given site.

Fortunately, the presence of radon gas is not nearly as troublesome in school buildings as it is in tight, energy-efficient homes. School buildings are almost always mechanically ventilated, while homes generally rely on the incidental infiltration of outside air. More specifically, the amount of ventilation currently required for instructional spaces in educational facilities is sufficient to overcome the dele-terious effects of nominal concentrations of radon gas. However, there may be areas within the building that are usually not as well ventilated, such as custodial work-shops, storage areas, and equipment rooms. These spaces may require special attention by educational facility planners. As a rule of thumb, normal ventilation requirements for instructional spaces are generally sufficient to offset the radon problem when the concentration of radon gas is not very high, between 1 and 2 pico-Curies per liter.

On the other hand, in areas where higher concentrations of radon are present, additional measures may be required. These remedies are aimed primarily at sealing the pathways of gas entry into the building. It is not within the scope of this text to deal with the engineering aspects of this type of remedial action. Suffice it to mention, however, that the usual points of entry of radon gas include porous cinder blocks, loose-fitting pipes, unsealed slab joints, cracks in walls and floors, exposed soil or granite, and from radon-contaminated ground or well water entering the building.

Harmful Dustlike Particles

Dust is a pulverized form of solid that is suspended in the air. Some types of dust are distressing but harmless. Some kinds of dust are temporarily irritating *and* potentially harmful. And some forms of dust can be deadly. These types of air pollutants are discussed briefly in the following paragraphs.

Non-Cancer-Producing Particles.   Wood dust is perhaps one of the most preva-lent forms of solid air pollutant that is encountered in educational facilities. Other forms of noncarcinogenic dust are sometimes found in spaces where students are working on arts and crafts projects and, to a lesser degree, in some of the homemak-ing rooms where lint and various powders may be present in the air.

Although the symptoms created by non-cancer-producing dust are usually temporary, their effects may be potentially harmful to persons who are repeatedly subjected to such irritants. Dust particles affect people in different ways, depending upon the concentration, type, and chemical content of the particles. They may irritate the skin, the eyes, and the respiratory system. Generally, the pain and discomfort associated with dust inhalation disappears when the person is no longer exposed to such irritants.

Educational facility planners have always been concerned with air pollution in school buildings. Their efforts to combat it have often been rewarding. For example, they were able to overcome the health hazards caused by wood dust by applying modern air purification methods. First, most of the dust particles were removed at the point of origin by a vacuum system. Then, air filters were installed in dust-producing areas to further improve the quality of the air. Architects and engineers successfully coped with this problem because they were aware of it during the planning process. For this reason planners should systematically examine each function housed in an educational facility and identify locations where harmful dust particles are likely to be produced. Once this review is completed, corrective measures can be taken.

Radon-Laden Particles.   The effects of radon in its gaseous form have already been discussed in considerable detail. There is, however, another phenomenon related to radon that should be mentioned. Radon molecules frequently attach themselves onto dust particles omnipresent in the air. Thus, concentrated radon gas could increase to significant levels through the accumulation of radon-laden dust in any nook or crook of the building.

Obviously, if radon gas is prevented from entering the building, radon-laden dust is nonexistent. But it is important for planners to be aware that radon gas may be carried by dust particles and to be on the alert, therefore, to situations that allow radioactive dust to enter the building; for example, fresh air ducts in the ventilation system or other openings.

Asbestos Dust Particles.   Asbestos dust is highly carcinogenic. As long as it remains solidified on pipes, walls, ceilings, and other surfaces it is relatively harmless. But when it crumbles and appears in the form of dust moving freely in the air, it becomes a deadly health hazard.

The removal of asbestos from a building creates treacherous conditions somewhat difficult to control. It presents a health hazard not only for those directly involved in removing it but also for others elsewhere in the building. Thus, special care is required. Furthermore, asbestos dust is so menacing to public health in general that a prescribed procedure must be followed in its removal, transportation, and final disposition.

The difficulty in dealing with asbestos stems from the nature of the material itself. After asbestos has been in place for a number of years, it becomes extremely friable. Consequently, as soon as it is disturbed, it pulverizes and forms a high concentration of dust that quickly permeates the air and ultimately spreads throughout the building. For this reason, it would be ideal to remove the asbestos when classes are not in session. If this is not possible, *extreme* care must be exercised, to prevent the asbestos dust from reaching locations occupied by students and staff. This procedure is covered in more detail under "Health Related Improvements" in Chapter 17.

Lead Paint and Lead Dust.   In school buildings constructed prior to World War II, the paint used for aesthetics and wood preservation usually contained lead. It has been found that even small amounts of lead ingested by children can have a deleterious effect on their mental and physical development. Research is being conducted to determine the extent to which lead is harmful to adults.

Lead paint can either be removed or sealed. In either case, special precautions prescribed by national codes must be taken in eliminating the source of lead poisoning. When lead paint is disturbed, even slightly, there is the possibility that dust particles containing lead may be formed. Recently, lead paint was being removed from a high bridge passing through a city in the Boston area. Special precautions were taken by state authorities to catch dust-laden particles in canvas sheets suspended below the bridge structure. Meanwhile, city officials continually monitored the air near homes located in the vicinity of the bridge and discovered that the amount of lead-laden particles escaping from the bridge area was becoming a health hazard. State officials were forced to take additional precautions to minimize the dispersion of lead-laden dust particles.

It is suggested, therefore, that any removal or sealing of paint containing lead be done when school is not in session. Furthermore, it is prudent that precautions similar to those employed by asbestos-removing contractors be specified in any contract awarded for the removal or sealing of lead paint. Custodians should not be expected to remove lead paint unless they are properly trained to do so and wear protective clothing, air filters, and goggles to shield them from the effects of lead-laden dust.

HAZARDS ASSOCIATED WITH NORMAL SCHOOL ACTIVITIES

Hazards are associated with many activities normally conducted in a school building. While such potential sources of danger cannot always be completely removed, they can and should be minimized or controlled as much as possible. School planners may wish to prepare a comprehensive checklist of specific dangers to be avoided in the design of school buildings in relation to students, faculty, clerical staff, and custodians.

Students

In reviewing plans of school buildings, each detail should be checked with the safety of the student in mind. A few questions suggest major areas of concern. If hot gases in the corridors block student egress from an instructional area, is there another means of escape? Are doors designed so they cannot be accidentally slammed into the faces of students? Are floors slippery in the corridors, wet shower areas, main entrances, and classrooms? Are there dangerous projections or protrusions in the corridors, classrooms, and other areas where students congregate? Are electrical circuit boxes and other controls properly shielded and located away from student access? Has every safety precaution been taken in normally hazardous areas such as shops, gymnasiums, laboratories, playgrounds, and stairways? Has adequate provision for first aid been made in the chemical laboratories? Is lighting in the various shops and laboratories adequate for the learning tasks to be performed? Is supplementary local lighting provided on power machines in the shops? Are electrical floor stubs avoided in teaching areas? Are catwalks, balconies, and other elevated areas fully protected? Can large expanses of glass be easily shattered by direct bodily contact by students? Are walks and drives planned for maximum safety, with a minimum of crossing of foot and vehicular traffic? Do driveways separate the building from play areas, thus causing a safety hazard?

Faculty and Staff

Many of the hazards listed above apply also to the faculty and staff. For the most part, schools are still designed without the work of the custodian in mind. Oftentimes, lights in auditoriums and gymnasiums are difficult to change and require the use of extra-long ladders. Pipes are seldom color-coded. Without such coding, custodians may be seriously burned by hot steam lines. Pipe trenches may be unlighted and studded with dangerous projections. Electrical equipment is not always completely free from shock hazards. Boiler controls and equipment are not always located for maximum safety. In multistory buildings, elevators are not always provided for the conveyance of heavy equipment from one floor level to another. These are a few of the hazards confronting custodial personnel. The health dangers produced by the use of cleaning agents in certain parts of the school are also of major concern to school plant planners.

PLANNING FOR COMFORT AND CONVENIENCE

Functional school planning has long been considered a fundamental concept of school design. However, in planning educational facilities, it is also important to include the dimensions of comfort and convenience.

It is generally agreed among educators that human comfort is conducive to effectual learning. Consequently, a school should feature comfortable lighting, humidity and temperatures, seating, colors, ventilation, and acoustical environment. A well-planned school should also provide for the convenience of its occupants. Convenience is important in location of rest rooms, design of traffic patterns, layout of equipment, location of storage and shelving, and grouping of areas of related activity. Convenience deserves careful consideration, especially when thoughts related to the functional aspects of the school are being crystallized. For example, while the functional aspects of the heating system are being discussed, it would be wise also to consider the safety and convenience of the custodian and engineer who will eventually operate the equipment. It is hoped, of course, that school planners will evolve a plan that is aesthetic, efficient, *and* convenient.

Architect Louis Sullivan believed that *form follows function.* The wisdom of this axiom cannot be overstated. Aesthetic integrity deserves careful consideration in the design of any educational facility, but if there is an unresolvable conflict between aesthetics and function, aesthetics must inevitably yield to function.

SANITARY FACILITIES

School planners are concerned with both the physical and the mental hygiene of those for whom schools are planned. Consequently, architects and engineers work as a team to create conditions that provide for the physical well-being of the occupants of a school building. By and large, the healthfulness of a building is determined by the design and function of the heating, cooling, and ventilating systems, and by its visual and acoustical environment. Healthfulness is also promoted by the selection of easily cleaned interior surface materials whose design reduces the accumulation of dust and air polluters. A building designed with the health of its users in mind also provides for emergency situations involving illness or injuries.

Plumbing Requirements

Plumbing requirements are often reduced to a simple formula with respect to the size and number of facilities, lengths of pipe runs, proper pipe pitch, and dollars and cents. Admittedly, all of these considerations are important, but the so-called "slide rule" approach to school planning often falls short of insuring healthful conditions in a school.

Local and national codes specify the plumbing requirements in various types of buildings. These requirements are realistic and are designed to meet the needs of modern society. The codes are reviewed by the plumbing industry periodically in order that the latest techniques and newly developed materials be incorporated in such codes. Consequently, there may be a wide discrepancy between the codes of today and those of a quarter of a century ago.

Many school buildings currently in use are over 30 years old and some of them may even be older than 50 years. Unless a building has been remodelled recently, the number of plumbing fixtures may not be sufficient to meet current needs. For those school administrators who wish to ascertain whether the existing number of plumbing fixtures in the older buildings are sufficient, Tables 10-1 and 10-2 are offered as guides. If the discrepancies between the number of existing fixtures and those specified in these tables are large, it is suggested that local building departments be requested to supply a copy of the latest plumbing requirements. With this information in hand, school administrators are in a position to take appropriate action to remedy any serious deficiencies.

Nationally recognized standards call for the following allocation of plumbing fixtures as specified in Table 10-1. The minimum quantity of plumbing fixtures in

TABLE 10-1 **Ratio of Students Per Unit Plumbing Fixture**

Type of School	Toilets Girls	Boys	Urinals Boys	Unit Lavatories	Drinking Fountains
Elementary School	35	60	30	50	75
High School	45	100	30	50	75

Source: Guide for Planning School Plants. (Columbus, OH: National Council on Schoolhouse Construction, 1964), pp. 78ff.

buildings serving adults, such as office buildings, factories, colleges, and universities, varies with the number of persons housed in the building. According to the New York State Labor Code, the minimum plumbing fixture requirements for buildings in which large numbers of persons are engaged in gainful pursuits are given in Table 10-2.

Toilet Facilities

A toilet room should be easy to clean, attractive, well ventilated, properly equipped, and uncongested. Every effort should be made to select fixtures, wall materials, and flooring that can be kept spotlessly clean with ease. The choice of

TABLE 10-2 **Required Number of Plumbing Fixtures in Public Buildings**

No. of Men	Toilets	Urinals	No. of Women	Toilets	No. of Men or Women	Lavatories
221–270	6	5	191–240	8	201–225	10
281–300	7	6	271–300	10	251–275	12
341–360	8	7	331–360	12	301–325	14
361–390	9	7	391–420	14	351–375	16
401–450	10	8	451–480	16	401–425	18
461–480	11	9	511–540	18	455–475	20
521–540	12	10	571–600	20	501–525	22
631–640	15	11	Above	1 additional	551–571	24
701–720	16	13	600	toilet per	Above	1 additional
721–750	17	13		30 women	600	lavatory per
761–810	18	14				25 persons
821–840	19	15				
881–900	20	16				
900 and above	1 additional toilet per 60 men	1 additional urinal per 50 men				

Source: New York State Labor Code.

colors in a toilet room is also quite important. The more attractive the space, the less likely it is to be defaced.

Congestion may be a problem in poorly designed toilet rooms. For example, the location of mirrors over lavatories contributes to congestion. It might be better to locate mirrors elsewhere in the toilet room. A shelf could be installed under mirrors for purses and other articles. In addition to distributing students within a toilet room, relocating the mirrors reduces maintenance of lavatory drains because less hair will be dropped in the lavatory. Then too, there is a significant increase in the potential utilization of the lavatory. One student can be engaged in washing, while another is combing his or her hair at a location removed from the lavatory fixture.

Cleanliness and ease of maintenance must be kept in mind in planning toilet rooms. Good lighting and attractiveness are desirable even there. School maintenance personnel affirm that attractive and well-illuminated toilet rooms are usually cleaner than those that are drab and dark. The use of interior surfaces that are easy to clean tends to improve the healthfulness of toilet rooms. Floor drains and hose outlets also promote cleanliness, because they permit custodial personnel to wash the floors with ease. Floor surfaces should be impervious to moisture and acid resistant, particularly in areas surrounding urinals.

The type of toilet fixtures selected may have an important bearing upon the healthfulness of toilet rooms. Although floor-type urinals possess many advantages, they present one serious drawback. Because of the difference between the coefficient of linear expansion of the china and the flooring material into which the unit is imbedded, a small crack eventually develops at the juncture between floor material and urinal. In time, body wastes collect in the crack and sometimes seep under the floor surface, producing an unpleasant odor, which can be removed only by tearing out the floor covering or tile. Wall-hung urinals avoid this problem and are less costly to purchase and install. Also, it is easier to clean the areas near the urinals. Wall-hung toilets are also desirable, because they permit the custodian to keep the toilet area clean more easily than do ordinary pedestal-type toilet fixtures. Wall-hung toilet fixtures are somewhat more costly than other types, so economy may dictate the pedestal-type fixture.

Ventilation is vital in toilet rooms. A mechanical ventilating system capable of producing about 20 complete air changes per hour in the room is essential. Natural ventilation through open windows would appear to be acceptable, but the lower portions must be kept closed for privacy, especially in single-story buildings. The upper sections, which are controlled manually, are not always open enough to provide the necessary ventilation. Mechanical ventilation, on the other hand, is effective and automatic.

Toilet seats and flush mechanisms should provide for maximum sanitation. Toilet seats of the open-front variety are highly desirable. Flush valves should be of the foot-operated type. Such flushing devices have been in operation in some institutions for almost a quarter of a century without presenting any unusual maintenance problem.

The location of toilet spaces deserves careful thought from the standpoint of their relationship to the educational function, public or school utilization of such areas, nature of the users of certain toilet rooms, and convenience. The accepted location of all gang toilets in most schools constructed before World War I was in the basement of the building—the boys' area on one side and the girls' on the other. After World War I, gang toilets were removed from the basement areas and distributed, in stack formation, on each floor. Generally, there was one set of gang toilets for each sex on every floor level. And, in most cases, such toilet facilities were placed adjacent to each other for reasons of economy. After World War II, however, toilets became more widely distributed throughout school buildings, and the use of single watercloset toilet rooms became common. Moving toilets from the basement to more convenient locations throughout the building was an improvement, but did not go quite far enough. The convenience of faculty was all but ignored in planning schools, although many teachers' rooms or lounges have been provided with toilets. But, in many situations, the toilets in the teachers' room are the only ones designated for faculty members. In large high schools or colleges, the teachers' lounge may be located far from many of the classrooms where teachers spend most of the school day. It would be highly desirable, therefore, to locate a simple toilet and lavatory space for men and one for women faculty members adjacent to each gang toilet provided for students. Such an arrangement would satisfy both the distribution and convenience requirements of such a facility.

Special attention should be given to the location and type of toilet facilities provided for students in kindergarten through grade three. Toilet facilities for these grades should be located adjacent to the classrooms to which they are assigned. The size of the toilet fixture and the height of the lavatory should be scaled down to accommodate the level of physical development of the children. In some instances, one common toilet room serves two adjoining classrooms. While this arrangement is economical, it increases the burden of supervision. The two teachers are never sure that the toilet is unoccupied when a student requests to use it. If the toilet is occupied, the student must return to his or her seat, disturbing the class twice. This may seem trivial, but if repeated several times a day, day in and day out in the two classrooms, the disturbance is significant.

There is, however, a possible solution to the problem. If an unobtrusive light were installed in each classroom indicating that the toilet is occupied, unnecessary class interruptions could be reduced to tolerable levels. This suggestion seems straightforward but is really not that simple. The question arises, "How would the lights be triggered?" In airplanes, for example, the triggering occurs when the occupant of the toilet locks the door. In primary grades, toilet doors must be left unlocked for safety reasons. Perhaps the lights could be controlled by opening and closing the doors. Each door could turn the light on when it is opened the first time and off when it is opened a second time. But what if someone enters the toilet area through the door in classroom A and leaves through the door to classroom B? Do the lights remain on in both classrooms when no one is in the toilet room? It is up to the electronic engineer to find a functional solution or to suggest an entirely different approach. Incidentally, there is always the alternative of providing one toilet and lavatory facility for each classroom in the primary grades.

Lavatories

Most lavatory fixtures found in educational institutions are not designed for both healthfulness and economy. While a few installations do satisfy the need for sanitation, they do not provide for economy of water consumption. A few installations reduce the waste of water, but ignore requirements of sanitation. The standard two-spigot faucets, one for cold water and the other for hot water, produce the most unsanitary conditions under normal school use. In this case, the student must plug the drain and fill the lavatory with a mixture of hot and cold water at the desired temperature. A lavatory used in this fashion soon accumulates dirt, since students do not ordinarily clean the lavatory after use. The spring-type or delayed-closing faucets, on the other hand, save water but do not permit students to wash their hands under sanitary conditions. When two spigots of this type are employed, the student can leave the drain open but cannot control the temperature of the water flowing from either spigot. Therefore, unless the hot water supply is tempered, he or she must wash with cold water. The other alternative, of course, is to close the drain and fill the lavatory bowl as described above. This procedure creates the same unsanitary conditions mentioned earlier.

What is desired in a hand-washing lavatory is an installation that saves water and promotes healthfulness. In public toilets, no student should have to wash his or her hands in water collected in a basin that is not thoroughly clean. Consequently, the use of a drain plug in a wash basin is ruled out. If economy of water consumption is not a major concern, an ordinary mixing faucet with a single spigot solves the handwashing problem. Students do not habitually leave faucets running after use. In discussing the operational aspects of such installations with school principals and custodians, the author found that in no case was there a feeling that water was wasted excessively. Another possible solution would involve the use of a temperature-controlled hot-water system in which each lavatory would possess a single delayed-closing spigot. In this situation, the student would depress the handle and wash his or her hands while the water continued to flow for a few seconds. Where such units are used, there is an almost constant problem readjusting the mechanism controlling the length of time the water continues to flow. Often the flow of water stops too quickly. The best solution is a foot-operated mechanism to control the flow of water. Under this method, water ceases to flow when the foot is removed from the pedal. Either a single-spigot mixing faucet or a controlled water temperature system can be used with the foot pedal.

Certain other handwashing needs merit attention. Soap may be provided in one form or another at locations convenient to lavatories. Liquid soap systems facilitate the distribution of soap, but added maintenance is required to keep the system from becoming clogged. Soap pads seem to have some advantage over bar, powdered, or liquid soaps. Some provision should also be made for hand drying in toilet rooms. Ordinarily, students use cloth rollers, paper towels, or electric hand dryers. Towels generally create a maintenance problem. The cloth roller must be laundered. Paper towels may be scattered over the floor or stuffed into lavatories and toilets. In either situation, however, the maintenance problem is not intolerable. Electric hand dryers are functional and satisfactory, provided they are furnished in sufficient numbers. Electric dryers are noisy and require more time for hand drying than other methods. Therefore they usually create some congestion, but maintenance is low and littering is avoided. The initial cost of such units is eventually off-set because there is no expense for paper towels or laundering cloth rollers.

Drinking Fountains

Water fountains should be readily accessible in areas where strenuous physical activity is carried on, such as playgrounds, gymnasiums, and playrooms. They should also be distributed throughout a school in convenient locations where water is already available.

The choice and installation of drinking fountains are of utmost importance in maintaining healthfulness in school buildings. They should be constructed of impervious materials and be designed to minimize the chance of contamination. Orifices should be located so that students' mouths do not come in contact with them and so that waste water does not fall upon the nozzle. The installation of water bubblers on the periphery of work sinks is not recommended, because students washing hands or equipment are apt to contaminate the bubblers during the washing process.

Nozzle heights are very critical, particularly in elementary schools, where there is a wide range in the age and development of the children. Acceptable heights for water fountains are as follows:

a. Twenty-four inches above the floor for kindergarten and primary grades.
b. Twenty-eight inches for upper elementary grades.
c. Thirty-two inches for junior high schools.
d. Thirty-six inches for senior high schools and colleges.

Water Supply

Unless the water supply system is part of a municipal system, it should be planned by a competent engineer. Where wells are used, a minimum supply of 25 gallons of water per day is required for each student for normal needs. Additional capacity of adequate storage is needed for firefighting equipment and special educational uses, such as laboratories, homemaking areas, and shops.

For obvious health reasons, drinking water should be free from nitrogenous or undesirable mineral content and harmful bacteria. It is of extreme importance that the plumbing system be designed to prevent back-siphoning from toilet fixtures, swimming pools, and the like.

Sewage Disposal

Unless it is part of a municipal sewer system, the sewage disposal system at any school should be designed by a competent sanitary engineer. Sewage disposal fields on school property can become a serious health hazard unless the system is properly designed. Soil percolation and terrain are critical factors in the design of a sewage disposal system. Only a well-qualified sanitary engineer can interpret the results of soil tests and drainage characteristics of the site in designing a healthful sanitary system.

THE THERMAL ENVIRONMENT

The effectiveness of the teaching-learning situation and the efficiency of school personnel are greatly influenced by the climate produced within the school building. The thermal environment should be designed to provide for the health and comfort of the individual. Comfort is determined primarily by the rate of exchange of heat between the individual and the environment. Thermal control of the environment simply regulates the net body heat loss or gain for given conditions. Contrary to popular belief, comfort is not necessarily a function of the air temperature alone. The temperature of the walls and other interior surfaces is more directly related to comfort than is the temperature of the air itself. For example, on very cold days, the exterior walls are relatively cool. Hence, the body radiates more heat to them than it receives and therefore experiences an uncomfortable cooling effect, even though the temperature in the room is about 72° Fahrenheit. Clothing insulates the body and reduces the radiational loss of heat, thus producing comfort on cold days. Discomfort, on the other hand, may be produced when the heat gained exceeds the heat lost. There is a considerable variation among individuals with respect to thermal comfort in any given set of conditions. This variation is due primarily to differences in basal metabolism that are dependent upon sex, age, activity, and individual characteristics.

Comfort and health are related, as noted above, to the equilibrium of heat exchange between the individual and the environment. The exchange is affected mostly by convection and radiation, and to some extent by conduction when the individual is sitting or lying down. Consequently, the temperature of the air and that of large surfaces become the major contributors to comfort. When walls are cool, air temperatures must be kept at a level considerably higher than normal if comfort is to be maintained. When wall and ceiling temperatures can be held close to that of the atmosphere within the room, an air temperature of 65°–68° Fahrenheit at shoulder height for kindergarten and primary-grade students, and of 68°–70° for older students, is both healthful and comfortable. Convection causes air temperatures to vary with height in any given space. The difference in temperature between the floor and the 5-foot level should not vary by more than 3° Fahrenheit.

The relative humidity in a space for learning strongly influences the comfort of the individual. The comfort index varies with respect to both temperature and humidity. At temperatures of about 72° Fahrenheit, a relative humidity of 60 percent is quite acceptable. As air temperatures rise, however, the relative humidity should decrease if comfort is to be maintained. The human body utilizes the principle of evaporation in order to achieve a comfortable equilibrium. Since evaporation is much more accelerated when the humidity is low, spaces in school buildings requiring higher temperatures, such as drying rooms and special science laboratories, should be dehumidified, if necessary, to keep the humidity in the vicinity of 40 percent.

Ventilation Requirements

Until recently, schools in many areas have been overventilated. The old rule of thumb specifying that every classroom provide 30 cubic feet of fresh air per minute for each student is now being replaced by fresh-air requirements that are more reasonable. Where state codes govern the ventilation capacities of mechanical systems in public schools, as in Massachusetts and New York, the ventilation requirement has been substantially reduced, because it is generally accepted among school planners that the 30-cubic-foot-per-student requirement is excessive and unnecessary in the ordinary school classroom.

The purpose of ventilation in schools is twofold. It is well recognized of course, that a major function of ventilation systems is to remove body odors from classrooms and obnoxious odors from toilets, laboratories, and kitchens. It is not as generally recognized, however, that cooling is really one of the most important functions of a ventilating system. When it is realized that human beings generate about 250 Btu (British thermal units) per hour, the need to remove heat from classrooms assumes new proportions. For example, the amount of heat generated by 300 persons occupying a multipurpose room can be as high as 75,000 Btu per hour, which equals the heating capacity of many home furnaces. Once a given instructional space in a school is heated to the desired temperature, ventilation for cooling must be provided unless the heat loss of the room exceeds the amount of heat generated by its occupants. In some spaces in a school building, such as shower rooms, drying rooms, and basement storage areas, it is necessary to provide ventilation to remove excessive moisture, as well as heat.

It is fairly well agreed among school planners and designers that a ventilation system providing between 10 and 15 cubic feet of fresh air per student per minute is adequate for the dilution and removal of obnoxious substances from the air in classrooms.

Heating, Cooling, and Ventilation Systems

It is not within the scope of this book to discuss the engineering aspects of the various mechanical systems commonly installed in school or college buildings, but a certain amount of descriptive information regarding these systems may be helpful to educational planners. As a rule, heating, cooling, and ventilating are conceived as a single system rather than three isolated and independent systems. Each could operate quite satisfactorily as an independent unit from the standpoint of engineering design, but it would not be economical, since many parts of an integrated system can be designed for dual or triple use. Basically, the mechanical system consists of a source of heat, a device for cooling, a method for ventilating (window, fans, closed systems), and a means of conveying heat from one point to another.

The design of mechanical equipment has reached a high level in terms of efficiency and automation. The choice of equipment is no longer as simple as it was a quarter of a century ago. Closely tied to the selection of equipment is the choice of fuel. While wood and coal were the only common fuels not too long ago, today heat energy can be derived from oil, gas, electricity, radioactive material, the earth's surface, the atmosphere, and the sun. The debate regarding the best source of heat continues. The greatest competition for the heating dollar has been between gas and oil and, to a lesser extent, coal. Electricity is no longer a serious challenge to oil and gas as a heat source. The choice of fuel is primarily a matter of economics, involving both the cost of the fuel and the operation of the equipment that converts the energy into heat. For example, while the cost of electricity per Btu of heat developed is generally higher than it is for other fuels, the system does not require the employment of a stationary engineer in a school, nor does it require the construction of a boiler room. It is the total cost over a period of time that should have a strong bearing on the selection of a fuel or form of energy. Again, the heating engineer can make an important contribution in this selection (see Chapter 9).

Heating. There are at least five basic types of heating systems, ranging from the heat pump to forced hot air. Each system has features that are best suited to a particular situation. For college campuses, a high-pressure steam system is most likely to produce the best results, particularly when a central power plant is provided. For high schools having a capacity of 1,000 or more students, low-pressure steam or a hot-water system can be used advantageously. In smaller educational facilities, it is possible to install forced hot-air, hot-water, or low-pressure steam systems.

The two less commonly used heating systems are heat pumps and resistance-type electrical heating units. The heat pump basically operates on the same principle as does a refrigerator. Heat is taken from one temperature zone and moved to another through the use of a compressor and a special fluid. During the winter, for example, heat is taken from coils placed in the ground or exposed to the air and conveyed to the interior of a building. During the summer, the cycle is reversed. Heat is taken from the interior and conveyed to the coils. Thus, a heat pump serves as an air-conditioning unit in the summer and as a heater in the winter. Another promising type of heating system consists of individual resistance-type, electrically heated baseboard convecters. In some instances, electrically heated coils are used to heat water contained in a radiator-type heat exchanger. This method provides so-called "wet-type heat" electrically.

Radiant-heat systems merit serious consideration for use in educational facilities. The system consists of a network of piping that is usually embedded in the floor or ceiling of the space being heated. When hot water is pumped through the pipes, the entire floor or ceiling is heated. Radiant-heated floors are ideal in kindergarten rooms where children often sit on the floor. The major advantage in radiant heating is comfort. Heat radiated from a large surface does not depend upon the intervening air medium for its effectiveness. Thus, it is conceivable that persons occupying spaces heated by radiant panels may be quite comfortable when the air temperature is several degrees below the usual 68° Fahrenheit.

Cooling. General air-conditioning is receiving much attention in the planning of educational facilities. The prospect that school and college buildings may soon be used year round strongly accentuates the need for cooling as well as heating. For this reason, general air-conditioning is commonplace in modern college buildings. The central air-conditioning system using ducts, which is found in home air-conditioning, is not very economical when entire sections of large buildings are involved. The most common method of cooling such buildings involves the use of chilled water. A three-pipe system with air handlers and traps to collect the condensate from the moisture in the air seems to be one of the most effective and economical methods of providing cooling in the various spaces in a school building. The additional cost of the third pipe and provision for trapping the condensate is nominal. If funds are not available to purchase cooling equipment during construction, it might be prudent to plan for future air-conditioning by installing the third pipe and specially designed air blowers at the time of construction. The cooling unit may be installed later.

The cooling unit is usually located on the roof. Two basic types are currently available. The compressor type, which is mechanically driven, is quite common in both home and industrial units. A second type is a diffusion method that uses heat to produce cooling. In this instance, the same steam boilers are used to produce space heating in the winter and space cooling in the summer.

Ventilation Methods. Many ingenious methods of ventilating buildings have been devised. In one instance, warm room air is drawn through the space between the top of the suspended ceiling and the bottom of the roof. Thus, the exhausted air provides a warm buffer between the ceiling and the roof. Another method simply exhausts the air through the corridors and ultimately out of the building.

Whenever air is exhausted, there is a corresponding intake of fresh air. In general, fresh air is preheated before it enters the classroom. The fresh air is often mixed with a certain proportion of recirculated air before it is introduced into the spaces to be ventilated. One frequently used method of providing a mixture of tempered fresh air and recirculated air is the unit ventilator. These units are generally installed along the outside wall of a building with a direct intake of fresh air from the outside. The unit can be adjusted to mix predetermined proportions of fresh and recirculated air. When unit ventilators are employed for air cooling, they can be set for the recirculation of air only. It should be pointed out, however, that a certain amount of fresh air is desirable even when the system is in the cooling cycle.

Special attention should be given to the ventilation of certain areas in school and college facilities. The gymnasium and natatorium are two facilities that merit special design considerations. The obvious problem in the natatorium, reduction of moisture, can be handled through an exhaust system which simply forces moisture outside of the building, or through a dehumidifier whose condensate can be fed back into the pool. Locker and shower areas deserve special consideration. Air is sometimes exhausted through the locker so that odors from soiled clothing are exhausted to the outside. Excessive moisture is also a problem in these spaces. Kitchen areas require ventilation primarily for cooling but also to prevent food odors from permeating the school building. And finally, special ventilation is required in spaces where noxious fumes are likely to be present, such as a paint room, chemistry laboratory, biology laboratory, and the like.

Control of Humidity. Although architects are currently not paying special attention to general humidity control in school buildings, both comfort and learning can be appreciably improved if *complete* air-conditioning, including humidity control, is provided.

NOTES

1. William Turner and Terry Brennan, "Radon's Threat Can Be Subdued," *Solar Age* (May 1985), pp. 19ff.

2. Marguerite Smollen, "Radon Remedies," *New Shelter* (June 1984), pp. 28ff.

3. Steve Bliss, "Breathing Free, Part I," *Solar Age* (November 1984), p. 42.

▶ 11

Acoustical and
Visual Environments

ERGONOMICS APPLIED TO EDUCATIONAL FACILITY PLANNING

Ergonomics is the science of human engineering. The words, *human engineering,* are somewhat misleading. They have nothing whatsoever to do with "engineering" human beings. Rather, ergonomics is concerned with engineering the *working situation* and the *architectural environment* to satisfy the physical and psychological needs of human beings. In short, human engineering is simply the science of planning buildings for people. This concept is undoubtedly as old as architecture itself, even though the science of human engineering is relatively new. In the past, architects were primarily concerned with the macroscopic necessities of human beings, such as heating, cooling, and ventilating, but largely neglected the microscopic elements of human needs. Human engineering, therefore, is a form of microarchitecture that focuses attention on the small details of building design that affect the health, safety, comfort, working conditions, and well-being of every person occupying a building, be it school, factory, or home.

Certain aspects of ergonomics have already been covered in this text. The psychological implications of educational facility planning and the special design of spaces for people working with computers were discussed in Chapter 2. The ergonomic elements of safety, health, and comfort were covered in Chapter 10. Matters related to human engineering concerning the acoustical and visual environment are discussed later in this chapter. And finally, ergonomic considerations related specifically to the planning of elementary schools, secondary schools, and colleges are described in the next three chapters. For those interested in delving more deeply into the science of ergonomics, it is suggested that they refer to the latest publications on either "ergonomics" or "human engineering." Both McCormick[1] and Popanek[2] have published comprehensive treatments on the subject in relation to industrial engineering. It is hoped that the authorities on ergonomics will someday concentrate their efforts on the "ergonomics of educational facility planning."

By and large, architects and engineers have given much thought to the comfort, health, and safety of school personnel and students, but their convenience and psychological needs have not always received the attention they merit. For example, one junior high school in central Illinois was designed so that on a cold wintry morning it took the custodian about 45 minutes to open dampers, close valves, and turn on switches located in different parts of the 1,500-student school. It would have been much more efficient if at least some of the equipment could have been operated by remote control and if the valves could have been located to permit more efficient use of the custodian's time.

The psychological well-being of faculty, staff, and students is also an important aspect of school planning. Architects have, to be sure, made a conscious effort to produce structures that are psychologically stimulating to the learner. However, much more can be done to plan schools that reflect the psychological needs of school personnel. School planners should also take into consideration design features that can reduce environmental causes of fatigue, such as background noises, glare, structural vibration due to mechanical equipment, and the like.

THE ACOUSTICAL ENVIRONMENT

Noise pollution is an ever-increasing public concern. It threatens the peace and quiet of residential neighborhoods and is a challenge for educational facility planners. Noise pollution refers to the presence of unwanted sound within a given space, such as a classroom. The techniques for reducing it are covered in detail in this chapter. Noise poses a real threat for students engaged in learning. Current research reveals that "noise levels of the magnitude of 75.5 decibels (A scale) deny an equal and adequate opportunity for students to be educated and for teachers to practice their profession."[3]

A significant portion of the instructional function depends upon good hearing conditions. Consequently, in designing a school building, it is imperative to plan for excellent hearing conditions just as for a first-rate visual environment. Recent research on the effect of noise on the learning process has shed new light on the reaction of students to the presence of disturbing noise levels. According to Glass, "In order to tune out the noise, the student also tunes out the instruction."[4]

Sound control in school buildings deals with two distinct types of acoustical problems. One is concerned with sound-conditioning within a given space, while the other is focused upon sound transmission from one space to another. Contrary to popular belief, sound-conditioning does not necessarily solve the sound transmission problem. The principles underlying the solutions to one type of problem are quite different from those related to the other.

Sound-Conditioning

Sound-conditioning refers to the treatment of interior surfaces of a given space to attain the desired reverberation time for the type of activity to be housed in the space. The persistence of sound within an enclosure after the source is shut off is called reverberation. Reverberation time, in the strictly technical sense, is defined as the time required for any given sound to decrease in intensity to one-millionth of its initial value. Optimal reverberation time is the recommended reverberation time for a specific space that is consistent with its volume and purpose. Table 11-1 contains a list of spaces commonly found in schools, together with their optimum reverberation times. Volume is a critical factor in dealing with reverberation times. The figures appearing in column 3 should be adjusted in situations where the

TABLE 11-1 **Optimal Reverberation Times for Selected Educational Spaces**

Type of Space	Volume in Cu. Ft.	Optimal Reverberation Time for Schools in Sec.	Estimated Number of Additional Sabins Required for Each Space
Kindergarten	13,200	0.60	847
Elementary school classrooms	9,900	0.63	556
Secondary school classrooms	9,240	0.63	509
Science laboratories	13,320	0.57	835
Homemaking	12,936	0.67	727
Business machines rooms or laboratories	9,240	0.63	528
Art rooms	12,320	0.65	698
Music rooms	12,150	1.09	260
Library reading room	19,800	0.59	1,220
Auditoriums (for schools)	95,160	1.13	1,412
Gymnasiums	145,920	0.84	6,427
Cafeteria	55,000	0.76	2,202
Conference room	5,500	0.66	
Shops and corridors	Maximum treatment within practical limits		

Source: Basil Castaldi, "Sound Control in School Buildings," Ed.D. dissertation, Teachers College, Columbia University, 1952, pp. 72, 75.

volume of the space in question differs from that appearing in column 2. The correction for volume is made as follows:

a. For volumes greater than those appearing in column 2, *increase* the reverberation time in column 3 by 0.0015 second for each 1,000 cubic feet of volume in excess of figures given in column 2. (Round off figures to the closest 1,000 cubic feet in all computations.)

b. For spaces having volumes less than those shown in column 2, *decrease* the reverberation time in column 3 by 0.0015 second for each 1,000 cubic feet of volume of difference between the space in question and the figure given in column 2.

Amount of Acoustical Treatment Required

The acoustical treatment of an enclosure is accomplished by covering certain areas of its internal surfaces with sound-absorbing materials, such as acoustical tiles or acoustical plasters. Different materials have different sound-absorbing characteristics. The total sound absorption within a given space is measured in "Sabins." One Sabin is defined as the quantity of sound that is absorbed by an open window having an area of 1 square foot. This unit of sound absorption is named after the "father of modern acoustics," Wallace C. Sabine, who was a professor of physics at Harvard University during the first part of the twentieth century.

Column 4 in Table 11-1 contains the number of additional Sabins of absorption that would be required in educational spaces of the type and volume indicated in columns 1 and 2, respectively. The number of square feet of acoustical material needed is determined by dividing the number given in column 4 by the sound absorption coefficient of the material to be used. The figures in Table 11-1 are based on the volume and optimal reverberation times required for each type of space. Without getting into technical details, the reverberation times shown in column 3 were determined by using a formula devised by Wallace Sabine, who was mentioned earlier. The figures in column 4 represent the number of sound-absorbing units (sabins) that must be added to each type of space in order to achieve optimal hearing conditions. Each figure takes into account the amount of sound absorption present in each type of space before acoustical treatment.

Table 11-1 should be used by school officials primarily for determining the financial feasibility of improving the acoustical environment of an existing instructional space. Once the amount of required acoustical material is known using Table 11-1, the approximate cost of sound conditioning a given space can be determined. It is suggested, however, that the exact amount of acoustical treatment required for any space be computed by an acoustics expert before a contract is awarded for the work.

Good hearing conditions in classrooms are not guaranteed by the common rule of thumb used by architects—treating the entire ceiling. Acoustical treatment should be computed on a room-by-room basis, depending its use, its size, and its shape. For this reason, educators should insist that competent acoustical consultants participate in planning a school in the same manner as the heating consultant, the lighting consultant, and the structural consultant.

Distribution of Acoustical Materials Within an Enclosure

A number of studies[5] have clearly demonstrated that acoustical materials are not as effective when applied over an entire ceiling as when they are applied in other locations. In some classrooms in which the entire ceiling is treated, the amount of sound absorption is excessive, and the quality of hearing conditions is substantially reduced. In order to produce good hearing conditions, it is necessary to

a. add sufficient sound-absorption materials to obtain optimum reverberation times within an enclosure, consistent with its function.
b. retain the sound-reflective properties of the ceiling to improve the transmission of sound from one end of the room to the other.

Only sufficient and necessary amounts of acoustical materials should be used, and they should be located at points of maximum sound pressure within a room. Applying such materials where sound pressure is at a minimum reduces the effectiveness of the materials and wastes money. For example, sometimes acoustical materials are installed in the concave depressions in corridor ceilings, using pan-type concrete construction. Acoustical improvement is insignificant under such an arrangement because very little of the noise generated in the corridor strikes the acoustical surface. Another example of inefficient use of acoustical materials is found in high gymnasiums where ceilings over 22 feet above the floor are fully treated with acoustical materials. Again, the acoustical results are quite disappointing. It would have been far better, in this case, to treat the upper walls of the gymnasium instead of the entire ceiling.

Acoustical materials should be located where the sound pressures are at a maximum, whenever possible. Theoretically, high sound pressures from noises generated within a room exist in areas where large surfaces intersect at angles less than 180°. In conventional classrooms where the intersecting angles of large surfaces approximate 90°, the sound pressure is very high at such intersections. When sound strikes in the vicinity of the intersection of two walls in a room, it usually undergoes two reflections before returning to the interior of the room where it can reach a listener again. Thus, if two adjacent walls are treated, the intensity of the sound ultimately reflected back into the enclosure after at least two corner reflections is substantially weakened.

For the most effective distribution of acoustical materials, and for improved hearing conditions, it is suggested that

1. acoustical materials be used at the edges of larger surfaces, where two surfaces meet, and at the corners.
2. no sound-absorbing materials be installed on the central areas of ceilings in classrooms or lecture rooms.
3. the edges of ceilings and upper edges of walls in classrooms be treated with acoustical materials.
4. acoustical treatment *not* be concentrated on one wall or ceiling of an instructional space.
5. sound materials be installed in panels or vertical strips about two feet wide in large rooms. Acoustical patches, uniformly but not symmetrically distributed, may also be used quite effectively in larger instructional spaces.

Noise Control in School Buildings

Thus far, we have been concerned with the judicious use of sound-absorbing materials to enhance a wanted sound produced in a room. The intelligibility of wanted sounds can also be significantly improved by the reduction of noise interference originating outside of the room.

Unwanted sounds may be controlled by

1. selecting a school site that is removed from sources of unwanted sounds.
2. suppressing them at the source.
3. isolating noisy areas from quiet ones.
4. *acoustically* (not necessarily physically) isolating noisy equipment from the rest of the structure.
5. designing partitions possessing the proper sound transmission loss.

In planning a school for sound control, it is also helpful to bear the following principles in mind.

1. It is uneconomical to reduce the intensity of a sound entering a room to a level much below the existing or normal noise level within the room.
2. For maximum economy, all sound paths into or out of a room should be insulated to about the same level against penetration of unwanted noises. For example, it is not justifiable to install a movable partition having a transmission loss of 40 decibels when the ceiling and duct work provide for, let us say, a 25-decibel transmission loss.
3. It is not economical to reduce the duct noises to a level much below that existing in the ordinary classroom environment.

The transmission of noise in any building is either airborne or structure-borne. Sounds normally produced in a classroom or lecture hall are airborne. Speech, music, and audiovisual equipment originate sounds that reach the listener through the intervening air. The containment of this type of sound within the enclosure where it originates is relatively simple. The introduction of massive, nonporous partitions and heavy acoustically stripped doors with double-glazed windows usually solves this problem. In most situations, it is not necessary to take all of these precautions to control airborne noises. Oftentimes, a well-designed, massive, airtight partition between two adjoining instructional spaces suffices.

The isolation of structure-borne noises, on the other hand, is a problem that is not easily solved once the building is constructed. Unless structure-borne noises are handled properly by the design of the building, noise control measures may be costly and only mildly effective. An excellent example of structure-borne sound in a school is that made by the impact of hard heels on concrete. Such sounds carry over long distances, without much attenuation through the structure of the building. Another source of structure-borne noises is the mechanical equipment in the building, such as fans, pumps, transformers, air-conditioners, steam pipes, and water systems. Isolation of noise sources from the structure is one of the best methods of coping with such structure-borne noises. Acoustical discontinuities in the structural design of a school also help to control structure-borne noises. Resilient platforms should be provided for noisy equipment, such as pianos, record players, drums, and other instruments resting on the floor. Stages, for example, are designed as resilient platforms to minimize structure-borne noises.

Noise from Ventilating Systems

A common source of unwanted noise is the ventilating system, which may give rise to motor noises, turbulent air at grille openings and within ducts, and "cross-talk." None of these sources of noise presents a technological problem. The science of ventilation is so advanced that none of these acoustical deficiencies need be tolerated in a well-designed school. "Cross-talk" refers to the transmission of sounds from one space to another through the ventilating ducts. This shortcoming can be readily corrected by installing a sufficient amount of duct liner inside ducts.

Acoustical Partitions

Walls separating one instructional space from another should be acoustically designed so that noise generated in one space does not interfere with the activities in the adjoining instructional spaces. With the advent of many types of movable partitions, it becomes of paramount importance that the partition selected possess at least the minimum required acoustical properties. It is also essential that permanent or destructible partitions be designed with sufficient acoustical transmission loss to satisfy the conditions under which they are to be utilized.

The following rule of thumb may be helpful in the design or selection of a partition separating instructional spaces: "The transmission loss in decibels of any partition should be equal to ten plus the difference between the outside noise level and the acceptable background noise for the space in question."[6] Stated in mathematical terms,

$$T.L. = 10 + (O_{db} - B_{db})$$

where:

      $T.L.$ = minimum transmission loss of the desired partition
       O = noise level in decibels on the outside of the partition
       B = noise level in decibels of background noises within
            the space to be enclosed.

The application of this formula, however, should be made by an acoustical consultant.

    Table 11-2 may be of some assistance in guiding educational planners in the choice of partitions to be used between various types of instructional spaces. In applying these figures, care should be taken that other paths of sound transmission have transmission losses equal to or greater than the figures given in the table. Other paths include ceilings, ducts, windows, and doors.

TABLE 11-2 **Minimum Sound Transmission Losses (in Decibels) Between Several Types of Instructional Spaces**

	Auditorium	Music Teaching Room	Office	Study Area	Classroom or Lecture Hall
Classroom or lecture room	45–55	45–55	35–45	35–45	35–45
Study hall	×	45–55	35–45	35–45	35–45
Office	×	45–55	35–45	35–45	35–45
Vocal music teaching room	×	50–65	35–45	45–55	45–55
Corridors	35–45	35–45	×	×	25–35
Shop	45–60	45–60	×	×	35–50
Gymnasium	45–60	45–60	×	×	35–50
Cafeteria	45–60	45–60	×	×	35–50
Toilet	45–55	45–55	×	×	35–45
Mechanical equipment room	45–55	45–55	×	×	35–45
Business machines room or laboratory	×	×	35–50	×	×
Band room	50–65	50–65	×	×	40–55

Source: Basil Castaldi, "Sound Control in School Buildings," Ed.D. dissertation, Teachers College, Columbia University, 1952, p. 132.

Construction of partitions possessing transmission losses of about 60 decibels is costly. Such walls can usually be avoided in the planning of school buildings simply by removing the exceptionally noisy spaces from the quiet zones. Only in very rare cases, therefore, will it become necessary to resort to the design of partitions having transmission losses in excess of 45 decibels.

Table 11-3 contains the transmission loss range for various types of wall construction.

Carpeting as a Substitute for Other Acoustical Materials

The use of carpeting as an acoustical material in school buildings is receiving increased attention by both educators and architects. At the present time, the major deterrent to the widespread acceptance of carpeting in school buildings is the luxury image associated with it in the past. Resistance to the use of carpeting in school buildings has all but disappeared. Following World War II, manufacturers of carpeting and the Educational Facilities Laboratories in New York made a number of studies showing that, due to lower maintenance, the pay-back period for carpeting

TABLE 11-3   **Sound Transmission Loss of Selected Types of Wall Construction**

Type of Construction	Average Transmission Loss in Decibels
A. 4" hollow pumice cement block, no plaster on faces	12
B. Single sheet $\frac{1}{4}$" plywood	22
C. Single sheet $\frac{1}{2}$" fiberboard	22
D. Single sheet $\frac{1}{8}$" glass	28
E. Double wall, $\frac{1}{4}$" fiberboard faces on 2 × 2-inch wood studs	28
F. Heavy wooden door, $2\frac{1}{2}$" thick; rubber gaskets, felt strip at bottom	28
G. Single sheet $\frac{1}{4}$" plate glass	33
H. Same as "A" above with $\frac{1}{2}$" of gypsum plaster on one side only	33
I. Same as "A" with $\frac{1}{2}$" gypsum plaster on both sides	38
J. $\frac{3}{4}$" plaster board on one side of 2 × 4-inch studs	38
K. 4" structural clay tile core of 4" hollow cinder block with $\frac{5}{8}$" plaster on both sides	42
L. 2 × 4 wood studs, $\frac{1}{2}$" gypsum plaster faces on $\frac{3}{8}$" gypsum lath, special nailing or resilient clip on plaster lath	42
M. 4" reinforced concrete wall	48
N. 8" brick walls, $\frac{1}{2}$" gypsum plaster faces	52

Source: Basil Castaldi, "Sound Control in School Buildings," Ed.D. dissertation, Teachers College, Columbia University, 1952, pp. 133–134.

was less than 12 years. The case for carpeting based upon the initial cost is no longer crucial, due to new methods of carpet installation that make it possible to replace finished wood or tile flooring with carpeting. Furthermore, with the ever-changing cost of materials, cost predictions become meaningless. The advice offered in the *Guide for Planning Educational Facilities* regarding carpeting is timely and sound. The guide suggests a logical approach, ". . . carpeting should be evaluated on the same basis as other floor coverings—initial cost, upkeep, and ability to do the job."[7]

The use of carpeting in spaces such as classrooms, seminar rooms, corridors, and libraries involves several considerations related to function, such as the need to

1. eliminate cold floors and conserve energy.
2. reduce the severity of injuries due to falls.
3. eliminate floor-generated noises due to the movement of chairs, desks, and the like.
4. absorb noises and improve the acoustical environment.
5. create an atmosphere that is quiet, aesthetically pleasing, and conducive to effective learning.[8]

THE VISUAL ENVIRONMENT

In the past, any discussion of visual conditions in school buildings was confined for the most part to artificial and natural lighting. In fact, until recently, natural lighting was considered the primary source of illumination in school buildings. For this reason, the maximum width of classrooms has been limited to about 22 feet. Since the light reaching the innermost part of a room enters through the upper portions of the windows, the width of classrooms has been determined to a large extent by the height of classroom ceilings. The old rule of thumb held that the width of a classroom should not exceed twice the distance from the floor to the top of the glass portion of a window plus 1 foot. Recently, the emphasis has shifted from natural to artificial illumination, which no longer fixes the width of any space in which adequate lighting is desired.

Visual environment is a much broader concept than school lighting, however. School planners must be concerned with natural and artificial lighting, with brightness differences, reflection coefficients, fenestration, and interior decoration. All of these factors affect the visual characteristics of a given space and the quality of the seeing conditions in school buildings. Every instructional area in a school building should possess an environment that promotes the visual health of its occupants.

Illumination Levels in Educational Spaces

The intensity of the illumination in any classroom is crucial to good seeing conditions, and the distribution of the light within the enclosure should be uniform and free from glare. The intensity of illumination required in school buildings depends upon the function of each type of teaching area and can vary widely from one to the other.

There is still no optimum value of light intensity that can be recommended for each space. The foot-candle values given above refer to minimum required levels of illumination. The unit foot-candle is defined as the intensity of light striking a surface at a distance of one foot from a standard candle. During the early part of this century, it was believed that, because the human eye is so extremely adaptable, light intensities ranging from 15 to 20 foot-candles were acceptable levels of illumination. In modern school design, however, the illumination levels have increased substantially. The accepted ranges of reasonable levels of illumination are shown in Table 11-4. When energy was abundant and inexpensive, there was a gradual trend toward raising the levels of intensity of illumination by substantial amounts. Research is still inconclusive regarding the absolute value of the level of illumination that should be maintained in various instructional spaces. Blackwell's work at the University of Michigan provided new insights on the problem of light intensity.[9]

In his research, Blackwell analyzed 31 samples of handwriting taken from a sixth-grade class in Toronto. To obtain a 90-percent visual efficiency, the intensity of illumination was varied from one foot-candle to over 80 foot-candles, depending on the writing samples. The study did not establish whether or not high intensities were absolutely necessary to protect the visual health of the students. It did, however, show that visual efficiency dropped below the 90-percent level for more than 40 percent of the class when the average intensity was reduced to below 63 foot-candles. It is not unreasonable to assume that students would not be asked to perform tasks as difficult as those included in the experiment for more than 15 minutes per day at the elementary school level. In view of the need to conserve energy (see Chapter 9), it is difficult to justify raising the intensity of illumination

TABLE 11-4 **Ranges of Illumination Recommended for Various Educational Areas**

Type of Space	Foot-Candles of Illumination Required
Classrooms, study halls, libraries, offices, art rooms, shops, and laboratories	30–40
Special education rooms, drafting rooms, typing rooms, and sewing rooms	50–70
Physical education, reception rooms	20–25
General service rooms, such as auditoriums, cafeterias, locker rooms, rest rooms, and stairways	15–25
Open corridors and storerooms	10–20

to the 60 foot-candle level in all instructional spaces for the relatively small gain in visual effectiveness.

According to Rankin, "The goal of school lighting must be to contribute to the creation of an effective, total environment for learning."[10] Rankin also points out, "Research indicates that age, experience, and fatigue greatly affect the quantity of light that a person needs to perform a task." Thus far, standards of illumination have been focused primarily on the nature of the task to be accomplished by the students and staff. Rankin suggests that the adoption of the concept of Equivalent Sphere Illumination (ESI) is a better method of specifying illuminance. In addition to the factors already included in the standards, as set forth by the Illuminating Engineering Society (Table 11-4), the proposed new scale for illuminance described by Rankin would also take into account the effects of glare and contrast within the visual field. Rankin hastens to add, however, that the present ESI suggested levels of illuminance shown in Table 11-5 are not yet ready to be recommended for general application. He believes that more research is needed before the levels of illuminance in various types of educational spaces can be finalized.

The Ontario Ministry of Education has adopted the ESI scale of illuminance presented in Table 11-5 as an interim step until additional research data become available. The illuminance figures presented in this table were determined by taking

TABLE 11-5 Recommended Illuminances by Ontario Ministry of Education as of 1982

Type of Spaces	Illuminance in LUX Units	Illuminance in Foot-Candles
Instructional Spaces		
1. Classrooms, study halls, art rooms, laboratories, music and seminar rooms	500	46.5
2. Drafting rooms, typing rooms, sewing rooms (with supplementary local lighting), shops	500	46.5
3. Kindergarten rooms	350	32.5
4. Gymnasium	250	23.2
5. Large room instruction (with capability of varying the intensity by 50%)	250	23.2
6. Laboratory demonstration desks	750	69.7
Supplementary Spaces		
7. Library reading rooms, cafeteria kitchen areas	500	46.5
8. Cafeteria serving areas	350	32.5
9. Auditorium, cafeteria dining areas, corridors with lockers, gymnasium locker and shower areas, library stack areas, mechanical and service spaces	250	23.2
10. Corridors without lockers, storage spaces	100	9.3

Source: John C. Rankin, "Lighting for Our Schools," paper presented at the annual meeting of The Council of Educational Facility Planners, 1982, p. 39. ERIC file no: ED 225287.

the figures recommended by the Illuminating Engineering Society shown in Table 11-4 and applying weighting factors to them to account for other elements that affect the visual environment, such as glare and contrast.

A comparison of the figures in Table 11-4, listing the standards of the Illuminating Engineering Society, and those in Table 11-5 reflecting the Equivalent Sphere Illumination recommendations reveals that the differences in the level of illuminance between the two tables for equivalent educational spaces are not really enormous. The major differences occur in two categories. The figures in Table 11-5 are slightly higher for classroom activities, 46.5 foot-candles compared to 40, and a bit lower than the standards set forth by the Illuminating Engineering Society in corridors and storage areas. This finding, however, is perfectly consistent with the goals and objectives of the Ontario Ministry of Education. Their level of illuminance seems to be a little higher in spaces where lighting is more critical for the visual task and lower than the Illuminating Engineering Society standards where the visual task is less demanding on the quality and quantity of light. This interim scale seems to be a step in the right direction. As indicated by Rankin, more studies are needed before levels of illuminance can be specified on a more scientific basis. There is every reason to believe that new research findings will provide new insights into the field of illumination—perhaps even shed more light on the subject.

Brightness Ratios.   Acceptable visual environments depend upon the intensity of the illumination and upon the brightness differences existing in any given space. An intolerable visual environment may be created in a room that possesses a high intensity of illumination, unless brightness ratios are maintained within acceptable limits. Brightness ratios are determined by comparing the brightness of the visual task with that of the surrounding field of vision. On the basis of the brightness goals adopted by the National Council on Schoolhouse Construction[11] for a total environment where critical seeing is necessary, the following criteria are suggested:

a. The foot-lambert brightness of any surface viewed from any normal standing or sitting position in the schoolroom should not exceed 10 times the foot-lambert brightness of the poorest-lighted task in the room.
b. The foot-lambert brightness of any surface viewed from any standing or sitting position in the schoolroom should not be less than one-third the foot-lambert brightness of the poorest-lighted task in the room.
c. The foot-lambert brightness of any surface immediately adjacent to the task should not exceed the brightness of the task and should be at least one-third its brightness.
d. The brightness difference between adjoining surfaces should be reduced to a minimum.
e. The brightness goals stated above assume a lighting system that provides from 30 to 50 foot-candles on the poorest-lighted task. As foot-candle levels are increased, sources of high brightness should be controlled to approach more

nearly the brightness of the task. The extent of the area of the surface producing the brightness has a measurable effect upon visual comfort. Generally, small areas of either extremes of brightness are less noticeable than are large areas of the same brightness.

f. Light distribution from any source should be such that direct and specular glare are eliminated for the observer to the greatest possible degree.

g. These objectives or goals should be achieved without the loss of a cheerful, friendly, and aesthetically pleasant classroom environment or of a balanced and acceptable thermal and auditory environment.

Reflectance from Interior Surfaces. The light reflection characteristics of interior surfaces, furnishings, and equipment are extremely critical in designing a well-balanced visual environment within an instructional space. The goals for achieving a first-rate visual environment were presented earlier in this chapter and a set of recommended brightness ratios were specified for educational spaces. The achievement of these goals and recommendations involves the control of three major elements that affect the visual environment. The first one is the color and texture of interior surface. The second component is the intensity and quality of the light within the room, both natural and artificial. And the third element is the shape, orientation, and design of the space itself. Simply stated, these goals demand that normally dark areas be made brighter and that sources of high brightness be reduced or controlled. More specifically:

1. *Floors should be as light in color as possible.* Floor surfaces should possess light reflection coefficients ranging between 30 and 40 percent.

2. *Walls, including the wainscoting, should be quite reflective.* The light reflection coefficient of walls should be greater than 60 percent.

3. *Ceilings should diffuse as much light as possible.* Reflection factors of over 90 percent are suggested for soffits and ceilings.

4. *Chalkboards should be as light in color as possible.* Since large areas of black chalkboards absorb a considerable amount of light, green or beige chalkboards are preferred. When perfected, whiteboards are ideal.

5. *Furniture surfaces, such as desk tops and chairs, should possess a light-reflecting factor of about 40 percent.*

6. *Adjoining surfaces should be finished in colors that create a minimum brightness difference.* For example, dark trim around windows violates criterion (d) because it presents too great a contrast to the brightness of the light entering through the window. Another violation of this principle is committed when door trims are painted or stained in dark colors in rooms with pastel-colored walls.

7. *High brightness should be controlled electronically, mechanically, or architecturally.* The common sources of high brightness are glare from the sky or snow cover, direct or reflected sunlight, and artificial light from incandescent bulbs or fluorescent tubes. Lighting engineers and architects have developed many very

effective solutions to the problem of glare. Educators and school plant planners should insist that the architect and the lighting engineer design the building with lighting fixtures and light controls that will satisfy both the specific requirements of illumination in a given space and the lighting goals described in the preceding paragraph. It is not within the scope of this book to discuss luminaries and the light distribution and glare characteristics of the various fixtures. Suffice it to say, however, that luminous ceilings merit serious consideration where high-quality general illumination for instructional spaces is required. Suspended light fixtures of both the fluorescent and incandescent type are also quite satisfactory, provided they illuminate both the ceilings and the floors, and provided that they are properly spaced and installed at a sufficient distance below the ceiling. There are instances where concentric ring-type incandescent fixtures, for example, have been installed so close to the ceiling that they create a series of light and dark spots on the ceiling surface. The same undesirable condition results when certain fluorescent fixtures are attached directly to the ceiling.

Fluorescent Lighting.   In the past, there has been some controversy over whether or not to install fluorescent-type fixtures in school buildings. Questions were often raised concerning possible health hazards associated with fluorescent-type illumination. It has been fairly well established, however, that the light source, whether it be sunlight, incandescent light, or fluorescent light, has no deleterious effect on the eyes of human beings, provided it satisfies the light goals described earlier. The choice of type of illumination, therefore, cannot be made on the basis of student health. From the standpoint of long-range economy, fluorescent lighting is demonstrably cheaper than incandescent fixtures. While the initial cost of fluorescent fixtures is substantially higher than that of incandescent lighting, the amount of light produced per kilowatt of power is almost 50 percent greater for fluorescent-type fixtures. One school district in the Boston area made careful cost studies of the two fixtures and found that within seven years the savings in the cost of power compensated for the initial cost and maintenance of fluorescent fixtures. As energy costs increase, the pay-back period decreases accordingly.

Control of Natural Light.   Bothersome natural light appears in the guise of snow glare, sky glare, and direct sunlight. Oftentimes, windows in instructional spaces facing north have not been equipped with light controls on the assumption that direct sunlight does not enter from this direction. True, it does not, but the visual environment in such a space leaves much to be desired. The light reaching the occupants of such a space from the sky is bright enough to cause headaches.

   Natural light can be controlled in many instances by the appropriate design of the building itself. Overhangs, horizontal or vertical louvres, and externally mounted slats or venetian blinds help to control natural light. Also, natural light can be controlled effectively by the judicious use of fenestration. Vision strips along the exterior walls of a building require a minimum of internal light control and satisfy the psychological needs of the students with respect to an environment that is conducive to learning.

The control of natural light within an instructional space may be achieved through the use of some type of window covering designed to shield the students from glare or direct sunlight. The most common device for controlling natural light is the translucent shade on spring-loaded rollers. In this case, separate opaque shades with special side channels are drawn over the translucent shades to insure complete darkening of teaching spaces when motion picture projectors are used. With the increased use of the rear projection screen and television, the traditional "blackout" is no longer necessary. "Brownouts" are preferred because students can take notes during audiovisual presentations. Venetian blinds are considered the best devices for internally controlling light in a classroom. They are, however, considerably more difficult to maintain than drapes, curtains, or reticulated light screens.

Types of Natural Lighting

The Window Wall.   Natural light may be introduced into an educational space in various ways. The most common method, of course, is the ordinary window. Architects have employed a wide variety of window arrangements in bringing natural light into the classroom. They have designed instructional spaces with window walls containing panes which extend from floor to ceiling over most of an outside wall. Their primary objective in this case is to create the pleasant and desirable feeling of transplanting part of the out-of-doors into the classroom.

The Windowless Wall.   In contrast is the windowless wall which permits no outside light to enter an instructional area. The major argument favoring the use of windowless classrooms stems from the need to reduce the amount of heat gain within an enclosure and hence to reduce the load associated with air cooling on hot days. Some architects have suggested that windowless walls tend to reduce student distractions caused by the outside world. On the other hand, many educators argue that students should not be isolated from the rest of the world while in school. They also maintain that it is psychologically desirable for the learner to be distracted once in a while during the learning process. The argument has also been posed that students should be able to look at distant objects from time to time in order to relax the muscles controlling the focusing mechanism of the eye. This eye accommodation cannot be made in a windowless classroom of limited dimensions. And finally, the opponents of the windowless classroom argue that a person does not feel comfortable if he or she is confined to a windowless area for long periods of time. Suffice it so say at this point that tradition and persistence of habit would dictate that visual contact with the outside world be maintained as part of the visual environment of the modern classroom.

Tognoli made a study on the effect of the classroom environment on student attitudes and retention.[12] He found that students rated embellished rooms as "more interesting" than plain classrooms and found classrooms with both windows and embellishments "more pleasant." This research suggests that windowless classrooms do not contribute to the visual comfort of students working within such enclosures.

The Limited Window Wall. There are several window arrangements that lie somewhere between the window wall and the windowless classroom. The most promising, at this time, seems to be the vision strip along most of the outside wall of a classroom. The height of the window sill, in this case, would be about 6 inches below the eye level of seated students, and the top of the vision strip would be located about 6 inches above the eye level of the teacher in standing position. Another scheme for admitting a limited amount of natural light into the classroom involves the use of floor-to-ceiling slits. These slits may be located near each end of the room. The surface between the two groups of slits is usually a large opaque wall. This pattern of fenestration allows the occupants to have some visual contact with the weather and the outside world. The primary purpose of this window design is to keep the amount of heat gain within the classroom at a minimum. Another less important but significant advantage of the slit pattern is the ease with which an instructional space can be "browned out" for audiovisual presentations.

Sky Domes. The unhappy experiences associated with skylights in the past have strongly prejudiced members of boards of education and boards of trustees against the introduction of top lighting in educational facilities. It is true, of course, that skylights installed in the past presented a serious problem because of water leakage, maintenance difficulties, and cold air entering directly below them.

Modern sky domes present an entirely different and exciting picture. The problem of leakage has been solved completely. If sky domes are installed according to the manufacturer's instructions, no water leakage whatever should occur. Sky domes are generally constructed of clear or frosted plastic. Modern sky domes are so advanced in design that condensation flows through weep holes that conduct the condensate away from the dome where it will evaporate harmlessly into the room. There is also an electrical heating element attached to the underside of the sky dome that prevents the downdraft of cold air into the classroom.

The visual and psychological effect of the sky dome is dramatic. Natural light floods the educational spaces and creates a feeling of psychological warmth and visual comfort. There is a sense of being outside, particularly when clear plastic domes are employed. On the other hand, unless frosted plastic is used to diffuse the incoming sunlight, glare can be quite annoying and uncomfortable. Fortunately, there are a number of devices that effectively control the sky dome glare and also make it possible to darken the room completely for audiovisual purposes (see Chapter 9).

Recent Improvements in Artificial Lighting Sources

While there have been no spectacular changes in the basic technology for producing artificial light, the improvements made on existing light sources are quite remarkable. There are basically two major sources of artificial light. One of them is the familiar incandescent bulb, which produces light by heating a tungsten filament to incandescence. The other is the well-known fluorescent lamp, which generates light through the process of ionization. Mercury and sodium lamps, which are discussed in more detail later, operate on the same principle as the fluorescent tube.

The incandescent light bulb paved the way for the development of the tungsten halogen lamp. The two lamps utilize the same principle, but they differ in the nature of the gases that surround the filament. In the common incandescent light bulb, the tungsten filament is placed within a glass enclosure filled with a mixture of nitrogen and argon. In the tungsten halogen lamp, on the other hand, the filament is placed in a quartz envelope filled with iodine vapor. The light output of the halogen lamp is significantly higher than that of the ordinary incandescent bulb.

Another version of the fluorescent-type lamp is the high intensity discharge lamp commonly called HIDS in technical publications. There are four types of HIDS. Each type produces light of a different basic color. The four types are created by filling the discharge chambers with mercury, metal halide, high-, or low-pressure sodium. The low-pressure sodium lamp produces an unappealing yellow, muddy-looking light, but all of the others are suitable for school purposes.

And finally, there is the high-output lamp that is often installed out-of-doors to illuminate play areas, walks, and drives. Like the high intensity discharge lamp mentioned earlier, these high-output lamps are filled with the same four gases: mercury, metal halide, high-, or low-pressure sodium. The mercury lamp produces light having a bluish color. The metal halide lamp generates light that is a little whiter in color than the mercury lamp. The high-pressure sodium lamp gives a "golden white" light. And the low-pressure sodium lamp develops a yellow light, which is not suitable for interior school lighting because it turns the color of whatever it strikes yellow or muddy.[13]

The construction of this high-output lamp, along with the process by which light is produced, is quite interesting for those who are technically inclined. The lamp consists of two glass envelopes, one inside of the other. The innermost envelope produces both visible light and a high concentration of ultraviolet rays that are designed to energize the phosphorus in the outer container. Thus, both envelopes supplement each other in the production of large amounts of visible light. Unfortunately, the small amounts of ultraviolet rays that are not absorbed by the phosphorus are emitted by the lamp. In this connection, a word of caution is in order. While there is practically no emission of ultraviolet rays associated with ordinary fluorescent light, these high-output lamps radiate ultraviolet rays that may affect people who have light-sensitive skin. For this reason, care should be exercised if these high-output lamps are installed indoors or in outside locations where students may be exposed to ultraviolet rays from these lamps at close range.

Color and Lighting

The color of an object within a room is determined by the color of the object (as seen in daylight) and by the color of the light that is illuminating it within the room. For example, if a wall is painted white, it looks white only when it is illuminated by full-spectrum light, such as daylight. If the source of light is red, the white wall changes color. It looks red, because it reflects all colors, and red is the only color in the room. Let us add another dimension to this example. What would happen if the white wall were painted blue, and if the color of the light from its source were still red? The blue wall would theoretically look black, because the blue-painted wall absorbs all colors except blue. Since there is no blue in the light source, the blue wall reflects no color and looks black. Actually, walls are not always perfect absorbers. They may retain a modicum of reflectivity. Thus, if the red light were quite intense, one might see a tinge of red from the blue wall. Let us pursue this phenomenon one step further. What would be the difference in the color of the blue wall if the color of the light source were white or if it were blue? There would be no difference. It would look blue in both instances. Clearly, the color of the light source is just as important in producing a visual environment as the color of the walls, furnishings, and furniture.

Chromatic Quality of the Light Source.   According to Birren, "Artificial lighting should be neutral and slightly warm in quality."[14] This can be achieved through a warm-type fluorescent lamp. The light emitted from incandescent light bulbs commonly found in educational facilities is a little richer in the yellow spectrum than Birren suggests. Nevertheless, the chromatic quality of light produced by the incandescent bulb is generally quite adequate for most of the functional requisites of an educational facility. There are, however, a few instructional spaces where full-spectrum illumination (daylight quality) is crucial, such as art rooms, clothing laboratories, and paint shops. In this connection, Hathaway suggests that, "Where high color rendition is of major concern, natural light or full-spectrum light may be used."[15]

The Physical Effects of Color on People.   For many years it has been suspected that there is some relationship between the color of the visual environment and the physical reaction of people to it. Recent research has demonstrated that certain colors are capable of producing measurable changes in some of the vital signs of the human body.[16] The research findings are impressive as well as informative. A red visual environment tends to raise the pulse rate and blood pressure and to increase the skin response (perspiration). Orange and yellow have the same effect as red, but to a lesser degree. Green is rather neutral. It has no observable effect on people. Blue, on the other hand, seems to have the reverse effect. It has a tendency to lower the blood pressure and pulse rate and to reduce muscular tension. These physical reactions to color have been well documented. But one aspect of the effects of color on people is sometimes overlooked. According to Birren, "Color effects are always temporary."[17] The body ultimately returns to normal after the initial reaction. This observation does not mean that color is not really important to the visual environment. On the contrary, Birren advocates the functional use of color by introducing, "A variety of colors in order to keep the human responses continually active and to avoid visual adaptation or emotional monotony."[18]

The Psychological Effects of Color.　　Studies on the emotional effects of color on *individual* human beings are not very conclusive.[19] Separate individual reactions to color do not seem to produce a consistent response to the same color when the same experiment is repeated with different individuals. Researchers endeavor to explain this and hypothesize that an individual response to a given color involves both conscious and unconscious reactions which may conflict with one another. Consequently, the results of studies concerning the psychological reaction of a given individual to a particular color are still open to question.

On the other hand, research findings on the general reaction of *groups of people* to different colors within a given space are somewhat more reliable. In this instance, researchers investigated the overall group reaction to a specific color that was dominant within a given visual environment. In these experiments, most people felt that red was a warm color, while blue and green were considered cool colors. Researchers found that, as a group, people had definite preferences in the choice of colors. The preferred colors were ivory, peach, pink, yellow, pale green, and aqua. The least-liked colors were purple and violet.

In his studies on color, Birren has explored various color arrangements that might be used in a room in order to produce a good visual environment. In so doing, he has taken into account color preferences along with brightness balance and reflective characteristics of various colors. Birren lists the following colors for ceiling and wall surfaces:[20]

1. Ceilings—white or off-white.
2. Sequence for walls—suntan or beige.
3. Light wall colors—peach, pink, yellow, pale green, and aqua.
4. Accent colors—coral, orange, gold, terracotta, green, turquoise, and blue.

NOTES

1. Ernest J. McCormick, *Human Engineering* (New York: McGraw-Hill, 1970).

2. Victor J. Popanek, *Design for the Real World* (New York: Pantheon Books, 1972).

3. Barney L. Kyzar, "Noise, Children and Learning," *CEFP Journal* (September–October 1983), p. 12.

4. Kenneth Glass, "Sonic Environment," *CEFP Journal* (July–August 1985), pp. 8–11.

5. Basil Castaldi, "Sound Control in School Buildings," Ed.D. dissertation, Teachers College, Columbia University, 1952, pp. 102–109.

6. Ibid., p. 113.

7. *Guide for Planning Educational Facilities* (Columbus, OH: Council of Educational Facility Planners, 1969), p. 125.

8. *Guide for Planning Educational Facilities* (Columbus, OH: Council of Educational Facility Planners, 1976), pp. 8–9.

9. Richard H. Blackwell, "Development and Use of Quantitative Method for Specifications of Interior Illumination Levels on the Basis of Performance Data," *Illuminating Engineer,* v. 54 (June 1959), p. 317.

10. John C. Rankin, "Lighting for Our Schools," Paper presented at the annual meeting of The Council of Educational Facility Planners, 1982, p. 8. ERIC file no.: ED 225287.

11. National Council on Schoolhouse Construction, *Guide for Planning School Plants* (East Lansing: Michigan State University, 1964), p. 130.

12. J. Tognoli, "The Effects of Windowless Rooms and Unembellished Surroundings on Attitudes and Retention," *Environment and Behavior,* v. 5 (June 1973), pp. 191–201.

13. Rankin, op. cit., p. 22.

14. Faber Birren, *Color and Human Responses* (New York: Van Nostrand Reinhold, 1978), p. 105.

15. Warren Hathaway, "Lights, Windows, Color: Elements of School Environment," Report given at the annual conference of Educational Facility Planners, 1982, p. 25. ERIC file no. ED 226423.

16. Birren, op. cit., p. 48.

17. Ibid., p. 33.

18. Idem.

19. Ibid., p. 43.

20. Ibid., p. 106.

Planning Elementary and Middle Schools

It is becoming increasingly difficult to classify schools, particularly at the elementary level. At one time, there were basically two types of common schools: the grammar school, grades 1 through 8, and the high school, grades 9 through 12. Then, after World War I, the junior high school, serving grades 7 through 9, emerged as an answer to the educational needs of the 1920s. As a result, three types of schools came into being: the school serving kindergarten or grade 1 to grade 6 became known as the elementary school; the school attended by students in grades 7 through 9, the junior high school; and the school housing grades 10 through 12, the senior high school. These grade-level organizations are by no means universal. In many parts of the United States the so-called 8–4 (eight-grade grammar school and four-year high school) organization persists. In Illinois, there are even separate elementary (1–8) and high school (four-year) districts within the same geographical area. In recent years, another type of school has emerged—the middle school, which usually houses grades 5 through 8. The grade structure associated with the adoption of the middle school concept is usually a K–4, 5–8, 9–12 organization. Under this grade grouping, the former elementary schools become neighborhood units that serve kindergarten through grade 4, and the high school houses grades 9 through 12. The case has yet to be made as to which grade organization is best. It does not matter what one calls a school. What really counts is the quality of education the student receives there.

The author has seen both superior and mediocre instruction in all types of schools. An excellent educational program can be provided under any of them. The organization for a given school district should be one in which the existing usable school facilities best serve the physical requirements of the educational program. Educators may honestly favor one type of organization on the basis of experience, personal preference, or conviction. There is to date, however, no documented evidence that strongly favors one type of grade organization over another. Often the reason for changing grade organization is to make the most effective use of available educational facilities within the school district. In some situations, such a change may significantly reduce the cost of maintenance and operation of the school plant without affecting the quality of the educational program. And, in a few instances, it may even improve the variety of learning experiences to which some students are exposed. Fundamentally, it is believed that instructional effectiveness depends far more on the interaction between students and teachers than it does upon the number of grade levels housed in a given building. Until educational psychologists uncover evidence demonstrating that a higher quality of learning occurs under a given grade organization, school plant planners should feel free to recommend the organization that best suits the needs of the educational program from the standpoint of cost, economy, student convenience, and safety.

For the purposes of this discussion, elementary schools refer to school buildings that are designed to house students under the age of 13, regardless of the grade organization. Under this definition, the elementary school building must provide for students at various stages of physical and mental development. School planners should be aware of these variations when they plan elementary school buildings. Table 12-1 indicates the magnitude of the differences among students who are likely to attend elementary schools. From Table 12-1 it is clear that the elementary school must be quite versatile if it is to satisfy the diverse needs of its occupants. In height, children will range from about 46 inches to almost 6 feet. In weight, they will range from a scant 27 pounds in kindergarten to a hefty 150 pounds in grade 6. Most seat heights in kindergarten will be 10, 11, or 12 inches above the floor; seat heights in grade 6 will be in the 13-, 14-, 15-, and 16-inch range. These differences in physical characteristics are accompanied by different levels of intellectual and social development. The range of differences does not seem to present any problems where the

TABLE 12-1 **Range of Physical Differences Between Students in Selected Grades**

Characteristic	Kindergarten	Grade 3	Grade 6
Weight in pounds	46.1	68	156
Height (with shoes) in inches	45	53	70
Eye height standing—above floor (inches)	35	49	65
Shoulder height standing—above floor	30.6	42.5	58
Seat height (inches) above floor	9.8	14.0	18.8
Eye height seated—above floor (inches)	26.6	31.3	49.6
Elbow height seated (above floor)	13.5	18.6	29.6

Source: Children's Body Measurements (U.S. Department of Education).

self-contained classroom is used; that is, where a group of students of a given age or intellectual level are taught in a single room by one teacher.

Until recently, the self-contained classroom was considered quite adequate for instruction at the elementary level, but educators are beginning to doubt the sanctity of this concept. The elementary school program is undergoing an orderly and systematic transformation. For this reason, school planners should give greater emphasis to the likely shape of the elementary school of tomorrow than to the pseudostable instructional practices of today.

THE CONTEMPORARY ELEMENTARY SCHOOL

A number of emerging concepts, which are discussed in the next section, are altering the conventional pattern of elementary schools. In some situations, the administrative organization seems to have changed, but the traditional practices still prevail. For example, a school district recently constructed a middle school. Actually, it was a middle school in name only. Grades 5 and 6 were still being taught in the same manner as they were in the former sixth-grade elementary school, and grades 7 and 8 in the new middle school were being treated as they were in the junior high school with almost complete departmentalization. The lower grades, under this arrangement, did not reap many of the benefits claimed for the middle school, and the upper grades experienced none of the significant educational changes predicted by the proponents of the middle school during the referendum that authorized construction of the school.

PRACTICES AND CONCEPTS

The Multipurpose Self-Contained Classroom

Under the traditional concept of elementary school education, between 25 and 30 children in one grade are assigned to a single room and a single teacher for all of the experiences they will undergo at that grade level. In some of the more advanced schools, supervisors of science, mathematics, and social sciences regularly meet with the teachers to assist them with their work. More often, the regular teacher in the self-contained classroom receives assistance and advice in the areas of music and art. Generally, students assigned to single classrooms in a conventional school use a common multipurpose room for physical education and indoor recreation.

Groupings Within the Regular Classroom. Even in the traditional self-contained classroom, there is provision for grouping. First of all, if there are two or more classrooms per grade, some school districts assign students of high learning ability to one room, average to another, and possibly slow learners to a third, if three sections per grade are needed.

Once the children are grouped in classrooms, the teacher in each classroom subdivides them into two or three other groups. Two methods are generally employed. The teacher may organize three permanent groups according to ability, in which case each group stays together regardless of the subject being taught. Or the teacher may organize three levels of instruction for each major area of teaching and assign students according to their ability in that area. For example, one could be a member of the top group in reading, the middle level in science, and the lowest group in arithmetic. This provides more effectively for individual differences than the first method. Both groupings, however, are aimed at meeting the individual needs of the students.

Functional Aspects of the Self-Contained Classroom. Under the aforementioned grouping, the teacher works very closely with about ten students at a time. When a group of about ten is being instructed by the teacher, the other 20 or so are studying, reading, drawing, or doing independent work.

Many activities take place within the conventional elementary classroom. Individual or group projects are conducted in science, social studies, or language in one part of the room. Report preparation and small-group work may be taking place in another. Construction of simple instructional projects is one part of the learning experience of the student. These projects may involve making plaster of paris topographical maps, use of simple machines and levers, cutting mathematical shapes out of cardboard to demonstrate the concepts of area and volume, using water to show the relationship of the volume of cubes and spheres, and work with musical strings.

To summarize, the self-contained classroom must be highly versatile and easily adaptable to a multitude of purposes. And it must accommodate several activities simultaneously without excessive interference between them.

Application of Promising Concepts

Elementary school education is approaching the threshold of a golden era. New concepts are challenging time-honored traditional practices. Multipurpose teaching aids are making a significant impact upon the quality of modern education through the enrichment of student experiences in the classroom. Newly developed techniques aimed at large-group instruction, effective use of electronic teaching aids, and cooperative instructional practices among groups of teachers are being tested. A more sympathetic attitude toward democratic administration on the part of principals and supervisors is also changing the character of the elementary school. Several promising concepts and practices were discussed in Chapter 2. A few of them are particularly suitable for elementary schools. When the administration and staff are receptive to new ideas, discussion of innovative practices can prove quite stimulating and often produce dramatic improvements in the curriculum. Where this adventurous spirit exists among staff, administrators, and generally in the community, the introduction of new concepts, studied carefully and implemented wisely, often generates a deep sense of pride within the community.

It is suggested that the concepts and practices described in Chapter 2 be reviewed and seriously considered in planning an elementary school. Special attention should be given to computer-oriented instruction, team teaching, the nongraded school, variable class size, and the epideikic (inquiry-demonstration) concept. The planners of elementary schools that are futuristic in concept should also review and consider other potentially sound and promising practices and concepts that may be in the developmental or emergent stage when an elementary school facility is being planned.

PLANNING CONTEMPORARY ELEMENTARY SCHOOLS

At some point architects and school planners must become concerned with the physical requirements, such as how many spaces are needed, how large they should be, and where they should be located in relation to each other. This type of information is contained in this section. Also, review Chapter 9 for energy conservation measures.

The school discussed in this section is based upon the self-contained classroom concept currently popular throughout the United States. The conventional elementary school is a proven concept which should not be viewed as obsolete or inferior in any way. It has had a long history of success and, it might be added, many leaders today are the product of either the self-contained classroom or the one-room school, which is a single classroom housing eight grades under the guidance of one teacher. It should be pointed out that the promise of the concepts discussed in the preceding section has yet to be validated through research findings. These new concepts have much in their favor and may become universally accepted in the not-too-distant future. For this reason, whenever a traditional school is being planned, it should be designed with the new concepts clearly in mind so that changes in the building can be made at a reasonable cost.

The Site

The minimum size of an elementary school site should be at least five acres plus one acre per 100 students of *ultimate* (includes future additions to the school) enrollment. In growing urban and suburban areas, boards of education should pinpoint the location of future school sites, so that sufficient acreage will be available when and where it is needed. In locations where land is available at reasonable cost, the above rule of thumb could be modified to read: "10 acres plus 1 acre per 100 students of ultimate enrollment." While these rules of thumb are helpful, they are not based on rigorous scientific study. More and more state agencies involved in educational facility planning are moving toward more objective methods in determining the size of school sites. They are relying less and less on empirical rules of thumb. The functional approach in determining the optimum size of a school site is discussed in Chapter 6. At the risk of being repetitious, it seems that it would be more cost-effective to spend capital outlay funds for educational improvements in the design of a school building than to purchase a school site that is larger than can be justified on a functional basis.

Building Height

A single-story building is preferred at the elementary school level. Some more advanced elementary schools, for example, have direct access from the classroom to an outside "classroom" during good weather. The outside classroom, separated from other outside classrooms by shrubbery, serves as a laboratory in the study of plants, solar heat, and weather. From the standpoint of building cost, there is no significant difference in cost per square foot of usable area between the single- and multiple-story school.

In cases where land is at a premium, a two-story building is preferable. Furthermore, it is desirable to locate the first floor about 10 or 12 feet above the ground when the site is small. In this case, the building would be supported by columns and the children would have a large covered area under the building for recreational purposes. "The school on stilts," so to speak, makes it possible to utilize almost the entire area of a small school site.

Maximum Size of School

There is, to date, no research that specifies a maximum or optimum size for an elementary school. It is generally accepted, however, that an elementary school of optimum size is one with about 15 teachers. The maximum size is considered to be about three rooms per grade, including kindergarten, or approximately 20 or 21 teachers. In cities, where the density of students is extremely high, the maximum size of an elementary school will necessarily be considerably higher than 21 teachers. In these situations however, it is strongly suggested that two or three schools within the same school be planned. For example, if a school of 50 classrooms is needed in a given area, three separate and distinct administrative units should be provided. When such a school is being designed, space should be provided for three principals, three secretaries, three teachers' rooms, and so on.

Required Spaces

Table 12-2 includes specific information about spaces commonly found in elementary schools.

TABLE 12-2 **Types, Number, and Sizes of Spaces in an Elementary School**

Type of Space	Number Needed	Normal Class Size	Suggested Net Area in Sq. Ft.
Kindergarten	1 per 20 pupils	20	1,000–1,200
Kindergarten storage, wardrobe, toilets	1 per room		300–350
Classrooms	1 per 25 pupils	25	850–900
Library	1 per 15 or fewer teachers		900–1,000
Remedial room	1 per 5 teachers	6–10	350–450
Special classrooms (retarded, gifted)	as needed	12–15	900–1,000
Storage for special classroom	1 per special classroom		150–200
Auditorium	a. 1 separate unit for schools with more than 21 teachers. Capacity: 50% enrollment		8 sq. ft. per person
	b. Combined with cafeteria in schools having 15–21 teachers		
	c. Multipurpose rooms in schools having fewer than 15 teachers		
Stage			600–800
Physical education	1 full-time use unit per 15 teachers		2,400–2,800
Storage for physical education	1 per P.E. Unit		400–450
Cafeteria			
(1) Dining	a. one unit having capacity of ⅓ enrollment		10–12 per diner
	b. Combined with auditorium in schools of 15–21 teachers		
	c. For smaller schools, combined also with physical education and assembly hall		
(2) Kitchen	1 per cafeteria dining		1½ per meal
(3) Food storage	1 per cafeteria dining		½ per meal
(4) Serving area	2 per dining area		0.8 per diner
Principal's office	1 per 21 or fewer teachers		200–250
Outer-office clerk	1 per school		250–300
additional clerk	1 for schools between 15–21 teachers		100–150
Health suite	1 per school		500–550

TABLE 12-2 *Continued*

Type of Space	Number Needed	Normal Class Size	Suggested Net Area in Sq. Ft.
Teachers' workroom and lounge	1 per school for 15 or fewer teachers		500–600
Custodial office-workshop	1 per school		500–550
Storage of outdoor maintenance equipment and instructional equipment	1 per school		300–350
Central storage of instructional materials	1 or 2 per school		0.8–1 per pupil
Book storage near classrooms	1 per wing and/or floor		80–100
Receiving rooms—incinerator	1 per school		150–200

Space Relationships

In the elementary school, with its self-contained classrooms and common spaces for indoor recreation, assembly, and hot lunch, the problem of space relationships is not over-complicated. Figure 12-1 suggests a desirable arrangement of spaces in an elementary school. The degree of relationship is indicated by the number of lines between any two spaces. No lines signifies no close relationship. The architect, in this case, may locate the space or cluster of spaces where they best fit into the plan. One line between two spaces denotes a weak relationship. The two spaces, for example, could be located on the same floor or wing. Two lines between any two spaces or groups of spaces means that there is a close relationship and that such spaces could be located across the corridor from each other. Three lines between two spaces denotes a very close relationship, in which case they should be contiguous.

Special Design Features

A school planning committee routinely explores many special ideas in planning an elementary school. A few of these special features are suggested in this section.

1. *Television reception.* Today every classroom, and the multipurpose room as well, should be equipped to receive a good television signal. In schools located near broadcasting stations, the problem is relatively simple to solve if the building does not have a steel framework. The use of "rabbit ear" antennae is adequate. In the majority of schools, however, the television signal is relatively weak and a master antenna system is required. It should be installed—with plugs in each classroom and

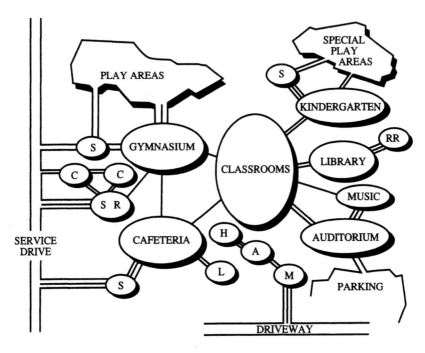

S – STORAGE   C – CUSTODIAN   A – ADMINISTRATION
S R – STORAGE AND   L – TEACHERS' LOUNGE   M – MAIN ENTRANCE
    RECEIVING   H – HEALTH   RR – REMEDIAL READING

FIGURE 12-1   **Schematic Diagram Showing Desirable Space
Relationships in Elementary Schools**

other spaces appropriate for the reception of open-circuit television broadcasts—
when the school is constructed. The excuse that "we don't have the conduit" is not
valid when, for an additional cost of just a few dollars per room, the entire reception
system could be installed at the time of construction, including provision for cable
television. (See Chapter 2.)

2. *Acoustical environment.* The topic of acoustics was covered in detail in Chapter
11. Suffice it to say at this point that a suspended acoustical ceiling should be
considered in planning elementary schools. The space above the tiles can be used
for many purposes, such as exhausting warm air from the room, so that a blanket of
warm air covers the classroom ceiling in winter. Above a suspended ceiling there is
also adequate space for installing pipes, cables, and wires at a later date. Furthermore, such a ceiling is not very costly. It provides a well-controlled acoustical
environment for classrooms where students may learn with fewer acoustical distractions and where teachers may teach with less fatigue.

3. *Visual surroundings.* The proper use of color is essential in any elementary school. Color can stimulate learning in the classroom, and its psychological effect upon learners should be explored in planning interior decoration. Age of the students, orientation of the classroom, and its purpose are all important in this regard. (See Chapter 11.)

4. *Health room.* The health room is frequently located near the administrative offices without much regard to its function. In small elementary schools where a nurse is not on duty even part time, the health room should be adjacent to the office of the principal so that either the principal or a staff member can quickly help or supervise a sick child.

The first-aid function should not be ignored. A general-use lavatory is not adequate for this purpose. It is suggested that a deep sink with gooseneck be installed in the health room area. Ordinary lavatories may be included in the toilet rooms, which should be adjacent to the health room. A small room, separate but adjoining the examination room in the health suite, should be provided for children who become ill during the school day.

5. *The elementary school library.* A library that is not staffed is really nothing more than a book storage room. As such, it does not serve the purpose of a library. Libraries should be provided in elementary school buildings and should be staffed by competent persons on at least a half-time basis. In surveying school districts, the writer was often dismayed when the superintendent of schools had to unlock the library room before it could be entered while school was in session. A library is essential in an elementary school, and groups of students should be allowed to use it under the guidance of the librarian. A rotating collection of library materials can be furnished to classrooms through properly designed library displays on casters. Such carts are loaded in the library and rolled into the classrooms where they may remain for a few days before being replaced by the librarian with another set of materials.

6. *Storage of students' wraps.* Two methods are in general use for storing students' outer clothing and overshoes during the school day in elementary schools. The most common method, particularly in the lower elementary grades, is to provide a cloakroom accessible directly from the classroom. This arrangement is quite adequate from the standpoint of supervision of students and their belongings, but it entails the loss of a wall for use as a chalkboard. Even when an interlinked system of horizontally swinging doors is used, it is difficult to keep exhibits attached to the doors. On the other hand, if a long counterbalanced panel that slides up and down is used, the wall space of doors enclosing the cloak closets becomes usable.

The second method involves corridor lockers for storing wraps. The corridor location for lockers is not as widespread at the elementary level as are wardrobes installed within the classrooms. There are three drawbacks to the use of corridor lockers in elementary schools. It is more difficult for teachers to supervise children in the corridor. The children, particularly in the lower grade levels, often forget combinations or lose locker keys. And, unless rubber bumpers are provided on the doors, lockers are noisy. On the other hand, corridor lockers utilize space already available in corridors and increase the amount of usable wall space in classrooms.

7. *The so-called multipurpose room.* The multipurpose room is sometimes called the "triple-threat" room, because it seems to be a threat to the three activities normally conducted in it. For example, the flat floor provides poor sight lines to the stage when this space is used for assembly. The chairs and tables must be removed before this space can be converted from a cafeteria to a play area, and vice versa when the room is transformed from a play area to a cafeteria. The use of in-wall tables facilitates the conversion, but they are expensive and not particularly suited to a good social situation during meals.

A serious objection to the multipurpose room is that it gives the appearance and assurance that all of the extra-classroom needs of an elementary school can be met by that single room. It is easy to assume that the single "triple-threat" room can meet certain extra-classroom needs. In reality, of course, such is not the case. In general, one multipurpose room can meet the needs for assembly, indoor recreation for all students for two periods per week, and dining for a school of about 12 classrooms. Beyond this point, a second large space is needed for a school not exceeding 20 or 21 classrooms. In this instance, two of the three functions are combined in one space. In the interest of operational efficiency, the assembly and dining functions are combined, and a separate space provided for indoor recreation. There are several advantages to this arrangement. The tables and chairs can remain in the room when the space is used for assembly. When more assembly capacity is needed, the tables may be replaced by chairs. The "cafetorium" may also be used as a large-group instructional space without removing tables and chairs. And finally, during inclement weather, the recreation room can be used by students who finish eating early.

8. *Classrooms.* It should be borne in mind that all student experiences, with the exception of physical education and perhaps music, take place within the self-contained classroom. Consequently, the room must be designed for instruction in art, science, language, social sciences, arithmetic, and music, if these activities are not conducted elsewhere. The room should be furnished with a work sink and work counters on both sides of it, primarily for experiments in science and art. There should be an alcove where students construct paper, cardboard, and wooden models of various types for science, art, arithmetic, and social sciences.

The classroom should be spacious and functional. It should, if possible, approach the shape of a square to simplify supervision. It should be designed to include two or three well-defined locations, such as a science and art area, a project area, a reading area, and perhaps an alcove where helping teachers may assist the teacher in working with small groups.

Fenestration has received much attention in recent years. Emphasis has ranged from one extreme to the other—from the complete window wall to the windowless classroom. Architects argue that it is easier and more economical to control the environment in a windowless classroom. This may be valid, but educators are mixed on this point. Some argue that it is not desirable to remove children from the world in which they live for the sake of easy temperature control. A few maintain that students are subjected to fewer distractions in a windowless school than in a conventional building; others counter this argument by pointing out that an inspiring teacher can hold the class's interest anywhere, even in a classroom where students may look out the window. The thinking on this matter is quite confused. Perhaps a compromise solution is in order. If artificial light is the primary source of illumination, it might be desirable to provide a simple vision strip across the outside wall of a classroom. In this case, the window sill should be about 6 inches below the eye level of the seated students, and the top of the vision strip should be approximately 6 inches above the eye level of a teacher standing in the classroom.

Again, it should be emphasized that a proper brightness balance must be maintained within a classroom in accordance with standards discussed in Chapter 11. Brightness balance should apply to the furniture and equipment as well as to the room itself. Color, acoustics, and brightness balance are all matters of major concern in planning classrooms that are conducive to effective learning.

9. *Site development.* In some instances, site development is left to chance or to "if funds are available," but site development is an integral part of a well-planned school plant. It seems ridiculous to acquire a site of, let us say, 8 acres without developing a major portion of it for recreation, parking, and educational purposes. In fact, the school site could also be planned for use by the public for Little League baseball, outings, and other recreation when it is not being used for school purposes. Summer recreational programs could also be accommodated on a well-developed school site.

The natural assets of a school site, such as trees or brooks, should be preserved whenever possible. Brooks lend beauty and interest to a school site, but too many school planners regard them as a liability that must be eliminated. A few imaginative architects and school planners have converted a liability to a beautiful asset by preserving, widening, or deepening a brook.

THE MIDDLE SCHOOL

The middle school, well-established in the United States, is an educational entity. It is neither an elementary school nor a junior high school. It is a school that is focused primarily on the educational and psychological needs of students in the 10- to 14-year age group. As a rule, middle schools are designed to house students in grades 5 through 8. In some instances, middle schools are planned for students in grades 6 through 8 or 9. These grade groupings may suggest that the middle school is a substitute for the upper elementary or lower high school level. It is not. The middle school, properly planned, is not a substitute for anything. It is uniquely a middle school.

THE EDUCATIONAL VIABILITY OF THE MIDDLE SCHOOL

The Concept of the Middle School

The middle school is not a new fad in grade grouping nor is it a novel building replete with new electronic gadgets. It is not a *thing* at all. It is simply an exciting idea that opens up an entirely new vista in the education of pre- and neoadolescents. For many years educators have strongly felt the need for some type of transitional program between the conventional elementary school, where children are mothered by a single teacher, and the high school where they are treated as adults. The junior high school, as currently conceived, does not seem to satisfy the psychological needs of the neoadolescent. As its name suggests, the junior high school has become a junior version of the more prestigious high school. It is true, of course, that the subject matter in the junior high school is taught at a lower level of sophistication than the corresponding courses in the high school, but the basic administrative organization and methodology employed in the junior high school are quite similar to those of the senior high school. It is self-evident that the special needs of the learner determine the specific nature of the educational institution serving them. Also, of course, the psychological and educational needs of 12-year-old students in junior high school are quite different from those of their 17-year-old brothers and sisters in high school. It follows, therefore, that the school required for the younger sibling must be significantly different in character from that attended by the older. That new and different school is called the middle school.

At the present time, the middle school has no precise definition or pattern. In practice, it seems to be anything that the local school district wants it to be. Unfortunately, it is sometimes nothing more than the last two years of a conventional elementary school and the first two years of a traditional junior high school, clumped together in a single building and labeled a middle school. It can be an ungraded school for students from 10 to 14 years of age organized for team-teaching, large- and small-group instruction, and variable-length class periods. It can be the traditional elementary-junior high school program with greater emphasis on specialized areas such as music, science, art, practical arts, and physical education for students in grades 5 and 6. And it can be a school in which there is a gradual and meaningful transition from the self-contained classrooms in grade 4 to the completely departmentalized organization in grade 9. The middle school is still a pliable concept, which is focused not so much on a building as on the special needs of the pre- and neoadolescent. Theoretically, at least, the middle school concept can be housed in any flexible building.

The word that best characterizes the middle school at the moment is "fluidity." It is in the process of becoming. Its shape, design, and function are limited only by the creativity of the human mind. It possesses an elasticity that encourages the introduction of a large variety of exciting instructional innovations. It has no tradition, no set pattern, and no preconceived educational characteristics to hinder its full development. The only fixed notion of the middle school at this time is its purpose—to satisfy the educational needs of preadolescent and neoadolescent students from the time they leave grade 5 or 6 until they enter grade 9.

The Strengths of the Middle School

The development and growth of the middle school can be justified psychologically, educationally, sociologically, and logistically. It is a direct outgrowth of a long-felt need for such an educational institution in the United States.

Psychological Need. For a number of years, educators have been concerned about the lack of a transitional period between elementary and junior high school. They have felt that preadolescent students change very abruptly from the sheltered and highly directed life in a self-contained classroom with a single teacher to the semidirected routine in junior high school under the informal guidance of several teachers. Under the middle school concept, students in grades 5 through 8 pass through the period of transition in a systematic fashion. The middle school makes it possible for students in grade 5, for example, to spend 75 percent of their time under one teacher and the remaining 25 percent under the guidance of two others. During the sixth and seventh grades, students may spend as much as 50 percent of their time under one teacher and the remaining time under a departmentalized organization. And, at the eighth-grade level, a student may spend about two periods per day under one teacher and the remainder of his or her time in departmentalized work. Thus, the psychological need for a period of transition between the elementary school and the high school can be satisfied by interposing the middle school.

The middle school is so adaptable that it can be conceived, planned, organized, and shaped to satisfy many psychological needs of pre- and neoadolescent students. Activities and instruction can be organized to give students a feeling of security and belongingness. Through small-group instruction, each one can experience feelings of accomplishment, self-confidence, and group acceptance. To be sure, these psychological objectives could theoretically be achieved in existing schools under certain conditions. Unfortunately, neither elementary nor junior high schools possess the required spatial flexibility or instructional versatility to accomplish these goals. The middle school is currently so pliable that any needed characteristic can be incorporated in it.

Educational Need. Lack of time for teaching is a matter of great concern to modern educators. There simply is not enough time to teach the desired subjects within present academic schedules. Our public schools seem to constantly add subjects to the educational program without curtailing any of those already being offered. The time will soon arrive when this procedure can no longer be sustained without drastic changes in the length of the school day, week, or year.

The middle school can be designed to increase the effectiveness and efficiency of the learning process. Some of the materials being taught in the high schools can be introduced in the middle school. New methods of teaching must be developed and perfected to meet this need for more concentrated learning in a shorter time. No longer, for example, can we afford the luxury of offering general science courses in the seventh, eighth, and ninth grades; oftentimes, one science course is no more than a rehash of the previous course at a more advanced level. Perhaps it would be more efficient to introduce a basic science program earlier, so that in, say, grade 5 students could conduct simple experiments using laboratory equipment instead of waiting until grades 8 or 9 to engage in purposeful experimentation. It may also be necessary to revise the course content and to reprogram the sequence of learning experiences for more efficient use of student time. The middle school is an excellent starting point for such changes. It is just taking form. It is still flexible and, hence, responsive to the needs of modern education. For creative educators and school planners, the middle school is both a challenge and an opportunity.

The middle school may be of value in meeting the problem of dropouts, a major national concern of both educators and government officials. Sometimes those who drop out of school are called "force-outs." They feel forced out, because the school failed to offer them challenging and meaningful experiences. Even though they may not drop out until high school, their decision to do so can sometimes be traced to a lack of interest first experienced in the lower grades. The middle school is so versatile that it can offer a wide variety of diverse experiences to a large number of students. Consequently, the middle school offers a ray of hope regarding the potential force-out who may choose to remain in school and thus become a greater asset to society.

Sociological Need. The middle school offers some relief to the problem of racial imbalance in the United States. If a middle school were planned for about 1,000 students, its attendance area would extend over a relatively large area. It is frequently possible to achieve racial balance in a school of this size by locating it strategically.

The middle school is sometimes an integral part of a school park where an elementary, middle, and high school may be located on one large multipurpose site. The school park plan is another attempt to break through the barriers that hamper attainment of racial balance within a school district.

Logistical Need. In many school districts, the middle school is the answer to the housing and transportation problems. By planning an intermediate grade school serving grades 5 through 8, it is frequently possible to convert present junior high schools to four-year high schools and to accommodate the increasing number of students in kindergarten through grade 4 in existing elementary schools. As four-year high schools ascend in popularity and elementary schools assume the role of neighborhood schools, the ideal link between the two increasingly appears to be the middle school. Under these conditions, the middle school solves the problem of logistics and often improves the sociological posture of the school district.

PLANNING A MIDDLE SCHOOL

A long step may be taken in the direction of the middle school concept without seriously alarming teachers, students, or parents in a stable, conservative community. After public acceptance of the middle school concept has been achieved, the board of education and superintendent of schools should develop policies governing the reorganization or redefining of the attendance areas for the respective schools.

The Special Characteristics of an Effective Middle School

The transition from the conventional elementary-junior high school concept to the middle school should be careful and evolutionary. The changes in instructional pattern may occur gradually at a pace that is comfortable for teachers and students. The middle school seems somewhat different but in reality is closely related to traditional patterns in many ways.

Grade Grouping. A gradual transition from the existing 6–3–3 or 6–2–4 to the 4–4–4 organization can be planned. It would not be surprising, therefore, to find that a middle school planned initially for grades 6 through 9 would later house grades 5 through 8.

Student Separation. Most modern middle schools are planned so that the lower two grades are assigned to one side of the building and the upper two grades to the other. While this practice has some merit, it should not be carried to such an extreme that specialized rooms, such as shops, homemaking suites, and science laboratories, are decentralized for the sole purpose of preventing a fifth-grader from crossing the path of a seventh-grader. In passing, however, it may be noted that parents who often protest against intermingling students of various age groups in school, where they are highly supervised, rarely seem to question the practice of transporting children of all ages in school buses, where practically no supervision is provided.

Team Teaching. Some provision is included in the modern middle school for the beginning of a team-teaching program. Seminar rooms are usually provided for the group activity of the team teachers, and a workroom of about 400 square feet is often located in the vicinity of the teachers' lounge. It is furnished with work tables and chairs and equipped with copiers, mimeographs, duplicating machines, a drawing table, art and drafting supplies, and photographic devices. The teaching team would thus be able to produce some of its own instructional materials. In the beginning, at least, most of the team teaching would be focused upon the upper two grades, but in time all of the students in the school could be exposed to some form of team teaching.

Variable Group Size.   The effective middle school can include provision for a limited amount of instruction in larger groups of about 60–80 students. In general, this is accomplished simply by including a few movable partitions between pairs of regular classrooms. A space about 78 feet long and 23 feet wide could be provided for teaching a group larger than the conventional 25 or 30 students simply by opening a partition. Provision for teaching in larger groups could also be made in the cafeteria and auditorium spaces. The expansible spaces may not seem very exciting or extraordinary at first glance, but in the hands of creative teachers and administrators their potential for educational improvement is greatly enhanced, provided their widths approximate 30 feet.

Number of Instructional Spaces for the Effective Middle School.   In planning a middle school, some regular, self-contained classrooms are usually retained while others are specialized. The distribution of regular and specialized classrooms, of course, depends upon the desired middle school program. In the middle school, it can be assumed that (1) students in grade 5 will spend 25 percent of their time in specialized rooms and the remainder under a single teacher; (2) students in grades 6 and 7 will spend half their time in regular classrooms and the remainder in specialized spaces; and (3) students in grade 8 will spend two periods (about 25 percent) of their time under one teacher and the remainder with several others. Under these conditions, the approximate distribution of instructional space is as follows:

Fifth grade: *Three units* of regular classrooms to *one unit* of specialized space.

Sixth and seventh grades: *One unit* of regular classroom to *one unit* of specialized space.

Eighth grade: According to programs—using formula below.

1. *Number of teaching periods needed.* The following formula may be used to determine the number of faculty periods per week required for each course:

$$Pwk = \frac{En}{C}$$

where:

Pwk = Number of periods per week required to staff a given course

E = Number of students enrolled in the course

C = Desired class size

n = Number of class meetings per week for the respective course.

2. *Teaching stations needed.* To convert *Pwk* into the number of teaching stations required, simply divide the sum of the *Pwk* for each subject by the number of instructional periods each classroom is available per week multiplied by 1.20. The computed number of teaching stations incorporates a surplus of 20 percent in order to provide sufficient leeway for scheduling difficulties and unavoidable variations from the desired class size.

To illustrate the application of the formula above, let us assume that the desired educational program for students in grade 5 is as follows:

Number of students to be served:	120	
Total number of periods in the school week:	45	
Desirable class size for all courses:	30	
Number of periods per week each student attends physical education classes:	2	
Periods per week per student for assembly, conferences, etc.:	3	
Number of academic instructional periods per week:	40	
Periods per week per student under a single teacher:	30	(in regular classroom)
Periods per week per student in a specialized *science* room:	5	
Periods per week per student in specialized *art* room:	2.5	10
Periods per week per student in specialized music room:	2.5	

The number of spaces required to house the program and enrollment in the example set forth above is computed as follows:

Regular classrooms—periods $= \dfrac{120}{30} \times 30 = 120$ periods per week

Science—periods $= \dfrac{120}{30} \times 5 = 20$ periods per week

Art—periods $= \dfrac{120}{30} \times 2.5 = 10$ periods per week

Music—periods $= \dfrac{120}{30} \times 2.5 = 10$ periods per week

To convert these period requirements to classrooms, divide each result by 40 and multiply by 1.2. Thus, the spaces needed for 120 students in grade 5 are:

Regular classrooms $= \dfrac{120}{40} \times 1.2 = 3.6$ teaching stations

Science rooms $= \dfrac{20}{40} \times 1.2 = 0.6$ teaching station

Art rooms $= \dfrac{10}{40} \times 1.2 = 0.3$ teaching station

Music rooms $= \dfrac{10}{40} \times 1.2 = 0.3$ teaching station

DIAGRAMMATIC FEATURES OF A MIDDLE SCHOOL

The computerized sketches presented in this section display selected components of a middle school planned for a capacity of 1,200 students. They also show how provision can be made for unforeseeable future needs. While the square footage figures shown for each type of space are within the normal range of the area needed for such spaces, they should not be construed as being fixed or standard sizes. The actual size of each space should be determined by local educational planners strictly on the basis of the area requirement perceived for each type of space. It is advised, however, that local school planners take a second look at their figures if they deviate by more than 50 percent in either direction, from those shown on the diagram. Such large deviations are not necessarily out of line. They only need to be confirmed and fully justified on the basis of unique local educational requirements.

Figure 12-2 presents the layout of several major components of an idealized middle school. It shows the degree of relationship between various parts of the educational facility. Three lines connecting two elements of the plan indicate a very close relationship. Two lines between two parts of the facility signify that a close relationship exists between them, while a single line means that the relationship is weak. The diagram also shows where future expansion should be located in order to preserve the educational integrity of the building.

It should be pointed out that the individual components of the school plant specified in Fig. 12-2 do not necessarily represent separate and distinct buildings. They simply denote function. Actually, all of the architectural components of the plan could be enclosed in a single building. The architect and local educators should determine how each component can best be integrated into a functional educational unit while preserving space relationships. It is realized, of course, that the topography of the site and cost considerations will have a direct bearing on the final design of the facility.

If any part of a school plant does not contribute to the educational function of the building, prudence dictates that it should not be built. A school plant should contain only those elements that are necessary and sufficient to house the desired curriculum.

Figure 12-3 focuses primarily on certain operational aspects of the educational facility. Only four major components are shown in Figure 12-3. These clusters were selected because they are especially sensitive to any weaknesses in their internal space relationships. Special attention is directed to the planning of cafeteria and custodial facilities. Sometimes, for example, there are situations where cafeteria food supplies must be wheeled through corridors because there is no direct access from the service drive to the food storage room. Similarly, custodial spaces are often planned without fully considering the functional requirements of such facilities.

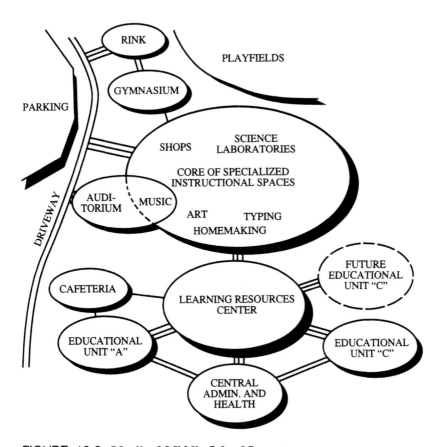

FIGURE 12-2 **Idealized Middle School Layout**

Figure 12-3 also calls attention to two other crucial components of a middle school: the administrative cluster, which represents a complex of closely integrated functions; and the learning resources center, which is surrounded by a cluster of ancillary spaces for remedial education and for the maintenance and storage of audiovisual materials. The most common deficiency within this complex is the lack of adequate space for storing special instructional equipment and materials associated with remedial education.

Figure 12-4 displays several clusters of highly specialized instructional spaces. Shop clusters deserve special consideration. They must be easily accessible from the service drive. It is frequently not realized that woods and metals shops receive and store a substantial amount of materials in bulk form. For this reason, direct access from the service drive to these two shops is mandatory. If the power mechanics shop deals only with small motors and electrical appliances, access from the

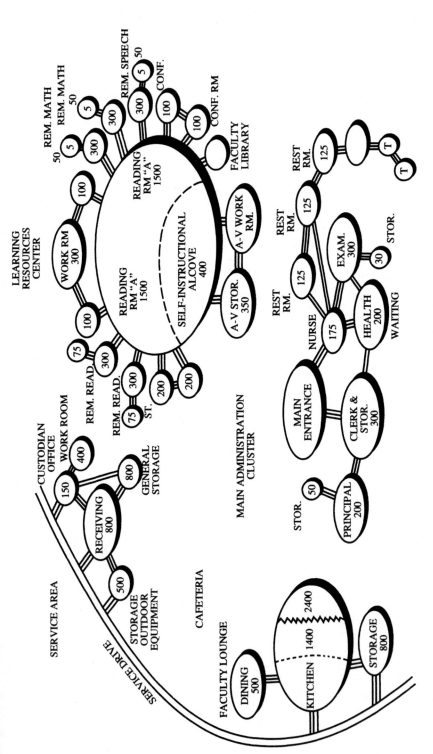

FIGURE 12-3 **Cafeteria, Custodial, Administrative, and Resource Center Clusters**

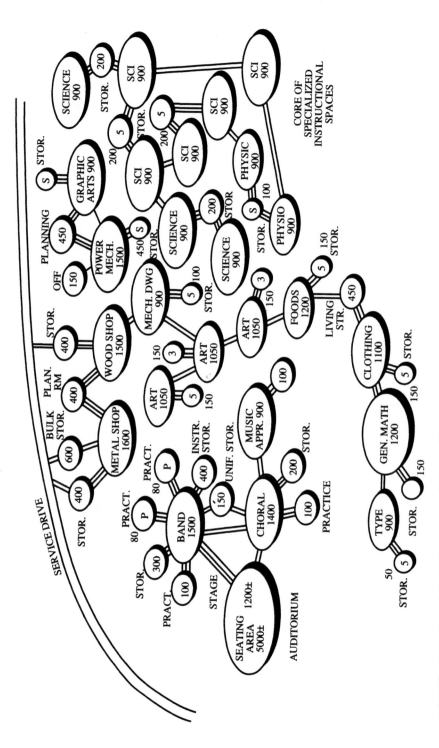

FIGURE 12-4 Specialized Instructional-Space Clusters

287

service drive is desirable, but not essential. It is also important to bear in mind that some shop areas tend to be very noisy. Thus, the woods, metals, and power mechanics shops should be placed at locations that are remote from the quieter parts of the building.

Figure 12-4 also shows other clusters of closely related spaces servicing specialized functions. The reader is invited to review an interesting progression of specialized spaces beginning with the typewriting room located on the lower left section of the diagram. The typing room is connected with the general mathematics room in which business mathematics is usually taught. The mathematics room is connected to the clothing room where measurements are an integral part of the course. The sequence continues to the art room and follows to the mechanical drawing room which, in turn, is related to the shops.

The science cluster is a self-contained unit which may be placed in any of several locations within the building. Logically, the biology room could start the science sequence by being positioned adjacent to the regular mathematics rooms. Or, the science cluster could be the link between the academic subject classrooms and the shop areas.

The auditorium and the music rooms are also closely related and form a self-contained, independent cluster. The placement of this cluster in relation to the rest of the building is very critical because of the high intensity of the sound generated within these spaces. If possible, this cluster should be acoustically isolated from the quieter areas of the building. The auditorium is also planned for community use. Thus, it should also be located close to the parking areas for the convenience of the public. (See Figure 12-2)

▶ 13

Planning Secondary School Buildings

Because of the current state of flux in grade organization, it is not always clear what grade levels are included in the secondary school grouping. For the purpose of this discussion, secondary schools are facilities designed to house students from 13 to 18. Students in this age grouping may attend middle schools, junior high schools, or senior high schools. The term used to designate a school is of little or no consequence in planning, but educational function and physical needs of students in this age group play an important role in the design, size, location, orientation, and interior treatment of school buildings.

In the absence of validated research regarding the design of secondary school buildings, the rationale underlying the various topics discussed in this chapter is based primarily on generally accepted practices in secondary school planning. Admittedly, it would be far better to rely on research findings, but they are not available. The Educational Facilities Laboratories in New York has sponsored important projects in school-building research, which are making a significant impact on the design of educational facilities in the United States and Canada. Nevertheless, the quantity of validated research on school buildings from the standpoint of educational function is still disappointing. For this reason, it is necessary to rely primarily on professional judgments and opinions that may or may not be based on research findings. School plant planners confronted with the problem of planning school buildings for the thousands of students who need school facilities today, or perhaps even yesterday, cannot afford the luxury of waiting until research findings are available.

CONTEMPORARY EDUCATIONAL PRACTICES
COMMON TO SECONDARY SCHOOLS

In planning secondary school facilities, it should be borne in mind that secondary school programs vary from district to district and sometimes even from school to school within the same school district. For this reason, there is no common or typical secondary school facility that can be described in definitive terms. Within these different facilities, however, there are a number of educational practices that are similar in most of them. The degree to which these practices are employed in each situation will vary somewhat from school to school, but they will generally appear in one form or another. The most prevalent version of each practice is described in the following paragraphs.

Complete Departmentalization.   Under prevailing practice, the secondary school is fully departmentalized by subject-matter area. A department head is usually given the responsibility of determining the course content, selecting textbooks, and choosing the type of instructional materials to be used in a given area of learning. He or she is the instructional leader and supervises the teaching and methods followed in the department. If the leader is imaginative, forward-looking, and sensitive to good human relations, the instruction may be superior. On the other hand, if the leader's appointment was not based on competence, the instructional effectiveness of the department may be disappointing, the methods obsolete, and teacher morale low. By and large, the department structure has operated at an acceptable level of efficiency for at least a half-century. Conscientious department heads have made the system work from an administrative point of view. Psychologists, on the other hand, might question the wisdom of compartmentalizing learning.

The Teaching of Classes.   In most situations, teachers instruct students in groups called classes. The usual class includes between 25 and 32 students for most courses. With good reason, teachers and administrators much prefer class size as close as possible to 25. The size of the group also depends upon the subject being taught. As a rule, most group sizes lie within the aforementioned limits, with the exception of classes in advanced sciences, art, and homemaking, where the maximum may fall well below 25. The class size in music may vary over a wide range. In some secondary schools, the group size for music instruction may range from 25 to 250, depending upon the type of musical activity. Industrial arts classes are often officially restricted to 20, but may actually reach 25 students. Physical education may be taught well, according to prevailing practice, in groups of 40 to 45, while typewriting may be taught effectively to groups of about 35 under the guidance of a single teacher.

The teacher instructs a given class for a period ranging from 45 to 60 minutes four or five times per week for a total of about 250 contact minutes per week per class. Each teacher usually offers instruction four or five periods a day for a total of about 1,250 minutes per week. The time spent by students in formal classes of various types ranges from 1,200 to 1,500 minutes per week at the upper secondary level of instruction. At the lower secondary level, it is customary to reduce the length of class period and to increase the number of periods the student must attend each week. For example, a 13-year-old student in grade 7 might enroll in seven courses for a total of 35 instructional periods per week. In this case, the length of the class period is usually reduced to about 40 minutes. A student in grade 12, on the other hand, may be assigned to only twenty 60-minute periods of formal instruction per week for a total of about 1,200 minutes in supervised classes.

Student Movement.   In the contemporary school, teachers are usually assigned to a given classroom where students come to them period after period for instruction during the school day. Under this system, the students move from one room to another where the different courses are offered. At the end of each period, a complete reshuffle of students occurs within the school. This situation creates a real problem in circulation within a secondary school. Students move not only from class to class, but also from classroom to library, to cafeteria, to gymnasium, to auditorium, to study halls, and to other supplementary spaces.

Grouping.   In the secondary school, students are grouped either homogeneously, according to some predetermined criteria, or heterogeneously in random fashion. Oftentimes, they are grouped according to reading ability, aptitude, general intelligence, curricula, and the like. When two or more sections of the same course are taught, homogeneous grouping reduces the range of differences in learning ability among the class. There is still much controversy regarding the value of homogeneous grouping over heterogeneous grouping. Both are found in secondary schools, depending on the philosophy of the administration and the board of education.

Once the group is formed, it remains intact during the entire semester or year. It is generally not combined with any other similar group. The teacher simply treats it as a class, introducing learning experiences appropriate to the group and subject matter being taught.

Teaching Aids.   The instructional tools of the prevalent secondary school consist primarily of books, chalkboard, and paper. Demonstrations are restricted primarily to the physical sciences, home economics, art, and industrial education. Motion pictures are available for classroom use on a limited basis. Overhead projectors are used in a few classrooms. Some teachers introduce slides into the curriculum at some point. Record players and tape recorders are usually available at the audiovisual center, but teachers do not, as a rule, avail themselves of such aids very frequently, preferring to use the book and chalkboard as major instructional tools. While electronic teaching aids such as television, computer instruction, and feedback systems could be effectively utilized in all schools, the orientation of the secondary school does not generally place a very high value on such aids or assign them a very important role in the educational program.

Large-Group Activity. In the contemporary secondary school, the major large-group activity is the school assembly. Secondary school principals often insist on facilities that can accommodate the entire student body at a single sitting for assemblies, which may be called as often as once a week or as infrequently as 10 times a year.

Secondary school principals can make a very strong case for the inclusion of an auditorium that can seat a minimum of the largest single class—usually freshmen—plus about 50 percent of that class enrollment. Often an auditorium that can seat one-half the student body is adequate. Under the contemporary concept of a secondary school, when the total enrollment exceeds 1,000 it is difficult to justify an auditorium capable of seating the total student body simultaneously for assembly and dramatics alone.

Student Detention. In-school student detention is being adopted by more and more school districts due to the changing character of the modern family. In the past, unruly and disruptive students, particularly at the secondary school level, were temporarily suspended from attending school. They were sent home and placed under the supervision and control of their parents. Today, there are often no parents at home to supervise them. This situation poses a real problem for school administrators. Suspension is no longer viewed as punishment by such students. Rather, they look forward to it as an opportunity to watch television or engage in whatever activity strikes their fancy. Thus, suspension simply reinforces their unruly behavior in school.

Educators are still searching for a constructive solution to this problem. Ideally, some method must be found to change the behavior of disruptive students, utilizing established principles of psychological therapy. In the meantime, school administrators have implemented a makeshift solution. Instead of suspending unruly students from school, they are assigned to a student detention room where they are supervised by school personnel.

Students assigned to the detention room are expected to do schoolwork in isolation. They are allowed to have whatever instructional materials are related to their course of study. They may not mingle with other students during school hours. Except for dining and meeting other bodily needs, they must remain in the detention room for the entire school day.

The planning of a student detention room must satisfy a number of crucial criteria. It should be located where it can be continually supervised by school personnel. It may be strategically placed in the administrative area or within the view of personnel working in the learning resources center. Its walls and doors must withstand abuse from students occupying the room. While conducting a school survey recently in a school system in western Massachusetts, the writer examined the student detention room, which was originally planned as the work room for the librarian. It was observed that the lower part of the walls were severely damaged by students trying to kick in the walls. Large holes were made in the gypsum board walls by students giving vent to their frustrations.

While the detention room restricts student freedom, it should not be planned as a jail cell. The space should be pleasant and comfortable. It should be a small lockable study room for one person and be equipped with a desk and chair. There should be glass vision strips on one or two walls between 3 and 5 feet above the floor for student supervision.

THE RELATIONSHIP OF EDUCATIONAL FUNCTION TO SECONDARY SCHOOL FACILITIES

A vital responsibility of educators involved in planning a school building is the translation of teaching and learning activities into the physical features of a building. The accent at this point is on activities, actions, and direct experiences of both students and teachers. We are more concerned at this juncture with the curriculum than with the broad educational program, although both ultimately play a crucial part in planning a secondary school.

The architect is not expected to be familiar with the curriculum of a given secondary school until given a clear picture of it by school officials. He or she should be presented with a document that translates curriculum into suggested space requirements, commonly called educational specifications (see Chapter 6) by educators and simply "a program" by architects. In any event, the architect is entitled to a fairly detailed set of educational specifications. They should be free from ambiguities and restrict the architect's work as little as possible. It should be borne in mind that the creative talents of the architect cannot be released if educators insist on making quasi-architectural sketches of the various spaces in a proposed school. It is far better to inform the architect about the activities and functions to be housed in a given space and to provide an estimate of the number of square feet required. Sometimes special features such as orientation, ceiling height, or length of a space are necessary to accommodate unusual equipment or instructional practice. In these instances, the architect would welcome specific information, but generally educational specifications should be prepared to give the architect as much freedom as possible.

METHODS AND FUNCTIONS ASSOCIATED WITH SECONDARY SCHOOLS

One or more of the methods listed below is employed in teaching both small and large groups of students. Some of them are easily recognized, and others are not.

Presentation Method. The most common method of instruction is one in which the teacher presents ideas to a group of students. The students receive instructional stimuli via sight and hearing. The learner, in this situation, is passive. The teacher transmits ideas by a number of means—books, locally prepared materials, the chalkboard, overhead projector, filmstrips, moving pictures, tape recorders, and the like. In all of these situations, however, the process is directive. The presentation is made by the teacher or by means of a teaching aid.

Demonstration Method. This method of instruction is somewhat similar to the presentation method. The major difference is in the manner in which the student receives the stimuli. In demonstrations, sight plays a major part in the transfer of ideas. In general, the teacher sets up an experiment to demonstrate a basic principle or phenomenon. Demonstration is a direct experience by the student as opposed to the vicarious experiences conveyed by the teacher using the presentation method.

Diagnostic and Evaluation Function. The diagnostic aspect of the instructional function is frequently overlooked by school plant planners. The testing, evaluation, and analysis of student progress is of paramount importance in any educative process. School facilities do not generally lend themselves to testing and diagnosing student work. In fact, cheating is made easy in the typical classroom by the proximity of one student to the other. Admittedly, the cost of providing individual cubicles in a room that is scanned by a rotating television camera might be difficult to justify solely on the basis of the need to reduce cheating. On the other hand, it is possible to introduce features that are likely to minimize the temptation for students to copy one another. Flexible seating arrangements, and electronic devices that permit immediate feedback from student to teacher, should be considered in planning a school plant. The function of testing, evaluating, and diagnosing a student's work should be borne clearly in mind when schools are being planned.

COMMON ELEMENTS OF SECONDARY SCHOOL PLANNING

The Secondary School Site

The requirements of the school site have already been discussed in Chapter 6. The rule of thumb regarding optimum size of a secondary school site varies considerably from source to source, but in practice a site of 10 acres (junior high school level) or 15 acres (high school) plus one acre for each 100 students of ultimate enrollment is generally accepted as a minimum. There appears to be no validated research thus far which indicates the optimum size of a secondary school site with respect to educational return. The increasing cost of land and the accelerated urbanization and suburbanization of the population reduce the availability of desirable land, and prices for school sites are rising rapidly. It is conceivable that the size of school sites may have to be drastically reduced in some areas. In open country, every effort should be made to meet or surpass the practical standard stated above.

Translating Program Requirements into Instructional Spaces

After the educational program has been fully worked out by the school staff and approved by the board of education, the number of students that will probably be enrolled in each course should be estimated. The number of periods per week that each course will be offered to a given number of students should also be noted. Two techniques may be employed in arriving at the required number of spaces.

The Conrad Method.[1] Conrad has developed a very accurate technique that indicates either capacity or number of needed teaching stations for a given student enrollment. (See Chapter 3, "Secondary School Capacity.")

The Castaldi Nomogram.[2] The nomogram consists of a chart from which the required number of spaces can be read directly for high schools organized on a 25-, 30-, or 35-period school week. For other administrative organizations of the school week, the Castaldi Formula shown below can be used directly. The formula takes into account that every student station (seat) in every classroom in a secondary school cannot be scheduled for occupancy 100% of the time. Thus, it provides for a student utilization factor of 80% in order to compensate for scheduling difficulties and variations in class size.

$$T.S. = 1.25 \frac{E}{C} \cdot \frac{n}{N}$$

where:

$T.S.$ = Required number of teaching stations
E = Number of students enrolled in a given course
C = Desired class size
n = Number of periods per week student attends a given class
N = Number of periods in the school week.

The formula may be used to answer questions such as: How many rooms are needed if 300 students are to be enrolled in art, which meets twice a week? The desired maximum class size is 25 and there are 40 periods in the school week.

$$T.S. = (1.25) \frac{300}{25} \cdot \frac{2}{40} = 0.75$$

In this case, 1.0 art room is needed. The 0.75 teaching station obtained by applying the Castaldi Formula is rounded off to the next highest integer.

Determining the Size of Various Spaces

The Functional Analysis Approach.   The most satisfactory way to determine the size of an instructional space is to list all the major activities expected to occur in it together with the type of equipment and number of students involved in each activity. A layout designating the space needed for the equipment and for each student or group of students will yield the approximate area needed for the activity in question. The total area included in a teaching space is the sum of the combination of activities carried on simultaneously that require the greatest floor space. It is presumed that other teaching experiences can be conducted effectively within the given space, even though the room is larger than it actually needs to be for the activity under consideration.

The Rule-of-Thumb Approach.   As mentioned earlier, validated research indicating optimum sizes or capacities of various types of instructional spaces is practically nonexistent. Since the need for school facilities is urgent, and the construction of school buildings cannot be postponed until such research findings become available, school planners have resorted to a rule-of-thumb approach. Although there is no proof that the specific figures in the rule of thumb apply to minimum, maximum, or optimum conditions or otherwise, there seems to be general agreement that spaces planned according to the rules of thumb function satisfactorily, at least when judged on a subjective basis. In the absence of other more specific data, the rule-of-thumb approach seems acceptable, and no apologies should be made for its use now in planning school buildings. It is important that school planners be aware of the subjective origin of the rules applied in the design of school buildings.

PLANNING CONTEMPORARY SECONDARY SCHOOLS

The so-called conventional school planned today often contains many characteristics of the school of the future. But, at the same time, the conventional school tends to be somewhat conservative in character, and its design and functional concept are generally not too far removed from the pattern of the past. Thus, innovations incorporated in such buildings are usually modest. The conventional secondary school should be designed with the potential innovations discussed in Chapter 2 clearly in mind.

SPECIFIC GUIDELINES FOR PLANNING SECONDARY SCHOOLS

Suggested Space Allocations

The specific sizes and comments presented in Tables 13-1 through 13-4 are not the product of research, nor are they attributable to any one person or group. They reflect the current thinking of both educators and school plant planners. Admittedly,

TABLE 13-1 Specialized Instructional Spaces in Secondary Schools

Type of Space	Suggested Max. Class Size	Suggested Area of Each Space	Suggested Area of Adj. Stor. Rm.	Comments
A. Art				
1. General art	25	1,000–1,200	100–150	North orientations not mandatory if adequate lighting is provided.
2. Arts and crafts	25	1,100–1,400	175–225	
B. Commercial Education				
1. Office machines	25	800–900	20–40*	Special attention should be given to sound transmission problems.
2. Office practice	25	800–900	20–40*	Electrical outlets should be available at every student station and at teacher's desk.
3. Typing	35	850–950	20–40*	
C. Homemaking				
1. General	24	1,200–1,400	50–75	It would be desirable to design this space so that by opening or closing partitions it could become part of either room adjacent to it.
2. Multipurpose area (living center)	4–8	400–500		
3. Clothing	24	900–1,000	50–75	
4. Foods	24	1,000–1,200	50–75*	
D. Music				
1. Band-orchestra	Varies	1,200–1,600	Cabinets	Music practice rooms should be slightly over-acousticized to prevent the blending of sounds. (See Chapter 11.)
2. Instrument storage space		250–300	Cabinets	
3. Chorus	Varies	1,200–1,400		
4. Practice room	1–6	100–125		High-grade stereophonic equipment should be installed in band and chorus room. One amplifier can serve more than one space.
5. Practice room	1–4	75–100		
6. Practice room	1–2	50–75		
7. Theory	30	700–850		
8. Office		150–200		
9. Listening and recording room and music library	6–10	350–450		One office per instructor needed.

(continued)

TABLE 13-1 *Continued*

Type of Space	Suggested Max. Class Size	Suggested Area of Each Space	Suggested Area of Adj. Stor. Rm.	Comments
E. Physical Education				
1. Gymnasium (one teaching station for physical education only)	40	3,700–4,400	300–400	The size of the gymnasium varies with bleacher seating capacity. Standard-size basketball court requires a gymnasium with an area of approx. 5,600. Add 3 sq. ft. per person for bleacher seating capacity.
2. Gymnasium (two teaching stations with folding partition)	40	5,600–7,000	250–350	Where more than two teaching stations are required, balcony area spaces should be considered for both movable seating and teaching space.
3. Corrective room	20	600–900		Adjoining gymnasium area.
4. Coach office		250–300		
5. Toilets (including public)	The total of areas 3–7 inclusive should be approximately 0.7 to 1.0 × total area of gym. Number of shower heads: Students 1:4 boys–1:3 girls			
6. Showers and locker rooms				In spite of opinions to the contrary, the American girl seems to favor stall showers.
7. Team room		700–900	250–300	
8. Other standard girls gym	40	3,000–4,000	250–300	
9. Auxiliary gym—one teaching station (girls)	40	2,000–2,400	14–16 ft. ceiling	
10. Lobby		800–1,000		Provision should be made for ticket office, checking, public toilets, and display.
11. Visiting team room		500–700		

	Pupils	Area (sq ft)	Per pupil	Remarks
F. Physical Sciences				
1. Biology	25	900–1,000	150–175	Science rooms should be "squarish" to permit use of peripheral laboratory units. Television jacks should be installed in all science spaces.
2. Chemistry	25	1,000–1,100	200–250	
3. General science	30	900–1,000	125–150	
4. Physics	25	900–1,100	200–250	
5. Growing room		200–300		Need not be exposed to the out-of-doors if controlled fluorescent lighting is provided.
6. Darkroom		60–100		May be related to either the art room or science area.
G. Industrial Arts (nonvocational)				
1. General (composite) shop	20	1,500–2,000	150–200	One locker, dressing-washing room per two shops, if possible.
2. Mechanical drawing	25	850–950	50–75	Avoid the use of loft storage areas in all shops.
3. General metals	20	1,700–2,000	150–200	
4. General woods	20	1,500–1,800	150–200	Provide high ceilings only in metals and woods shops.
5. Electrical shop	20	900–1,200	100–150	
6. Power mechanics	20	1,600–2,200	150–200	
7. Metal shop	20	1,600–2,000	150–200	
8. Wood shop	20	1,400–1,600	150–200	
9. Graphic arts	20	1,000–1,100	150–200	
10. Planning room		400–450		
11. Other finishing room		100–300		
12. General storage space			100–125 per shop	Planned as a single large space.
H. Occupational Education				
1. Agriculture shop plus agriculture	20	2,400–2,600	500	
green house		1,400–1,600		
2. Auto repair	20	5,000–5,400	500	
3. Auto body shop plus	20	5,000–5,400	300	Storage area fireproof.
frame straightener		450–500		
spray booth		450–500		

(continued)

TABLE 13-1 *Continued*

Type of Space	Suggested Max. Class Size	Suggested Area of Each Space	Suggested Area of Adj. Stor. Rm.	Comments
4. Baking	20	2,400–2,600	400	
5. Boat building	20	2,800–3,200	300	
6. Cabinet making finishing room	20	3,000–3,400 300	400	Dust-free and well ventilated.
7. Carpentry	20	3,000–3,400	400	
8. Commercial art	20	1,400–1,600	200	
9. Cosmetology	20	1,400–1,600	150	
10. Data processing	15	1,100–1,300		
11. Dental lab	20	1,600–1,800	200	
12. Distributive ed. rm. plus store	25	1,000–1,200 500		
13. Drafting	20	1,500–2,000	150	
14. Electronics	20	1,200–1,500	100	
15. Electrical shop plus	20	1,800–2,000	150	
electrical lab—machinery		800	100	Storage for unfinished work.
electrical lab—appliances		500–600	100	Storage for unfinished work.
16. Food trades area plus dining and sales	20	2,000–2,400 800	400	
2 dressing rooms		50 each	20	Storage for specific clothing.
17. Machine shop plus inspection room	20	3,000–3,200 300–400	400	
18. Medical assistant	20	1,100–1,300	150	
19. Medical lab	20	1,200–1,400	200	
20. Metal fabrication	20	2,800–3,200	400	
21. Optical tech.	20	1,400–1,600	200	
22. Painting and decorating	20	1,500–1,700	200	
23. Pattern making	20	1,900–2,100	200	
24. Plant maintenance	20	2,800–3,000	250	Storage—fireproof.

25. Plumbing	20	2,000–2,400	300	
26. Practical nursing	20	1,800–2,200	350	
27. Printing	20	3,600–3,800	300	
28. Sheet metal	20	2,000–2,400	300	
29. Upholstery	20	1,500–1,700	200	
30. Welding	20	2,400–2,600	350	
31. Clothing textiles	20	1,600–1,800	200	
32. Consumer economics	20	800–900		
33. Dietician's assistant	20	800–900		
34. Family living	20	800–900		
35. Fashion design and merchandising	20	1,000–1,200		
36. Foods and nutrition	20	1,500–1,800	300	
37. Home aides				
a. Geriatric aides	20	1,000–1,200	300	
b. Pediatric trng.	20	1,000–1,200	300	
38. Nursery school aides	20	1,200–1,400		
39. Kindergarten aides	20	1,000–1,400		
40. Related classrooms	20	800–900		
I. Other Specialized Spaces				
1. Mathematics lab.	25	850–900	100–125	Located near similar rooms.
2. Language arts lab.	30	900–1,000	75–100	Located near similar rooms.
3. Social studies lab.	30	900–1,000	75–100	Located near similar rooms.
4. Other				
J. Nonspecialized Instructional Spaces				About one-third of the nonspecialized classrooms should be grouped in pairs separated by a movable partition having a noise reduction coefficient in excess of 38 decibels. Television reception and origination jacks should be installed in these rooms.
1. Large classrooms	35	800–850	20–40*	
2. Medium classrooms	30	750–800	20–40*	
3. Small classrooms	25	650–700	20–40*	
4. Core curriculum	30	850–900	75–100	
5. Commercial	30	750–800	20–40*	

*Optional.

TABLE 13-2 **Supplementary Instructional Spaces in Secondary Schools**

Type of Space	Suggested Area of Each Space	Comments
A. Auditorium		An auditorium that seats 350 persons is needed for any secondary school. For larger schools, the absolute minimum should be an auditorium that seats the largest single grade plus 50. But it is recommended that the auditorium seat at least one-half the ultimate capacity of the building.
1. Stage	1,800–2,200	
2. Audience space	7–8 sq. ft per student	
3. Check room	200–300	
4. Lobby	1,500–2,000	
5. Public toilets		
6. Storage space (as near stage as possible)	250–300	Maximum capacity—seating the whole student body at one time, provided its seating capacity is not greater than 1,200–1,500.
B. Audiovisual (related to library)		
1. Work room— preview room	250–300	
2. Storage space	350–450	Adjoining workroom
C. Library (Instructional Material Center)		
1. Reading room (40– 75 capacity)	1,200–2,000	Reading space should accommodate about 10 percent of the enrollment, plus carrels (3–5% of enrollment). Minimum capacity—about 40, and maximum about 75 students. For larger schools, plan two or more reading rooms.
2. Office (librarian)	125–150	
3. Book processing room	150–200	Space for receiving, recording and cataloguing new books and for repairing worn or damaged books.
4. Conference room(s)	150–300	One per each 300 students of enrollment.
5. Storage space	175–240	
6. Carrels for self-instruction. Provide carrels for 3–5% of school enrollment.		Approximate—25 sq. ft. per carrel. Allocate about one square foot per student based on total school enrollment.
D. Cafeteria		
1. Kitchen	2 sq. ft. per meal, minimum	Plan to feed the ultimate anticipated enrollment in not more than three shifts.

TABLE 13-2 *Continued*

Type of Space	Suggested Area of Each Space	Comments
2. Dining area	12–15 sq. ft. per diner	The capacity of the dining area of the cafeteria should not be less than
3. Serving space	0.5–0.8 sq. ft. capacity of dining area	$^1/_3$ of the ultimate anticipated enrollment plus 50. Consider continuous feeding, which can add up to 20 percent of the capacity of the cafeteria.
		For secondary schools whose enrollments are less than 300, plan to seat at least $^1/_2$ of the ultimate anticipated enrollment. (This allows more time for the use of this area for other activities such as music, study, and assembly.)
		Locate one or two hand-washing areas adjacent to the cafeteria.
		Plan one serving line for every 200–250 students dining in each shift.
		Kitchen area—allow at least 2 square feet per meal to be served.
		Dietitian's office—one per cafeteria.
		Lavatory and dressing room facilities—one per cafeteria.
4. Storage space and can wash area	approx. 0.8 sq. ft. per meal	Easily accessible from service drives.
5. Toilets		
6. Handwashing area		
7. Teachers' dining area	12 sq. ft. per diner	Located near but separate from student cafeteria.
E. Remedial Instructional Spaces		
1. Reading	400–500	Remedial rooms may be located in
2. Speech	400–500	library area and planned for
3. General	400–500	supervision by the librarian
4. Computer lab	See Chap. 2	through the use of vision strips. Privacy gained by closing draw curtains when needed.
F. Student Activity		
1. Activity room	450–600	Size depends upon the nature of its uses.
2. Storage space	80–100	Location within view of main office.
G. Study Hall		
1. Study room	15–20 sq. ft. per pupil	Storage is needed if study hall is used as a multipurpose room.
2. Storage space		

TABLE 13-3 **Administrative and Related Areas**

Type of Space	Suggested Area of Each Space	Comments
A. Administration		
1. Principal	200–250	One principal's office per school.
2. Vice-principal	150–200	One assistant principal's office for each 500 students in excess of 400.
3. Clerk-waiting	300–350	
area	100 per clerk	One general office per school.
4. Storage (office supplies)	75–100	
a. Vault	50–75	
5. Toilet	40–50	
6. Conference rooms	250–300	
B. Guidance		
1. Guidance counseling office(s)	120–150	
2. Guidance director's office	150–200	This suite should possess a pleasant and informal atmosphere with drapes, carpets, and easy chairs.
3. Guidance library and waiting room	200–250	One guidance counselor's office for every 300 students of ultimate anticipated enrollment.
4. Space for guidance in small groups	125–150	
5. Space for individual testing	40–50	One guidance counselor library-waiting-browsing room per guidance suite.
6. Storage space	30–40	One testing cubicle for every 3 guidance counselors.
C. Health		
1. Office (nurse)	150–175	Should be located adjacent to guidance
2. Exam room	275–300	suite on the opposite side of
3. Waiting space	100–150	administrative suite.
4. Restrooms (2 cots)	100–125	At least one waiting room per suite.
5. Toilets	30–40	One nurse's room.
		One exam room.
		At least two dressing-rest rooms.
		One dental room, if the community has a school dental program.
D. Teachers' Rooms		
1. Common lounge	700–800	The size of this space depends upon the number of teachers to be served. The suggested size would be adequate for a faculty of about 30 teachers.

TABLE 13-3 *Continued*

Type of Space	Suggested Area of Each Space	Comments
2. Toilets–restrooms (one or more) for each sex	250–300	At least one teachers' restroom per school for each sex. At least one common teachers' lounge and workroom per school. A small teachers' lavatory related to each gang student toilet is desirable.
3. Workrooms	300–350	This function could be housed in the faculty dining room if it is properly designed for a dual function. Simple movable partitions could be used to screen one or two work alcoves.
4. Storage	30–40	
5. Faculty library	450–500	Located within the library complex.
6. Faculty office	100–120	One office for each three teachers.

TABLE 13-4 **Service Areas**

Type of Space	Suggested Area of Each Space	Comments
A. Custodian		
1. Office	100–150	Located near the general receiving
a. Storage	50–75	room and boiler area. At least one office per building.
2. Toilet and shower	100–125	
3. Workshop	250–300	At least one workroom.
4. Storage of custodial supplies	150–200	Storage space for custodial supplies and cleaning agents. Shower and locker facilities.
5. Service closets (with slop sinks)	20–25	These closets should be located adjacent to each gang toilet and near each of the large spaces, such as auditorium, gymnasium, and cafeteria.
6. Receiving room	150–200	Adjoining storage spaces.
7. Storage of outdoor equipment	100–150	Should be at grade level so that wheeled equipment can be driven or pushed into the storage room.
B. Other Service Spaces		
1. Book storage at various locations	40–50	One serving each wing and floor of the building.
2. General storage of instructional supplies	½ sq. ft. per pupil in school	One or two per school depending upon the size and plan of the building.
3. Toilets		See Chapter 10.

the quantities listed in Tables 13-1 to 13-4 are likely to change from time to time as research becomes available or as educational practices undergo certain transformations. It is felt, however, that school planners will deviate from the figures presented in Tables 13-1 to 13-4, of course, when the educational and service functions demand more or less space in certain situations.

Relationship of Clusters of Spaces to Each Other. Figure 13-1 shows the arrangement of groups of spaces in a traditional secondary school building. Essentially, the groupings are divided between quiet and noisy areas. They are also arranged with regard to the need for proximity to the service drive, outdoor play areas, or main entrance.

It should be reemphasized that the space arrangements shown in Figure 13-1 conform to current accepted practice. For example, it is generally agreed that all science rooms should be clustered together, that locker and shower rooms and play

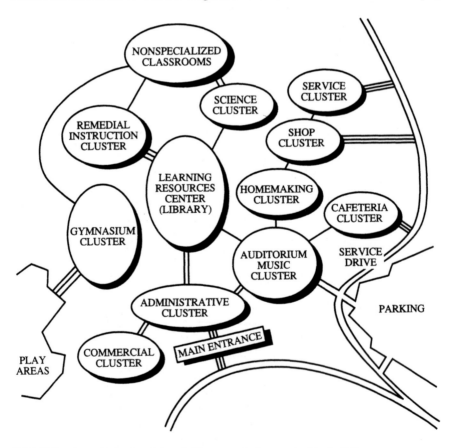

FIGURE 13-1 **Relationship of Clusters of Spaces to Each Other**

areas should be adjacent to the gymnasium, and so forth. The degree of relationship is indicated on the diagrams by the number of lines drawn between each element. Three lines denote a very close relationship, in which case one space should adjoin the other. Two lines means that the two spaces should be in the same general area, perhaps no farther apart than a corridor's width. One line between two spaces for clusters indicates that it is desirable but not essential that the two spaces be located in the same general area. An absence of lines between any two spaces or groups of elements means that no relationship exists between them. In this case, the architect may locate the space wherever he or she believes it will best fit into the architectural scheme of the building.

The art cluster is sometimes related to the stage rather than to the industrial arts cluster or home economics cluster on the premise that the art room is used in relation to the painting of scenery. While this argument has some merit, the functional relationship between art and mechanical drawing, between art and interior decoration, and between art and clothing design is more obvious. In some plans, the fine arts areas are completely divorced from related instructional areas, but such an arrangement is perhaps more a matter of architectural convenience than it is of educational function.

The Administrative Cluster. The administrative cluster is made up of three distinct but functionally interrelated parts, as indicated in Figure 13-2. The location of the guidance suite is crucial in this cluster. It should be between the general office and the health suite. If possible, the student entrance to the general office should be completely divorced from the entrance to the guidance-browsing-waiting area. It is often possible to locate the entrance to the general office around the corner from the entrance to the guidance room. This arrangement keeps the disciplinary function of

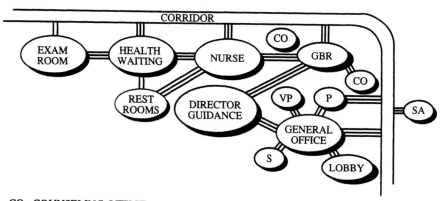

CO - COUNSELING OFFICE
GBR - GUIDANCE BROWSING ROOM
P - PRINCIPAL

VP - VICE PRINCIPAL
SA - STUDENT ACTIVITY ROOM
S - STORAGE

FIGURE 13-2 **The Administrative Cluster**

the principal's office completely dissociated from the guidance function. Internally, however, these two activities are closely related. Records kept in the general office are of basic concern to the guidance counselor. Conversations between the principal and the guidance people are also part of an effective guidance program.

The health and guidance functions are closely related. Many times, guidance counselors find that student difficulties arise from health problems. In such instances, the nurse and the guidance counselor work as a team in seeking to help the student. The nurse's office and health records should be easily accessible to the guidance counselors, and these two spaces can be closely related externally as well as internally, since the functions involved are psychologically compatible.

The Commercial Cluster. It is desirable, but not essential, to locate the commercial cluster near the general office. Those who advocate relating this cluster (Figure 13-3) to the office do so on the premise that some of the students may get actual office experience in the school office. Also, it is argued that where school funds are restricted, some of the office machines in the classroom may also be used by regular office employees. These reasons have merit, but if the architectural scheme does not permit the location of commercial classrooms near the office, no serious educational handicap is likely to result.

The Library Cluster. The library itself is surrounded by a large number of spaces occupying a first order of importance. In Figure 13-4 these spaces are connected to the library by three lines. It is essential that these spaces be arranged in the library area so that they can be easily supervised by the librarian. This can sometimes be achieved by installing vision strips in certain spaces and by locating others for direct supervision. Regular classrooms should be located in the general library area if such an arrangement is feasible. Sometimes the library is isolated when it serves both the school and the community.

School planners do not generally view the isolation of the library from nonspecialized classrooms with any degree of alarm, although it would be convenient to place regular classrooms in the library area.

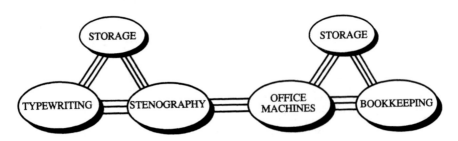

FIGURE 13-3 **The Commercial Cluster**

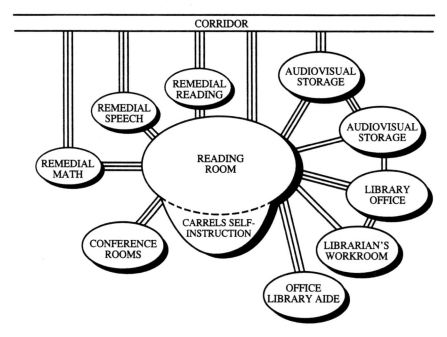

FIGURE 13-4 **The Library Cluster**

The Science Cluster. If the architectural scheme permits it, the science cluster might well adjoin the rooms in which mathematics is taught. While the specific location of the science cluster (Figure 13-5) itself is not critical, the clustering of the individual science rooms in one area is essential, partly to facilitate the movement

FIGURE 13-5 **The Science Cluster**

of costly equipment used for demonstration purposes from one laboratory to another. It is also important that the science teachers be able to work as a team and exchange ideas freely.

The Shop Cluster. This group of related instructional areas may be located wherever the architect feels it best fits into his or her total concept, provided it is at ground level near a service drive and that it is far enough away from quiet instructional areas not to disturb them. The progression shown in Figure 13-6 starts with the heavy industrial shops and culminates with arts and crafts shops. Existing shop clusters suffer most from a lack of sufficient storage. The need for storage in shop areas is three-fold. Space is needed for the storage of large tools, unfinished student projects, and materials and supplies. Small tools are often stored in the shop itself in lockable wall cabinets. The storage room for materials and supplies should be easily accessible to the service drive for unloading lumber, steel, and sheet material. It should also be convenient to students in the adjoining shops.

Planning rooms, one serving two shops, are essential in shop areas. Some educators feel that it is just as important for students to learn how to plan and detail projects on the drawing board as it is to learn how to use tools to construct the project itself. Planning rooms can also be used by teachers giving special instruction to individuals or groups of students working on a given project.

The Auditorium-Music Cluster. The auditorium and music areas are closely related. Dual-purpose use of dressing rooms is necessary to justify such spaces, for

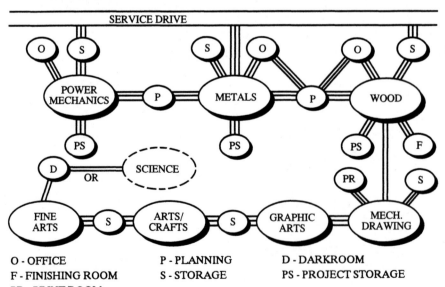

O - OFFICE   P - PLANNING   D - DARKROOM
F - FINISHING ROOM S - STORAGE   PS - PROJECT STORAGE
PR - PRINT ROOM

FIGURE 13-6 **The Shop Cluster**

they will be required very few times during the school year. The author has seen a number of dressing rooms near auditorium stages filled with broken chairs, desks, and other school equipment. Instead of being used for junk storage when not used for dressing, these spaces can be utilized efficiently at all times as combination music practice-dressing rooms. Figure 13-7 is self-explanatory. The music areas

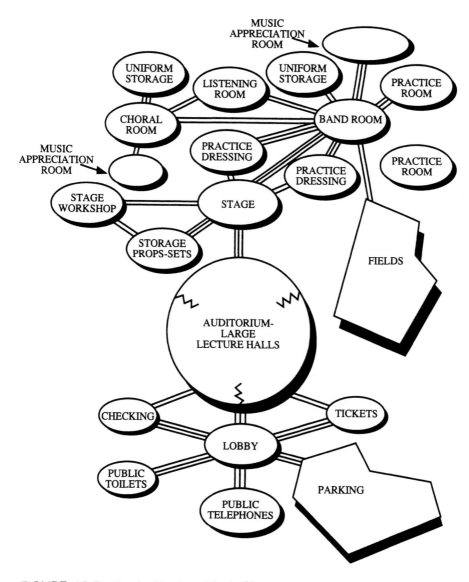

FIGURE 13-7 **The Auditorium-Music Cluster**

shown in this cluster should be designed and located so that the sounds emanating from them do not interfere with quiet activities in the auditorium or in other instructional areas.

The Gymnasium Cluster. In addition to what is shown in Figure 13-8, it should be pointed out that no driveways should be interposed between the gymnasium and the play areas of the school. Also, students should be able to travel directly from the locker and shower area to the out-of-doors without walking through the gymnasium.

A few special requirements of this area are worth noting. Each teaching area of the gymnasium should be provided with a storage room and instructor's office. At least two corrective rooms should be included directly off the floor of the main gymnasium, one for the girls and one for the boys. Drinking fountains should not be installed in the main gymnasium area, but in an alcove of the gymnasium or in a corridor. In the Midwest, architects ingeniously provide additional teaching sta-

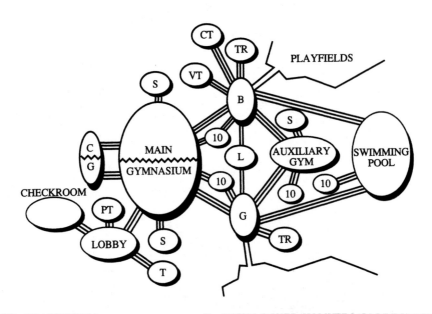

CT - COACH/TEAM
PT - PUBLIC TOILETS
CG - CORRECTIVE GYM
TR - TOWEL ROOM
G - GIRLS LOCKER/SHOWERS
L - LAUNDRY

B - BOYS LOCKER/SHOWERS/CORRECTIVE
VT - VISITING TEAM
T - TICKETS
IO - INSTRUCTOR'S OFFICE
S - STORAGE
C - CORRECTIVE

FIGURE 13-8 **The Gymnasium Cluster**

tions by locating supplementary spaces on balconies that are also used as seating capacity when folding bleachers are open. In the closed position, the bleachers form a partial wall between the upper main gymnasium and the auxiliary balcony gymnasium.

The Homemaking Cluster. The specific location of this cluster (Figure 13-9) is not very critical. However, if a nursery program is to be served by this cluster, it is essential that it be located at ground level adjacent to a play area for the four-year-old children who participate in the program.

In the past, some school planners insisted that the homemaking cluster be located next to the cafeteria. There is little basis for this. The homemaking suite serves an instructional function, while the cafeteria is a service. Some school people argue that the homemaking teacher should be near the cafeteria to supervise the cafeteria personnel. Such an added duty overburdens the homemaking teacher and shortchanges students. To avoid this questionable practice, it might be desirable to remove the homemaking cluster from the vicinity of the cafeteria, as is customary in many conventional secondary schools.

The Cafeteria Cluster. The individual elements in the cafeteria cluster are shown in Figure 13-10. Of primary importance is the strategic location of the kitchen, dishwashing area, and storage room. Two flow charts should be prepared when this cluster is being planned. One chart should show the student circulation from the point where they enter the cafeteria to the point where they leave the area after dining. The other chart should indicate the flow of food from the storage room to the food preparation and cooking area, and to the serving counter. The chart should also show the movement of dishes from the clean-dish storage to the serving areas, to the dishwashing machine, and back to the point of origin.

FIGURE 13-9 **The Homemaking Cluster**

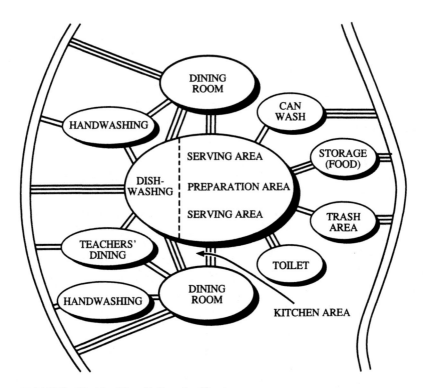

FIGURE 13-10 **The Cafeteria Cluster**

The location of the service drive is critical to the kitchen function. The delivery zone should be designed so that bulk foods may be easily unloaded at the storage areas. And there should be provision for the storage and removal of trash from this area, a feature that is usually overlooked in planning a kitchen area. Empty food cans are unsightly and usually attract flies. It is suggested that a special screened-in can wash and storage area be provided in a location convenient to the service drive.

The Service Cluster. The basic feature of this cluster of spaces is its location next to the service drive. Very few schools provide adequately for receiving and storage of supplies and for maintenance facilities. Storage often seems to be located wherever the architect has excess space rather than where it is needed. It is true, of course, that a few odd spaces cannot be avoided in any school plan. The use of such spaces for storage is most acceptable. In addition to these spaces, however, special-purpose storage spaces are needed in specific areas properly related to other spaces. Figure 13-11 indicates the type of spaces that should be located in the service cluster.

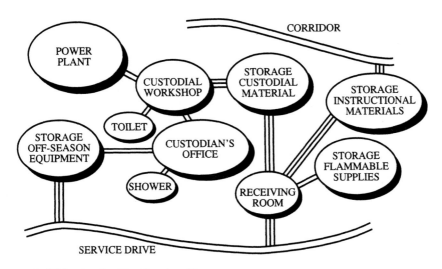

FIGURE 13-11 **The Service Cluster**

NOTES

1. Marion J. Conrad, "A Technique for Determining Operating Capacity of Secondary School Buildings," Doctoral dissertation, Ohio State University, 1952.

2. Basil Castaldi, *The Castaldi Nomogram* (Cambridge, MA: New England School Development Council, 1953).

► 14

Planning Colleges
and Universities

The demand, following World War II, for additional capacity at colleges and universities has all but vanished. However, there is still a definite need for the modernization and rehabilitation of many existing facilities of higher education. For this reason, a chapter devoted exclusively to planning of colleges and universities might provide some useful information for planners. A textbook on educational facilities would be incomplete without it.

The basic principles of planning discussed earlier in this text are valid for all types of educational facilities. But the procedure involved in developing long-range plans for colleges and universities differs substantially from that described for other educational facilities. The major difference lies in the composition of the planning team. In higher education, there is a much greater emphasis on faculty participation.

LONG-RANGE PLANNING FOR COLLEGES
AND UNIVERSITIES

In literature on long-range planning of colleges and universities there is little information on planning for higher education. The procedure described is often quite superficial. An architect engaged by the board of trustees is instructed to work with the college president, who in turn entrusts the major responsibility for educational matters related to campus planning to a faculty member on an overload basis. In some instances, although the designated faculty member may lack both the time and technical competence for planning school facilities, he or she may find it difficult to refuse a request from the college president. Faculty members who find themselves in such a position may grope along, hoping that the architect will pull them through somehow.

Some major universities employ a full staff of architects and engineers to plan their academic buildings, laboratories, and halls. The writer has observed on several occasions that such a group may plan admirably for heating, for cooling, for lighting, for acoustics, for safety, and for health, but rarely does it plan for education as a prime objective. Apparently, such architects and engineers simply assume that if all features affecting the comfort of people are properly designed, the resulting building automatically becomes an efficient educational tool. This assumption is not necessarily true. Fortunately for such planners, lack of emphasis on educational planning has not become a source of embarrassment to them, because the methodology of instruction in higher education has not changed significantly for centuries. Nevertheless, when unsound or uninformed educational planning by this professional team is coupled with the services of a faculty member who is not knowledgeable in the field of school planning, the resulting building may be strong in aesthetic charm, character, and architectural distinction, but often weak in educational efficiency. This outcome may be a tribute to the planners from the standpoint of architecture and engineering, but it does not speak well for the educators who have allowed these weaknesses to occur by default. Certainly, it is unfair to blame architects and engineers for educational shortcomings in a building, and it would be equally unjust to lay the blame on the overworked faculty member. The fault lies squarely with the planning procedures frequently employed by the administrative officials in colleges and universities.

THE NATURE AND ORGANIZATION OF COLLEGES AND UNIVERSITIES

Before discussing effective procedures for college and university planning, a brief review of the nature and organization of the several types of institutions of higher learning might be helpful. An institution of higher learning may take the form of a university, a college, a community college, or an institute of technology. While the pattern of organization of these institutions is quite similar in many respects, their primary educational functions may differ widely.

Purposes

The primary purpose of every college and university is to provide instruction to qualified students, but the scope, goals, and programs of each type of institution may differ extensively. Each basic type is discussed briefly below.

The University. In general, the three fundamental functions of a university are teaching, basic research, and service to the community or to the society that supports it. The university, then, represents a multipurpose, multilevel institution that must be capable of providing advanced instruction, of performing research at the frontiers of knowledge, and of rendering service to society. The university is also a major center for the storage and retrieval of knowledge, for the development of human talents, and for the creation of new knowledge in every field of human interest. In general terms, the university should be a fountain of knowledge that generates a dynamic force in a progressive society. The university is concerned with every aspect of human endeavor and thought, and it transmits a body of knowledge from generation to generation.

The College.   The major function of a college is teaching. To students who complete a prescribed program of studies, undergraduate colleges may award degrees at levels below the doctorate. College programs are generally restricted to specific fields, such as liberal arts, education, law, medicine, commerce and industry, graduate studies, and the like. While research and service may also be carried on at some of the colleges, these are secondary. Some colleges are colleges in name only, however, because what is called a college may really be a university in both function and organization.

The Community College.   The community college is unique in several respects. It offers both a terminal and transfer program for students who have completed high school or its equivalent. It is designed for students desiring a two-year program in technical, semiprofessional, and undergraduate training. The community college is the only institution of higher learning that offers comprehensive training in the technical and semiprofessional fields of learning.

The complex and comprehensive nature of the two-year community college program confronts school planners with the special problem of unifying three separate distinct programs of studies. In a well-planned community college, no attempt is made to isolate students by programs and buildings. On the contrary, every effort is made to encourage and stimulate the intermingling of students from all programs. More specifically, students enrolled in the college transfer program might be assigned to classes in physical education with students from the technical and semiprofessional programs. Certain courses in mathematics and English may be required of all students. Planning common and special facilities at the junior college level is critical from the standpoint of functional relationships. It is essential that all common-use spaces be identified during the planning process so that they may be centrally and conveniently located with respect to the specialized spaces associated with each major curriculum.

The Commuter College.   The commuter college is emerging as a public necessity. Both two- and four-year colleges are fulfilling this need. Community colleges are almost always designed as local or regional commuting colleges. Four-year colleges, on the other hand, are usually envisioned as residential colleges. However, those located in densely populated urban areas are sometimes planned for both residential and commuting students. As tuition and college fees rise higher and higher, students and parents of modest means are becoming increasingly interested in the commuting or drive-in college. Naturally, many students want to go to college away from home, and a significant number of parents are willing to make financial sacrifices to send them to resident colleges. Unfortunately, spiraling college costs make attendance away from home a financial impossibility for many. Thus, the college where students learn while living at home is becoming the college of affordability for more and more students.

Common Elements of Organization for Colleges and Universities

All institutions of higher learning, whether public or private, are governed by a board of trustees or its equivalent. They all possess an administrative head, usually called the president, who is the chief executive officer of the board of trustees and the operational head of the institution. The number of administrative staff and line positions below the rank of president varies widely from one type or size of institution to the other.

In general, the principal administrative officers of a university consist of a president, a provost (the dean of deans), college deans, and a financial and business officer. Several staff positions may also be part of the administrative structure of the university. Staff members are usually persons responsible for university-wide services that are indirectly related to the academic function. Such persons may include the university librarian, the director of student personnel services, the director of university research and development, and the director of physical plant.

Certain administrative functions must be performed at all institutions of higher learning regardless of size. The principal administrative functions in any institution of higher learning are admissions, records, personnel, academic affairs, student affairs, business affairs, physical plant, and planning and development. The number of persons employed depends upon the size and scope of the institution. For example, in a small college it is more than likely that the president will be concerned with academic affairs and professional personnel in addition to other duties. The college dean may be involved in student as well as academic affairs and so on. Every institution of higher learning relies heavily upon the director of physical plant and the persons responsible for the long-range development of the institution for its school plant planning.

BASIC PLANNING PROCEDURES FOR COLLEGES AND UNIVERSITIES

Every institution of higher learning needs a planning bureau. Where such a bureau does exist, the planning team does not always include an educator who has the technical competence to plan institutions of higher learning. Admittedly, a faculty member is almost always brought into the planning process, but as mentioned earlier, he or she is not always competent in college facility planning. A knowledgeable faculty member is often overruled by the chairman of the planning group, who is usually either an architect or engineer.

It is strongly recommended that an educator competent in the field of school plant planning be made part of the planning team. If possible, he or she should have the final word on all building matters that affect the educational function of the school.

The College and University Planning Group

A planning team is essential if a college facility that is both architecturally imaginative and educationally functional is to be designed. The team should include at least the persons listed below.

1. As chairman, the institution's educational planner or educational consultant.
2. The planning architect and institutional architect if one is employed.
3. The dean of the college concerned.
4. The head of each department concerned.
5. The president or someone representing the president.

This group is viewed as the primary or executive planning team. It has full responsibility for planning and equipping the building and for much of the administrative work. It is concerned with educational, architectural, structural, legal, and budgetary matters. Through the president of the institution, this group assumes the function of a building committee for the board of trustees. In many small colleges and community colleges, the president may choose to serve on this committee.

The Advisory Committee.   The faculty members should be organized, perhaps by department, to supply ideas and suggestions to the planning team and to make a continuous evaluation of plans as they are being developed. The planning team should meet with the college faculty as a whole from time to time, and frequently with each department to insure that every educational detail of the plan is known to those who will use the facility.

College planners should never forget that many experts in the various subject-matter fields are available for consultation on the campus itself. Of course, it may be necessary, at times, to turn to other campuses for needed expertise. Many excellent ideas may be gleaned from local faculty, whose morale is often favorably affected by direct involvement in planning their school. The planning mechanism should be designed to enable each faculty member to react to plans and to submit ideas to the planning team through the advisory committee or directly.

BASIC TYPES OF INSTRUCTIONAL PRACTICES IN COLLEGES AND UNIVERSITIES

Instructional methods employed in institutions of higher learning have remained fairly static for centuries. Some colleges of education have dared to introduce bold innovations in teaching college- and university-level students, but many courses are taught by substantially the same methods employed by Aristotle, Plato, and Socrates. To be sure, the present-day environment for teaching is perhaps more conducive to learning than it was in the Greek schools, and the introduction of teaching aids in the modern classroom has done much to enrich the content of instruction. But, on the whole, the methods employed by instructors and professors today do not differ materially from basic practices in vogue two thousand years ago. Perhaps substantial change is long overdue, but until changes are conceived, developed, and tested, colleges and universities will continue to offer instruction using many of the methods of the past. No criticism of these methods is intended, nor is there a desire to downgrade the instructional practices of the great teachers of the past. Our purpose is simply to point out that few fundamental changes have occurred in the methods of instruction employed in institutions of higher learning over the past few centuries. Four basic methods are still in use today.

The Lecture Method of Instruction

The most common method of instruction of the college and university level is the lecture. The procedure is relatively simple. A group of students ranging from perhaps 5 to 500 are seated in a room or hall where the professor lectures to them. The instructor may cite and recite subject matter, demonstrate various principles through the use of experiments, or employ a chalkboard or overhead projector to supplement the oral presentation. The student, in this case, usually listens and takes notes. He or she may, of course, ask questions related to the material. In groups of fewer than 30 students, instruction may be conducted in a less formal setting, which may result in an appreciable increase in student participation.

The Seminar Method of Instruction

The seminar is an effective instructional procedure if used judiciously. Basically, small groups of about 10 or 15 students and instructors engage in a free interchange of ideas concerning a given subject. The atmosphere is usually informal, but the proceedings are sufficiently structured to promote fruitful discussions. Seminars are most productive when all participants are well acquainted with the topic. Sometimes, the seminar method is improperly used as a substitute for the lecture-recitation method in which the instructor serves as the primary source of information while students participate to the extent of their ability. It is still an instructor-oriented procedure. On the other hand, in the seminar, all participants are knowledgeable about the topic and able to make a contribution to the discussion. In situations where students are not well acquainted with the topic, the seminar becomes a pooling of ignorance. Its instructional purpose is thus defeated.

The Laboratory Method of Instruction

The laboratory approach to instruction exposes students to direct, as opposed to vicarious, learning experiences. In a science laboratory, for example, students conduct experiments in which they gain first-hand experience in demonstrating principles and phenomena. The laboratory concept has been expanded to include any activity in which students gain knowledge primarily through a directed form of self-instruction. Originally students performed series of predetermined experiments to supplement the lectures. The expanded notion of a laboratory includes such facilities as language laboratories, where students may gain aural proficiency in a foreign language through the use of electronic devices. In general, a laboratory is an area where learning occurs through the concentrated participation of the student in a given learning activity.

A laboratory class is usually restricted in size and scope. Generally, a laboratory at the college level is planned for no more than 25 students. In more advanced classes where the experiments are more complex, the laboratory class may consist of only 10 or 15 students. In graduate schools, it is not unusual to find laboratories for one or two students. The scope of the work conducted in a given laboratory space is also governed by the highly specialized equipment often associated with a certain laboratory.

The Conference Method of Instruction

In colleges and universities, it is not unusual to find a professor holding a conference with one or more students in his or her office. Such conferences may consist of a direct interchange of ideas between the professor and student on basic concepts or philosophies. The urgent need to teach large numbers of college students has almost eliminated this type of instruction at the undergraduate level. Fortunately, most graduate colleges still retain the conference method as an integral part of the instructional process.

THE COLLEGE AND UNIVERSITY CAMPUS

The basic elements of school plant planning discussed earlier in relation to elementary and secondary schools apply equally to all types of institutions of higher learning. Some are associated with aesthetics, safety, and convenience, while others stem from the educational functions envisioned for the institution.

The Size of a College and University Site

The selection of a site for a campus is an important duty of the board of trustees. Since many institutions educate students in residence on campus, a proper learning environment is fundamental in selecting a site. Size, location, aesthetics, potential development, accessibility, and topography are matters of basic concern.

There is currently no standard by which to determine the optimum size of a college or university site. Its size will obviously depend upon the availability and cost of land in the general area where the school is proposed. A rule of thumb, derived from a review of current practices, calls for sites of at least 50 acres per thousand students of ultimate enrollment. Many colleges are located on campuses that are proportionately much larger, where land is available and reasonably priced. Because urban campuses, of necessity, are highly restricted in area, they should be located on the periphery of urban areas rather than crowded into high-rise buildings in the middle of the city. Political influences and forces not necessarily concerned with educational matters often induce boards of trustees to select mid-city campus sites, often against their better judgment. Every effort should be made by such boards to resist politically inspired forces if location in the center of a business district cannot be justified on educational grounds.

The college campus is much more than a collection of educational facilities. It is in reality a total environment that stimulates teaching, learning, introspection, and creative thinking. The college campus should be intellectually inspiring and aesthetically exciting. In addition to land for the buildings, the college campus must provide abundant space for walks, trees, shrubs, fountains, pools, open centers of aesthetic interest, stone walls, and lawns. The well-designed campus contains many elements of art and beauty conceived by an imaginative architect. Students who enter the college campus must feel they have stepped into an intellectual world that is pleasant and aesthetically exciting. To achieve this, the architect requires land and a great deal of it. Regardless of enrollment or urban location, the minimum size of any campus should be about 50 acres of usable land.

Essential Features of a Campus Site

The number of desirable characteristics of a campus site discussed below is necessarily limited. It is hoped, however, that they will suggest other ideas pertinent to the selection of a campus site.

Location. The college or university site should be readily accessible to students and faculty by both private and public transportation. It should be located near, but not necessarily in, an urban center capable of providing the many services required by the institution and the people associated with it. And finally, the campus should be located in an area where existing development is compatible with that of the institution.

Natural Beauty. The general environment surrounding a college campus is as important as the site itself. Natural beauty is vital. Closeness to majestic mountains, oceans, lakes, or rivers, or to beautifully landscaped golf courses, is highly desirable. In areas with rolling hills, a campus that overlooks a wide vista is also desirable. Of course, natural beauty cannot always be found, but every effort should be made to select a site with an abundance of natural beauty or one where beautiful surroundings can be developed.

For many reasons, a campus within the boundaries of a built-up city cannot always be avoided. In such instances, college planners need not be discouraged. An imaginative approach to campus planning can create much natural beauty within the confines of the campus itself. Much more attention must be given to internal landscaping, and more money must be spent to compensate for the lack of scenic beauty. A city college campus site presents a real challenge to the creativity and ingenuity of the architectural planner.

Freedom from Danger. Safety hazards are a prime consideration in selecting a college site. For example, a campus should not be located in the flight path of aircraft landing at a nearby airport because of the danger of accidents during inclement weather. Major highways present a safety hazard when they adjoin a college campus, unless special precautions are exercised. Campuses in industrial areas should avoid locations near any source of explosions.

Freedom from Health Hazards. College campuses should not be located where noxious gases or smog tend to accumulate. Areas downwind from municipal incinerators, fertilizer and rendering plants, and the like are also undesirable campus sites, as are those near industries, such as oil refineries and paint factories that produce fumes. Air pollution is sufficient grounds for rejecting an otherwise desirable campus site.

Freedom from Noise, Vibrations, and Other Distractions. The campus site should be situated well away from any source of noise, vibration, or other factor that would interfere with the student's ability to concentrate on learning. Such distractions range from jet whines to structural vibrations transmitted through the building itself. In urban locations, students could be distracted by the noise from normal automotive traffic. Under certain conditions, the building as a whole might vibrate as high-speed railroad or subway trains pass in the vicinity of the campus. The vibration is objectionable for two reasons. Not only is it a source of student distraction, but it may also cause malfunctioning in a delicate scientific instrument such as a minimum thermometer, thermograph, barograph, or sensitive balance.

Locations near sources of distractive odors are also undesirable. For example, the odors from a chocolate, potato chip, or fish factory might not be injurious to health, but they might create some annoyance among the students and faculty.

The Master Campus Plan

Some college and university planners object to the use of the term "master plan" in campus development. They seem to feel that once the plan is formulated they become its slave. This notion could not be further from the truth. It is axiomatic that a long-range developmental plan is a *sine qua non* in planning an expanding campus. Without such a plan, the campus would grow haphazardly. Indeed, this has been the case in many large universities. In contrast, many obviously follow a well-conceived plan of campus development.

No growing college or university, large or small, can afford to develop without a flexible master plan. Many of the principles mentioned in Chapter 4, under long-range planning also apply to a college or university. To reassure those who fear the dominance of the master plan, the postulates and assumptions underlying the plan should be reviewed before any appreciable capital funds are spent. If the master plan is still valid and adequate, there is no reason why the long-range plan embodied therein should not be implemented. On the other hand, if the assumptions underlying the original master plan are no longer true, it would be in the best interest of the college to postpone major capital expenditures until the master plan has been revised to take into account any changes in the financial program or in the educational goals of the institution. College and university administrators will find it easier to justify the raising and expenditure of capital funds if the proposed action fits into a professionally developed master plan of the campus.

The Master Plan as a Fulfillment of Future Educational Needs

The master plan should advance the achievement of educational goals of the college or university and promote its research and service programs. Indeed, the master plan should clearly reflect the future educational needs of the institution. To some college planners, the master plan is simply a site plan of the campus showing the main malls and the location of existing and future buildings. This rather narrow approach covers only a small segment of the long-range planning normally associated with an institution of higher learning. Each major element of the campus long-range plan is discussed below.

Future Enrollment. In most instances, future enrollment is determined primarily by the capacity of the college facilities. Generally speaking, future enrollment at a specific campus is extremely difficult to predict. Statistical data on the number of college-age students anticipated nationally year by year are available through federal agencies. Whether such increases will reflect later as registered students at a particular campus is pure conjecture.

Available space does not attract a student to an institution. There are a number of other considerations; cost of tuition and fees, strength of the academic program in a field of interest, location, and prestige. Thus, prudence dictates that expansion of facilities proceed with caution and with a sound, well-conceived goal in mind.

This goal may simply involve an increased capacity due to a demonstrated need. It may be aimed at attracting more students. Or it may focus on the need to introduce a new academic program to strengthen the college offerings. In any event, expansion should not be undertaken for the sake of expansion alone. There should be a well-documented rationale. For example, assuming that program improvement can increase student enrollment, it might be fruitful to initiate a study of the academic program. If after such a study is completed it is found that the academic offerings are weak in some major discipline such as engineering, business, fine arts, or architecture, it might be advantageous to provide a facility that fulfills that need. The primary purpose of the expansion is to provide a more balanced program and hopefully to attract more students. Consequently, the institution may be in a better position to compete with other colleges for students.

Clearly, future enrollment is almost impossible to predict. Obviously, the more prestigious and popular institutions operate at full capacity year after year. But, for most of the others, enrollments are unpredictable. Therefore, if additional capacity is warranted, it is suggested that additional space be provided for disciplines that are likely to attract more students.

Future Institutional Programs. The long-range plan should show clearly how and where future programs in teaching, research, and service will be staffed, financed, and housed. Listing the amounts to be expended for each category is a good beginning but it is not enough. All future programs should be set forth in detail. Descriptions should indicate courses and content, showing how future courses are integrated with those offered at present. There should be some indication of the number and type of personnel needed and the anticipated operational cost of the instructional program. All of the foreseeable general areas of research and service likely to be undertaken by the institution should be listed, together with information about personnel needs and future operational costs.

Facilities Needed. Anticipated enrollment and future programs should then be translated into educational facilities. The program dictates the type needed, and the enrollment and extent of research and service activity fix the size or capacity. The master plan could include a detailed description of each facility, but such specific information could better be deferred until a facility is about to be planned. Several years may elapse between the time when the need for a certain facility is identified in the master plan and the time the facility is actually built, and details applicable earlier may have become obsolete by the time the building is actually being planned. The master plan should simply identify facilities needed by general type and approximate size or capacity and include a cost estimate for each one. For example, the master plan might call for a three-million-dollar physical education building containing a swimming pool, eight teaching stations, and associated spaces.

The Capital Outlay Program. Once the cost and type of needed facilities are listed in order of educational priority, it is possible to determine the overall cost of campus development. In private institutions, fund-raising campaigns and gifts account for the major part of capital funds. The financial officer must develop a realistic capital outlay program. His or her study may well show that the program set forth by the educators is somewhat more ambitious than the anticipated accumulation of capital funds can support for a given year. In such instances, the time factor must be extended or the anticipated capacity for a given year must be reduced, or both. It is the responsibility of the financial officer and educational planners to determine a realistic financial program for the balanced educational development of the institution.

The Master Plan as a Guide to Future Action
The master plan not only insures that future educational needs can be met in a systematic fashion but also provides a clear and orderly plan of action for future expansion of facilities within the limits of the financial resources of the institution. A number of basic decisions must be made by the board of trustees before long-range campus planning can proceed intelligently. One major consideration related to campus planning is discussed below.

The General Layout of the Campus. As soon as future educational facility needs have been clearly specified in the long-range plan, the campus planner, together with educators, can begin to develop the layout of the campus as a whole, using planning concepts that fit the educational function of the institution. On a new campus, proven concepts of expansion can be implemented simply by drawing and redrawing fresh lines on paper. On an established campus, however, the introduction of such principles may present a real problem, unless the campus was laid out in the first place according to a functional and logical plan of development. In any event, it is the responsibility of the campus planner to create a plan that embodies a desired conceptual pattern within the framework of existing facilities. Obviously, compromises will have to be made, but the new parts of a campus can begin to give form and direction to its ultimate development.

Fundamental Policies That Shape the Master Plan
The long-range plan that guides the future action of boards of trustees and college administrators is a carefully drawn document that describes a series of sequential steps linking the present with the future. In formulating such a plan, administrators, faculty, and members of boards of trustees must come to grips with a number of fundamental issues which, in turn, shape the resulting long-range plan. Some of these issues are discussed below.

The Compact Campus Plan. There is no ideal or recommended layout for a college campus. In the past, college buildings have often been located as though they were separate and distinct schools of learning, particularly on campuses with an abundance of land for both immediate and future development. The facilities of a small college, under such circumstances, might consist of three or four individual structures, such as an academic or humanities building, a science building, a physical education building, and perhaps a separate library-auditorium building. Larger institutions might include, in addition, a fine arts building, an engineering building, and perhaps a graduate college building. In some large universities with enrollments in excess of 12,000 students, not only is the number of buildings increased but each facility is more specialized. For example, instead of a science building, one might find a chemistry building, a physics building, a biology building, and an astronomy building. Instead of an engineering building, there might be an electrical engineering building, a mechanical engineering building, and a civil engineering building. And the fine arts building might be replaced by a music building, band building, art building, and architecture building. Good campus planning requires that all related buildings be clustered in the same general area.

In the absence of a well-conceived campus plan, however, the compact concept cannot always be applied. In many instances, the location of a given building is determined more by the availability of land on the campus than by functional or conceptual considerations. The rapid growth of many colleges and universities emphasizes the need for compactness in campus planning. As enrollment increases, more and more separate buildings are erected to provide the needed additional capacity. In many institutions, this proliferation of buildings creates such a distance between buildings in distant corners of the campus that students can no longer walk from class to class. In one large midwestern university, it became necessary for students to ride buses to reach classes in distant buildings within the 10-minute interval between periods.

College and university planners are giving serious consideration to the compact campus plan. Under this concept, most educational buildings are located in a central core surrounded by a circular peripheral driveway. No vehicular traffic is allowed on the central mall. Service trucks approach each building from the rear, which is oriented toward the peripheral drive.

Figure 14-1 shows the campus plan for a New England college campus. It is designed as a compact campus for an initial enrollment of about 3,500 students. If two more buildings, a humanities and a science and engineering building, were added, the campus would have a total balanced capacity for about 7,000 students. If a capacity of 15,000 students should be needed, it is planned simply to locate the parking spaces on the other side of the peripheral driveway and construct needed facilities on space formerly used for parking. The architect who conceived the campus design created a highly flexible plan for expanding the central core of the campus. Even at the 15,000-student capacity level, the walking distance between

FIGURE 14-1 **A Campus Plan**

any two educational buildings could be covered by the average student within the time allowed between periods.

The compact campus plan has much in its favor. Distances for students to walk from building to building are shorter and so are utility and communication lines. The compact plan encourages greater contact among faculty members and promotes the interchange of ideas among the community of scholars. The compact campus also offers greater architectural cohesion than does the decentralized campus plan.

Psychologically, the compact plan lends itself more readily to an intellectually stimulating atmosphere than do other plans. The individual buildings surrounding the core can be architecturally exciting and harmoniously designed. Imaginative landscaping of the central core can add a feeling of beauty and serenity. The arrangement of the various related buildings within the visual field of the student can present a panorama symbolic of the entire spectrum of human knowledge. The architect designing a compact campus can create a unity of architectural concepts in a single field of vision, blending the beauty of nature with that created by man and creating an atmosphere that pleases the eye, relaxes the body, and stimulates the intellect.

Centralization versus Decentralization of Common Facilities.   When an institution of higher learning is being planned, the question of centralization of facilities utilized by the entire student body is almost certain to arise. There is no hard and fast rule regarding centralization or decentralization of the various functions. Some aspects of this topic are discussed in the following paragraphs.

1. *The library.* The centralization of the library is strongly recommended by librarians. On a compact campus, such as that described earlier, there is little reason to disperse the library collection among the various instructional buildings. All library books should be available to the entire student body and faculty. When doing research, for example, it is annoying to learn that a book is located in a building at the other end of the campus.

The departmental faculty often insists on maintaining its library in its own building. While this is more convenient from the standpoint of students who may spend most of their time in the departmental building, the books stored in the departmental library are not so readily available to the rest of the faculty and student body. From the standpoint of students engaged in research, the decentralized library is neither desirable nor functional, for it contributes little to the efficient utilization of research time.

The establishment of a central library serving the entire institution is generally favored by campus planners. Under this plan, duplicate copies of materials may be stored and read in the departmental library, provided they are cataloged and processed through the central library. Under this arrangement, a researcher, for example, may have access to at least one copy of every volume in the institution's holdings in the main library itself. If the copy stored in the main library is in circulation, he or she may still refer to any available duplicate copies normally shelved in departmental libraries.

Although the case for the departmental library has some merit, librarians generally maintain that library materials are of little value unless they are readily accessible to potential users. Decentralized storage of library materials, according to this view, does not accomplish the basic purpose of a campus library. It is further argued that the overall cost of staffing branch libraries with qualified personnel is greater than it is for a centralized library. And finally, librarians believe that greater control on circulation is possible and better service can be rendered under the centralized arrangement. It seems that an excellent case can be made for the centralized campus library, particularly on a compact campus. On a large campus where departmental buildings are far apart, however, there seems to be some basis for combining a centralized library with departmental libraries in which duplicate copies and reference material are stored.

2. *Food services.* On any campus on which both resident and commuting students are accommodated, the problem arises as to whether or not a single dining hall should be provided for all students. There is no single answer to this problem, but a number of workable solutions are possible.

If the dormitories can be located adjacent to the student union building, centralization is the obvious answer. Resident students may use special dining halls adjacent to the central kitchen, or they may simply utilize a central cafeteria dining area that is open to all students, faculty members, and institutional employees.

If for any reason the dormitories must be located in a remote part of the campus, complete centralization is not feasible. In this situation, it may be possible to centralize the kitchen in the student union building and transport prepared foods to the dining halls in the dormitories. Of course, if the dormitory complex houses over 500 students, it may be just as economical to decentralize the food services, in which case two separate kitchens would be operated by the institution.

3. *Instructional materials production center.* All supplementary teaching materials that can be utilized by instructors in two or more disciplines should be centralized in one campus location, perhaps in the library building. Every campus should provide an instructional materials production center for faculty members who need special charts, transparencies, films, tapes, or other supplementary teaching materials. This service should be rendered by professional artists and technicians operating within the instructional materials production center.

4. *The computer center.* Many campuses install their computer in the business office, in the engineering building, or in the mathematics department. Because of its location, the computer often becomes the special property of one operational unit, when actually it is a campus facility that should be readily available to all departments through a central control system. It is suggested that the computer center be housed in the library building, if possible, although the physical location of modern computers is not crucial to their efficient operation. The computer service should be centralized and under the control of the general administration of the campus so that proprietary claims to the computer made by departments and business office may be kept to a minimum. In large institutions where more than one computer may be needed, at least the most sophisticated unit should be under centralized control.

5. *The television production center.* This function might well be centralized in the library building where resource materials are readily available. Programs may originate from many parts of the campus, but videotapes and associated equipment should remain in the television center. On existing campuses, it may not be possible to centralize the television studios and allied spaces in the library. While proximity of the television production center to the library is highly desirable, it is not crucial to the efficient operation of a closed- and open-circuit television system.

6. *Student personnel services.* If possible, all student personnel services should be centralized in a single area or building. Health services, personal aid service, financial service, and guidance and testing should be centralized for the entire campus.

7. *Campus maintenance and operation center.* The activities of the director of physical plant should be centralized in one building, perhaps in the vicinity of the power plant. Storage of custodial and maintenance supplies and materials should also be centralized in one area. The building or area should be designed so that the distribution of such materials can be controlled. Office space should be provided for the recording and storing of complete data on inventories, cost, and condition of all equipment owned by the institution, regardless of where the equipment is used and stored on the campus.

8. *Campus transportation center.* Most colleges and universities own various types of vehicles ranging from snow plows to buses. A centralized motor pool in the vicinity of the maintenance center would be highly desirable. If the institution owns a fleet of vehicles, it is suggested that the institution provide its own maintenance garage.

9. *Administrative center.* Every campus should provide a central administrative area for its general academic control and business affairs. In small colleges, this centralized function may require no more than the equivalent of two classrooms located perhaps in a wing of the main building.

10. *Centralized warehousing.* The storage of instructional equipment and supplies may not present a serious problem on campuses with enrollments of about 1,000 students. When enrollments reach 5,000 however, storage will require warehousing of a large number of items. In such instances, a centralized warehouse should be provided for receiving, checking, recording, and distributing equipment, supplies, and food commodities received in bulk. The dollar volume of materials, foods, and supplies reaches into the hundreds of thousands at many institutions. It is essential that such a large investment be properly stored, equitably distributed, and protected against pilferage, spoilage, and destruction by fire.

11. *Centralized printing.* If the institution has an enrollment exceeding 3,000 students, it might be advantageous to establish a centralized printing and material duplication center on the campus. The most practical location for such a unit is in the vicinity of the administration center, which is usually responsible for approving materials produced by such a center.

12. *Centralization of related instructional functions.* In formulating the master campus plan, it is functionally efficient to cluster facilities housing closely associated fields of learning in a single building or in the same area of the campus. For example, the English, social sciences, and foreign language buildings could be grouped together in the same general area of the campus. Or all of these subject-area fields could be housed in the same building where separate buildings are not needed.

Architectural Aspects of the Master Plan. The general architecture of the campus merits serious consideration in any master plan. Broad policies regarding the type of architecture, height of buildings, and materials of construction should be set forth prior to the development of a master site plan for the campus. For example, it may be the policy of a board of trustees to permit only Georgian architecture on the main campus quadrangle and to limit the heights of all buildings to four stories. On the other hand, a board of trustees may wish to construct only contemporary structures regardless of the architecture of existing buildings. The campus planner should be made aware of any architectural limitations that may be imposed. Ideally, the governing board should supply broad written policies and a minimum of restrictions to guide in planning a campus that is creative in design, functional in character, and economical in cost.

Other Policy Statements Influencing Campus Development. Campus planning may be influenced by other matters that may determine the nature, direction, and speed of campus development. A few examples of policies affecting campus development are listed below.

1. No vehicular traffic shall be permitted in the central campus.
2. The use of certain facilities, such as the library, auditorium, and small halls, by the public shall be encouraged.
3. Professional meetings of various types shall be encouraged on the campus.
4. The institution shall serve as a cultural center for the area in which it is located.
5. The institution shall remain primarily a commuter college.
6. Faculty members may rent institutionally owned homes located on the campus for not more than two years.
7. Dormitory facilities shall be planned for approximately 40 percent of the student body.
8. Provision shall be made for housing married students on the campus.

9. Closed-circuit television shall be planned so that programs may be received or may originate in any classroom, laboratory, or auditorium.
10. Special emphasis shall be placed upon the use of self-instructional devices which serve all disciplines.
11. Information retrieval from the informational resource center shall be available to all students and faculty.
12. An electronic feedback system shall be installed whenever groups larger than 50 students are instructed.
13. All faculty members shall have secretarial services readily available regardless of the location of their office or operational unit.
14. Parking space shall be provided for all students and employees, with or without a parking fee.
15. All normal student and faculty service spaces, such as cafeteria, bank, post office, and barber shop, shall be provided on the campus.
16. A limited number of hotel-like rooms should be provided for visiting lecturers, resource persons, and governmental dignitaries.
17. An institutional reception center shall be included in the master plan.
18. Student and faculty recreational and health facilities shall be included in the campus plan.
19. Natural features of the site, such as trees, brooks, and lakes, shall be preserved as much as possible.
20. Bomb shelters with sufficient capacity for students, faculty, and citizens in the area shall be constructed on the campus.
21. The development of the campus shall promote dignity and elegance in every possible way.
22. All buildings shall be designed to blend with the natural beauty of the campus and its surroundings.
23. All architectural design and masses shall be in complete harmony with the existing buildings that will surround them.
24. If basic architectural concepts change from one building to another, there shall be a transitional zone between them.
25. Buildings shall be constructed far enough apart to prevent noises, obnoxious odors, and other distracting influences from interfering with the instructional or research functions carried on within them.
26. All buildings shall be provided with service drives to be used by authorized vehicles only.
27. All parking areas shall be hidden from direct view from the main campus mall.
28. All sidewalks shall be provided with heating devices designed to melt ice and snow.
29. All students shall be able to move at a normal pace from one instructional area to any other instructional space on the campus within an interval of eight minutes.

30. Insofar as possible, students shall be grouped according to year level. For example, freshmen would use facilities primarily on one part of the campus or in one end of a given building for certain types of instruction.
31. Students shall intermingle as much as possible within a given classification. Segregation of students shall be kept at an absolute minimum.
32. All student activities shall be concentrated in a single part of the campus or a single building, such as the student union.
33. All buildings shall follow a specific type of architecture, such as Gothic, Georgian, contemporary, etc.
34. All buildings shall reflect contemporary design regardless of the style of buildings surrounding them.
35. A wide variety in type of architecture is permitted provided that the architecture of a given building does not clash aesthetically with that of its surroundings.

FUNCTIONALLY DESIGNED SPACES IN COLLEGE AND UNIVERSITY FACILITIES

Unlike secondary schools, each type of space on a college or university campus serves an established and distinct function. Each space serves well-defined functions which are usually specified by a faculty committee. Since the space requirements vary from campus to campus, it is suggested that the college and university planning group carefully analyze its spatial needs and prepare a set of detailed educational specifications, as described in Chapter 6, for the proposed campus.

The types of spaces that require special attention are listed below. It is recommended that the planning group determine the functions that it envisions for each type of space, and then visit other campuses that have already addressed similar needs and profit from their experiences.

Typical Spaces on a College or University Campus

The typical spaces normally found on a university campus are included in, but not limited to, the list presented below. Detailed specifications, including size, location, and general features, should be prepared by the planning group for each type of space.

1. Instructional Spaces

    a. Small seminar rooms accommodating about 15 students.
    b. Small lecture halls with a capacity of about 50 students.
    c. Large lecture halls with risers serving about 300 students.
    d. Student laboratories of various types with a capacity of about 25 students.
    e. Small laboratories for faculty or graduate students for individual experiments.

2. Administrative Spaces

   a. Offices for individual administrators.
   b. Ancillary spaces for communication equipment, mail handling, administrative computer system, materials distribution, etc.
   c. Conference rooms for administrative personnel.
   d. Secretarial offices.

3. Faculty Spaces

   a. Faculty offices.
   b. Faculty secretarial space.
   c. Departmental conference rooms.

4. General University Facilities

   a. Library.
   b. Computer services center.
   c. Television production and processing center.
   d. Central storage and warehouse spaces.
   e. Campus maintenance and operations center.
   f. Gymnasium, fieldhouse and other athletic facilities.
   g. Fine and performance arts center.

5. Student Services

   a. Dormitories.
   b. Dining rooms.
   c. Health services.
   d. Parking spaces.
   e. Spaces for student guidance and advisement.
   f. Student recreational areas.
   g. Student placement center.

▶ 15

Planning Child-Care Facilities

Child care has existed for centuries among royalty and the very rich members of society. It has been only within the past two centuries that child care has been extended to children of the working class. Today, the need for child care is even greater in industrialized nations where the economic demands of society impose an ever-increasing financial burden on the family.

The traditional family that existed a half century ago is gradually fading from the scene. While a variety of child-care facilities are appearing here and there to fill the gap created by this situation, the general public is not yet fully aware of the consequences of the changes occurring in both the structure and function of the family. Neither has any public agency, private group, or governmental body assumed the responsibility for funding and promoting universal child-care service. The efforts, thus far, have been sporadic, fragmented, and ineffective, perhaps because the public still believes that child care is the sole responsibility of the parents and should be provided at their expense.

THE EVOLUTION OF CHILD-CARE PROGRAMS

There has been a deep interest in child-care services on the part of a few enlightened educators for over a century. A few social reformers in Europe were inspired by the writings of Rousseau and Pestalozzi, who observed that young children learn rapidly and retain easily. With these concepts in mind, a number of European social reformers embarked on a venture to improve child development by exploiting these perceived childhood talents. They focused their attention on helping to develop nursery schools for the children of the poor. Although these early childhood schools were well intentioned, they were available to only a small segment of the population.

Early Child-Care Programs

The early childhood programs were designed to achieve a limited number of specific goals. They started by concentrating on only one or two major objectives. Later, a few of the more progressive childhood schools felt the need to stimulate the intellectual and creative interests of the child and expanded their programs accordingly.

Infant Schools. During the middle of the nineteenth century, the infant schools of Europe were created for the purpose of developing character and laying the foundation for good mental health.[1] The founders of infant schools were more concerned with the development of the child than they were with custodial day-care services. They believed that it was the duty of the mother to care for and raise her own children at home.

A few years later, the content of early childhood programs shifted from character building to matters related to health and sanitation. The quality and substance of childhood programs continued to improve over the next few years. In the late 1880s, prekindergarten child-care programs were much broader and more attuned to the needs of the very young. Many programs were rewritten. The new ones gave high priority to the physical, emotional, and social development of the child.

Kindergartens. In 1837, Freidrich Froebel, an eminent German educator, felt that there was a need for a special program for children who were four and five years old. He believed that children within that age bracket should be engaged in a program designed to develop motor skills and manual dexterity, and to promote interrelationship of ideas. He also saw a need to provide for the education of mothers and nurses in order to improve child rearing at home. He hoped that state-supported institutions would ultimately embrace the kindergarten concept.

The growth and expansion of the kindergarten movement was very slow at first. It took over a century before the kindergarten concept was accepted in other parts of the world. Kindergartens were introduced into the United States by a German immigrant, Margarethe Meyer Schultz, in 1855. By 1880, a quarter of a century later, only two districts in the United States—St. Louis, Missouri and Forrestville, Illinois—had adopted kindergartens. The spread of kindergartens, as part of the public school system, proceeded very slowly over the next 40 years. By the end of World War I, 40 states had enacted laws establishing kindergartens.[2]

Montessori Schools. At the turn of the twentieth century, Maria Montessori, the first woman to graduate from the medical school at the University of Rome, became deeply concerned that mentally handicapped children were intermingled with insane persons in public institutions. She was so moved by this situation that she single-handedly established a separate school for the mentally retarded and prepared a special curriculum for them. She resigned from the directorship of the school two years later when she accepted another challenging opportunity to work in behalf of children's welfare.

In 1907, a developer constructed a large number of apartments in a slum area of Rome. The developer was soon plagued by an unexpected problem. He discovered that while their parents were at work, the children who were too young to attend school damaged the property. The owner of the apartments came to the eventual conclusion that it might be more economical to develop a school that these children could attend during the day than to pay for repairs to the damaged buildings. Maria Montessori was hired to create and oversee a school for children ranging in age from 2.8 to 7.0 years.

She developed a curriculum that was specially adapted for children within this age group. In addition to providing day-care facilities, her program trained parents on the basics of child development and taught them the skills needed to administer the cooperative parental ownership of the school. She also instituted a program whereby children taught themselves various skills of their choice by trial and error. Furthermore, the children received instruction in the three R's as soon as they were ready for such learning. She also encouraged gifted children to delve into academic-type learning if and when they were inclined to do so.

This version of the Montessori-type day school was rejected by educators in the United States in the 1920s, but the concept lived on. The Montessori school was revived during the 1950s by a small number of educators who had complete faith in Maria Montessori and in her school. A modified version of the original school was established in Greenwich, Connecticut in 1958.

The American Montessori Society was established for the purpose of reviving and supporting the ideals and goals of Maria Montessori. Montessori-type schools are currently fashionable in the United States. Many of them are built and operated by private enterprise and are promoted by the American Montessori Society.

The Development of Child-Care Services in the United States. The child-care movement emigrated to the United States in 1854 when a Nursery School for Children of Poor Women was established in cooperation with the Child's Hospital of New York City.[3] Child-care services for the children of poor women remained scarce in the United States for the next half a century. It was not until the 1930s that the federal government first participated in child-care services. During the Depression, it subsidized all-day child-care programs in order to improve the well-being of the children and to find work for unemployed teachers. A quarter of a century later, the federal government again funded a number of child-centered programs. These early childhood programs included Head Start, day-care services for migrant workers, and day-care programs for children whose parents were involved in certain manpower programs.

CHANGES IN THE LIFE-STYLE OF AMERICAN FAMILIES

The traditional family, in which the husband works and the wife is at home full time caring for the children, is gradually becoming less fashionable in our ever-changing society. The parental roles within the family are changing from day to day. The economic demands on the family are increasing more rapidly than income. Thus, in many instances, it becomes necessary for both parents to work. These changes are often detrimental to the well-being of a large number of preschool and school-age children.

According to Haberman, "The time has come for universal day care that is educational as well as custodial and that begins no later than the child's first birthday."[4] Although educators have generally responded quickly to the demands imposed by society, they have been slow in reacting to the impending demise of the traditional nuclear family. For too many years, educators have simply assumed that the life of a child began when a child entered kindergarten. Life before kindergarten was none of their concern. Legally, it was not. Morally, there is an obligation on the part of educators to assist in mitigating the adverse impact of social change on the children who are attending their schools. Educators are in the unique position of serving as catalysts in coping with the child-care problem. They might find it fruitful to join with other educators in sponsoring conferences involving private entrepreneurs, local school boards, state and federal officials, social workers, and parents for the purpose of finding creative and affordable solutions to the problem of early childhood care.

Statistical Data on the Status of the American Family

The statistics concerning changes in the life-style of families in the United States are somewhat alarming. The following statements underscore the magnitude and urgency of the problem:

1. Hodgkinson points out in a recent article that:
   a. in 1955, 60 percent of households in the United States consisted of a working father and a housewife mother, and that by 1980 that traditional family unit existed in only 11 percent of the homes.
   b. in 1988, over 50 percent of women were in the work force.
   c. in 1988, there were over four million "latchkey" children (children who had no direct adult supervision from the end of the school day to the time that either parent returned home from work).[5]

2. Kenney reports that the pregnancy rate in the United States was (in 1987) the highest in the western world.[6]

3. Hodgkins indicates that in 1991:

    a. almost 50 percent of all children under the age of 18 were being raised by a single parent.

    b. about 4.3 million children were living with an unwed mother.

    c. for children raised by a single mother, child care is vital to the survival of the family.

    d. the 2.5 million fathers raising children by themselves also have a vital need for child-care services.[7]

DIVERGENT CHARACTERISTICS OF CURRENT CHILD-CARE SCHOOLS

Child-care centers are often called schools because it is presumed that some form of developmental learning is occurring in such centers. Actually, the quality and quantity of learning varies widely from center to center. The activities in child-care facilities for both toddlers and pre-kindergarten-age children may range from a well-planned educational curriculum to a well-supervised baby-sitting operation. Facilities housing child-care services may vary from a specially designed and professionally staffed child-care center to a private home operated by an individual who is certified by state authorities.

Unlike the planning of an elementary school, where a single facility can be easily designed for both primary and upper-elementary-age students, the diversity in the developmental needs of children whose ages range from infancy to 12 years is so great that special-purpose facilities must be planned for specific subgroups. Thus, the solution to the child-care problem is much more complicated. It is a multifaceted housing problem. Different facilities are needed to serve infants, toddlers, pre-school-age children, and the older latchkey students.

OWNERSHIP AND MANAGEMENT STYLES OF CHILD-CARE SCHOOLS

Private Schools

Privately owned and operated day-care facilities, including nurseries for infants, have been available to working parents for several decades. They are operated as professionally administered, profit-making businesses and are supported primarily by parents who pay a fee for services received. They are somewhat expensive, but the services are usually first class and the center is customarily staffed by professional teachers and health personnel.

Parent Cooperatives

The creation of a Parent Cooperative Association is a common method of funding and administering a child-care facility. It is less costly for the parents because they contribute time as well as funds to the enterprise. There are several variations of parent cooperatives. Some cooperatives own the facilities, administer the school, and finance the program. In other instances, the cooperative association rents the space from private entrepreneurs, but manages the facility and administers the program with the help of parents who also pay fees for the day care of their children.

Residentially Centered Operations

Finally, child-care services are provided in a countless number of private homes throughout the United States. All of these child-care units are self-supporting and entirely funded by parents. They tend to be rather costly and are generally not within the reach of many working parents.

In many states these operations are strictly controlled by child-care agencies. These residential units, as well as other forms of child-care facilities, must be approved by state authorities and be professionally staffed in accordance with state regulations. Special attention is given to the health and safety features of every facility. The operators of such facilities must be licensed and are subject to unannounced inspections by state authorities.

BASIC FUNCTIONS OF TYPICAL CHILD-CARE FACILITIES

In order to better understand the nature of child-care schools, it might be fruitful to review a few of the major functional features of each type of child-care school. It is also important to have a clear perception of the variety of interrelated functions that are conducted within each type of facility. This task is much more difficult than it appears because there is considerable *intermingling* of functions and activities within a child-care facility.

Nursery Schools

It might be helpful to identify the clientele that is usually served by nursery schools. The largest group of children comes from homes where both parents work. More and more mothers are opting to return to work within a short time after giving birth to their child. Another increasing number of young children come from single-parent families. And a smaller group comes from the skyrocketing increase in teenage pregnancies. For the latter group, some of the more progressive school districts are already providing nurseries in their schools so that teenage mothers may be able to complete their education.

Nursery schools normally serve both infants and toddlers. It is self-evident that facilities for infants are completely different from those provided for toddlers. Consequently, child-care facility planners are confronted with two distinctly different sets of circumstances. Theoretically, what is needed is a single facility consisting of two separate and distinct parts—one for infants and one for toddlers. In order to avoid this conflict, some child-care centers simply restrict the enrollments to either infants or toddlers. There is, however, one noteworthy advantage for housing both infants and toddlers in a single child-care center. When infants become toddlers, they are simply transferred to another section of the same facility without inconveniencing parents and without a loss of enrollment.

Infant-Care Schools

There is very little difference between the nursery schools described earlier and so-called infant schools. The infant schools will admit babies, while some of the nursery schools may prefer toddlers. For the moment, let us focus on the child-care functions associated with infants.

Infant-care schools must provide specialized space for several basic functions. A relatively large space is needed for the feeding and care of the infants. Additionally, space must be provided for rest periods, personal hygiene of infants, food preparation, and linen storage. There should also be space for a laundry and for the storage of trash materials and soiled diapers. Finally, many of the larger child-care facilities include space for a health room where children may be examined by the nurse and be held until the arrival of the parent or guardian of the child.

The infant school must also accommodate a few adult functions. Supplementary space should be provided for parents who are waiting to place their babies in the hands of the staff or to retrieve them at the end of the day. There should also be toilet facilities for the staff, and a lounge where staff can rest while the infants are napping.

In planning spaces for the staff, it should be pointed out that staffing is very intensive in infant-care schools. The staffing ratios vary from state to state, with one adult typically in charge of two to four babies. A ratio of one adult for each two babies is extremely expensive, resulting in fees that are out of reach for most mothers. The National Academy of Early Childhood Programs recommends a ratio of 1:3 for groups of six babies under the care of the nursery.[8]

Toddler and Prekindergarten Schools

A wide variety of instructional activities must be accommodated in a facility for toddlers and prekindergarten children whose ages may range from one to five years. These activities are specialized and diversified. They are designed to reinforce the normal physical and social development of the child. More specifically, they are focused on the development of motor skills, manual dexterity, social relationships, and self-expression, in the form of art, music, and drama. Some prekindergarten schools also endeavor to stimulate intellectual curiosity by providing space for science projects. A workshop is provided for the development of manual skills. Space is also needed for group listening and indoor play activities.

Toddlers and prekindergarten children require supplementary spaces to accommodate a number of other essential functions. Space is needed for dining, food preparation, and personal hygiene. Facilities must be provided for napping and for children who become ill during the day. A substantial amount of space is required for storing food, toys, books, printed matter, audiovisual materials, children's wraps, incompleted children's projects, and instructional supplies. Outdoor spaces are needed to supplement the developmental activities conducted within the building.

The facility should also include space for adult-oriented functions. In schools where several staff members are employed, there is a need for a conference room, a lounge, restrooms, closets, and cloakrooms. As was mentioned in connection with nurseries, parents drop off and pick up their children each day. It is important, therefore, that parents or guardians have space where they can be sheltered while waiting for their children at the end of the day.

CARDINAL SPECIFICATIONS FOR CHILD-CARE FACILITIES

A number of fundamental concepts related to the planning of any educational facility were presented in Chapter 6. With this information in hand, educational facility planners are in a position to develop a set of specifications that apply to any type of educational facility, be it an elementary school, a high school, or a child-care center.

The special characteristics of child-care facilities presented in this section have a direct bearing on the physical and developmental welfare of the children housed in the facilities. Some of these common features focus on the safety and health of the children, while others are intended to improve the educational efficiency of the child-care center.

The inclusion of similar design characteristics in all child-care facilities is not intended to result in the standardization of such facilities. The common features suggested in this section are specifically aimed at satisfying functional needs. Thus, it is expected that child-care facilities will continue to differ from one another in size, form, and shape, depending on the ingenuity of the architect.

While it is encouraged that child-care facilities be designed creatively and functionally as separate entities, planners of such facilities must recognize that a number of basal functions are common to all child-care facilities. The specifications listed below represent features that are essential to any child-care facility.

The importance of each one of them is self-evident. They deserve serious consideration by the planners of such facilities.

Design Features Common to All Types of Child-Care Facilities

Admittedly, a large number of child-care services are currently housed in converted residential space. It would be unrealistic to expect that all of the desirable features described below can be implemented in former residential buildings. It is hoped, however, that at least some of them can be incorporated in plans involving the conversion of residential buildings into child-care facilities.

1. *Safety within the Building.* All safety hazards should be viewed from the standpoint of the child rather than the adult. For example, while sharp projections from shelves and furniture at the eye level of the child pose a real safety hazard, they could be inadvertently overlooked by adults. Furniture and equipment that can be easily toppled also poses a potential safety hazard for the child.

2. *Playground Safety.* Outdoor equipment should be selected on the basis of operational safety. The placement of such equipment on the site should be carefully considered from the standpoint of safety. Equipment in active play areas should be arranged so that children playing on one piece of equipment do not pose a danger to those playing on another one next to it.

3. *School Site Safety.* No vehicles should be permitted in or near children's play areas. Poisonous vegetation should be avoided or removed from the site. Outdoor electrical outlets and wires should be installed out of the reach of children. Equipment that may tip over easily should either be anchored firmly to the ground or not placed on the site. Obstacles on the site should be painted in bright colors so that they are clearly visible to the child from his or her point of view.

4. *Site Cover Safety.* The surfaces of outdoor play areas should protect children from falls and abrasions. While grassed areas contribute to a pleasing aesthetic environment, they do not necessarily protect children from injury or abrasions. Contrary to common belief, a grassed surface is not as soft as it appears. Grass growing on a clay-type soil, for example, does not effectively protect children from abrasions. On the other hand, a thick layer of loose, small pea stone or its equivalent is a safer ground cover under playground equipment, such as swings, slides, and climbing bars.

5. *Health and Sanitation.* The building and site should provide a healthful and invigorating environment. Special care should be taken to assure that all interior surfaces can be easily maintained and kept spotlessly clean. The selection of play equipment and toys should be strongly influenced by whether or not such items can be thoroughly washed and cleaned after use.

6. *Incidental Learning.* It is not generally realized that incidental learning contributes significantly to the education of young children. Such learning may occur subconsciously under unpredictable circumstances. According to Shaffer and Shoben, "The concept of unconscious learning represents a very great discovery of modern psychology, for which we are mainly indebted to Sigmund Freud."[9] Children are capable of learning without realizing that learning is taking place.

Incidental learning represents an educational bonus in any school. Architects should exploit this psychological discovery by planning school buildings that will stimulate such learning. For example, the metal cover over room thermostats can be replaced with a clear plastic cover so that children can see the inner workings of this control device. Science equipment and instruments used in conducting science projects, such as thermometers, lenses, simple machines, and volt-ohm meters should be visible to children at all times. They can be stored on shelves and in cabinets that are enclosed by transparent materials, such as glass or clear plastic.

There are many other opportunities for incidental learning on the school site and in the building. Animals and gardens promote this type of learning. The physical plant is another rich source of material for incidental learning. The internal mechanisms of selected heating, cooling, and electrical equipment could be exposed to the view of children through transparent covering material. Needless to say, labels with information about each item are not too effective, because most children in child-care centers are not yet able to read.

In order to promote incidental learning, teachers must point out and describe the various items that are designated for such learning. They should discuss only one or two of them at a time and explain their function. Teachers might also caution the children about any dangers posed by any of them. Once this exercise is completed, the children, who are naturally curious at that age, may subconsciously look at these items from time to time, and remember what was explained to them by their teacher.

Since many teachers have not specialized in science or engineering, it would be advantageous for the school administration to offer staff seminars aimed at stimulating incidental learning. The architect who designed the facility might be asked to explain the function of each item designated for incidental learning and indicate where each one is located.

7. *Destructible Partitions.* The use of destructible partitions facilitates future changes in the configuration of the internal spaces within a building. As explained in Chapter 7, such partitions provide a practical and economical solution to the problem of planning for unforeseeable future needs.

8. *Movable Partitions.* Movable partitions add flexibility in the use of the instructional areas. In the case of child-care schools, however, such partitions should be of a type that strongly attenuates the transmission of sound. (See Chapter 11.)

9. *Efficiency in Child Development.* The concept of educational efficiency discussed in Chapter 6 can be adapted to promote developmental efficiency in child-care facilities. The design of any child-care facility should stimulate and promote the maximum achievement of desired developmental objectives.

10. *Visual Environment.* The visual environment within the main activities center should be pleasing and stimulating. High-quality artificial lighting should be provided. Glare should be avoided from all sources of light and from highly reflective surfaces, such as mirrors and glass. Snow and sky glare should be controlled.

The artificial lighting should be diffused and evenly distributed throughout the room. Activity centers may be accented, provided that such highlighting blends into the general lighting of the room. Chapter 11 offers additional information on the visual environment.

11. *Acoustical Environment.* The acoustical environment should provide for good hearing conditions. Carpeting should cover the floor, except in wet areas, and acoustical materials should be placed on the ceilings and upper walls to create a quiet atmosphere within the room. The amount of acoustical treatment is specified in Chapter 11.

12. *Color.* The positive psychological effect of color should be exploited. It has been well established that color has a definite psychological effect on the occupants of a room. Young children prefer warm colors, for example. See Chapter 11 for additional details.

THE TRICHOTOMY OF CHILD-CARE SERVICES

Child-care services were originally provided for children who had reached the toddler age. But changes in the family structure over the past quarter of a century have broadened the demand for child-care services. Today, there is a pressing need to provide child-care services for children ranging from infants to teenagers. The increased age span of children requiring child-care services suggests that a second look be taken at the way young children are grouped. The age categories of the past no longer suffice.

The time has come when child-care services must be differentiated on the basis of the type of services needed. Three separate groups of children—infants, toddlers, and latchkey students—need three separate types of child-care service. Unfortunately, the facilities required for each of these three categories are extremely different from each other. Thus, it will be necessary to provide three types of facilities to accommodate the total child-care population.

Ideally, child-care facilities should be functionally designed to house specific child-care services. Since the services differ from group to group, it follows that different facilities should be designed for different groups. Therefore, the present practice of designing facilities for children that fall within certain age groups leaves much to be desired.

Grouping children according to age is a carryover from the public schools, which divide the child population into three or four age brackets. This grouping has been very practical in the public schools because the differences in child development within each group are within manageable limits. The situation is quite different in dealing with very young children. It is not too difficult to imagine, for example, the difficulties that might be encountered in attempting to plan a single unit that would satisfy all the needs of both infants and preschoolers in the same room.

Based partly on tradition and partly on established public-school practice, child-care specialists have divided young children into two major age groups. The first group, known as infants and toddlers, includes children from birth to the age of 1.9 years. The second group, called preschoolers, consists of children between 2 and 4.9 years of age.

From the standpoint of planning child-care facilities, however, grouping by chronological age alone poses a number of difficulties because of the large span of functions within some groups. For planning purposes, it would seem much simpler and more productive to categorize children according to their level of physical development rather than by their chronological age. For the purpose of this text, therefore, children are classified under three groupings based on the functional needs of the children: Infants are envisioned as a single group which can be housed in a nursery school until they become toddlers; Toddlers are preschool children who are housed in a facility referred to in this text as a prekindergarten school; And latchkey students are those who could be housed after school in existing school buildings.

The rationale underlying the groupings employed in this text stem from two functional and realistic considerations. First, there are very few similarities between facilities for infants and those designed for older children. And second, toddlers, who represent the remainder of the preschool population, all have similar developmental needs. Such needs tend to differ in degree rather than in kind. For example, both younger and older toddlers within this group enjoy slides. Generally, low and high slides are provided. While the neotoddlers would be more inclined to use the low slides, a few of the more adventurous toddlers might utilize the higher slides. On the other hand, most of the older children are likely to use the high slides, but a few of the more cautious older children might prefer the lower ones. The point is that many of the facilities under this grouping can be utilized by both younger and older toddlers. Thus, only one type of child-care facility is needed for this grouping of prekindergarten children.

In view of the foregoing discussion, two types of child-care facilities will be treated in detail in this text—the nursery school and the prekindergarten school. There will also be a brief discussion of facilities for the latchkey children, who, as mentioned earlier, can be adequately housed in existing school buildings.

The planning of new child-care facilities will be presented in two parts. One part will discuss the planning of nursery schools, while the other will deal with the design of prekindergarten schools. The planning process discussed in Chapter 6 should be reviewed and relevant procedures should be adapted for the planning of child-care facilities.

THE DEARTH OF INFORMATION ON CHILD-CARE FACILITIES

At the moment, architects seem to be vigorously probing for specific information on the planning of child-care facilities. Passantino, an architect, states, "At this writing, there is no uniform national code for the design or operation of day-care centers."[10] The author was also unsuccessful in his search for a compendium on the planning and design of child-care facilities. There were, however, several excellent articles dealing with child-care services, but they touched only lightly on matters related to facilities. This poses a real problem for the planners of such facilities. There is no source of professionally developed specifications available to the planners of child-care facilities. There is no "standard" facility that the architect can use as a model. There is no consensus among the providers of child-care services as to what constitutes an ideal child-care facility. The architect is faced with a myriad of existing child-care facilities, each of which has been planned in accordance with the whims and philosophy of its proponents and within the budgetary limitations imposed by the entrepreneur.

By comparison, architects planning elementary and secondary schools find themselves in an enviable position. They have a superabundance of information describing current practices related to such facilities. Architects planning child-care facilities, however, are at a distinct disadvantage. They seem to be operating in an informational vacuum. At the moment, however, there is a modicum of helpful information from accreditation agencies and child-care associations. They are making a great effort to infuse some sense and sensibility into the planning of child-care facilities.

This situation raises a number of pertinent questions. "Can we find a rational solution to this problem?" "Can we provide some positive guidelines for the planners of child-care facilities?" And, "Is it possible to suggest a logical starting point for architects engaged in planning child-care facilities?" The answer to these questions is a qualified, "yes." We can accomplish all of these goals if there is a united effort among the national and international organizations concerned with early childhood education listed by Decker.[11] This objective may seem idealistic at this time, but past experience with public schools gives us a ray of hope. Chapter 1 described the evolution of educational facility planning for the public schools. There is no reason why such a successful evolutionary process could not be adopted by the child-care organizations in the United States as well as those in Europe.

A PROPOSED TECHNIQUE FOR PLANNING CHILD-CARE SCHOOLS

Due to the diversity in the types, sizes, and management styles of child-care facilities, there is currently no universal starting point for the planning of such facilities. A new approach is needed. The concept proposed in this text involves the creation of a self-contained *operational unit*. It is envisioned that this operational unit will house a specific combination of child-care activities required for a given number of children at a certain level of development. Each basic unit can then be combined with others to form a single, integrated child-care facility that is tailor-made for a particular situation.

This proposal is intended to simplify the planning of a child-care facility. Under this plan, architects can work with the client in designing one self-contained unit at a time. Once the plan of each desired unit is worked out, architects can blend them together in a variety of combinations to form a single, functional child-care center.

More specifically, each basic operational unit is conceived as a separate entity consisting of a *primary activities center* together with related *ancillary spaces*. The primary activities center is defined as a single large room with space allocated for a variety of activities. The designated space for each activity is formed within the primary activities center by the arrangement of movable furniture and space dividers. The ancillary spaces, on the other hand, consist of several special-purpose rooms that adjoin the primary activities center.

The cluster of spaces comprising the primary activities center *and* all of the ancillary spaces associated with it form the basic operational unit. The area of each space within the basic operational unit is specified later for both nursery schools and prekindergarten centers. These areas represent net space inside of each room. They are suggested as starting points for the architect. Local planners should feel free to modify these space allocations within reasonable limits. It is cautioned, however, that any reduction in space exceeding 20 percent from that suggested in the specifications may seriously hamper the operational function of the unit.

Under this concept, the operational unit becomes the basic building block of any child-care facility. For maximum simplification, therefore, the number of different types of building blocks should be kept as small as possible. For the purpose of this text, the number of basic building blocks has been reduced to two. They are the *nursery operational unit* and the *prekindergarten operational unit*.

The choice of only two types of operational units does not restrict the size, shape, or scope of any proposed child-care center in any way. For example, a center may contain only prekindergarten operational units and serve only toddlers. Or, it may contain a combination of both types of operational units and serve both infants and toddlers. Under the procedure suggested in this text, an architect has complete freedom in planning a large variety of child-care schools by simply combining any number of either type of operational units in accordance with the wishes of the client.

THE OVERALL SIZE OF A CHILD-CARE FACILITY

The size of a child-care facility can range all the way from a single operational unit to one that has as many as 10 or 15 units. Under the proposed planning concept, the overall size of the building is not fixed until the number of units to be housed in it and the number of the ancillary spaces have been determined. Thus, the size of the building is not predetermined by child capacity alone. It is an outgrowth of the functional planning of each component of the facility.

PLANNING A NURSERY SCHOOL

For the purpose of this text, a nursery school is defined as a facility that houses only infants. This definition in no way prohibits the planning of a child-care center that houses both infants and toddlers. In these instances, however, special care must be exercised to prevent the encroachment of one function on the other.

Preparation of Educational Specifications

As was the case in planning elementary and secondary schools, the preparation of educational specifications for the guidance of the architect is of paramount importance. Unless the architect is given a detailed and comprehensive description of all the developmental experiences that are to be offered to the children, the resulting facility is likely to be a disappointment. It is suggested that the information related to the preparation of educational specifications in Chapter 6 be reviewed.

The School Site

The school site for a nursery school is not a major consideration since infants are not likely to use the site for play purposes. Of course, as infants become toddlers, there might be a limited use of the site by them before they are transferred to a toddler facility.

The nursery school site merits another look, however. In planning for the unforeseeable, as explained in Chapter 7, the size of the site is an important consideration. If planners were positively certain that the nursery school would never become a prekindergarten school, the size of the site would need to be sufficient only for the building, landscaping, driveways, and parking for staff and for parents dropping off and picking up children from the school. Prudence, however, would dictate otherwise. Whenever possible, the site for a nursery school should be similar in size to the one recommended later under "Planning a Prekindergarten School."

The Nursery Operational Unit

The nursery operational unit, which is the building block for nursery schools, is presented below, together with suggested sizes of various spaces (Tables 15-1 and 15-2). As mentioned earlier, the nursery operational unit includes both the primary activities center, Group A below, and all of the ancillary spaces listed under Group B. When these two groups are merged into a single functional unit, they form an independent, self-contained element of the child-care center.

The primary activities center, which is discussed later, is a single large room in which the staff performs almost all of the functions that are directly related to the care of infants and neotoddlers.

A. The Primary Activities Center: Group A
   1. *Functional Description.* The primary activities center is designed to care for six infants. It will require a staff of at least two adults, and perhaps three. Smaller infant-care units are generally not economically viable when they are to be housed in facilities requiring a substantial capital outlay. Such small units are usually accommodated in a remodeled residence.
   2. *Space Allocations within the Primary Activities Center.* The space allocations listed in Table 15-1 are located within a single room.
B. Ancillary Spaces: Group B
   The ancillary spaces listed in Table 15-2 are separate rooms with direct access to the primary activities center.

TABLE 15-1 **Space Allocations for the Primary Activities Center: Group A**

Purpose of Space	Suggested Space Allocation (in Square Feet)
a. Sleeping area holding six cribs.	150
b. General activity and feeding area.	500
c. Hygiene area with two changing counters, including bathing equipment and sanitary storage and disposal.	100
d. Two story-reading nooks.	50
Total area of Group A	**800**

TABLE 15-2 **Ancillary Spaces**

Purpose of Room	Size of Each Room (in Square Feet)
a. Staff workroom with infant bathing counters, sanitary disposal facilities, and storage for supplies.	100
b. Food storage and preparation room with work counters, range, microwave unit, and refrigerator.	125
c. Staff lounge and lavatory.	125
d. Parent's waiting room and lobby.	150
Total area of Group B	500
Total area for one nursery operational unit (Group A + Group B)	1,300

Space Needed for Multiple Units. The areas suggested in Tables 15-1 and 15-2 represent the net space needed for a single nursery operational unit. The area of the primary activities center (800 square feet) will remain the same for each of the multiple nursery units. The total area required for ancillary spaces, however, will vary as the number of operational units increases, in accordance with the rule of thumb presented below.

> *Rule of thumb for the distribution of space allocated to ancillary functions shown under Group B*
>
> a. A staff workroom having an area of 100 square feet should adjoin each primary activities center.
> b. A food preparation room with an area of 125 square feet should adjoin each primary activities center.
> c. The total allocation of space for lounge and lobby should follow the figures shown in Table 15-3. The distribution of space among these two facilities is left to the discretion of the architect.

An example is presented to illustrate the application of the suggested space allocations for a nursery school containing five nursery operational units. The space allocation would be as follows:

1. Five separate primary activities centers at 800 square feet each, for a total of 4,000 square feet.
2. Five separate staff workrooms at 100 square feet each for a total of 500 square feet.
3. Five separate food storage and preparation rooms at 125 square feet each for a total of 625 square feet.
4. A total area of 1,100 square feet (from Table 15-3) for a lobby and faculty lounge.

TABLE 15-3   **Space Allocation for Staff Lounge and Lobby**

Total Number of Operational Units	Space Allocation for Staff Lounge and Lobby (in Square Feet)
1	275
2	500
3	700
4	950
5	1,100
6	1,300
7	1,400
8	1,600
9	1,750
10	1,950

It should be mentioned again that the above areas are based on inside dimensions. Thus the net area, excluding corridors and space for heating and cooling equipment, required for this hypothetical five-unit nursery school is approximately 6,200 square feet. The amount of space required for corridors, wall thicknesses, and mechanical equipment varies widely from building to building depending upon the design of the building and the type of equipment that is housed in it. If it is assumed that the net area represents 70 percent of the total area of a nursery school, the amount of construction area envisioned for this five-unit facility is in the vicinity of 9,000 square feet. A rough estimate of the cost of such a facility may be computed by multiplying 9,000 by the prevailing construction cost per square foot in any locality. It might be of interest to entrepreneurs to note that capital costs can be lowered by reducing the space devoted to circulation and other noneducational uses. Chapter 8 provides additional information on economy measures related to the planning of school facilities.

The Primary Activities Center

The primary activities center is the operational heart of both nursery school and prekindergarten child-care facilities. It is a multipurpose room that serves a number of child-centered developmental activities. Although it has been stated earlier in this chapter that a nursery school deals with infants, it cannot be assumed that all of the children enrolled in a nursery school are babies. Even if they are babies when first enrolled at the center, they soon become crawlers and later reach the toddler stage. Realistically, a nursery school must be planned to serve children from babies to neotoddlers.

Under these conditions, nursery school planners must envision a heterogeneous group of children consisting of babies, crawlers, and perhaps even a few teetering toddlers. Incidentally, as soon as teetering toddlers gain a little more confidence and stability, they should be transferred to a prekindergarten child-care facility where a variety of appropriate developmental opportunities are available to them.

The planning of a primary activities center for a nursery school is not quite as complex as that for a prekindergarten school, but it is sufficiently complicated to challenge the ingenuity of the architect. Let us review some of the major activities that take place in the primary activities center in a nursery school. Babies require intensive personal care. They need specialized space for sleeping, feeding, bathing, and related matters. A few months later, they become more aware of the world around them and the development of communication skills begins to take place. At this stage, quiet space should be provided where the staff can read to them and converse with them as much as possible.

Soon, children reach the crawling stage, which has important implications for the design of the primary activities center. Safe and ample space must be provided for the crawling activity. The floor must be soft and carpeted. The furniture should be sturdy and sufficiently movable so that nonwalkers can pull themselves up and balance on it. The crawling space should be well defined and free from small items that can be swallowed, and clear of objects with sharp protruding edges or corners. Items such as floor and desk lamps and end tables that can be easily tipped over should be removed from the crawl space area. All electrical outlets should be covered with appropriate devices and all radiators or heating baseboards should be screened so that crawling children will not suffer burns.

Crawlers and neotoddlers are reaching the age when they are ready to embark on the development of manipulative skills. Another part of the primary activities center should be set aside as a play area with blocks and other toys appropriate to their stage of development. Space should be provided for the storage of toys and other materials, such as finger paints, used by the children. It is suggested that toys and materials stored on shelves, bins, and the like be easily accessible by the children, who may wish to use them at a time of their choosing.

Finally, the primary activities center should provide for the needs of the so-called teetering toddlers who are about ready to be promoted to prekindergarten facilities. Remember that each nursery primary activities center, as defined in this text, serves only six children, so the different activities do not involve large groups of children. And further, the developmental stages of the six children in this group range from infancy to neotoddler, so there is no pressing need for a large variety of spaces for motor development.

A summary of the various activities conducted in the primary activities center will give planners a general idea of its complexity. Briefly, the center must provide space for the sleeping and rest periods of the children. It must provide space for the crawlers. It must provide space to develop manipulative skills. It must include space and materials to stimulate the creative skills of the children. And it must provide space for the neotoddler. All of these activities take place in a single room that permits the free flow of staff and children from one area to another. Most importantly, each activity must be easily supervised by the staff from any part of the room. Blind spots due to the design of the building or the placement of furniture should be avoided.

Space Relationships

Child safety is strongly dependent on the level of supervision that can be exercised by the staff, particularly when one adult is responsible for the care of two or three infants. Staff members must have the ability to supervise the operational unit at all times. Frequently, they find themselves in the position of having to deal with several child demands at the same time. More often than not, each demand must be handled in a different part of the primary activities center or in one of the ancillary spaces. It can be seen, therefore, that the relationships between certain ancillary spaces and the primary activities center are quite critical.

For the most part, the staff members are either in the primary activities center, in the workroom caring for a child, or in the food preparation room. For this reason, it is imperative that the workroom and the food preparation room be directly accessible from the primary activities center. A vision strip should be installed at eye level in the wall separating these two spaces from the activities center in order to facilitate supervision and promote visual contact.

The location of other spaces in the operational unit complex also merits the attention of facility planners. The lobby, or parents' waiting room, should be located as close as possible to the primary activities center. If the lobby adjoins the primary activities center, it might be advantageous to install a one-way vision strip in the wall separating the waiting room from the activities center so that parents can see their children without distracting them.

The lounge is often used to give the staff members momentary relief when the children are sleeping. The location of the staff lounge is not very critical unless only one staff member is employed to care for two or three infants. In this case, the lounge should also adjoin the primary activities center and a one-way vision strip should be installed in the wall separating the lounge from the center. In this way, the staff member can see into the primary activities center while retaining his or her privacy.

Finally, there is a close affinity between certain parts of the building and the site. Obviously, the lobby should be easily accessible from the parking lot. There should also be direct access to the site from the primary activities center whenever possible. Such an arrangement provides ready access to the outdoor play areas for some of the children and allows the staff to take the infants outside for fresh air when weather conditions are favorable. Of course, it may not be architecturally possible to provide this close relationship in large nursery schools containing several operational units.

Figure 15-1 shows the relationship among the various spaces in the nursery operational unit. Three lines between two elements indicates that a very close

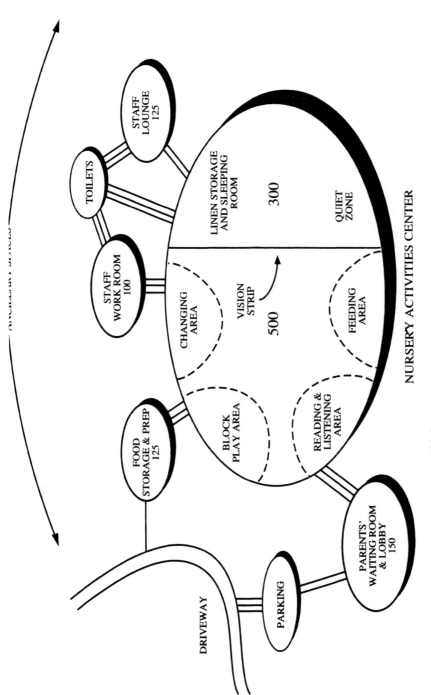

FIGURE 15-1 The Nursery Operational Unit

relationship exists between them. These spaces should adjoin each other. Two lines between two elements denotes that the relationship between them is still close, but they need not necessarily be contiguous. A single line between two elements indicates that only a loose relationship exists. These units should be located as close as possible to each other within the general configuration of the facility.

PLANNING A PREKINDERGARTEN CHILD-CARE FACILITY

There are a number of noteworthy differences between a prekindergarten child-care facility and a nursery school. In a prekindergarten school, the age span of the children is three times greater. The number of children that can be cared for by one adult is more than tripled. The number of different activities is quadrupled. And the number of levels of difficulty for each activity is tripled. This introduction is not intended to frighten planners of prekindergarten facilities. Quite the contrary, it is hoped that it will prepare such planners for the complicated task of blending a wide variety of activities into a well-integrated prekindergarten child-care center.

The Prekindergarten Activities Center

The Interest Center. Space is needed in the prekindergarten activities center for a variety of developmental activities. Each activity is conducted within an interest center which is designated for that purpose. Interest centers are not isolated spaces. They tend to flow into one another to form a continuous sequence of interrelated working areas. Some of them may be planned to provide a little privacy for the child who wishes to play alone for a few minutes. Such privacy is achieved by the arrangement of low furniture and cabinets.

Each interest area should be well defined in some distinctive manner, such as using differently colored walls or carpeting. It is also important to keep these areas flexible by using space dividers or furniture to subdivide the space within the prekindergarten activities center. And last but not least, it is imperative that the staff be able to supervise the entire room from any standing position.

Types of Interest Centers. The area allocated for each interest center is determined by the nature of the activity that is conducted in it. Suggested space allocations for each interest center are presented in Table 15-4. The most common types of interest centers are described below.

TABLE 15-4 **Space Allocations for the Prekindergarten Activities Center: Group A**

Purpose of Space	Suggested Space Allocation (in Square Feet)
a. Block play center	100
b. Art center	80
c. Dramatic play center	125
d. Music center	100
e. Sand play area	75
f. Water play area	100
g. Microcomputer area	150
h. Five private play areas	120
i. Circulation space	<u>100</u>
Total area for the prekindergarten activities center	**950**

1. *The block play center.* This center should accommodate up to four children. A child may work alone in this area or with others.
2. *The art center.* This center should contain a sink with running water and space for storing supplies and children's art work. It should accommodate about four children.
3. *The dramatic play center.* This has a sort of housekeeping appearance. It is furnished with dolls, doll beds, toy stoves, and the like. This activity is apt to be somewhat more space consuming than the other centers due to the spread of toys and the nature of the activity.
4. *The music center.* This area is used for singing and dancing. It should be located in a remote area of the prekindergarten activities center.
5. *The sand play center.* Sand play sometimes invites conflicts. For this reason, a box with sides should be provided to contain the sand within the area. Furthermore, the architect should provide carpeting or a metal grate through which sand will fall and not be tracked to other parts of the primary activities center.
6. *The water play center.* This area should be properly situated within the primary activities center near a source of water and supplied with proper floor drains. Special tables about 2 feet wide should be provided for child play. The architect should pay special attention to slip-proof floors.
7. *Concept and microcomputer center.* This center is designed to stimulate the intellectual development of those children who are ready for such learning. It should be a quiet area where three or four children might work with computers, read, or solve puzzles.
8. *Places for animals and plants.* No specific center is designated for animals and plants. Plants may be placed on window sills or near window areas. Animals should be located away from the main flow of traffic and be placed in appropriate confinement on sturdy tables.

The Outdoor Playground Activities

The following type of equipment and interest centers should be provided on the school site:

1. Swings and slides. These are intense motor activities. This equipment should be separated from passive activities and placed so that its users do not collide or interfere with other children.
2. Climbing equipment. Special attention should be given to the type of ground cover under this equipment as well as under slides.
3. Sand pit area.
4. Water play area.
5. Wading pool.
6. Gardens.
7. Outdoor animal cage areas.

The Prekindergarten Operational Unit

As indicated earlier, the planning concept presented in this text is predicated on the use of operational units as the building blocks of a child-care facility. The nursery operational unit was discussed in the preceding sections of this chapter. A similar approach is used in developing the prekindergarten operational unit.

    A. The Prekindergarten Activities Center: Group A
       The prekindergarten activities center houses all of the indoor interest centers described in the preceding section.
       1. *Functional Description.* The prekindergarten activities center is designed to care for 16 children under the supervision of two staff members.
       2. *Space Allocations within the prekindergarten activities center.* The space allocations shown in Table 15-4 are located within a single room.
    B. The Ancillary Spaces: Group B
       The ancillary spaces listed in Table 15-5 are separate rooms adjoining the prekindergarten activities center.

Space Needed for Multiple Units.   The areas suggested above represent the net space needed for a single **prekindergarten operational unit.** The area of the prekindergarten activities center (950 square feet) will remain the same for each prekindergarten operational unit in the complex. The total area required for ancillary spaces, however, will vary as the number of operational units increases, in accordance with the rule of thumb figures presented in Table 15-6.

TABLE 15-5   **Space Allocations for the Ancillary Spaces: Group B**

Purpose of Room	Size of Each Room (in Square Feet)	Percent of Total Area
a. Staff workroom-lounge, and storage for supplies.	200	12%
b. Food storage and preparation room with work counters, range, microwave unit and refrigerator, and dining area.	400	26%
c. Napping room and health room	400	26%
d. Toilet rooms (2)	90	6%
e. Cubbies for children wraps	60	4%
f. Parents' waiting room & lobby	400	26%
Total area of Group B	**1,550 Square feet**	
Total area (Group A + B) for the prekindergarten operational unit	**2,350 Square feet**	

Rule of thumb for the distribution of space allocated to ancillary functions shown under Group B

Table 15-6 shows the total suggested allocation of space for ancillary facilities for each grouping of operational units. The distribution of space among all of the ancillary spaces is suggested in column (3) in Table 15-5, but may be modified at the discretion of the architect depending upon local requirements.

TABLE 15-6   **Space Allocation for the Cluster of Ancillary Spaces**

Total Number of Operational Units	Space Allocation for All Ancillary Spaces (in Square Feet)
1	1,550
2	2,750
3	4,075
4	5,350
5	6,575
6	7,800
7	9,025
8	10,250
9	11,475
10	12,700

To find the net area for any proposed facility containing 10 or fewer prekindergarten operational units, multiply the number of proposed units by 950 and add the figure shown in the right-hand column of Table 15-6 corresponding to the number of units proposed for the facility. For example, if a four-unit facility is proposed, multiply 950 by 4 and add 5,350 (from Table 15-6) for a total net area of 9,150 square feet.

It should be remembered that the space allocations suggested for Groups A and B are for a comprehensive prekindergarten child-care facility. These space allocations are intended to house a first-class program. If reductions in space must be made due to limited resources, the entrepreneurs and planners should decide in the early stages of planning which programs are to be eliminated or limited in scope, using the distributions shown under Group A as a guide. It should be pointed out that reduction of spaces under Group A has little effect on the spaces needed under Group B, which house basic auxiliary functions. It is possible, however, to reduce the total area specified in Group B by providing spaces of minimal size for each function and by making dual use of some spaces. For example, the dining area could be planned with bench-type tables that fold into the wall. This space could then be used for parent waiting when children are not dining. Dual or triple use of certain ancillary spaces will promote economy but may increase the cost of personnel needed to convert a space from one function to another. The potential consequences of planning multiuse spaces should be carefully considered before final decisions are made.

Educational Specifications

The importance of preparing a set of detailed educational specifications cannot be overstated. The procedure has been discussed in Chapter 6 and also in connection with the planning of nursery schools. It is suggested that Chapter 6 and the information presented earlier in this chapter be reviewed. Educational specifications should be prepared describing all of the desired features that should be incorporated into the design of the proposed facility.

Functional Features of Sites for Prekindergarten Schools

The site for a prekindergarten school is an integral part of the child-care facility. Its primary function is to supplement all of the motor development activities normally conducted within the building. The site serves a multitude of related functions, ranging from active play to passive observation of plant growth. It must provide for the safe interaction among several strenuous activities utilizing swings, slides, and climbing equipment, and it must be relatively flat for the use of wheeled toys and for activities involving water play and sand boxes. It should also provide space for projects that involve gardens and animal sheds. Finally, the site must be sufficiently large to accommodate the building, landscaping, parking, walks, and driveways.

Unless a child-care facility is being built on an open site, some outdoor activities may be restricted due to the topography of the land or the lack of space. Most governmental regulations require a minimum of 75 square feet of site area per child enrolled in the school. Compared with the standards presented in Chapter 12 for elementary schools, this allocation of space for child-care sites is miniscule, since enrollments in child-care centers are usually very low compared to those in a minimum-size elementary school.

In fairness to the operators of child-care schools, however, it must be mentioned that their source of funding is very limited and that the cost of land is extremely high. Furthermore, child-care facilities are usually located in highly populated areas where open land is a very scarce commodity.

Determining the Minimum Acceptable Size of a Site for a Prekindergarten Child-Care Center

It is strongly suggested that the functional approach be employed in determining the minimum acceptable size of a site for a child-care center. This procedure is discussed in Chapter 6. It does not rely on arbitrary rules of thumb. Once the number of operational units planned for a child-care facility is known, it is possible to compute the minimum size of the site required by using the procedure described in the following paragraphs.

First, determine the number and type of each outdoor interest center that is needed for the desired program. With this information in hand, the architect can compute the amount of outdoor activity space that is required for a single operational unit. Multiply this figure by the number of proposed operational units. This figure represents the total net space needed for the outdoor activities associated with the program.

Second, compute the area that is needed for the other functions that must be accommodated on the site: (1) Allow 300 square feet per car to be parked on the site, (2) Add additional space for walks and driveways, and (3) Provide space for the storage of outside equipment and space for the building itself.

Third, estimate the amount of site needed for the building as follows: (1) Multiply the total net area of a single operational unit (indicated earlier as the sum of Groups A and B) by 1–4. This figure represents the gross area needed by one prekindergarten operational unit. (2) If more than one unit is planned, multiply the figure obtained in step 1 by the number of proposed units in order to estimate the amount of site area needed for the building. This computation is based on the planning of a single-story building.

The sum of the spaces required to accommodate all of the items mentioned above represents the absolute minimum size of the site. If land is available at an affordable cost, it might be wise to acquire a site that is at least twice the size of the minimum acceptable site. It might be surprising to planners of child-care schools to discover that the minimum size of the site computed using the above procedure is less than that based on some of the rules of thumb that are currently in vogue.

In addition to size, however, a school site should fulfill a number of other requirements. It should be located where it can be reached conveniently by parents. It should be situated in an area that is free from noxious gases, disagreeable odors, high noise levels, and heavy traffic. Its topography should be somewhat convex and slightly higher than the roadway. Finally, the site environment should be aesthetically pleasant.

Space Relationships

Space relationships are just as important for prekindergarten facilities as they are for nursery schools, but some of them are not so critical. A few of the more noteworthy relationships are mentioned here.

1. There should be direct access to the toilet rooms from both the prekindergarten activities center and the outdoor play areas.
2. The staff workroom should adjoin the activities center and have a vision strip installed in the wall separating these two spaces so that the staff can maintain visual contact with the children in the activities center.
3. If it is planned to use the dining area as a combination dining room and parents' waiting room, it should adjoin the entrance lobby.
4. The health room, serving one or two children who may become ill during the school day, should be in a quiet area, preferably near or adjoining the napping room.
5. The food preparation and storage area should be easily accessible from the service drive for the delivery of supplies, and should adjoin the dining area.

Figure 15-2 shows the relationship among the various spaces in the prekindergarten operational unit. Three lines between two elements indicates that a very close relationship exists between them. These spaces should adjoin each other. Two lines between two elements denotes that the relationship between them is still close, but they need not necessarily be contiguous. A single line between two elements indicates that only a loose relationship exists. These units should be located as close as possible to each other within the general configuration of the facility.

FACILITIES FOR LATCHKEY CHILDREN

Fortunately, the facilities for latchkey students already exist. It might be helpful, however, to define what is meant by "latchkey" students. This term refers to children who have no supervision from the time they leave school to the time

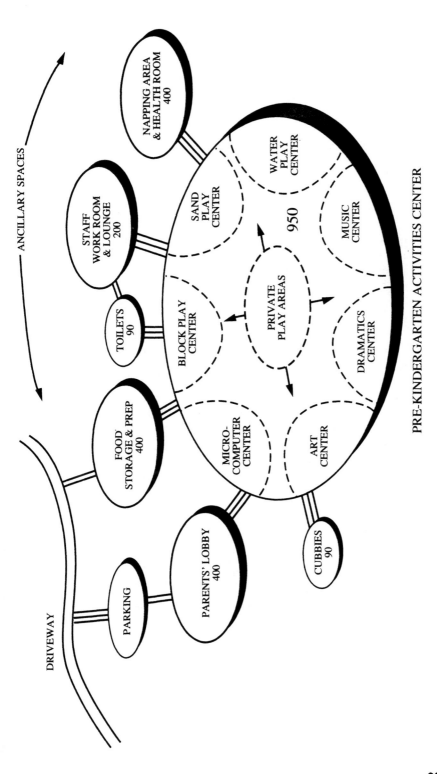

FIGURE 15-2 The Prekindergarten Operational Unit

that parents return home from work. Thus, during that period of time, such children are often free to do whatever they want, wherever they wish to do it and with whomever they wish to associate. Young children under the age of 14 or 15 are particularly vulnerable to peer pressure and tend to be greatly influenced by forces outside of the home. Both parents and educators, as well as the public in general, are deeply concerned about these children during their formative years of development.

There is definitely a moral obligation on the part of public and private school authorities to face this problem without further delay. The need is urgent. The remedy is relatively simple and could even be financially profitable for the school district. Some of the more progressive school districts are already making school facilities available to latchkey students after school hours.

Educators must assume the leadership in solving this crucial problem. Some school districts are already deriving additional income by utilizing school buildings from 6:00 A.M. to 8:00 A.M. and from 2:00 P.M. to 6:00 P.M.[12] This practice is highly beneficial to the school district, to the children affected, and to society in general. The school district can derive substantial income by making unused facilities available to parent groups. It can provide a safe and well-supervised space for countless numbers of children. And it has the potential to reduce the crime, drug, and early pregnancy problems that now plague society by keeping some of the latchkey children off the streets.

The use of school facilities for latchkey children does not impose a noticeable administrative burden on school officials. This program can be fully managed and staffed by parents. Generally, the parents form an association which works closely and directly with school administrators in the operation of before-, after-, and summer-school activities. School districts may charge the association a reasonable fee for the use of school facilities. This practice is feasible, timely, and profitable for many school districts.

THE OUTLOOK FOR CHILD-CARE SERVICES

There is a dire need for expanded child-care services, from birth to at least age 14. The facts presented earlier strongly support the need for a united effort on the part of educators, social workers, health organizations, and legislators to address the child-care problem. Federal officials are already proposing legislation to fund and give national impetus to the creation of child-care centers.

But the general public has not yet shown a willingness to commit energy, effort and funds for child-care facilities. The main impetus, thus far, stems from working parents. While some of them can afford to enroll their children in well-designed child-care centers, such as those described in this chapter, many others must rely on relatives, or individuals who offer child-care services in their homes for a nominal fee.

The outlook for the advancement of child-care services in the United States is not entirely hopeless. The urgency underlying the need for early childhood care is escalating day by day. The plight of the latchkey children is becoming more and more evident. The increasing number of teenage mothers is posing an unanticipated burden on our schools and on society. For these reasons, state and local governments will become much more involved in early childhood care. The gravity of the child-care problem is reaching the point where federal action is forthcoming within the foreseeable future.

Current Trends and Future Outlook

Facilities for young children are not expected to be standardized in the near future. It is anticipated that they will appear in a myriad of forms, sizes and shapes. Some of them will be unifunctional, while others will be comprehensive centers housing children of all ages. Some will be operated by an individual homeowner, while others will be administered by corporations. Some will be managed by a group of parents, while others may be under the jurisdiction of school districts. Some will be funded entirely by parents, while others will be funded by foundations and public service organizations.

There are currently many varieties of child-care facilities. As indicated earlier, there is no standard or model facility. There is only one common ingredient in all of them—young children. While it can be stated categorically that all forms of child-care facilities will provide some sort of service for children, the level and scope of such service will differ greatly from facility to facility. The nature and character of each child-care facility will depend on the philosophy of its founders, the level of funding, the expectations of parents, and the local demand for a given type of child-care service.

While the size, type and operational characteristics of future child-care facilities are not easily predictable, it is expected that as the need and demand for child-care services becomes more pressing, the number of child-care facilities will increase accordingly. It is hoped that the fundamental concepts underlying child-care facilities discussed in this chapter will form the basis for a new generation of child-care facilities. It is anticipated that changes in the size, scope, and diversity of activities in future child-care centers will be evolutionary. If state and federal funds become available for such facilities, their numbers will increase enormously and the number of controls on their design and function will increase accordingly. It is also expected that more and more school districts will provide space for latchkey students and for teenage mothers. The increasing availability of child-care facilities bodes well for the future. The need for such facilities is great now and promises to be even greater in the foreseeable future.

NOTES

1. A. L. Kuhn, *The Mother's Role in Childhood Education: New England Concepts 1830–1860* (New Haven, CT: Yale University Press, 1947), p. 27.

2. N. C. Vandewalder, "Facts of Interest about Kindergarten Laws," *Childhood Education,* v. 1 (1925), p. 324.

3. Celia Anita Decker and John R. Decker, *Planning and Administering Early Childhood Programs* (Columbus, OH: Charles E. Merrill, 1984), p. 5.

4. Martin Haberman, "An Education Platform in Search of a Candidate Who Wants to Win," *The Phi Delta Kappan* (March 1988), p. 520.

5. Harold L. Hodgkinson, "Facing the Future," *The School Administrator* (September 1988), p. 28.

6. Asta M. Kenney, "Teen-age Pregnancy: An Issue for Schools," *Phi Delta Kappan* (June 1987), p. 729.

7. Harold L. Hodgkinson, "Reform vs. Reality," *Phi Delta Kappan* (September 1991), p. 9.

8. *Accreditation Criteria and Procedures* (Washington, DC: National Association for the Education of Young Children, 1984), p. 24.

9. Lawrence Shaffer and Edward Shoben, *The Psychology of Adjustment* (Boston: Houghton Mifflin, 1956). p. 139.

10. Richard J. Passantino, "Day-Care Centers to Stimulate Learning," *The School Administrator* (September 1989), p. 9.

11. Decker, op. cit., pp. 360–372.

12. John Hodge Jones, "Use Child Care to Extend School Day, School Year," *School Administrator* (October 1989), p. 30.

▶ 16

Postplanning Procedures and Construction Costs

After architectural plans have been developed to the satisfaction of the planning team and the board of trustees or board of education, they must be translated into a school building by the cooperative efforts of the architect and the builder. The conversion from plans to building is a crucial part of school plant planning. It includes bidding, supervision, and a good working relationship between architect and general contractor.

PRUDENTIAL CONTRACT STIPULATIONS

Construction Time

It is generally agreed that the number of working days allowed for construction should be stated in the contract. If the expected completion date of the project is clearly specified, the contractor will not be tempted to shift his work force from one project to another of higher priority and thus postpone the completion of the building.

In specifying a completion date, however, both parties should agree that the length of time allowed for construction is reasonable, whether or not penalties are involved.

Penalty Clauses in the Contract

The insertion of penalty clauses in a construction contract is not an unmixed blessing to the owner. Generally, where penalties are imposed upon the contractor on a per diem basis for exceeding the stipulated construction time, he is allowed a stated bonus for each day in advance of the specified completion date that he completes his work. Unless the allocated construction time is reasonable, a penalty clause in the contract is likely to cause a significant increase in the contract price of the job.

Even where a penalty clause exists, there is really no positive assurance that the contractor will be legally penalized for not completing the project on time. In most situations, change orders of one form or another are bound to be made. If penalties are involved, the contractor will always seek a time extension whenever a change order is requested. In one instance, a contractor requested a 10-day extension of time to move two electrical outlets from one part of a wall to another. The owner has little choice under such circumstances. If he wants the change, he must accept the extension of time. In a state project having an area of about 120,000 square feet, the contractor requested and received a total time extension of 240 calendar days as a result of numerous change orders. The penalty clause in the contract was never invoked, although about 1,000 students were deprived of the use of the facility for an additional academic year.

The Liquidated Damage Clause

Under this clause, the builder agrees to complete the project on a given date, but the owner does not automatically receive payment in the event that he fails to do so. The owner must prove damages directly resulting from the delay in completion of the project in order to collect damages. As a rule, it is difficult to prove that damages are directly traceable to the builder's failure to comply with the contract. For this reason, the liquidated damage clause is not always effective in assuring completion of educational facilities on time.

Insurance

In any contract between a school district or college board and the builder, provision should be made for various types of insurance. The liability insurance is usually carried by the contractor and the fire insurance by the owner. A northern Illinois school district found that it was less expensive for the district to carry both the liability and fire insurance. As a result, it requested the contractor not to include the cost of liability insurance in his bid price. It is suggested that boards of education or boards of trustees explore these alternatives and select the one that provides adequate insurance coverage at least cost.

Performance Bond

According to Strevell and Burke, "This (performance bond) is an assurance that the person or firm to whom the contract is awarded will faithfully perform the contract including all provisions of plans and specifications."[1] The performance bond should not be executed prior to the execution of the construction contract. The terms of the performance bond must meet with the approval of the owner. The premium for this bond may be paid by either the owner or the contractor. It is important, therefore, that the owner specify who will pay the premium for this bond at the time bids are requested.

BIDDING PROCEDURES

The accepted method for selecting a contractor is competitive bidding. This procedure, generally followed by private enterprise, is almost always required by state and local statutes for the construction of public buildings. Bids are not always given to the lowest bidder. Most laws simply require that contracts be awarded to the lowest responsible bidder.

The usual procedure is to invite bidders to submit a proposal and then to supply them with plans and specifications to use in preparing cost estimates. Invitations are usually issued through the press or construction publications. Such invitations include the name of the project and the time and source from which plans and specifications may be obtained. The announcement must also state when and where the bids must be filed and the documents returned, and whether or not a deposit is required for the drawings. Very frequently the bidders must give some assurance that they will accept the bid if it is offered. This assurance usually takes the form of a deposit of a certified check or the filing of a bid bond. The amount of the deposit is usually specified in the statutes.

Time for Preparing the Bid. The contractor should be allowed ample time to make cost determinations and prepare the bid. Usually a period of about four weeks is allowed, but in less complicated projects two weeks is generally sufficient. Sometimes, extension of bidding time is necessary. In such cases, all bidders should be notified of the extension at least 48 hours before the original opening time. At times, the architect may be required to issue explanations and clarifications during the bidding period. When such action is necessary, he or she should be sure to issue all supplementary information to all the bidders.

Opening of Bids. In general, bids are opened at the appointed time in public and are tabulated by the architect. After prices and alternatives are carefully weighed and compared, the successful bidder is selected. Before receiving the contract for the project, however, the successful bidder is usually required to post a performance bond for the full amount of the contract. This bond serves as a guarantee that should the contractor fail to complete his work satisfactorily, the bonding company will assume the financial obligation for the completion of the building.

Awarding of the Contract.[2] The contract for the construction of the school is signed by both the awarding authority and the contractor. It is strongly suggested that legal advice be sought at this point to make certain that the document is properly prepared and fully protects all concerned, and that persons signing the contract are legally authorized to do so.

Upon signing the contract, the builder is customarily required to submit to the architect a breakdown of the estimates concerning items set forth for the work of the various building trades listed in the specifications. He or she also submits a schedule of dates for the completion of the various aspects of the construction project, such as footings, foundations, electrical roughing, plumbing, and heating.

BUILDING THE EDUCATIONAL FACILITY

Once the contract is let, the builder must commence construction within the time specified in the contract. The building of a school, as mentioned earlier, is basically a cooperative effort on the part of both the contractor and the architect. In order to be sure that work is performed in accordance with specifications, continuous supervision should be provided. Unless the project is fairly large, in excess of, let us say $500,000, it is difficult to justify the employment of a full-time clerk-of-the-works, even though the employment of such a person is highly desirable in any project.

The Supervisory Responsibility of the Architect.[3] Contrary to popular belief, the architect is *not* responsible for continuous supervision on the job, unless this is specifically stated in the contract. On the other hand, the supervision provided by the architect should be sufficient to insure that the building is constructed according to specifications. On small projects, the architect may supervise the work as infrequently as one afternoon per week, while on a multimillion dollar project he or she might provide a full-time resident architect or engineer.

The builder cannot deviate from the plans and specifications without the approval of the architect. Neither can the builder devise his or her own method of construction unless it is approved by the architect. Oftentimes, the architect is called upon to verify shop drawings produced by fabricators of the several components of construction. Also, the owner makes no payments to the builder without the authorization of the architect.

The Clerk-of-the-Works. In fairly large projects, a clerk-of-the-works is employed by the owner to supervise and inspect every detail of the construction on a full-time basis. He or she reports any irregularities to the architect, who then takes the necessary corrective action.

The clerk-of-the-works is often worth many times his or her salary. He or she makes certain that the contractor delivers a full measure in materials and workmanship. The writer had an experience that clearly demonstrates the value of a competent clerk-of-the-works. While visiting a school building under construction, he was conversing briefly with the clerk-of-the-works. In the middle of the conversation, the clerk-of-the-works departed abruptly and climbed a ladder leading to the roof where a workman was installing a flashing around the chimney. Upon his return, he stated, "Just as I thought, they were using $3/_4$-inch copper nails instead of the required inch and a half." When he was asked how he had detected this deficiency at a distance of 300 feet, he answered, "Whoever heard of driving a one-and-one-half-inch roofing nail with a single blow of the hammer?"

Change Orders.   A change order is defined as a change made in the plans of a building while construction is in progress. The number of change orders should be kept to a minimum, but where the function of a school plant can be substantially improved, or serious deficiencies corrected, change orders should be made.

In general, change orders are more costly than the same changes would have been if they had been included in the original working drawings. They need not be so costly, but because of the very nature of competitive bidding, the contractor's profit is often not included in a deductive change order. On the other hand, an additive change order is often treated as a single project without competitive bidding. Thus, the amount that is added to the contract is ordinarily greater than it would be if competitive bidding entered the cost estimate. For example, a school district in central Illinois had awarded a substantial contract to a contractor for pointing the mortar joints in the exterior of a fairly large junior high school. While work was in progress, it was discovered that the parapet was loose and constituted a safety hazard. The board of education voted to remove it from the building. The contractor was asked to quote a price on a "change order" basis for the removal of the parapet, on the assumption that he was already on the job and his price would probably be lower than others. As a matter of academic interest, one of the board members suggested that several other quotations be sought. To the surprise of all concerned, the price of the contractor on the job was about 25 percent higher than that supplied by others! Needless to say, no change order was issued.

Relationship Between the Contractor and School Officials.   Generally speaking, there is no direct relationship between the owner and the contractor. The owner deals with the contractor through the architect. It is true, of course, that the owner retains the right to inspect the work during construction, but the builder is usually not required to take orders directly from the owner.

It should be pointed out, however, that the builder generally has complete jurisdiction within the contract limits of the project during construction. He or she almost always has the authority to prevent anyone from trespassing within the contract limits. Builders are reluctant to permit persons not having official business in the construction zone because of legal liability in case of accidents.

MANUAL FOR ADMINISTRATION AND STAFF

The normal procedure after the school facility is ready for occupancy is relatively simple. The board of education accepts the building. The contractor turns the keys of the building over to school officials and, at some early future date, an open house is held for the public under the auspices of the board of education. Speeches are made, the taxpayers are congratulated, and the school band plays on. This marks the end of the major construction works, on the part of the contractor, the architect, and educational consultants. Of course, all parties may be called in to correct problems that may arise during the "shake down" period of the building operation.

Eventually, all parties responsible for the planning and construction of a building will become disassociated with the occupied school facility. And after a decade or so, very few people will know who these parties were, without reading the bronze plaque that is usually affixed to one of the walls in the lobby area of the building. There is nothing improper or unusual about this sequence of events. However, the administration and staff assigned to the building inherit a complicated educational facility which they are required to operate for many years in the future. In some instances, no one will remember or know the intended function for each space in the building nor how the mechanical and electrical equipment should be maintained and operated.

In order to avoid this situation, it is suggested that the architect be required to prepare a manual regarding the maintenance and operation of the school building. The manual should describe:

1. how each space was intended to be used when the building was planned.
2. all of the lighting, heating, and ventilating controls, where they are located, and what they control.
3. how each critical building or working surface and each piece of mechanical equipment should be maintained, including cautionary statements as to "what not to do."
4. how the building is planned for expansion and the specific points in the electrical, mechanical, and architectural systems where extensions can be made.

The manual should also show the "as built" plans in logical segments on several pages of the booklet, so that future modifications of the building can be made economically and intelligently.

COMPARISONS OF CONSTRUCTION COSTS

As many architects and educators readily admit, comparing the unit cost of one school with that of another is meaningless and often misleading. Costs simply indicate the number of dollars that are spent for a unit area, volume, or student. This much of the comparison is quite specific and definite. On the other hand, there are several aspects of a school plant that are not revealed in unit cost figures. In computing any type of unit cost, there is only one figure that is certain, namely, the total cost. For this reason, unit costs in school construction are really quite vague. Unit costs are determined by dividing cost by another item, usually number of students, number of square feet, number of cubic feet, or number of classrooms. Since only the numerator or cost figure is definite, the unit cost loses much of its significance.

Inadequacy of Unit Cost Comparisons

Unit cost figures alone are quite meaningless in making cost comparisons. There are several shortcomings inherent in all unit cost figures applicable to school buildings; others are peculiar only to certain unit costs.

Inadequacies Common to All Unit Cost Figures.   A cost of a school building per square foot, per cubic foot, per classroom, or per student cannot be used by itself in comparing school building costs sensibly for the reasons listed below.

1. It does not indicate what is actually included in the building in terms of unusual spaces, laboratory units, and special built-in equipment.
2. It does not reveal the quality of the construction materials selected by the architect and educational boards.
3. It does not tell anything about extraordinary site conditions.
4. It fails to indicate the type, extent, or quality of mechanical equipment used in the building.
5. It neglects to provide an index of economy regarding the cost of operation and maintenance of the building after it is completed.
6. It omits any information regarding the educational efficiency of the structure.
7. It does not reveal the extent to which the building may be over-planned for future expansion.
8. It fails to indicate how much site development and educational equipment are included in the cost figure.
9. It does not reveal how efficiently the space within the building can be utilized.

Additional Shortcomings Peculiar to the Use of Cost Per Square Foot or Per Cubic Foot of School Buildings.   Such a unit cost is also deficient for the reasons listed below.

1. It fails to indicate what areas or volumes are included in obtaining the total areas or volumes. For example, is attic space included in the volume? Are pipe trenches counted as area or volume?
2. It does not reveal how overhangs, enclosed walkways, and covered walks have been treated in the computation.

Shortcomings of the Use of the Cost Per Classroom or Per Student.   These unit costs are even less reliable than those listed above, for several obvious reasons.

1. The capacity of a school building is not fixed or uniform for every school of the same type. There is no standard of measuring building capacity. In most cases, it is simply an "educated guess."
2. The cost figures do not reveal the number of square feet in a school building per student or per classroom. Clearly, a building with inadequate instructional spaces costs less to construct than one with adequate spaces.

How to Make Reliable and Meaningful Unit Cost Comparisons

The view of unit cost comparisons expressed in the previous paragraphs is not altogether dismal. Up to this point, it has been assumed that a board of education or board of trustees seeks to compare simply by reviewing unit costs supplied by architects, school personnel, or educational consultants. Such figures, as indicated earlier, are quite meaningless, except in making crude estimates of school building costs. Unit costs can be extremely valuable, however, when they are compiled by a central statistical agency.

Which Is the Most Reliable Unit Cost Figure?   The author made a study of two of the unit costs in common use; 129 elementary units were included in the study. Costs were derived from the official records of the Massachusetts School Building Assistance Commission. A coefficient of correlation was computed between the construction cost of a school and (a) the cost per square foot and (b) the cost per student. It was found that the coefficient of correlation between cost per square foot and total construction cost was 0.92, and the coefficient of correlation between cost per student and total construction cost was 0.71. Obviously, the cost per square foot is a more accurate predictor of the total cost of a building. This fact is not surprising. Architects have used this method since the beginning of architectural costs analysis.

Obtaining Reliable Cost Figures.   Sensible cost comparison using cost per square foot can be made if the instructions listed below are followed.

1. Start with the basic data. Use working drawings of the various buildings and request a breakdown of the costs involved.

2. In measuring areas, observe the following rules:

   a. Use all outside dimensions of the buildings.
   b. Include only usable floor spaces. For example, storage rooms in the basement would be considered part of the area of the building, while unfinished spaces and pipe trenches would not.
   c. Divide the areas of all covered walks and overhangs by three before adding them to the area of the rest of the building.
   d. Divide enclosed corridors by two before adding them to the area of the rest of the building.
   e. Staircases should be included at each level at full value for each level.
   f. The area of elevator shafts should be included only once, but the wall thickness at all levels should be included in the spaces surrounding the elevator shaft.

3. Costs should be treated as follows:

   a. Construction cost should include the cost of the structure, all equipment attached to the building, and the cost of site development for about 25 feet around the building. Care should be taken in comparing costs of buildings in which expensive laboratory equipment or air-conditioning is installed. In these cases, be sure that buildings compared are similar. Otherwise, the cost of the highly specialized equipment must be omitted from the total cost.
   b. Exclude architectural, legal, and other fees.
   c. Exclude the cost of the site development and site acquisition.

If these guides are observed, any central office can accumulate a reliable set of cost figures for both predicting and comparing school building costs. This service can best be rendered to school districts by the various state departments of education and by the statistical branch of the U.S. Department of Education.

NOTES

1. Wallace H. Strevell and Arvid J. Burke, *Administration of the School Building Program* (New York: McGraw-Hill, 1959), p. 411.

2. Harold W. Boles, *Step by Step to Better School Facilities* (New York: Holt, Rinehart and Winston, 1965), p. 151.

3. *Guide for Planning Educational Facilities* (Columbus, OH: Council of Educational Facility Planners, International, 1976), p. M–8.

▶ 17

Modernization of Educational Facilities

The terms *rehabilitation, remodeling,* and *modernization* are common in the parlance of schoolpeople, but they often have different meanings to different people. As used in this text, *rehabilitation* is a form of deferred maintenance. The school building is simply restored to the same condition it was in when it was built. Old equipment and worn parts are replaced. Interior walls, floors, and ceilings are repainted and refinished and the exterior of the building is reconstructed wherever necessary to make it weather-proof again. These changes are essentially cosmetic.

Remodeling goes one step beyond rehabilitation. It also includes changes in the size or shape of any space within the building. To this extent, a remodeled school facility could improve its function as an education tool.

The term *modernization,* as defined in this text, is a process whereby an existing school facility is brought up-to-date structurally, educationally, and environmentally. In this process, certain spaces within the school building may be reshaped to accommodate modern educational practices. Worn mechanical equipment, weathered parts of the structure, and unsightly and unsafe interior surfaces may be restored to their original state. Modernization also includes the installation of more efficient mechanical and electrical equipment and the addition of energy-efficient materials to the exterior walls and roof. And finally, modernization accommodates a forward-looking educational program, improving the health and safety of the students occupying the building, and provides for special education services as described in the section entitled, "A Guide for Planning New and Renovated Schools," in *Facilities for Special Education Services.*[1]

AN OVERVIEW OF SCHOOL FACILITY MODERNIZATION

School facility modernization is a more complex and time-consuming task than planning a new facility. It is much easier to change lines on paper than it is to move partitions, reroute electric wires, cut and rejoin pipes, and redesign the structural members of an existing building. On the other hand, educational facility planners and architects are presented with both a challenge and an opportunity to transform an obsolete school building into one that is educationally efficient, structurally safe, and environmentally healthful. Several aspects of school facility modernization are outlined in the following sections.

IMPROVEMENTS IN EDUCATIONAL FUNCTION, ENERGY CONSERVATION, AND ENVIRONMENTAL QUALITY

The interrelated improvements in a school facility can be illustrated best by introducing a hypothetical situation involving the Smith Elementary School, typical of those built in 1923. It is a two-story building with a flat roof and parapet. It contains eight classrooms, and features a principal's office on the second floor over the main entrance. It has a brick exterior, wooden sash and frames, and two basement play areas with toilets adjoining each room. The classrooms are fairly large, each containing slightly over 900 square feet. A cloakroom about 10 feet wide and 22 feet long adjoins each classroom. The central corridors and lobbies are constructed of fire-resistant materials. The ceilings and walls are plaster on wooden lath, except in the corridors and exterior walls where plaster is applied directly to the brick walls. The lighting system in each room consists of four suspended globe-type fixtures furnished with 200-watt incandescent bulbs. The heating system consists of a coal-fired steam boiler and cast-iron radiators in the classrooms and corridors. The ventilating system is capable of providing about 25 cubic feet of fresh air per student per minute.

After a review of the findings of a school survey recently completed by a team of educational consultants from Home State University, the board of education decided to follow the recommendation in the long-range plan calling for modernization of the Smith Elementary School. The study described some of the school's shortcomings as follows: "The wooden floors in the corridors and classrooms are dark, warped, and creaky. The window sashes are loose and in need of repair. There is no suitable place for physical education and assembly. There is also no health room or workroom for the teachers. The building, as a whole, is in excellent structural condition but the atmosphere found in the classrooms is not conducive to effective learning. . . . " On the basis of this report and a study of the curriculum, educational specifications were developed and the following was accomplished.

In addition to a face-lifting around the front entrance and main lobby, the Smith Elementary School was modernized as follows:

1. The foundation was examined, repaired wherever necessary, and insulated with panels of styrofoam or equivalent structural insulating materials.
2. A gas hot water heater, separate from the boiler, was installed in the boiler room and piped through insulated pipes to the cafeteria, adjoining lavatories, and to the multipurpose room. A small, self-contained electric hot water heater was installed near the principal's office and teachers' lounge. (This eliminated long hot-water pipe lines from the central hot-water heater.)
3. A gas hot-water heater was installed in the boiler room and hot water piped to all lavatories.
4. Two cloakrooms on each floor were converted to modern toilet rooms, one for boys and one for girls. Ceramic tile was installed on the floor and walls, and new lighting and improved ventilation were provided. Wall-hung fixtures were used throughout, and foot control, single-spigot faucets with tempered water were introduced.
5. A new base was installed on all of the wooden floors in the corridors and classrooms, and light-colored vinyl asbestos tile was laid over it.
6. The upper part of all classroom and corridor walls was repainted in pastel colors. A warm wood-toned formica-type material was installed on the lower walls of the classrooms.
7. The ceilings in all of the classrooms and corridors were lowered to a height of about 10 feet, using a mechanical steel grid system. Acoustical tile was installed on all ceilings.
8. The lighting in corridor and classroom areas was replaced by continuous-strip fluorescent fixtures. The school was completely rewired.
9. The wooden window sashes and frames were replaced with modern anodized aluminum units with insulating glass.
10. The parapet was removed and new flashing was installed to give the building a modern, sleek appearance and to correct a leaking roof.
11. The three outside doors were replaced with modern glass doors.
12. All stairs were resurfaced using abrasive, nonslip materials.
13. The single wooden handrail was replaced by a modern, metal double handrail set at two heights.
14. Cloak closets with vertically sliding panel doors were built in the classrooms along the corridor walls.
15. The gray slate chalkboards were removed, and the walls beneath were replastered, refinished, and painted. Vertical standards four feet apart were installed

in all areas where chalkboard and tackboard were needed. Movable, metal chalkboard panels were hung on these standards. The two chalkboard panels in front of each room were equipped with a source of ultraviolet light so that luminous chalk could be used.

16. Similar standards were installed in the main lobby to support display cabinets and shelves.
17. The lower walls in all corridors were sprayed with plastic-type paint to a height of about four feet.
18. At least two duplex electrical outlets were installed on the opposite walls of each classroom and in strategic locations in the corridors.
19. The old shades in the classrooms were replaced by vertical-type venetian blinds for improved light control.
20. Eight solar hot-water heating panels, each having an area of about 40 square feet, were installed on the roof facing south and tilted at an angle from the horizontal, approximating the latitude on which the Smith School was located. This unit was tied into the new gas hot-water heater.
21. One cloakroom on each floor was converted to a remedial room for speech therapy, reading, and arithmetic.
22. The remaining cloakroom on the first floor was used for storage of instructional and custodial materials. Locks were installed on the doors.
23. The principal's office on the second floor was enlarged, refinished, relighted, paneled in birch, and converted into a teacher's lounge. All of the floor was carpeted except the area surrounding the work space and the sink-refrigerator-range combination, where vinyl tile was used. This space was enlarged by removing the wall between the principal's office and the adjoining cloakroom. Part of the cloak area was added to the teachers' lounge and part of it was designed as a workroom.
24. The two basement playrooms with relatively high ceilings were converted into a kitchen and cafeteria for the hot-lunch program. The ceiling was dropped about 6 inches below the former ceiling and covered with acoustical tile. Surface-type, plastic-covered fluorescent strips were attached to the ceiling. Wooden paneling was used on the walls and gaily colored vinyl asbestos tile was installed on the floor. A movable raised platform was placed at one end of this space.
25. Modern, movable, colorful plastic chairs and plastic-surfaced tables were provided.
26. Lounge furniture and a comfortable work table were provided in the teachers' room.
27. The two large toilet areas in the basement were reduced in size and completely restyled with new fixtures, ceramic tile floors and walls, better lighting, and improved ventilation.

28. A general storage area for instructional materials was developed in the basement of the building.
29. A fire-resistant area for storage of cleaning agents was built in the basement area.
30. New partitions were installed in the basement areas to separate the kitchen from the dining area, the boiler room from the rest of the basement, and the storage spaces from the spaces around them.
31. The walls between four pairs of classrooms were replaced with movable partitions having a rated sound transmission loss of about 40 decibels.
32. The bricks on the exterior walls were steam-cleaned and repainted. The outside walls and the roof were insulated and basement walls were repaired and waterproofed.
33. An addition to the Smith Elementary School was also built. The new section was connected to the side entrance by an attractive carpeted corridor. The addition was designed so that it could stand by itself architecturally and structurally if the main building were to be demolished at a later date.
34. The new addition contained the following spaces:
    a. One 1,200-square-foot kindergarten room of modern design with wall-to-wall carpeting, except in the dressing space and in the wet work areas.
    b. One library room having an area of about 1,500 square feet, plus space for storing audiovisual equipment.
    c. Four regular classrooms, each about 950 square feet in net area. Wall-to-wall carpeting was installed in all except wet work areas.
    d. A multipurpose room having an area of about 2,500 square feet, plus space for a stage and chair storage room.
    e. A clerk and principal's office and a health suite with office and examination room. A toilet and hospital-type sink were also located in this area. These areas also had wall-to-wall carpeting.
35. The four regular classrooms mentioned in item 34 were located in a circular cluster so that movable partitions between them could be opened to produce a single unified space for about 120 pupils.
36. Television reception jacks were installed in both the new and original classrooms of the Smith Elementary School.
37. A special conference room was located adjacent to the library. It was directly connected to the library for the convenience of team teachers using this space in the preparation of their work. It was furnished with comfortable chairs and trapezoidal tables.

Thus, Smith Elementary School in Hometown, U.S.A. was extensively modernized. The cost? Hundreds of thousands of dollars. Was it worth it? Probably not. A formula will be presented in the latter part of this chapter to assist school planners in making this crucial decision.

HEALTH-RELATED IMPROVEMENTS

The modernization process demands that educational facility planners concentrate heavily on matters related to the safety and health of the occupants of a building. Lighting, temperature and humidity control, sound pollution, water quality, ventilation, fire protection, and potentially dangerous situations should be improved to the maximum possible degree. Any flaw in the design of the building or construction material that may have a deleterious effect on the health of the occupants must be corrected in its entirety, notwithstanding economic considerations. One example of this type of health hazard is cited in the next paragraph.

Medical research scientists have discovered that asbestos is a cancer-producing agent. Immediately following World War II, asbestos was widely used in the construction industry because of its excellent thermal properties. It was fireproof and a good heat insulator. It appeared in several forms. It was pulverized and made into a cementlike substance that was plastered around boilers or steam pipes. Often, the asbestos insulating tubes were covered with fabric. During this period, the walls and ceilings were constructed of materials containing asbestos. Sometimes, asbestos and other sound-absorbing materials were sprayed on ceilings for acoustical and insulating purposes. School administrators should not wait until a school building suspected of containing asbestos is modernized. All asbestos materials should be replaced immediately with noncarcinogenic materials. In situations where asbestos materials cannot be removed immediately, a temporary solution may be considered once the mechanics of the asbestos danger are understood. As long as the asbestos remains where it was installed, there is no real danger from it. But, since it is a cementlike substance, it ultimately pulverizes and becomes airborne. When such air is inhaled, the danger of developing cancer is real and imminent. There are currently on the market resinous sprays that can be applied to the surface of materials containing asbestos. This treatment seals the asbestos-laden material temporarily and prevents the asbestos powder from becoming airborne. A word of caution is in order. This is not a permanent solution to the asbestos problem in school facilities. Funds should be provided to remove asbestos materials from a school building as soon as possible.

MODERNIZED FACILITIES FOR SPECIAL EDUCATION SERVICES

In Chapter 6, a few guidelines were presented in relation to the planning of new facilities for the needs of exceptional students suffering from physical impediments and learning disabilities. The same goals and objectives apply to modernized educational facilities. Accordingly, all special features and design characteristics planned for exceptional students in new school facilities should be embodied in the plans of a modernized school facility. It is suggested that the publication, *Facilities for Special Education Services,* cited earlier, be studied before planning facilities for exceptional students. It is replete with extremely valuable information on the needs of these students. It is further suggested that the sections in Chapter 6 dealing with facilities for special students' needs be reviewed during the design stages of school facilities that are being modernized.

TO MODERNIZE OR TO REPLACE

One of the most perplexing questions confronting citizens within a school district is whether the existing school facility should be modernized or replaced. Many approaches are possible, but there seems to be no single line of reasoning that will satisfy everyone.

Paradox and Controversy

For various reasons, the issue of modernization or replacement is often fraught with paradox and controversy. There seems to be a natural tendency among many citizens to favor modernization over replacement for two reasons. They may feel a sense of loyalty to the grand old school that served them and their predecessors well in the past. There seems to be a common belief that modernization automatically means greater economy because part of the old structure is preserved. Unfortunately, the average citizen sees only part of the picture, unaware that school buildings, like automobiles, become functionally obsolete. Too few citizens realize that the educational process today is considerably different from what it was when they attended school. Consequently, when citizens' committees examine today's school buildings, they often fail to perceive the presence of educational obsolescence. Under these circumstances, they cannot be expected to make valid judgments of the educational worth of an existing school building. Nonetheless, citizens do make judgments about their schools, arrive at conclusions, true or false, and act accordingly. Having convinced themselves, with or without a valid basis for judgment, that a building is educationally useful, citizens frequently presume that it is more economical to modernize it than to replace it. This line of reasoning is perfectly understandable from the standpoint of the taxpayer, who, after all, sees an apparently useful educational structure that represents a real value in dollars and cents. Why abandon it only to replace it with another structure? During a recent controversy regarding the question of modernization or replacement, the mayor of a large, conservative New England city said, "The city has no use whatsoever for that (high school) building except as an educational facility. There's been talk of turning it into a new City Hall, but it would cost millions to turn classrooms into office space. Abandoning that building as a school would be abandoning a facility valued at some $6,000,000, private assessors have told me." This statement or one similar to it is quite familiar to educators in all parts of the country. Whenever the question of modernization versus replacement arises, someone is almost certain to remind the voters of the replacement value of that wonderful old school building in the middle of town. This subtle emotional appeal and the desire for economy lend considerable power to such statements. This argument places economy above educational values, and it is very difficult to combat it with reason, logic, common sense, or a promise of a better educational program for all of the children of all of the people.

Modernization is both a blessing and a curse. When modernization is warranted in terms of the criteria presented in this chapter, it is usually easier to "sell" to the public than other proposals. On the other hand, when new construction is preferable to modernization, the issue may become highly emotional and controversial. The resistance to new construction seems to stem from the feeling of some citizens that a perfectly good building is being abandoned only to be replaced by a new one on the same or on another site.

MODERNIZATION OR NEW CONSTRUCTION

The decision whether or not to modernize a given building requires time, study, vision, and courage. A comprehensive study of all aspects of the problem is a necessary first step. Time and imagination are needed to identify and explore alternatives and to study and evaluate the consequences and educational returns associated with them. A hasty and ill-conceived decision to modernize a school may penalize the education of children yet unborn. School officials and members of boards of education should identify the real issues and act in the best interest of the public and the school district.

The Castaldi Generalized Formula for School Modernization

A thorough search of the literature of school modernization uncovered virtually no information about what factors should determine whether or not a school should be modernized. The author asked himself the question that at some time or other has confronted all school planners, "When should or should not a school be modernized?" Only two rules of thumb were discovered. They are as follows:

1. According to Linn, the decision to modernize a building is questionable if the cost of modernization exceeds 50 percent of the cost of a new project. He suggests that a 40 percent figure would be more realistic.[2]

2. The second rule of thumb was proposed by building experts who believe that when any two of the following items are required, modernization should be questioned. The items include major replacement of plumbing and heating; total replacement of electrical wiring; basic structural changes involving space arrangements; complete replacement of roofing; or complete revamping of the fenestration pattern.

There is, to be sure, much merit in both of these guidelines to modernization. Both statements focus upon economic considerations, but the Linn statement is more precisely related to the actual expenditure that may be required for modernization. The rule of the building experts, on the other hand, does not require that the cost of modernization be converted into dollars before a decision is made. Also, since the decision whether or not to modernize is based upon the need for any two of the major projects noted above, the actual cost that serves as the determinant in making the decision may vary over fairly wide limits. This does not mean that the second rule of thumb is of little value. The rule of the building experts serves a most important function in alerting boards of education and school planners to take a second and even a third look at the advisability of modernizing an existing school.

Another approach to the financial aspect of modernization is proposed here. In developing a generalized formula for school modernization presented in this book, the author has sought to set forth a mathematical expression that:

1. Separates, insofar as possible, the total cost of modernization into its major component parts: cost for educational improvements, cost for improvements in healthfulness, and cost for improvements in safety.
2. Takes into account the educational adequacy of the modernized school, which also includes the school site.
3. Clearly indicates whether or not modernization would be of financial advantage to the school district over an extended period of time.
4. Places replacement cost and modernization cost on a comparable basis.

This formula is based upon the rate-of-depreciation concept, and contains both a determinant and a hypothesis (underlying the formula).

The fundamental determinant in the proposed formula for school modernization is the annual rate of depreciation of school facilities. It is hypothesized that the lower the effective rate of depreciation[3]—represented primarily by the amount of capital required to provide a school plant that is adequate in every respect—the sounder the expenditure of public funds. It is postulated therefore, that the determinant of financial advantage on the part of a school district is not the initial cost, but the *rate* at which the initial cost is likely to depreciate over a period of years.

The general formula is stated as follows: Modernization is justifiable if:

$$\frac{(C_E + C_H + C_S)}{(L_M)(I_A)} < \frac{R}{L_R}$$

where:

C_E = Total cost of educational improvements

C_H = Total cost for improvements in healthfulness (physical, aesthetic, and psychological)

C_S = Total cost for improvements in safety

I_A = Estimated index of educational adequacy (0–1)

L_M = Estimated useful life of the modernized school

R = Cost of replacement of school considered for modernization

L_R = Estimated life of new building

Discussion of the General Formula. The three terms in the parentheses include many items that are not readily apparent. For example, C_E may include, in addition to remodeling, the expansion of the site, new wiring for educational television, and accommodating new teaching practices. C_H may involve an improved heating system, improved lighting, redecoration, refenestration, resurfaced floors and ceilings, and better ventilation. And finally, C_S may cover items such as structural repairs, fireproofing corridors and stairways, elimination of loose plaster, or repairing loose shingles.

I_A is an index of educational adequacy, ranging in value from 0–1, that is applied to the school for which modernization is being proposed. The value of the index is determined in relation to the educational adequacy of a replacement for the school in question. Often, when a school is modernized, compromises must be accepted. They may appear in the form of inconveniences to students and teachers or as restrictions of the educational function of the school. The school site is a case in point. The author does not hold that an inadequate site, per se, is sufficient reason for arbitrarily deciding that a school can neither be replaced nor modernized at a given location. The size of a school site is an important factor, but it is only one of many that must be considered in deciding where a school should be located. In situations where school sites do not meet desired standards, the site deficiency should be reflected in the index of educational adequacy unless the replacement school would also be located on an inadequate site. It is important to bear in mind, however, that the index of educational adequacy applies to the entire school plant, of which the site is only one element. Since the index of educational adequacy is determined subjectively and represents a professional judgment, it might be desirable to obtain an evaluation of educational adequacy both from professional persons within the school system and from one or two qualified professionals outside the school district.

L_M refers to the estimated number of years of useful life remaining in the school in question after it is modernized. It is quite possible that under certain circumstances, the expected life of the modernized building can be extended through structural improvements.

R and L_R represent the cost of a school that would replace the building under consideration and the number of years it is likely to remain in operation, respectively. Admittedly, both the modernized school and a new building would require maintenance over an extended period of time. And it might even be argued that the average annual cost of maintenance could differ considerably between the modernized school and its replacement. For the purpose of the generalized formula, it is assumed that the average annual cost of maintenance for the modernized building is the same as that for its replacement. It should be pointed out, however, that a well-designed modern school may have a greater life expectancy than the building designed in the past.

Application of the Formula. The figures required in the formula should be determined as accurately as possible and entered in their proper places in the formula. If the left side of the formula is numerically smaller than the right, modernization would be financially advantageous to the school district. The smaller the numerical value of the left side in comparison with the value of the right, the greater would be the financial advantage of modernization to the school district. If both sides are approximately equal, the author would favor replacement over modernization. A word of caution is in order, however. The formula should be the determining factor only if the prerequisites mentioned later are met.

Comparison of the Linn Rule with Results from the Generalized Formula. It will be remembered that Linn suggested that modernization may be justified if the cost of modernization is about 40 percent of the cost of replacement. It will also be recalled that, in the life cycle of a building, 40 seems to be the age at which most schools are considered for modernization. Let us assume that a school building is 40 years old and is estimated to have a remaining life of 30 years after modernization. Let us further assume that the modernized school would contain a few unavoidable compromises so that its educational adequacy is judged to be about 90 percent of that expected for its replacement. It is also assumed that the replacement would have an expected life of 65 years.

$$\frac{\text{(cost of modernization)}}{(30)(0.90)} < ? \frac{\text{(cost of replacement)}}{65}$$

But, according to the Linn hypothesis, if cost of modernization equals 0.40 (cost of replacement), modernization is justifiable. Let us test the Linn hypothesis in the general formula for the situation in this example. Substituting 0.4 (cost of replacement) for the cost of modernization in the general formula, we have,

$$\frac{0.4 \text{ (cost of replacement)}}{(30)(0.90)} < ? \frac{\text{(cost of replacement)}}{65}$$

$$\frac{0.4}{(30)(0.90)} < \frac{1}{65}$$

$$0.0148 < 0.0154$$

Since the left side of the expression is less than the right, modernization is justifiable according to the generalized formula. It can be concluded, therefore, that the Linn hypothesis is a special case of the general formula presented in this report, and is valid for schools similar to the one described above. It should be noted, however, that the Linn hypothesis would not agree with the generalized formula when the school considered for modernization is more than 45 years old.

REQUISITE CONDITIONS FOR MODERNIZATION

Before modernization can be justified as the best expenditure of public funds in any school district, the answer to *every* question listed below must be *in the affirmative*. It cannot be overemphasized that a negative response to any *one* of the criteria listed below is a sufficient reason for rejecting a proposal to modernize a given building unless a blue ribbon committee mentioned under question 7 and on page 391 deems that there are extenuating circumstances. These statements may appear to be exacting and uncompromising. They are meant to be just that. School officials and boards of education cannot afford to yield to selfish pressures when the welfare and education of students are at stake and when tax funds would be used inefficiently.

1. *Is the school building under consideration needed in its present location for at least 75 percent of its remaining useful life after modernization?* Stated differently, the question might be, "Why spend money to modernize a building that will be phased out of operation in the very near future?"

2. *Is it impractical to distribute the student load of the school considered for modernization among other nearby adequate schools?* In some instances in large cities, it is possible to abandon an obsolete school building after reassigning students to other schools. This alternative, when feasible, should take precedence over modernization.

3. *Does the structure lend itself to improvement, alteration, remodeling, and expansion?* If the answer is "no," the cost of remodeling or expanding such a building could be unreasonably high and/or the educational function could be restricted because of the technical impracticability of accomplishing certain necessary structural changes.

4. *Does the modernized building fit into a well-conceived long-range plan?* There are situations in which a modernized building can be justified on all other counts. On a short-range basis it does provide for an immediate and predictable need. But a short-term perspective is sometimes costly where modernization is concerned. Let us illustrate this point. A northern Illinois school district was operating a single, centrally located high school enrolling about 1,000 students. The building was about 30 years old and in fairly good repair, but it was situated in the middle of the city on a site of about 4 acres. The site was hemmed in by business enterprises on three sides and was bounded by homes in the rear. The school district was confronted with the problem of providing space for an anticipated increase in enrollment of approximately 1,100 students within three years. The district had several alternatives: (1) it could change the grade organization so that it could house the lower level of the secondary school in the existing building with only a few modifications and construct a new building for the upper level on an adequate site; (2) it could sell the school for use as an office building and construct a single large high school on a site of about 30 acres located less than one-half mile from the existing school; or (3) it could modernize and expand the existing school.

After a great deal of controversy, the school district chose to modernize and expand the existing building. Although this action satisfied a number of criteria favoring modernization, it failed to pass the test of fitting into a plan designed to meet the long-range needs of the school district. Nevertheless, the adjoining block of houses was acquired by the board of education for the expansion of the school. This addition pushed the rear boundary of the site back to a railroad track which served as a major railroad trunk line.

Two years after the project was completed, it became obvious that the expanded school lacked sufficient capacity to house an additional 400 students. The board of education found itself in a dilemma. It did not feel that it could justify construction of a separate high school for this enrollment, but there was no free space on the already crowded $7^1/_2$-acre site to construct the needed facility. Furthermore, the board of education realized that the present site was already severely overloaded. It recognized, too, that it would be folly to add student capacity to an already inadequate site and simultaneously reduce its land area still further by placing another structure on it.

This unwelcome situation could have been avoided if the electorate had been better informed when the decision to modernize was made. At least two of the criteria for modernization discussed here were not met. Indeed, the site could not be expanded to the minimum size needed for the ultimate enrollment, and the modernized building did not fit into a long-range plan for the school district. Nonetheless, in this particular instance, the board of education recommended—and the electorate supported—the modernization and expansion of the original high school building.

5. *Can the site of the school considered for modernization be expanded to meet minimum standards for the ultimate enrollment envisioned on the site?* In the example cited in the previous section, it was clear that the school district had not developed a long-range plan to guide its action. But the modernization proposal would have been indefensible on the basis of site considerations alone. The original building housing about 1,000 students was situated on a 4-acre site. A $3^1/_2$-acre block was added to the original site. Consequently, the board recommended that a 2,100-student high school be situated on a $7^1/_2$-acre site. When it is realized that the board of education could have purchased about 30 acres of open farmland less than half a mile from the existing high school, the case for modernization is considerably weakened.

6. *In accordance with the Castaldi Generalized Formula, is the annual cost of capital outlay for modernization less than it would be for a replacement building?* Regardless of the purported value of an existing building or the initial cost of new construction, it is the rate of consumption of capital outlay funds that is significant in the choice between modernization and new construction. Figure 17-1 illustrates the application of balance to modernization.

7. *Has a blue-ribbon committee concluded that educational obsolescence of a given building can be substantially eliminated through the process of modernization?* A team consisting of the superintendent of schools, a member of the board of education, a qualified educational consultant, an architect, and a citizen selected by a group or person (mayor) outside of the school should be organized when a building is considered for modernization. This group should review, study, and discuss the educational aspects of the building, particularly its limitations, and then

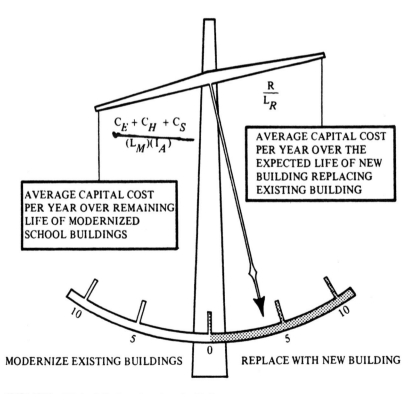

FIGURE 17-1 **Modernization in Balance**

decide whether or not it is *physically* possible to correct its educational shortcomings. The team should also make an estimate of I_A, the index of educational adequacy of a modernized building. This figure should then be substituted in the Castaldi Generalized Formula.

SEQUENTIAL STEPS IN PLANNING FOR SCHOOL FACILITY MODERNIZATION

As school districts develop, expand, and reach maturity, the cumulative investment of public funds for educational facilities becomes progressively larger. It is not long before this total dollar investment in school buildings by a school district over a period of years represents an enormous accumulation of capital assets. The dollar and cents value of this investment may be quite impressive from the position of an economist, but may look quite different from the standpoint of an educator. In a few cases, the educational value of this large capital investment may even be close to zero. This low educational assessment of capital expenditures occurs when the existing school plant is no longer capable of sustaining, reinforcing, and promoting an effective program of instruction.

In many instances, school buildings become outmoded only after 20 or 30 years of occupancy. A few become obsolete even sooner, particularly if they were not designed to accommodate foreseeable changes in future educational practices. In the natural course of events, however, obsolescence ultimately sets in. This phenomenon cannot be evaded or sidestepped in spite of the imaginative and advanced features that might have been built into a school building when it was conceived. The reason for this unavoidable outcome is quite clear. The educative process is inherently dynamic and is in a continual state of flux. School facilities, on the other hand, are rigid, fixed, and quasi-permanent. Thus, educators find themselves constantly trying to fit a changing educational activity into a static and immutable structure. As the gap between the needs of the educational program and the original design function of the building widens, it becomes more and more difficult to house the desired educational program in a building that was not planned for it. Consequently, in due time an existing school building becomes obsolete. Unfortunately, too many school buildings must be continued in operation even after they become obsolete because there is insufficient bonding capacity to replace them. This situation exists in many of the fast-growing school districts throughout the country. Hopefully, some of the suggestions presented in this chapter can help to remedy this situation at a reasonable cost.

The modernization of obsolete school buildings is perhaps one of the most controversial and difficult decisions confronting a board of education. The first basic question that must be answered is whether or not a given obsolete school facility should be remodeled or replaced. This question has already been discussed in this chapter. It must be stressed again that no decision should be made to modernize an obsolete school building until it has been demonstrated beyond any doubt that such modernization is in the best interest of the school district. The criteria set forth in the preceding section are developed to assist school plant planners and boards of education in arriving at a decision regarding this issue.

This discussion is intended primarily for those school districts that have come to a well-reasoned conclusion that the modernization of an obsolete school building is clearly warranted. In this connection, it should be mentioned that, in most cases, modernization of obsolete school facilities is not a wise expenditure of public funds. This rule is especially true in situations where a school district has a choice between modernization and replacement. A sound rule of thumb to bear in mind is, "When in doubt, do not modernize." In some instances, however, modernization of obsolete school buildings is justifiable and appropriate. The suggestions and procedures described in this chapter are therefore dedicated to the sound planning and design of such obsolete school buildings. In presenting the practical aspects of modernization, it is presumed that an obsolete school is needed in its present location, fits into a valid long-range plan, and has the potential of being transformed into a facility that is educationally and economically equivalent to a new building.

A Suggested Plan of Action

At the risk of being repetitious, it is strongly recommended that all persons involved in the consideration of whether or not to modernize an existing school facility concentrate heavily on Task Unit I, below. This is one task that deserves as much time as is required in order to arrive at the solution that is in the best interest of the school district. Take time, think clearly and objectively, and act logically.

Task Unit I: Can the Obsolete School Building Considered for Modernization Be Fully Justified Educationally, Structurally, Geographically, and Economically?

It is suggested that the section in this chapter entitled, "Requisite Conditions for Modernization" be reviewed and studied carefully. It is further suggested that each question be listed on a blank piece of paper and that the answers to each item be committed to writing by all persons contributing information related to the decision on whether or not to modernize a given building. At some point in the decision-making process, such persons should meet as many times as needed to share and exchange views on the issue. If the answer to any one of the first six questions is "no," the modernization issue requires further study and analysis. The findings of the "blue-ribbon" committee under question 7 should be given very serious consideration since this group recommendation is made by a majority of its members, representing citizens, school officials, experts, and the board of education, which, of course, must make the official decision on the issue. It should be mentioned that it is the people, except in some cities, that really make the final choice by supporting or not supporting a referendum authorizing funds for the modernization project.

A word of explanation regarding the answers to the questions on the modernization issue is in order at this point. A "no" answer to any one of the first six questions does not necessarily kill the project, but certainly places it in serious jeopardy. For example, if the site is inadequate and cannot be improved at a reasonable cost, it may still be advantageous to modernize an existing school facility, provided the "yes" answers to the other questions are preponderantly positive. Or, the modernization cost of an existing school may not be in the best financial interest of the school district according to the Castaldi Formula, but the school district may find itself in such financial straits that its bonding capacity is not sufficient to replace the building. Although modernization is not the ideal solution in this instance, the decision to modernize would be more in line with the financial capability of the school district.

The modernization of a school facility should not be ruled out *a priori*. It is well known among educators that modernization is often justifiable and in the best interest of the school district. On the other hand, a modernization project should not be undertaken until every facet of the problem is studied in depth. Such a study is required under Task Unit I. In conducting this study, it is important that the first six questions mentioned earlier be fully addressed and that the recommendation made by the "blue-ribbon committee," described under question 7, be positive and supportive of the modernization proposal. If, upon completion of this investigation, a decision is made to modernize an existing school facility, proceed to Task Unit II.

Task Unit II: Developing a Set of Ideal Educational Specifications

At this point in the planning process, it is assumed that the decision has been made to modernize a given building for a specified capacity and a stated grade grouping. For example, "The Jones Elementary School shall be modernized to serve 750 pupils in Grades 5 through 8." Once these two elements have been stipulated, educational planners should develop educational specifications for a school facility designed to house the desired educational program. Modernization should be temporarily disregarded. It should be stressed that one of the premises leading to a decision to modernize was that the modernized building would approximate the function of a new facility. In order to achieve this goal, it is essential that the educational specifications be exactly the same as those prepared for a new building. Obviously, compromise will need to be made in a later stage of the planning, but it is imperative that an ideal set of educational specifications be prepared at this stage.

It is suggested that the procedure described in Chapter 5 be reviewed and followed as much as possible. Information contained in Chapters 6, 12, 13, and 16 will also have a direct bearing on the preparation of educational specifications.

Task Unit III: Fitting Available Spaces in the Existing Building into the Ideal Educational Specifications

This is one of the most difficult and crucial steps in modernizing an existing school building. Obviously, the present structure does not contain very many spaces that conform to the educational specifications. If it did, the existing structure would not be considered obsolete. The major objective at this point in the planning is to search for the most effective use of existing spaces in relation to the spaces specified in the educational specifications prepared under Task Unit II. Before attempting to develop a variety of options designed to satisfy the educational specifications—more or less—it is suggested that the next section of this chapter, entitled "Practical Considerations in School Modernization," be read very carefully. This section provides helpful approaches designed to assist school plant planners in developing a multitude of options for consideration by the board of education.

Task Unit IV: Preparing a Revised Set of Educational Specifications

After completing the time-consuming procedure suggested under Task Unit II, the board of education is in a position to approve the combination of options that make the most effective use of existing spaces. Once these options are defined, the educational consultant or some designated school official should revise the original specifications and rewrite them in relation to the building to be modernized.

Let us cite an example illustrating the nature and type of revision.

"The ideal educational specifications for the learning resources center call for a total area of 7,000 square feet distributed as follows:

Reading area	3,500	sq. ft.
Librarian's office	250	" "
Librarian's workroom	300	" "
Audiovisual storage	500	" "
Audiovisual workroom	350	" "
Television workroom	350	" "
Television studio	750	" "
Self-instructional area	500	" "
Conference Room	500	" "

The present auditorium containing 5,000 square feet will be converted as part of the learning resources center. The three regular classrooms across the corridor from the present auditorium, together with the intervening corridor, will become part of the learning resources center. The architect will develop various schemes of this area incorporating the space relationships described in the ideal specifications. Existing walls may remain. Vision strips should be installed in all walls separating operational units in the learning resources center. Such vision strips shall be approximately 3 feet high. The bottom edge of the strip should be about 3 feet above the floor. Where vision strips cannot be installed, supervision will be conducted using closed-circuit television."

The instructions to the architect should be as flexible as possible. Specifics should be included only when they have educational significance. Otherwise, the architect should be given as much freedom as possible. For example, in the above illustration, the upper edge of the vision strip is specified at a level about 6 feet above the floor. There is a specific functional reason for this. It is extremely annoying when an obstruction is located in a vision strip at eye level. One finds oneself subconsciously either standing on tip toe trying to look over the obstruction or bending down to look under it. Such annoyance is not conducive to effective teaching or learning. The remedy is simple and not costly. Educationally important details should be clearly stated in the educational specifications. This is the only way that the architect will know what is desired.

Task Unit V: Architectural Planning of the Modernized Building

The revised educational specifications described in the previous section become the basic educational requirements which the architect will make every effort to satisfy. As plans develop, the architect will discover a large number of previously unknown obstacles. For example, he or she may find that a major waste line is imbedded in the wall that was scheduled for removal. As these problems arise, the consultant, school officials, and the architect will convene and discuss alternatives, arriving at the best resolution in each instance.

The general procedure from this stage to the awarding of the bids for a modernized building is similar to the one described in Chapter 5, beginning with step 10. It will be the responsibility of the consultant to make certain that the plans conform to the requirements stated in the educational specifications. From this standpoint, the consultant will be devoting far more time to a modernized building than to a new one. Under new construction, lines can be changed quickly and easily. In a modernized building, it is definitely more difficult to move or remove existing walls.

Task Unit VI: Generating Public Support

The importance of gaining public support for any school project has already been discussed in Chapter 5. There is no evidence showing that it is easier to win a bond referendum for modernization than it is for a new building. Whenever public funds are being expended, it can be anticipated that opposition to such expenditures will develop. The extent of such opposition, however, is unpredictable. It is therefore essential that early attention be given to the matter of public support.

It might be helpful to review the section in Chapter 5 dealing with public support and the strategies that might be used to develop a favorable attitude toward the project among the citizens. Unless this support can be generated prior to the referendum, the project may be doomed to failure.

PRACTICAL CONSIDERATIONS IN SCHOOL MODERNIZATION

The modernization of an existing school plant is far more complex and time-consuming than planning a new school building for the same educational program and capacity. The design, construction, and structural system of an existing school facility often impose serious physical constraints upon the architect. Some of these obstacles are frequently difficult, if not impossible, to overcome. To say that school modernization is a challenge to ingenuity of school plant planners is an under-statement of high order. The best that can be expected in the modernization of a school building is finding a solution that contains the lowest number of least harmful compromises. For this reason, school planners often develop several options that are designed to satisfy the educational specifications. In most cases, none of the options completely meet the requirements of the educational program. Con-sequently, choices are usually made so that each compromise solution has the smallest negative effect on the educational program. A number of guidelines are presented in this section to assist planners in the search for solutions that are least harmful to the educational function.

1. *The modernized school facility should be equivalent to a new building housing the same educational program.* When a decision is made by school officials to modernize an existing school building instead of replacing it with a new one, the implied assumption is that the modernized facility is equivalent to a new building that would be constructed to replace it. Very rarely do school officials feel that this equivalency cannot be achieved when the decision is made. The decision to mod-ernize is usually made in good faith with the full expectation that such equivalency is possible.

In the real world of planning, however, it is almost impossible to modernize an existing school building without making a number of significant compromises. The validity of this premise is well recognized by most school plant planners. Thus, the architect often presents several options to a board of education. It is suggested that the principle of "least educational compromise" be kept clearly in mind when choices are being made among a number of reasonable solutions to a modernization problem.

2. *The least costly conversion from one space use to another is one that requires only a change in room label.* In the interest of economy, school plant planners should actively seek out spaces that can be used effectively almost as they are, for one or more instructional purposes. There are frequently many spaces in an existing building that can be well utilized for functions different from those currently housed in them. For example, a large regular classroom can be used as a drafting room. A large typewriting room can be utilized for large-group instruction. A shop planning room can be converted to a room for small-group discussion. The educational specifications should be scanned to identify existing spaces that meet the physical requirements of the desired educational program.

Decisions of how to best utilize existing spaces, however, require extreme care and sound educational judgment. When the educational specifications are compared with the physical features of existing spaces, it is often quite possible to find a number of existing spaces that satisfy the size requirement stated in the specifications. Many of these properly sized spaces, however, cannot be used effectively in a modernized building, because they may not be well related to other spaces functionally associated with them. For example, the small-group discussion room mentioned in the preceding paragraph may be isolated at the end of a wing of a building. Thus, even though it meets all other criteria for a small-group discussion room, it lacks the proper functional relationship to other associated instructional activities.

On the other hand, it is frequently quite surprising to discover how many of the existing spaces can be utilized for other uses without making any major changes in the spaces. Oftentimes, when two or three spaces in a given area of an existing building are remodeled and converted to specialized uses, they may be surrounded by a cluster of spaces that could be adapted for functions associated with the remodeled area. In some instances, these related spaces may be adequate and suitable as they are. Consequently, the decision of which rooms to remodel in an existing building becomes quite crucial. It is important, therefore, to look for clusters of spaces that are logically associated with the spaces considered for major modernization. This precaution could result in substantial savings through a more efficient utilization of existing spaces.

3. *The conversion of existing large spaces into smaller ones can be financially rewarding.* It is frequently advantageous to subdivide a large space in an existing building into smaller ones. Obviously, any space, large or small, that can be utilized effectively in its original location and design should be continued in operation with minimal changes. There are many instances, however, when existing large spaces are no longer adequate, suitable, or needed in their present form. Oftentimes, such spaces are replaced by new additions to the modernized structure. Consequently, there are situations when a large existing space can be considered for new educational uses.

The subdivision of large spaces into effective smaller instructional areas is an important aspect of school modernization. The multitude of potential uses of large spaces presents a wide variety of exciting options in the redesigned version of a modernized school building. In order to explore a large number of possibilities, it is suggested that the total usable area of each existing large space destined for conversion be determined and recorded, and that the total area included in each cluster of related spaces be computed from an analysis of the educational specifications. All clusters that contain areas approximating the areas of the various large spaces should be given further study. School plant planners should prepare several options in which combinations of related functions can be housed in existing large spaces. Each combination should then be evaluated in terms of educational effectiveness, considering both the advantages and disadvantages of each proposed use of available space.

There are a few common uses of large spaces that are worthy of note. They are mentioned only as ideas that will hopefully suggest many other possible solutions to local school planners. An obsolete assembly hall, for example, has a number of possible uses. It can be converted into a library on two levels. The lower level might contain bookshelves, together with carrels, a librarian's office and workroom, a television center, and an audiovisual center. The second level could be designed as a mezzanine for expanded library services. It may be possible to include remedial rooms for speech, reading, and mathematics on the mezzanine level, with direct entry to such spaces from the second-floor level in a two-story building. This same large space could be converted into a two-story classroom area. A 6,000-square-foot assembly hall, for example, could be converted into approximately ten classrooms, five rooms on each floor. It may be possible to use certain large spaces for one or more clusters of related specialized rooms, such as science, homemaking, art, and business programs. Large spaces can also be subdivided into offices for administration, health, guidance, and faculty work stations (offices).

Sometimes one large space function can be substituted for another. For example, an outmoded gymnasium with a relatively high ceiling (20′–22′) could easily be converted to a sloping floor auditorium, particularly if it was originally designed as a gymnasium-auditorium with a stage and proscenium opening. Cafeterias can frequently be converted into multisized teaching areas for large-group–small-group instruction through the ingenious use of interlocking movable partitions. Shop areas are usually large, single-story, high-ceiling enclosures. If these areas become available, it is often advantageous to consider using these spaces for specialized classrooms that require water, gas, and electricity. The functions that might be most appropriate for these areas are homemaking, art, drafting, business programs, and science. In school districts that provide student-activity-type facilities, a properly located large space can often be converted into spaces for student lounge, quiet study areas, television viewing areas, and small film projection viewing rooms. These facilities are essential in secondary schools where the open-campus concept is embraced by the school philosophy. Under this concept, students are free to leave the campus whenever they are not in scheduled class activities. In some instances, students do not leave the campus but congregate in the corridors and lobbies when no other facilities are available. Under these circumstances, the corridors become sources of distracting noise and teachers have found it difficult to conduct classes in adjoining classrooms. Consequently, when the open-campus concept is adopted, student activity centers are basic to the success of the plan.

4. *Housing large-space functions in a cluster of small spaces.* Although it is much simpler to convert a large space into a number of smaller ones, it is sometimes possible to house large-space functions within a constellation of smaller spaces. The learning resources center function is one that can often be accommodated in a cluster of smaller spaces. Let us illustrate the application of this concept by citing an example. In this illustration, it is assumed that the educational specifications call for 5,000 square feet of space for the learning resources center. What is needed in this instance is essentially a 5,000-square-foot block of spaces that can become a self-contained operational unit of the school. This large block of space might be located at the end of a wing or it might occupy a major part of one floor level in an existing building. If such an isolated area cannot be found, it may be possible to remodel the existing building slightly to create this condition. Normally, a 5,000-square-foot block of space in an existing school building contains several classrooms, a small storage room or two, a main corridor, and possibly toilet areas. The boundaries of this block of spaces should be clearly outlined on a plan of the existing building in pencil or ink. Hopefully, in designing the learning resources area, this main corridor can be "dead-ended" and become an integral part of the learning resources center. Entrance to one end of this center can be gained from the terminus of the remaining corridors through a set of doors at that point. In this situation, it is not necessary to remove entire walls to create the feeling of a library. It may be advantageous to simply install vision strips in the intervening walls so that the bottom of the vision strip is about 3 feet above the floor. The height of the top of the vision strip should be not less than 6 feet above the floor. Such vision strips provide visual coherence to the area and simplify supervision of the area. Obviously, it may not be possible to install such strips in all walls because of the location of utility pipes and wires in some partitions. Closed-circuit television can be utilized for supervision in these instances. In spaces where privacy is needed at certain times, it is a simple and inexpensive matter to install draw-curtains across the vision strips. If double glazing is used on the vision strips, each cubicle or room can be acoustically insulated from adjoining spaces, thus making it possible to use different audiovisual materials for group viewing in adjoining rooms.

In some existing buildings it might be possible to convert classrooms, corridors, and small storage spaces into a cafeteria. If a sufficiently large block of space could be found with one end of it easily accessible to the service drive of the school, it might be feasible to convert this block of space to cafeteria uses. The cafeteria effect can be created through the judicious use of vision strips. There may be some decided aesthetic and functional advantage in using a series of smaller spaces in contrast to the usual institutional-type cafeteria. Special attention should be given to the circulation patterns established under this concept. Generally, classrooms already have two means of egress. These can be incorporated into the traffic flow pattern of the cafeteria function, which would be housed in a series of adjoining spaces.

5. *From the standpoint of cost and structural considerations, the removal of load-bearing partitions should be kept to the absolute minimum.* In school buildings constructed prior to World War II, many of the interior walls of the building were load bearing. This was particularly true of the walls on both sides of the main corridor. In addition to being load bearing, these corridor walls were also constructed of fire-resistant materials. The question is frequently asked as to whether or not a load-bearing wall can be removed. In some instances, it can be removed entirely; in others, it can be eliminated only partially. Technically, walls can be removed and a new structural system can be substituted for the original wall in most situations. Indeed, all this can be accomplished, but usually at an enormous cost to the owner. Is such a tremendous cost justifiable? Not very often. These high costs can be supported only in rare cases where no other alternative is possible.

As a practical matter, therefore, it is suggested that the removal of load-bearing interior partitions be avoided as much as possible. Vision strips or closed-circuit television, as described in the preceding section, often solve the problem of visual contact very inexpensively. Nonbearing partitions, of course, do not present serious structural problems, except when utility pipes are located within them. The cost of removing nonbearing walls is often quite reasonable and justifiable. When vision strips do not serve an educational function, the cost of removing a non-load-bearing partition should be compared with the cost of installing a vision strip. In some instances, it could actually be less expensive to tear down the wall, remove the rubble from the premises, and patch the ceiling, floor, and walls than it would be to install a vision strip.

6. *If the modernized building is to be expanded, it might be advantageous to plan large and specialized spaces under the new construction.* There are many reasons why existing school buildings become obsolete. The rooms may be too small for modern educational practices. There may be no provision for water, electricity, or gas in certain areas. The space for physical education may be too small. There may be no suitable space in which to install automated instructional equipment. Most often, however, the reason that school buildings are considered obsolete stems from the absence of adequate and suitable specialized classrooms and the lack of sufficiently large spaces for large-group activities such as assembly and physical education. Frequently, spaces that were originally designed for specialized uses can no longer support the more sophisticated teaching practices that require more space and more advanced equipment. These deficiencies must be taken into account during the modernization process. Consequently, the plans of the modernized facility must contain design elements that correct such deficiencies.

When modernization also includes new construction, it is often financially rewarding to locate specialized classrooms and large-space functions within the new construction. The benefits resulting from this suggestion are twofold. Since many of the specialized spaces in the original building are usually nothing more than oversized classrooms, it is educationally sound to use these existing spaces as regular classrooms. Also, most of these spaces can be used without any appreciable expenditure of capital outlay. In many instances, the conversion of a former specialized space to a regular classroom requires simply changing the label on the door. This type of modernization is inexpensive and educationally sound. The reason for including large-space activities under new construction, however, is usually more a matter of necessity than choice. Generally speaking, there are usually no spaces within an obsolete building that can be expanded or converted into suitable large-space use. For this reason, many additions to school buildings frequently include a gymnasium, an auditorium, and a cafeteria. Of these three, the gymnasium is the space that is most often included in new construction.

7. *Rehabilitation of obsolete school buildings.* It is important to bear in mind that obsolete school buildings have often been occupied for several decades. After this long period of time, it is highly probable that the electrical, mechanical, plumbing, and heating systems in the building will require special attention when the building is modernized. It is also anticipated that there will be a certain amount of deferred annual maintenance that can be dealt with at the same time.

As mentioned earlier in this chapter, modernization is comprehensive in scope. It includes both remodeling and rehabilitation. Several aspects of remodeling have already been discussed in the preceding six sections. Rehabilitation alone does not produce a modernized building. It simply brings the physical plant to the same level of appearance and function that it possessed when the building was occupied for the first time. Thus, when a building constructed in 1940 is rehabilitated in 1985, it improves physically but not educationally. It is the combination of remodeling and rehabilitation that transforms an obsolete school building to one that is aesthetically pleasing, mechanically functional, and educationally effective.

Rehabilitation is primarily concerned with the restoration of the physical plant to its original condition. Consequently, all spaces and equipment within a school building are subject to rehabilitation, regardless of whether or not it was remodeled. Ceilings and walls may need to be repaired or replaced. Floors may require resurfacing. Lighting fixtures may need to be replaced with more efficient units. Interior surfaces will undoubtedly need to be cleaned and redecorated. Masonry must be examined for evidence of deterioration, and corrective measures must be taken. Plumbing fixtures may be in need of repair or replacement. The heating system may be obsolete and inefficient. There may be a need to change from one form of heating energy to another because of changes in the cost of various sources of energy, such as gas, oil, coal, and electricity. Ventilation equipment may require new motors and control systems. These are only a few of the many items that could be included under rehabilitation. In rare cases, the total cost of rehabilitation may well exceed that of remodeling. The writer has observed on several occasions involving modernization that members of boards of education were frequently surprised to learn that the cost of rehabilitation was sometimes as high as 40 percent of the cost of modernization. This is especially true when the architect is trying to bring the level of the modernized building up to the standards of a new building.

Remodeling without rehabilitation leaves much to be desired. Although the educational function of certain spaces will be improved, the general atmosphere within the school may not be conducive to effective learning. The cost of rehabilitation varies over a wide range. In school districts where there is a systematic program of maintenance and upgrading, the cost of rehabilitating an obsolete school building is relatively small. Unfortunately, when a school district must operate within budgetary cutbacks, funds for maintenance are among the first to be deleted from the budget. As a result, the cost of rehabilitation rises in direct proportion to the amount of deferred maintenance accumulated over a number of years. In spite of these situations, every effort should be made to fully rehabilitate a building that is scheduled for modernization. To do less means that the modernized building is not equivalent to a new structure that could have replaced it.

NOTES

1. Allen C. Abend, Michael Bednar, Vera J. Froelinger, Yale Stenzler, *Facilities for Special Education Services* (Reston, VA: The Council for Exceptional Children, 1979).

2. Henry Linn, "Modernizing School Buildings," *American School and University,* v. 24 (1952), p. 401.

3. Effective depreciation includes both educational adequacy and capital outlay.

▶ 18

Maintenance
and Operation

School officials and boards of education have realized for a long time that the construction and operation of a school building involve a substantial expenditure of public funds. The investment for construction represents only the initial cost of a school facility. Operational costs for power, maintenance, and custodial staff become an important item in the annual budget. The sequence of events is quite familiar to all educators. Once the building is completed, the keys are turned over to school officials. Power and fuel are supplied to the building and, for the first time, are charged directly to the school district as school expenses. The switches are activated, and the building—hopefully—provides a comfortable and inspiring environment for learning. Ideally, once energized, all systems and equipment should operate flawlessly. In practice, this situation almost never occurs. In most cases, there is a "shake-down" period when all equipment and controls are adjusted, rebalanced, or replaced. In due time, however, the new or modernized building becomes operative and begins to fulfill its intended purpose.

As soon as the teachers, students, administrators, and physical plant staff begin to function normally within the spaces specifically designed for them, the building is said to be "operational." This is the point in the life of a school building when the aging process sets in. The materials and surfaces of the structure begin to deteriorate very slowly, and each piece of mechanical equipment starts to wear out at its own predictable rate. The aging process is natural, universal, and inevitable. It cannot be eliminated. For this reason, a well-conceived program of maintenance is an integral part of the daily operation of a school building. The details concerning the development of such a program are presented in this chapter. A number of promising practices dealing with the periodic care and maintenance of school buildings are also included in this chapter.

Several publications have been prepared on the routine maintenance of school buildings. They contain a large number of details pertaining to a wide variety of daily housekeeping duties normally performed in a school building. A discussion of these matters is not within the scope of this book. Consequently, this chapter will deal primarily with the major concepts of school building maintenance covered in such texts. One of the earliest publications in this field was entitled *Housekeeping Handbook,* written by Dr. Henry H. Linn at Columbia University.[1]

There is no scarcity of custodial handbooks. Many of the larger school districts and most departments of education publish handbooks for custodians for the purpose of prolonging the life of a building and improving the environment for learning. Several custodial handbooks describe the work of the custodian in meticulous detail. As indicated earlier, a discussion of such details does not fall within the scope of this text. However, the availability of such practical information fulfills a basic need for the custodial work force. With such information in hand, the custodian is well armed to cope with extraordinary janitorial situations or unforeseen building emergencies.

Two recent publications on building maintenance and management might be of interest to school business administrators and school building personnel. They contain essential technical information on newly developed materials and outline procedures for minimizing the operational costs of buildings. The Association of School Business Officials has published a manual for school business officials dealing with a wide variety of topics and procedures related to school building maintenance and operations.[2] A second publication was sponsored by the National Research Council, which is affiliated with the National Academy of Sciences.[3] Although this report was prepared by a committee of experts selected to review maintenance and operations activities of governmental agencies, the findings from this study apply equally well to school buildings. The report contains a wealth of technical information on the maintenance of buildings and offers a number of recommendations aimed at improving the management and operational efficiency of buildings.

Dr. O. Barker Harrison prepared a comprehensive handbook for custodians dealing with both building maintenance and the care of mechanical controls and devices in a school building. According to Harrison,

> The school custodian is co-responsible with the principal for a building worth many thousands of dollars, its care and operation, and indirectly responsible for the priceless lives of hundreds of children and their teachers, as their lives relate to the proper operation of the school plant.[4]

The great contribution made by physical plant personnel in maintaining a comfortable and healthful environment in a school building is rarely recognized by school officials, boards of education, and the general public. Admittedly, the work of the school custodian is physical, time-consuming, and not particularly glamourous. Nevertheless, an alert and knowledgeable custodian can save the school district thousands of dollars in future maintenance costs by paying attention to the "little things," such as water leaks, lubrication of equipment, erosion of soils adjacent to the building, excessive condensation of humidity around cold pipes, and replacement of defective temperature controls.

The men and women in the physical plant work force also play an important part in the educational function of the school. It is these men and women who provide and maintain an environment that is conducive to effective learning. And they do all this without interfering with the educational process. These dedicated people do most of their work after the teachers and students have left the building for the day or before they return to it in the morning. This often unseen work force performs an indispensable service that benefits the students, teachers, administrators, clerical personnel, and the taxpayers. It is this group of people that improves learning by providing a proper environment and saves the taxpayers thousands of dollars over the life of a school building by giving immediate and prompt attention to the little things before they become big and costly problems.

THE ROLE OF CENTRAL ADMINISTRATION IN OPERATION AND MAINTENANCE

The central administration of a school district has an important part to play in the operation and maintenance of all of the school buildings within its jurisdiction. It develops district-wide policies concerning the working conditions of physical plant personnel, their rate of pay, fringe benefits, and other forms of compensation. It sets work standards and procedures that are implemented by the individual school principals. And it develops instructions designed to help the entire physical plant staff to better preserve and maintain the school buildings to which they are assigned. But, according to Glass, one more ingredient should be added to the maintenance menu—commitment. He points out that, "A good facility maintenance program *requires* commitment from board, administration, staff and community that maintenance of district facilities is a high priority and must be provided each year with adequate funding."[5]

Determining the Size of the Work Force

The central administration of a school district has the basic responsibility of making certain that custodial personnel are not being overworked. It also has an obligation to the taxpayers of the school district to keep the number of personnel at a minimum. There are currently several rules of thumb that can be used to compute the number of custodians normally required in a given school building. Any one of them could be used to determine the theoretical custodial staffing required in a school. One of the nationally accepted methods, known as the "factoring formula," is presented in this section. Although this rule of thumb is completely empirical, it does give the superintendent of schools or his or her assistants a valuable point of departure. In applying the formula, one should bear in mind that there may indeed be situations where the conditions within a particular school building make it necessary to assign more personnel to it than the formula would indicate. For example, the building may be old and hard to keep clean and maintain, or it may be a new building that is severely overcrowded and used more hours per day than is customary. On the other hand, any staffing in existing school buildings that deviates substantially—too high or too low—from the theoretical staffing computation described previously should be studied and justified by the central administration. If the present staffing is too low compared to the theoretical result, the custodial staff is probably overloaded and relief for them should be sought. On the other hand, if the present staffing exceeds the theoretical need, such additional personnel should be justified on the basis of extenuating circumstances. If this cannot be done, the excessive staff should be reassigned to school buildings where staff deficiencies may exist. A work sheet for implementing the factoring formula is presented in Table 18-1.

There is another rule of thumb for determining the number of needed cleaning personnel, which is simpler and not as analytical as the factoring formula. According to this unsophisticated approach, the number of cleaning personnel needed is simply one cleaning person for each eight or nine teachers assigned to the school building. The weaknesses inherent in this formula are obvious. It disregards student load, which contributes directly to the work of the custodian. It ignores the condition, number, and size of teaching areas in the school. It does not take into account the size of the school site and school walks. And it makes no provision for the amount of custodial work required due to the overall size of the building. In spite of these shortcomings, this formula does offer a simple first approximation to the staffing need in a given building.

In addition to adjusting the custodial staff load for each school building, the central administration can also utilize information regarding the number of physical plant personnel needed in each building for purposes of planning, budgeting, and reassignment of custodians within the school district. If a study of custodial needs within the total school district reveals that the number of existing staff is too small, the central administration has two options. It may choose to employ additional custodians to correct the overloaded conditions. Or, if funds are not available for additional staff, it can reassign personnel among the various schools in order to distribute the overload equitably among all of the custodians on the work force.

Selection of Custodial Personnel

The central administration establishes the qualifications for hiring custodial personnel. It conducts the search for qualified candidates for existing vacancies, and sets up a screening procedure to identify the best candidates. In many school districts,

TABLE 18-1 **Worksheet for Estimating Custodial Staffing Using the Factoring Formula**

Factor 1	Number of teaching stations* divided by 11.		
	$\dfrac{\text{(No. of T.S.) (\quad)}}{11}$ = _____		Line 1
Factor 2	Number of teachers divided by 8.		
	$\dfrac{\text{(No. of Teachers) (\quad)}}{8}$ = _____		Line 2
Factor 3	Building capacity divided by 25.		
	$\dfrac{\text{(Bldg. Capacity) (\quad)}}{25}$ = _____		Line 3
Factor 4	Gross area of building divided by 15,000.		
	$\dfrac{\text{(Bldg. Area) (\quad)}}{15,000}$ = _____		Line 4
Factor 5	Area of site in acres divided by 2.		
	$\dfrac{\text{(Site in Acres) (\quad)}}{2}$ = _____		Line 5
Factorial Sum	(Add Lines 1–5) _____		Line 6
Final Computation of Staff Need	Divide Factorial Sum by 5.		
	$\dfrac{\text{(Enter Line 6) (\quad)}}{5}$ = _____		Custodians Needed
		(Round off to next higher whole number.)	

*A teaching station is equivalent to about 900 square feet in which teaching is conducted. Divide area of gymnasium floor by 1,000 to determine the number of teaching stations for it.

the final selection is made jointly by the central administration and the school principal where the vacancy exists.

Qualifications. School districts should develop a set of job qualifications tailored for their particular situation. Some districts may have special needs, such as the requirement of custodians to be bilingual. There are, however, a number of qualifications that would apply to most school districts. These are presented below in outline form for the purpose of assisting local school districts in preparing their own job specifications for custodial positions. The set of qualifications given below contains items that would apply to most school districts. This list should be revised, expanded, or shortened according to the specific requirements of a given school district.[6] Hopefully, it will serve to suggest other pertinent qualifications.

The candidate:

1. should be physically capable of performing duties required by the position.
2. should be of good moral character, clean habits, and clean speech.
3. should possess sufficient ability to carry out duties in an intelligent manner.
4. should at least be able to read and write and should have a ninth-grade education.
5. must be free from communicable diseases and should be free from chronic disturbances that could cause him or her to be absent from the job excessively.
6. shall present a neat, clean appearance.
7. should be dependable, and able to get along with people—teachers, principal, and patrons.
8. should be orderly and willing to learn new techniques for housekeeping.
9. must be able to plan and organize his or her work and the work of the staff, and to supervise the efforts of the staff in the proper housekeeping of the plant.
10. should be even-tempered and possess a good disposition.

Maintenance and Operation Budget

In addition to staffing, the central administration is responsible for providing funds for custodial supplies, cleaning and maintenance equipment, normal wear and tear of mechanical equipment, and preventive maintenance. Unfortunately, these are usually items of low priority in the school budget. It is true, of course, that when funds are limited, these expenditures can often be deferred without penalizing the educational function of the school. But this relief is only temporary. Sometimes the cost of deferral is much greater than providing the funds when they can do the most good. For example, it may be possible to postpone the replacement of boiler tubes for a year or two on the premise that "we'll just have to make do." In the meantime, the school district will be spending more money for fuel because the old tubes are not as efficient as new ones in transmitting heat from the combustion chamber to the water or steam flowing through the tubes. Thus, in the long run, the school district is paying a penalty for such a postponement.

Procurement and Use of Custodial Supplies. In this connection, the central administration has two major responsibilities. The first one, obviously, is to include sufficient funds in the school budget to purchase custodial supplies. The second, and equally important, obligation on the part of central administration is to make certain that the most efficient and least damaging cleaning agents are provided for each school building in the district. Some person in the central staff should be charged with the responsibility of conducting the necessary study and research regarding the proper selection and appropriate use of various maintenance supplies and cleaning agents. The importance of this task cannot be overstated. For example, one coat of ordinary paint over an acoustical plaster ceiling can destroy most of its sound-absorbing capability. The daily or prolonged use of abrasive powders on glazed materials, stainless steel, and chromium-plated fixtures can permanently damage their surfaces. The application of acid solutions on ceramic-tiled floors tends to weaken the mortar joints between each tile unless the floor is sealed perfectly. Consequently, the improper use of cleaning agents can be very costly to a school district over a period of time.

The selection and proper use of cleaning agents is usually the responsibility of the superintendent of buildings or the director of plant operations in large school districts. In the smaller school districts, however, this function is often delegated to the head custodian of the building. Obviously, the superintendent of schools in these small school districts cannot be expected to conduct the necessary study and research pertaining to the selection and use of cleaning agents. The best protection for the school district, in these cases, is to employ a high-level, well-trained, and well-paid head custodian with at least 10 years of experience in a large school district working under the supervision of a director of physical plant.

Hiring a competent custodian, however, does not completely solve the maintenance problems of the small school district. The superintendent of schools in such districts cannot afford to give a low priority to the maintenance and care of school facilities on the grounds that he or she simply does not have time for it. Admittedly, time is limited and other duties are more pressing. There are a few measures that the superintendent can take, however. He or she can make arrangements with counterparts in the larger school districts in the area to have the head custodian participate in training sessions held in the large school districts; purchase approved lists of cleaning agents researched and prepared by the larger school districts; and, finally, obtain a copy of a custodian's handbook from one or two of the larger school districts at a nominal cost. Armed with this material, the school superintendent in a small school district can feel fairly secure in the choice and proper use of cleaning agents, if he or she has selected an experienced and competent head custodian trained to use them appropriately.

Although it is simply good business to procure custodial supplies through a central purchasing office, care should be exercised to make certain that the needs of each building are reflected in the unified purchasing process. Centralization does not imply uniformity of need in each building in the school district. Each building should be considered unique regarding the type and amount of supplies. There are, to be sure, a wide variety of supplies common to all buildings. There are a few supplies that are needed in all buildings but in different quantities depending upon the age, size, and type of construction of the building, and there are certain supplies that may be peculiar to a given school building. For example, a school building that uses energy pumps for heating and cooling may require a small supply of refrigerant to recharge the system, while other buildings may have no need for such material.

Normal Wear and Tear of Mechanical Equipment

Seldom, if ever, does one find a school district that has been able to set aside funds in advance to replace all equipment that is completely worn out through normal use. The practice of establishing reserve funds for equipment depreciation is commonly found in business. It is a financially sound policy. In many states, however, school districts are prevented by law from establishing reserve funds. This may be the reason why school districts have generally not become involved in reserve or sinking funds commonly found in business.

Nevertheless, it is both economically sound and financially wise to anticipate the replacement of sometimes costly equipment. If each piece of equipment were classified in terms of its normal life expectancy, it would be possible to determine its rate of depreciation in terms of dollars per year. Then, it would be relatively simple to determine the total cost of depreciation for mechanical equipment each year. If this amount of money, representing the total cost of depreciation, could be placed in a reserve fund, all of the mechanical equipment owned by the school district could be replaced when it was no longer operable. This practice would apply to items such as water circulators, motors in the ventilating system, motor vehicles, power equipment, fuel burners, electric resistance-type heaters, vacuum cleaners, machine scrubbers, typewriters, business machines, and photocopiers. If this practice were instituted, the tax levy each year would include a proportional amount of money for equipment replacement. Thus, the cost of replacing mechanical equipment would be spread over the expected life of the item, rather than having the entire cost of such items fall upon the taxpayers in a single year.

If laws prohibit the establishment of reserve funds for equipment depreciation, every effort should be made to have them changed. If business finds this practice sound and in its own best long-range interest, it would seem reasonable and proper that public agencies be allowed to engage in the same healthy fiscal practice.

It might be possible, even under existing laws, to develop a program of planned replacement. It is suggested that the rate of depreciation be determined for each mechanical item and that the total annual cost of depreciation be computed for the entire school district. The next step in this suggested process is to examine the condition of each piece of mechanical equipment and set forth the cost of equipment that needs to be replaced or will require replacement sometime during the next fiscal year. Find the total cost of equipment that should be replaced. Compare this total replacement cost with the total annual cost of depreciation. If they are approximately equal, simply include the cost of equipment replacement in the budget. If the cost of depreciation is greater than the total replacement cost, include at least the replacement cost in the budget. This type of imbalance occurs whenever replacement of worn equipment has been deferred in the past. Under the reserve plan practiced by business, this circumstance would never occur because the accumulated reserves would balance out the cases where the cost of replacement would exceed the total annual depreciation figure.

The above suggestion does not solve the depreciation problem. It simply eases it by focusing attention on the need for replacing mechanical equipment on an annual basis. Through this procedure, there would be an opportunity to include funds for equipment replacement each year on a systematic basis. Without this approach, or one like it, school districts would find themselves replacing worn crucial equipment from time to time on an emergency basis. Mechanical equipment of lower priority would probably be continued in use at a high maintenance cost to the school district. Such practice is certainly not prudent from the standpoint of economic efficiency. It represents an unnecessary waste of public funds. It can be corrected only when educators make responsible legislators aware of the situation.

THE ROLE OF THE SCHOOL PRINCIPAL IN OPERATION AND MAINTENANCE

The school principal is the key person in the school district responsible for the operation and maintenance of the school building to which he or she is assigned. The principal is the direct operational supervisor of all physical plant personnel assigned to the building. In some school districts, the custodian has a dual administrative responsibility. He or she reports to the school principal for all functional matters associated with the operation and maintenance of the assigned school building and is accountable to central administration for all technical matters related to his or her work. For example, the custodian may be responsible to the principal for scrubbing a certain classroom floor at a given time on a specified day, but may be responsible to the central office staff for the type of cleaning agents used and the procedures to be followed. Thus, he or she is functionally responsible to the principal and technically responsible to the central administration. These two responsibilities are compatible, easily differentiated, and administratively consistent.

Custodial Obligations

In the daily operation of a school building, the principal can reasonably expect that the custodian will fulfill these requirements:[7]

1. Have a knowledge of the principles of heating, ventilating, sanitation, and care of school buildings.
2. Have a knowledge of the best tools, materials, cleaning agents, and methods to use in various phases of custodial work.
3. Have a knowledge of the correct use of mechanical equipment of school buildings.

4. Have skill in using proper tools, materials, cleaning agents, and methods of procedure for the different kinds of custodial jobs under various conditions.
5. Possess a scientific attitude toward the study of various phases of custodial services, in order to effect the greatest efficiency and economy of time and energy.
6. Possess attitudes that will lead to serious, wholehearted, and unselfish attention to the duties of custodial service.
7. Possess attitudes that make for harmonious cooperation with students and with the administrative, educational, and custodial forces.
8. Have ideas of what constitutes good custodial service and of the importance of the service to both the educational work of the school and the protection of the school property.
9. Have an appreciation of beauty, harmony, and cleanliness in and about the school grounds.

Maintenance and Operational Responsibilities of the Custodial Staff

The school principal has the right to expect his or her custodial force to perform the duties listed below. They are presented in two groups. The first category deals with tasks related to the maintenance of the school building. The second group includes routine operational responsibilities subdivided into three classifications—daily operations, weekly operations, and periodic operations. The principal may hold the custodians responsible for the performance of these tasks.

   A. *Maintenance responsibilities*[8]
      1. Replace broken door and window glass.
      2. Make minor repairs to locks, hinges, door closers, etc.
      3. Repair and adjust faulty window shades.
      4. Keep stair handrails tightly in place.
      5. Make minor repairs to students' and teachers' lockers.
      6. Replace faulty lamps, fuses, etc.
      7. Keep all fire-fighting equipment securely in place.
      8. Maintain towel racks, soap dispensers, and tissue racks.
      9. Maintain students' and teachers' furniture.
      10. Render minor repairs to heating and plumbing equipment.
      11. Make minor repairs to playground equipment.
      12. Repair or replace pencil sharpeners as needed.
      13. Lubricate heating and ventilating fixtures.
      14. Paint rusting and corroding metal surfaces with inhibitors in small areas. Report large-scale rusting or corrosion to the principal.
      15. Correct minor leak problems and report major leaks to the principal.

B. *Operational responsibilities*
  1. Daily operations
     a. Display the flag as weather permits.
     b. Clean and dust all classroom areas.
     c. Clean and dust all administrative areas.
     d. Clean and dust all stairway and corridor areas.
     e. Clean and service all restroom areas.
     f. Clean chalkboards and erasers.
     g. Service all entrances, walks, and drives as weather permits.
     h. Clean and service physical education and auditorium areas.
     i. Inspect and service playground equipment.
     j. Dispose of trash, waste, and ashes.
     k. Clean and care for custodial rooms, supplies, etc.
     l. Clean and service heating plant area.
     m. Clean drinking fountains.
  2. Weekly Operations
     a. Clean or dust doors and door glass.
     b. Spot clean soiled floor and wall area.
     c. Clean restroom walls, doors, and partitions.
     d. Polish floor areas as assigned or scheduled.
     e. Clean inside glass as assigned or scheduled.
     f. Clean furniture as assigned or scheduled.
  3. Periodic Operations
     a. Clean, finish, and polish floor areas.
     b. Clean window glass inside and outside.
     c. Clean or dust window shades.
     d. Clean ceiling, walls, bulletin boards, and trim.
     e. Clean lighting and heating fixtures.
     f. Care for yard and ground area.
     g. Inspect and clean storage areas.
     h. Attend to custodial maintenance functions listed under section A.

TIME STANDARDS, SCHEDULING, AND DESCRIPTION OF CUSTODIAL DUTIES

The general duties of the custodial force were listed in outline form in the preceding section. No reference was made to the allocation of these tasks among the custodial work force, nor to the operational features of a care and maintenance program for a given school building. In order to accomplish this task, it is necessary to make a job analysis of the individual custodial tasks together with the time required to complete each one of them.

Time Standards for Selected Custodial Tasks

It is helpful to both the principal and the head custodian to know how much time is normally required to complete a number of specific custodial tasks. It is also important to establish the frequency with which these jobs must be repeated in maintaining a high level of custodial services. Table 18-2 contains a list of jobs normally performed by most custodians assigned to a school building. It also includes the frequency of each task and the time normally required to perform it.

Custodial Work Load

The time standards and frequency with which each task is to be repeated form the basis for determining a reasonable work load for the custodian. In developing a custodial work schedule, it should be remembered that the time standards listed in Table 18-2 do not include preparation time. For example, the time required to mop and rinse a 900-square-foot classroom is 40 minutes. Additional time is required by the custodian to fill a water bucket, add detergent to it, place the container with the cleaning agent back on the shelf, locate the mop, and carry these materials from the custodial closet to the classroom. The time standard of 40 minutes does not include the time necessary for the custodian to return to the custodial closet, clean the mop(s), dispose of the dirty water, and rinse out the buckets. Depending upon the location of the custodial closet with respect to the classroom, the additional time required could easily be 10 percent higher than the standards would indicate. It should also be borne in mind that it takes the custodian time to reach the custodial closet from some other part of the building. Thus, the time standards should be used judiciously. They serve as starting points. The other conditions related to each task should be taken into account and the time requirement should be adjusted accordingly.

Custodial Work Schedule

The schedule of work for each custodian should be structured so that it interferes minimally with the educational function. Custodial tasks are dovetailed with the instructional uses of the building. For example, classrooms can be dusted and swept before school, after school, and when they are not in use during the school day. For this reason, some school systems stagger the hours on which the custodians report for work. In general, most of the custodians are on duty at the close of the school day when the bulk of the cleaning tasks can be accomplished.

Barker Harrison has developed a sample daily schedule that could be adapted in many school buildings.[9] This example applies to a school building employing a head custodian, a helper, and a maid. This building would house 20 to 25 secondary school teachers and serve between 550 and 600 students depending upon the grade

TABLE 18-2 **Time Normally Required to Complete Selected Custodial Tasks**

Task	Frequency	Time Required
Classroom (Assumed area of 900 square feet)		
a. Dusting	Daily	5 min. per rm.
b. Sweeping	Daily	12 min. per rm.
c. Damp mopping	As needed	23 min. per rm.
d. Wet mop and rinse	As needed	40 min. per rm.
e. Machine scrubbing	As needed	25 min. per rm.
f. Machine polishing	As needed	15 min. per rm.
g. Wet vacuum pickup	As needed	14 min. per rm.
Servicing classroom	Daily	15 min. per rm.
a. Removing waste paper		
b. Sweeping floor with treated mop		
c. Dusting chalk tray, window sills, etc.		
d. Closing windows and adjusting shades		
e. Adjusting temperature controls		
f. Making note of needed repairs		
Servicing men's lavatory	Daily	35 min. per lav.
Servicing women's lavatory	Daily	38 min. per lav.
Lavatory area		
a. Cleaning lavatory	Daily	1 min. per fixture
b. Cleaning toilet bowl and seat	Daily	1 min. per fixture
c. Cleaning urinals	Daily	2 min. per fixture
d. Cleaning urinal trap	Weekly	2 min. per fixture
e. Cleaning wash sink	Daily	2 min. per fixture
f. Mopping toilet floors	Daily	2 min. per 100 sq. ft.
Stairways		
a. Damp mopping	Weekly	4 min. per flight
b. Sweeping	Twice Daily	6 min. per flight
Other		
a. Cleaning drinking fountains	Daily	1 min. per fixture
b. Dusting fluorescent tubes	Monthly	12 tubes per min.
c. Sweeping auditorium	Daily	15 min. per 1,000 sq. ft.
d. Sweeping corridors	Twice Daily	8 min. per 1,000 sq. ft.
e. Sweeping gymnasium floor	Daily	5 min. per 1,000 sq. ft.
f. Washing glass	As needed	1 min. per 10 sq. ft.
g. Buffing and reconditioning plastic-finished floors	As needed	50 min. per 1,000 sq. ft.

TABLE 18-2 *Continued*

Task	Frequency	Time Required
h. Machine scrubbing traffic areas		
1. Light-soil areas	8–24 months	90 min. per 1,000 sq. ft.
2. Medium-soil areas	Every 6 months	100 min. per 1,000 sq. ft.
3. Heavy-soil areas	Every 3 months	110 min. per 1,000 sq. ft.
i. Refinishing floors (waxless finish)	As needed	20 min. per 1,000 sq. ft.

level and class-size policies. The sample schedule is presented in Table 18-3. This schedule applies to a relatively small school building where all custodial staff are employed during the day. In some of the larger schools, this schedule might have to be changed substantially if night crews are hired to perform some of the work listed in the sample schedule. Regardless of the time when each member of the custodial staff reports for work, however, it is essential that each person be scheduled for his or her entire eight-hour tour of duty.

Preventive Maintenance Program

Boards of education are often not aware of the potential savings that could accrue to a school district by instituting a well-defined plan of preventive maintenance. Over an extended period of time, it is economically advantageous to avoid the complete breakdown of mechanical equipment and the serious deterioration of the physical elements of a school building. It is far better, for example, to repair a hairline crack on the exterior surface of the roof when it is barely visible and is still harmless, than it would be to do it later. In time, the extreme changes in temperature, and the repeated melting and freezing of ice, can enlarge the crack to such an extent that water can seep into the building and discolor ceiling tiles in a classroom directly below the deteriorated roof. Under these conditions, the lack of preventive maintenance could subject the school district to the cost of redecorating a classroom ceiling at best, and the possible replacement of the entire ceiling under less favorable circumstances.

Developing a Preventive Maintenance Plan. The creation of an effective plan of preventive maintenance is highly technical. It is not something that can be delegated to the school principal or head custodian. The central administrative staff should

TABLE 18-3 **A Sample Custodial Schedule**

Time	Custodian	Helper	Maid
7:00–7:30	Raise flag Open building Check heating plant Check fire bells Check building		
7:30–8:00	Dust all class- rooms, principal's and secretary's of- fices, library, and any other room to be used during the day.	Same	Same
8:00–10:00	Sweep sidewalks Check with office Install glass if needed Check heating plant Make minor repairs	 Wash sweeping mops	Begin dusting in corridors Clean some inside hall glass Sweep stairs and corridors if needed
10:00–10:30	*High School—* Check all toilet rooms—see that all fixtures are flushed, if needed Insure proper ventilation Pick up paper from floor Replenish towels, paper, and hand soap as needed *Elementary School—* Same as H.S. but completed immediately following the morning recess	 Same	 Same
10:30–11:00	Check boiler Check with office Walk building to check for needed repairs	Return to dusting and cleaning in halls	 Same as helper

TABLE 18-3 *Continued*

Time	Custodian	Helper	Maid
11:00–12:00	Check toilet rooms	Lunch	Check drinking fountains and wash sinks (clean and replenish soap and towels)
	Shake out doormats		
12:00–1:00	Lunch	Brush and pick up papers in corridors Clean sweeping brooms and mops	Lunch
1:00–1:30	All toilet rooms— same as 10:00–10:30	Same	Same
1:30–2:40	Check drinking fountains and wash sinks Burn (dispose of) paper and rubbish collected during day Clean some inside door glass and any writing from walls (In H.S., right after noon recess)		
2:40–3:00	Ready equipment and materials for afternoon cleaning Give help 5-minute rest period	Same	Same
3:00–5:00	Sweep all classrooms and halls Clean all toilets Mop toilet floors Carry out trash and paper Empty pencil sharpeners	Same	Same
	Custodian begin checking behind help so entire building is checked prior to day's end	Classrooms No. ____, ____, ____, ten rooms with halls and other areas and two toilets	Same
	Secure building Take down flag		

take an active role in the development of such a plan. Except in very large school districts, the necessary expertise will not be available to create a maintenance prevention plan. The accomplishment of this task requires the talents of an architect, a heating and plumbing engineer, an electrical engineer, and a structural engineer. These services should be secured by the school district on a per diem basis. When a new building is being planned and constructed, the architectural firm can supply these services gratis or at a nominal fee because each expert is intimately familiar with all of the materials and systems included in the new building. Although the breadth of the talents required to produce a maintenance prevention plan is wide, the amount of time required by each expert is quite minimal. Each expert should be able to list the items requiring preventive maintenance in a given situation within a period of one or two days. The basic question to each one of these experts should be, "What can I do on a regularly scheduled program to extend the life of each piece of major mechanical equipment, and to preserve the physical properties and function of the building itself?"

Once the plan is developed, it is the responsibility of the building principal to implement it. The custodian or assistants are required to perform all of the work called for in the preventive maintenance program. The principal should hold the head custodian accountable for the proper execution of the plan. The success of this program depends largely upon the commitment of the building principal to it. If he or she carefully supervises the work of the custodians and maintains some form of check on whether or not certain work has been performed, the success of the plan is assured. And with such success, the school district can reap rich financial rewards in the form of reduced cost of school building maintenance.

Implementing the Preventive Maintenance Plan. In any prescribed maintenance program, the list of tasks to be performed is described in detail. The frequency and nature of the work are clearly stated. The materials to be used are specified in considerable depth. And the manner in which the work is to be accomplished is expressed in simple language.

It is suggested that the head custodian develop a reliable system for accomplishing all of the required work. He or she may wish to record each task to be performed on a card. This may include a description of the task and the tools and materials to be used. These cards may well serve as a "tickler file" or a reminder to the custodian as to when the task should be completed. He or she should note on the card the date of the next time when the work is required and file all of the cards chronologically by date, starting with the current date. In this way, the custodian will know at a glance what needs to be completed within a given month, week, or day. Once the work is completed, he or she can record what was done on the back of the card. The principal can scan through these cards from time to time to assure that the preventive maintenance program in the building is effective and in full operation. He or she may also wish to compare the work described on the card with that stated in the preventive maintenance plan developed under the auspices of the central administration.

The maintenance plan described in the preceding paragraphs can be made more cost-effective through the use of a district-wide computerized data base management system. In addition to providing a list of items needing preventive maintenance at certain specified times, a computerized building file can generate a wide variety of up-to-the-minute reports on matters related to the maintenance and operation of the building. A district-wide system can project maintenance costs within specified categories and allocate such costs to each educational facility in the school district. It can generate current information on the inventory and rate of consumption of supply items. And it can provide an up-to-date list of student-station utilization factors for each instructional space in the school district. In view of these benefits, it is suggested that the implementation of a computerized data base management system be considered for the maintenance and operation of educational facilities on a district-wide basis. According to Borowski, "The installation of a space and equipment inventory system improves the use of resources and offers a wealth of information for the management of these resources."[10]

NOTES

1. Henry H. Linn and Leslie C. Helms, *The School Custodian's Housekeeping Handbook* (New York: Bureau of Publications, Teacher's College, Columbia University, 1948).

2. *School Facilities and Operations Manual* (Reston, VA: Association of School Business Officials, International, 1988). ERIC file no. ED324823.

3. *Committing to the Cost of Ownership: Maintenance and Repair of Public Buildings.* (Washington, DC: National Research Council, 1990). ERIC file no. ED322581.

4. O. Barker Harrison, *Suggested Methods for Custodians for the Routine Care of Schools* (Nashville, TN: Yearwood and Johnson, 1973).

5. Thomas E. Glass, "Planned Maintenance Programs: A Memorandum to Facility Officers," *CEFP Journal* (May–June 1984), p. 13.

6. Harrison, op. cit., p. 55.

7. Ibid., p. 56.

8. Ibid., p. 159.

9. Ibid., p. 131.

10. Paul D. Borowski, "Maintaining a Computerized Building File," *CEFP Journal* (September–October 1984), p. 18.

Technique for Determining the Approximate Location and Capacity of New Construction Employing an Indirect Approach

In utilizing the indirect approach for determining the location and capacity of needed facilities when accurate census data are not available, it is suggested that:

1. an enrollment projection of the entire school district be made using the percent-of-survival technique or its equivalent, and the desired grade organization be established for the school district by the board of education.

2. the capacity of each serviceable building that would make most effective use of each school be determined by use of techniques discussed in Chapter 4.

3. the total available capacity in the school district for each grade grouping be computed and deducted from the total projected enrollment in the respective grade groupings for the key planning year. The difference, then, represents the additional capacity that should be provided somewhere in the school district for the respective grade groupings.

4. the present attendance areas be drawn on a map of the school district, and present enrollment and the capacity of the respective buildings in each area be shown in each attendance area.

5. a qualitative estimate be made regarding the likely increase or decline of student population in each attendance area, and each area be shaded in by distinctive colors or cross-hatching indicating the extent of the estimated change.

6. present enrollment in each attendance area plus estimated increases of enrollment in the future, as determined by the percent of expected population change, be compared with the present capacity in each attendance area, and a symbol be entered in each area showing whether an excess or deficiency of capacity is expected in each attendance area.

7. attendance areas be revised as follows:

    a. Excess and deficient capacity areas should be balanced as much as possible through minor adjustments of attendance lines, or by transporting students from one area to the other.

    b. Attendance lines should be adjusted, if possible, to shift student population from insufficient areas to those with excess-capacity.

    c. When deficient capacities exist in several adjoining attendance areas, attendance lines should be altered so that the total deficiency is concentrated in an area where present facilities or availability of sites offers a logical solution to the problem of increased capacity for that general area.

8. after attendance line adjustments have been made according to paragraph 7, above, the amount of the additional capacity and its possible location be determined for each reconstructed attendance area. Where excess capacity is available, its location should be noted for possible use later in formulating the final long-range plan.

9. the sum of the additional capacity envisioned for each attendance area under paragraph 8, above, be subtracted from the overall district capacity deficiency computed in paragraph 3. In school districts that are relatively stable, a balance between the sum of area needs and the overall district capacity needs may be reached at this point. If balance is not achieved, readjust the estimates of growth within the attendance areas accordingly.

10. in growing school districts, the areas of potential population growths be defined and drawn on a map of the school district. Priorities as to areas where the most rapid growth is likely to occur should be indicated on the map. New facilities should be strategically located in these areas of potential growth.

11. the long-range building program provide for the construction of schools in locations specified under paragraph 10, above, and a balance between total capacity and expected enrollment in the key year be attained.

It is realized, of course, that this procedure for determining the location of additional capacity in a school district is more qualitative than quantitative. A scientific approach to this problem would require that the school district be subdivided into small permanent census tracts without regard for attendance areas, and, further, that an annual census be taken of preschool and in-school students. The reason for taking a census of students who are in school as well as those below school age is to provide a check on the validity of the preschool data. By comparing the number of students in the first grade, for example, with the number of first-grade students reported by the census-takers, it is possible to determine the percent of under-enumeration and thus provide a basis for adjusting the preschool figures.

Index